NEGIMA!

37

Ken Akamatsu

TRANSLATED AND ADAPTED BY
Alethea Nibley and Athena Nibley

LETTERING AND RETOUCH BY
Scott O. Brown

KC
KODANSHA
COMICS

A word from the author

THANK YOU FOR FOLLOWING *MAGISTER NEGI MAGI* THESE PAST NINE YEARS.

NOW, THE NEXT VOLUME, VOLUME 38, WILL BE THE GRAND FINALE!

WHAT... ...WILL HAPPEN!?

The next volume will be the last!!

WHAT WILL HAPPEN TO ASUNA!? WHO WILL WIN IN THE NEGI VS. NAGI(?) FIGHT!?

ALL WILL BE REVEALED IN VOLUME 38, SO PLEASE CHECK IT OUT.

...Now enjoy the classmates' final brouhaha. (^^;)

Ken Akamatsu's home page address*
http://www.ailove.net/

*Please note Akamatsu's website
is in Japanese.

Honorifics Explained

Throughout the Kodansha Comics books, you will find Japanese honorifics left intact in the translations. For those not familiar with how the Japanese use honorifics and, more important, how they differ from American honorifics, we present this brief overview.

Politeness has always been a critical facet of Japanese culture. Ever since the feudal era, when Japan was a highly stratified society, use of honorifics—which can be defined as polite speech that indicates relationship or status—has played an essential role in the Japanese language. When addressing someone in Japanese, an honorific usually takes the form of a suffix attached to one's name (example: "Asuna-san"), is used as a title at the end of one's name, or appears in place of the name itself (example: "Negi-sensei," or simply "Sensei!").

Honorifics can be expressions of respect or endearment. In the context of manga and anime, honorifics give insight into the nature of the relationship between characters. Many English translations leave out these important honorifics and therefore distort the feel of the original Japanese. Because Japanese honorifics contain nuances that English honorifics lack, it is our policy at Kodansha Comics not to translate them. Here, instead, is a guide to some of the honorifics you may encounter in Kodansha Comics.

-san: This is the most common honorific and is equivalent to Mr., Miss, Ms., or Mrs. It is the all-purpose honorific and can be used in any situation where politeness is required.

-sama: This is one level higher than "-san" and is used to confer great respect.

-dono: This comes from the word "tono," which means "lord." It is an even higher level than "-sama" and confers utmost respect.

-kun: This suffix is used at the end of boys' names to express familiarity or endearment. It is also sometimes used by men among friends, or when addressing someone younger or of a lower station.

-chan: This is used to express endearment, mostly toward girls. It is also used for little boys, pets, and even among lovers. It gives a sense of childish cuteness.

Bozu: This is an informal way to refer to a boy, similar to the English terms "kid" and "squirt."

Sempai/Senpai: This title suggests that the addressee is one's senior in a group or organization. It is most often used in a school setting, where underclassmen refer to their upperclassmen as "sempai." It can also be used in the workplace, such as when a newer employee addresses an employee who has seniority in the company.

Kohai: This is the opposite of "sempai" and is used toward underclassmen in school or newcomers in the workplace. It connotes that the addressee is of a lower station.

Sensei: Literally meaning "one who has come before," this title is used for teachers, doctors, or masters of any profession or art.

-[blank]: This is usually forgotten in these lists, but it is perhaps the most significant difference between Japanese and English. The lack of honorific means that the speaker has permission to address the person in a very intimate way. Usually, only family, spouses, or very close friends have this kind of permission. Known as *yobisute*, it can be gratifying when someone who has earned the intimacy starts to call one by one's name without an honorific. But when that intimacy hasn't been earned, it can be very insulting.

Ken
Akamatsu

NEGIMA!

MAGISTER NEGI MAGI

37

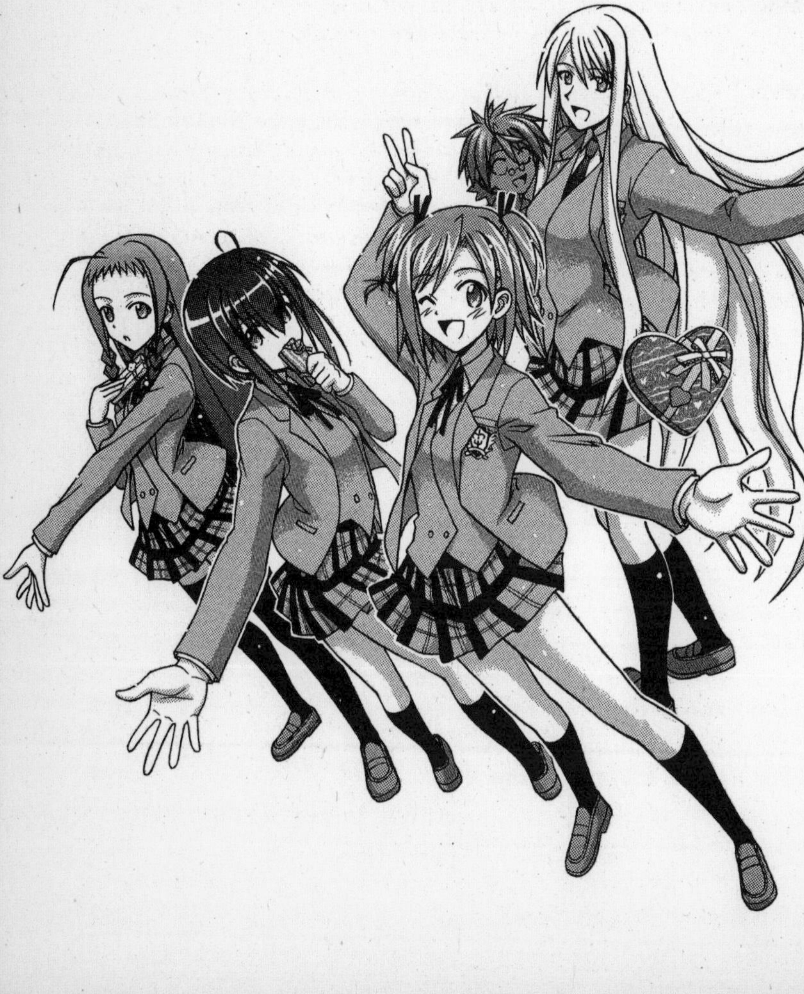

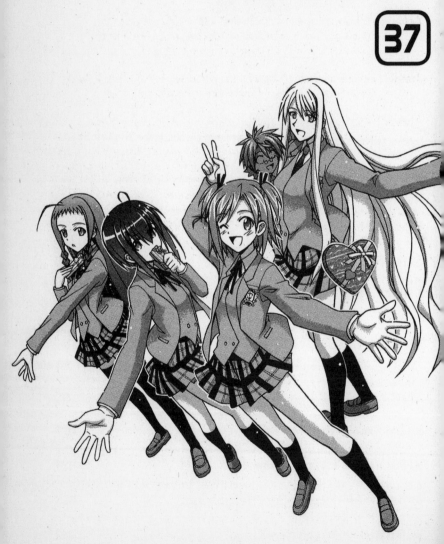

CONTENTS

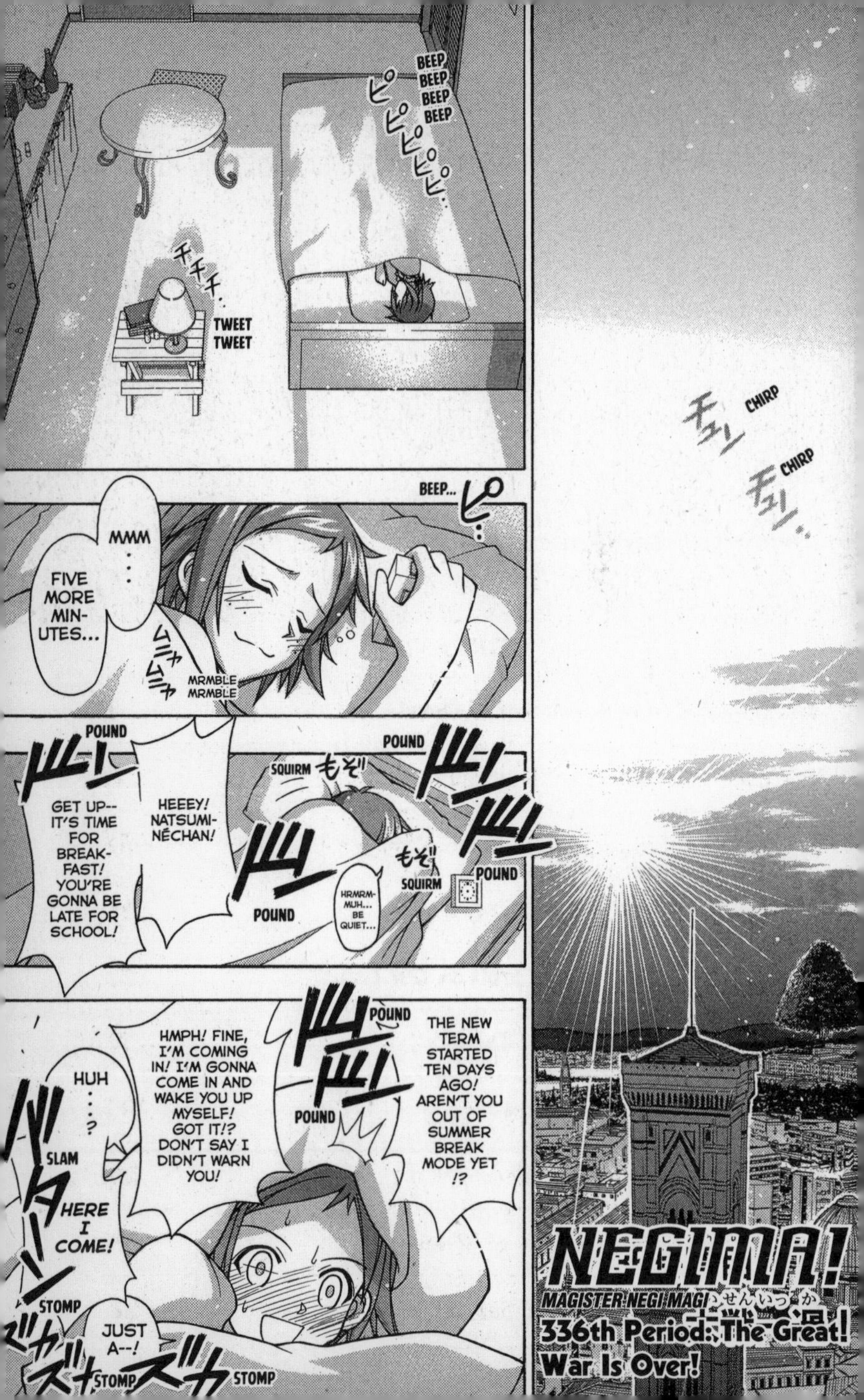
CHIRP
CHIRP
NEGIMA!
MAGISTER NEGI MAGI
336th Period: The Great! War Is Over!
BEEP BEEP BEEP BEEP
TWEET TWEET
BEEP...
MMM... FIVE MORE MIN-UTES...
MRMBLE MRMBLE
POUND
SQUIRM
POUND
POUND
HRMRM-MUH... BE QUIET...
SQUIRM
POUND
HEEEY! NATSUMI-NÉCHAN!
GET UP-- IT'S TIME FOR BREAK-FAST! YOU'RE GONNA BE LATE FOR SCHOOL!
POUND
THE NEW TERM STARTED TEN DAYS AGO! AREN'T YOU OUT OF SUMMER BREAK MODE YET!?
POUND
POUND
HMPH! FINE, I'M COMING IN! I'M GONNA COME IN AND WAKE YOU UP MYSELF! GOT IT!? DON'T SAY I DIDN'T WARN YOU!
HUH...?
SLAM
HERE I COME!
JUST A--!
STOMP
STOMP
STOMP

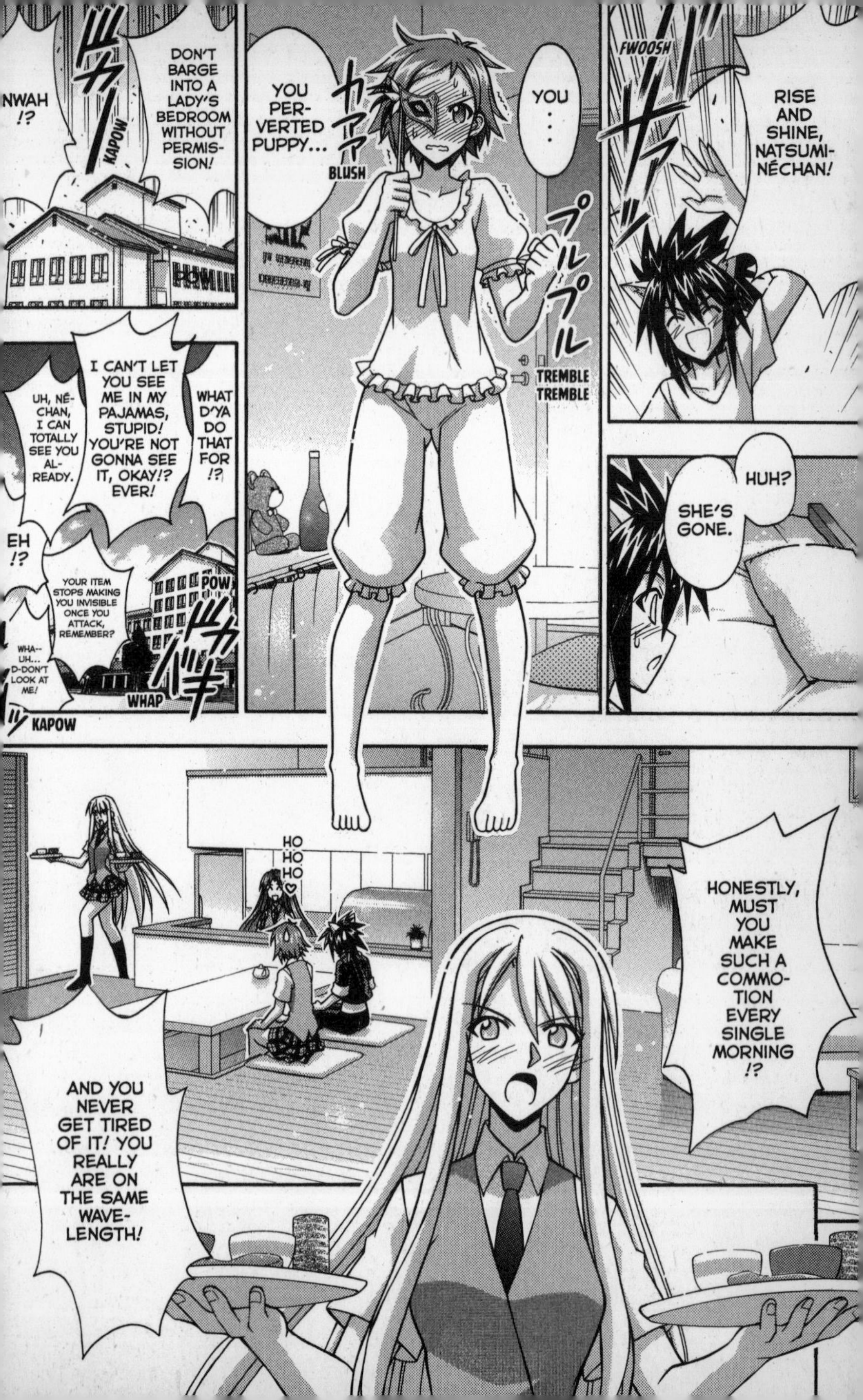
FWOOSH
RISE AND SHINE, NATSUMI-NÉCHAN!
HUH?
SHE'S GONE.
YOU...
YOU PERVERTED PUPPY...
BLUSH
TREMBLE TREMBLE
DON'T BARGE INTO A LADY'S BEDROOM WITHOUT PERMISSION!
KAPOW
NWAH!?
WHAT D'YA DO THAT FOR!?
I CAN'T LET YOU SEE ME IN MY PAJAMAS, STUPID! YOU'RE NOT GONNA SEE IT, OKAY!? EVER!
UH, NÉ-CHAN, I CAN TOTALLY SEE YOU AL-READY.
EH!?
YOUR ITEM STOPS MAKING YOU INVISIBLE ONCE YOU ATTACK, REMEMBER?
POW
WHAP
WHA-- UH... D-DON'T LOOK AT ME!
KAPOW
HONESTLY, MUST YOU MAKE SUCH A COMMOTION EVERY SINGLE MORNING!?
HO HO HO ♥
AND YOU NEVER GET TIRED OF IT! YOU REALLY ARE ON THE SAME WAVE-LENGTH!

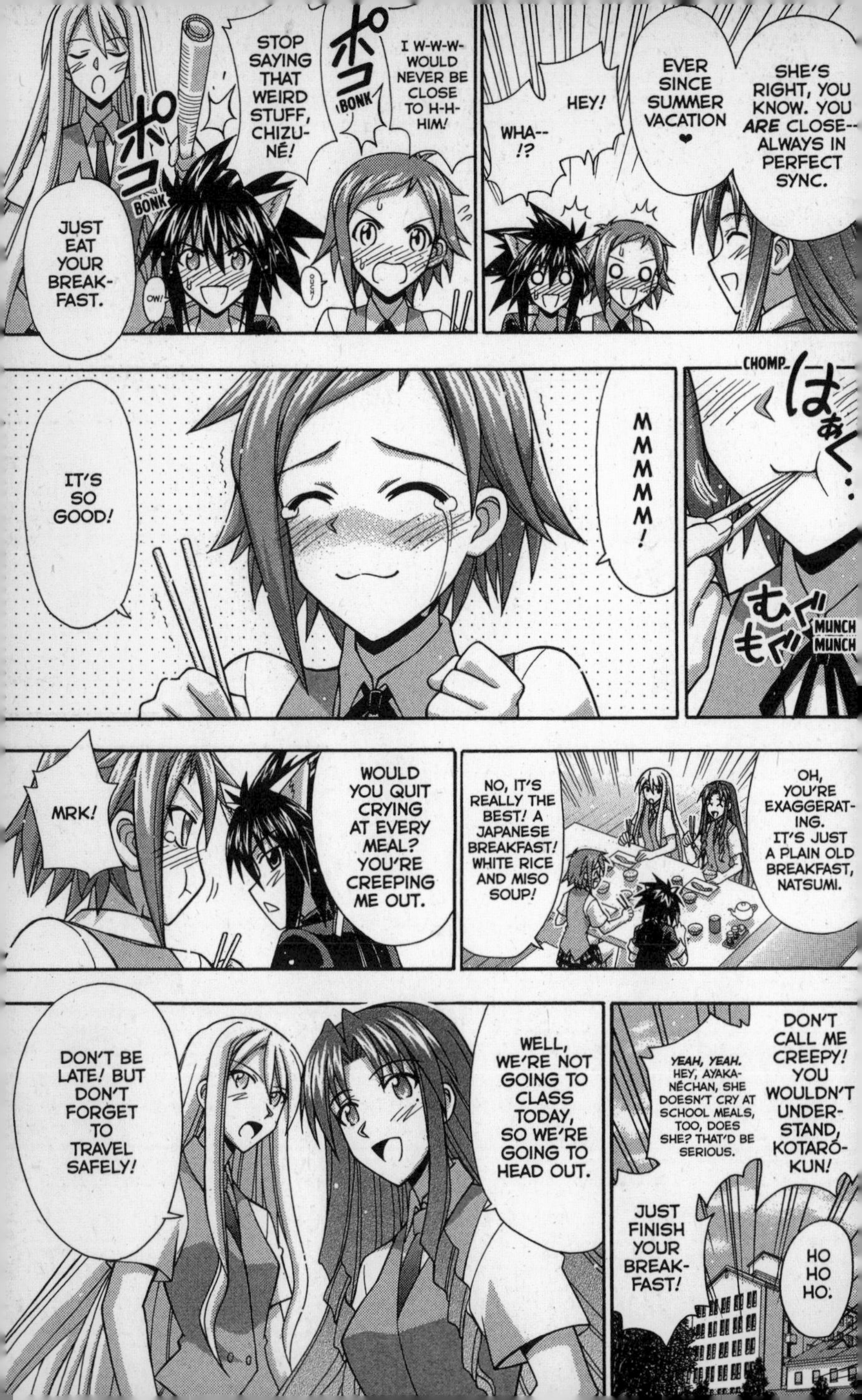
SHE'S RIGHT, YOU KNOW. YOU *ARE* CLOSE-- ALWAYS IN PERFECT SYNC.
EVER SINCE SUMMER VACATION ❤
HEY!
WHA-- !?
I W-W-W-WOULD NEVER BE CLOSE TO H-H-HIM!
ポコ BONK
STOP SAYING THAT WEIRD STUFF, CHIZUNÉ!
ポコ BONK
JUST EAT YOUR BREAKFAST.
OUCH
OW!
CHOMP
むぐもぐ MUNCH MUNCH
MMMMMM!
IT'S SO GOOD!
OH, YOU'RE EXAGGERATING. IT'S JUST A PLAIN OLD BREAKFAST, NATSUMI.
NO, IT'S REALLY THE BEST! A JAPANESE BREAKFAST! WHITE RICE AND MISO SOUP!
WOULD YOU QUIT CRYING AT EVERY MEAL? YOU'RE CREEPING ME OUT.
MRK!
DON'T CALL ME CREEPY! YOU WOULDN'T UNDERSTAND, KOTARŌ-KUN!
YEAH, YEAH. HEY, AYAKA-NÉCHAN, SHE DOESN'T CRY AT SCHOOL MEALS, TOO, DOES SHE? THAT'D BE SERIOUS.
JUST FINISH YOUR BREAKFAST!
HO HO HO.
WELL, WE'RE NOT GOING TO CLASS TODAY, SO WE'RE GOING TO HEAD OUT.
DON'T BE LATE! BUT DON'T FORGET TO TRAVEL SAFELY!

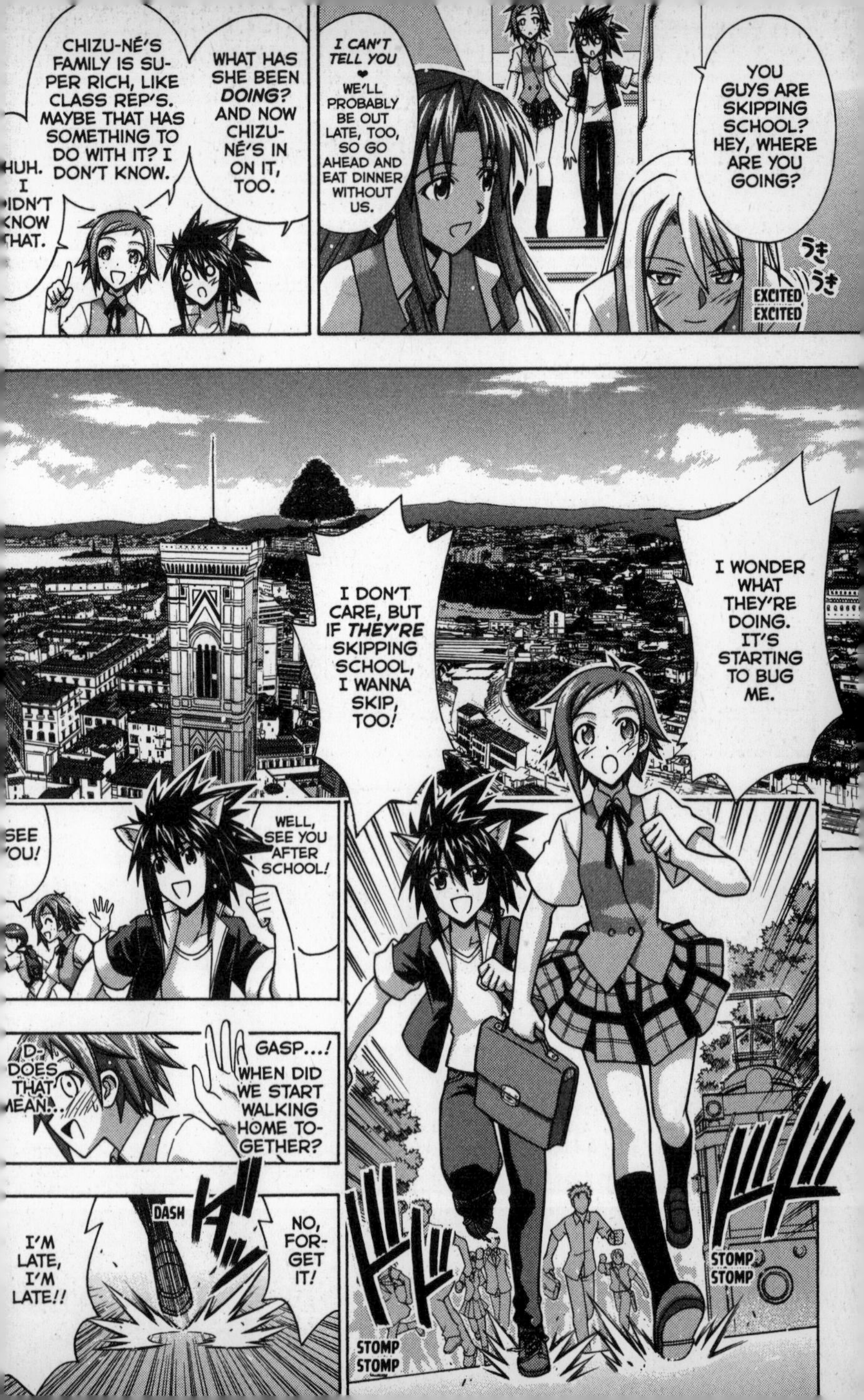
YOU GUYS ARE SKIPPING SCHOOL? HEY, WHERE ARE YOU GOING?
うき うき
EXCITED EXCITED
I CAN'T TELL YOU ❤ WE'LL PROBABLY BE OUT LATE, TOO, SO GO AHEAD AND EAT DINNER WITHOUT US.
WHAT HAS SHE BEEN DOING? AND NOW CHIZU-NÉ'S IN ON IT, TOO.
CHIZU-NÉ'S FAMILY IS SUPER RICH, LIKE CLASS REP'S. MAYBE THAT HAS SOMETHING TO DO WITH IT? I DON'T KNOW.
HUH. I IDN'T KNOW THAT.
I WONDER WHAT THEY'RE DOING. IT'S STARTING TO BUG ME.
I DON'T CARE, BUT IF THEY'RE SKIPPING SCHOOL, I WANNA SKIP, TOO!
STOMP STOMP
STOMP STOMP
WELL, SEE YOU AFTER SCHOOL!
SEE YOU!
GASP...! WHEN DID WE START WALKING HOME TOGETHER?
D-DOES THAT MEAN...
NO, FORGET IT!
DASH
I'M LATE, I'M LATE!!

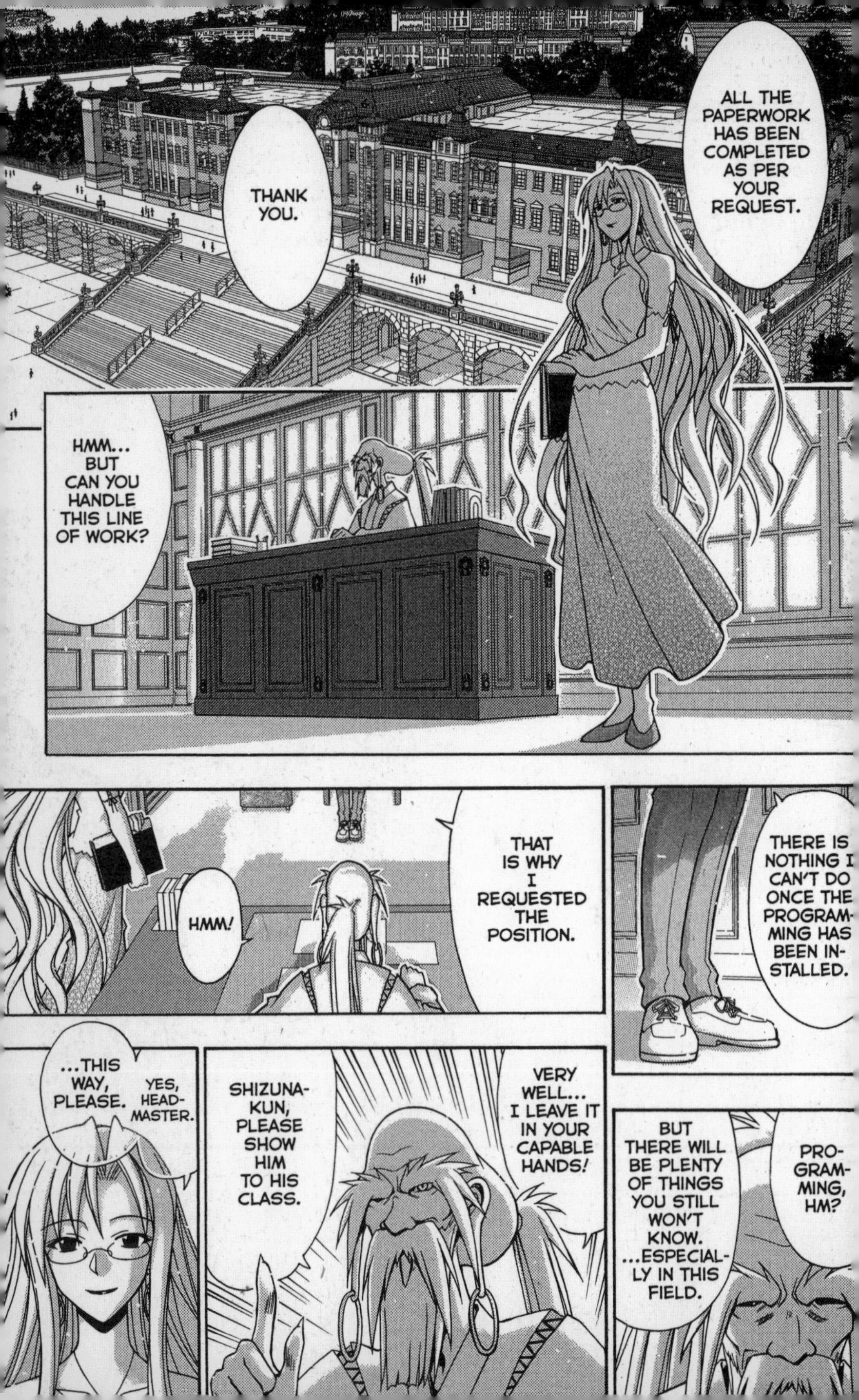
ALL THE PAPERWORK HAS BEEN COMPLETED AS PER YOUR REQUEST.
THANK YOU.
HMM... BUT CAN YOU HANDLE THIS LINE OF WORK?
THERE IS NOTHING I CAN'T DO ONCE THE PROGRAMMING HAS BEEN INSTALLED.
THAT IS WHY I REQUESTED THE POSITION.
HMM!
PROGRAMMING, HM?
BUT THERE WILL BE PLENTY OF THINGS YOU STILL WON'T KNOW. ...ESPECIALLY IN THIS FIELD.
VERY WELL... I LEAVE IT IN YOUR CAPABLE HANDS!
SHIZUNA-KUN, PLEASE SHOW HIM TO HIS CLASS.
YES, HEADMASTER.
...THIS WAY, PLEASE.

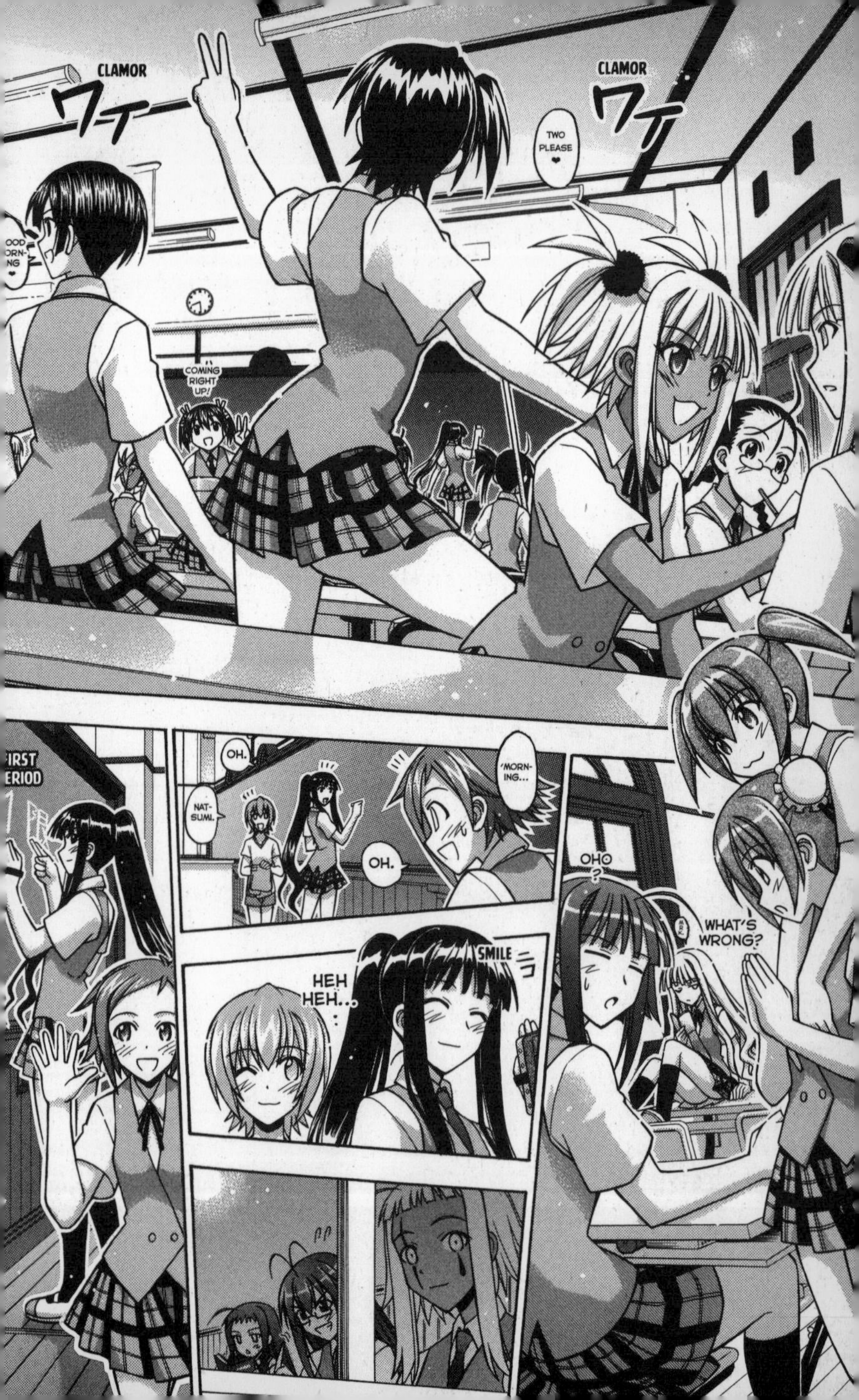
CLAMOR
ワァ
TWO PLEASE ❤
CLAMOR
ワァ
COMING RIGHT UP!
OOD ORN-NG ❤
OHO ?
WHAT'S WRONG?
'MORNING...
OH.
NAT-SUMI.
OH.
SMILE ニコ
HEH HEH...
IRST ERIOD

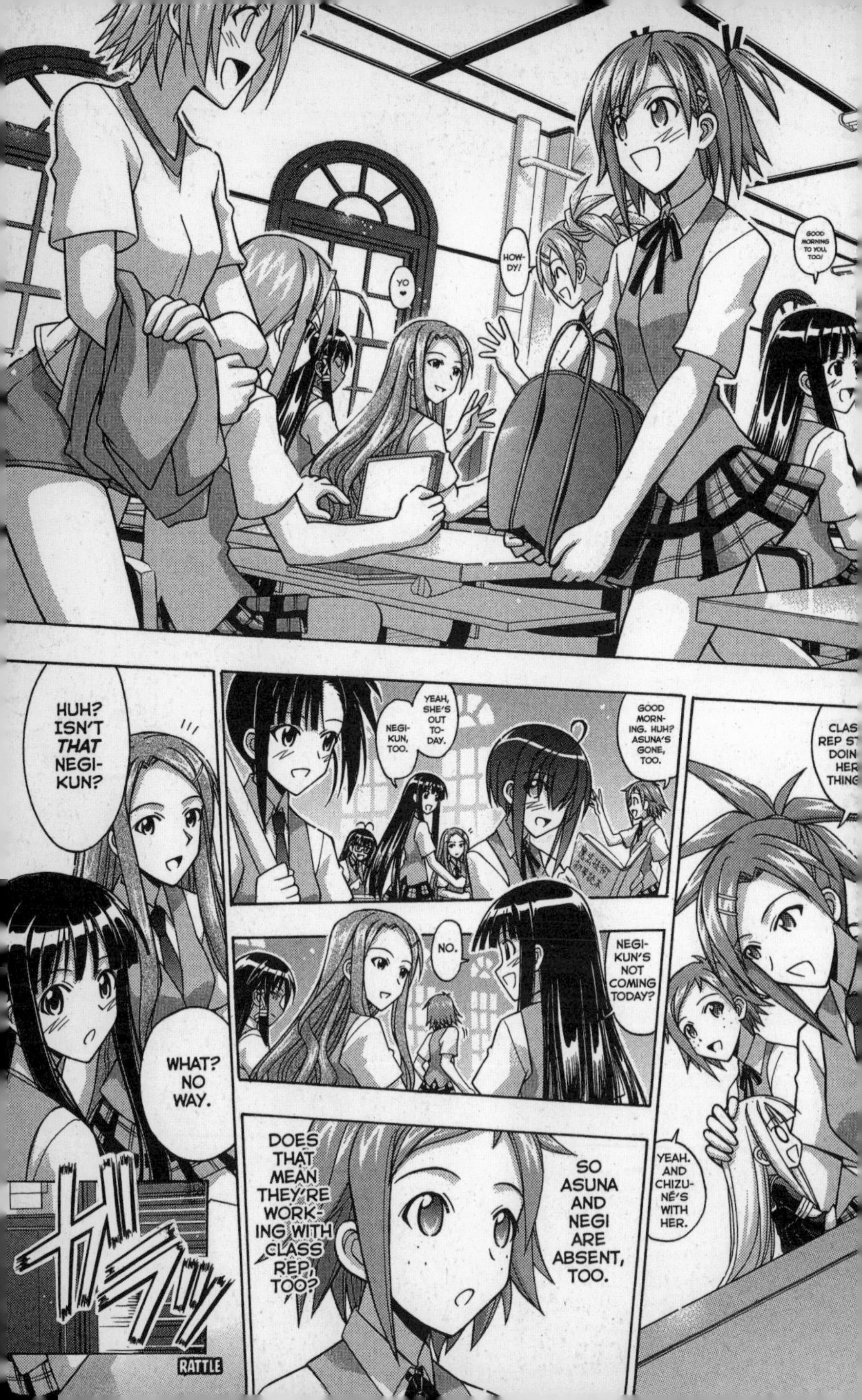
GOOD MORNING TO YOU, TOO!
HOW-DY!
YO ❤
CLAS REP ST DOIN HER THIN
YEAH. AND CHIZUNÉ'S WITH HER.
GOOD MORN-ING. HUH? ASUNA'S GONE, TOO.
YEAH, SHE'S OUT TO-DAY.
NEGI-KUN, TOO.
NEGI-KUN'S NOT COMING TODAY?
NO.
SO ASUNA AND NEGI ARE ABSENT, TOO.
DOES THAT MEAN THEY'RE WORK-ING WITH CLASS REP, TOO?
HUH? ISN'T *THAT* NEGI-KUN?
WHAT? NO WAY.
RATTLE

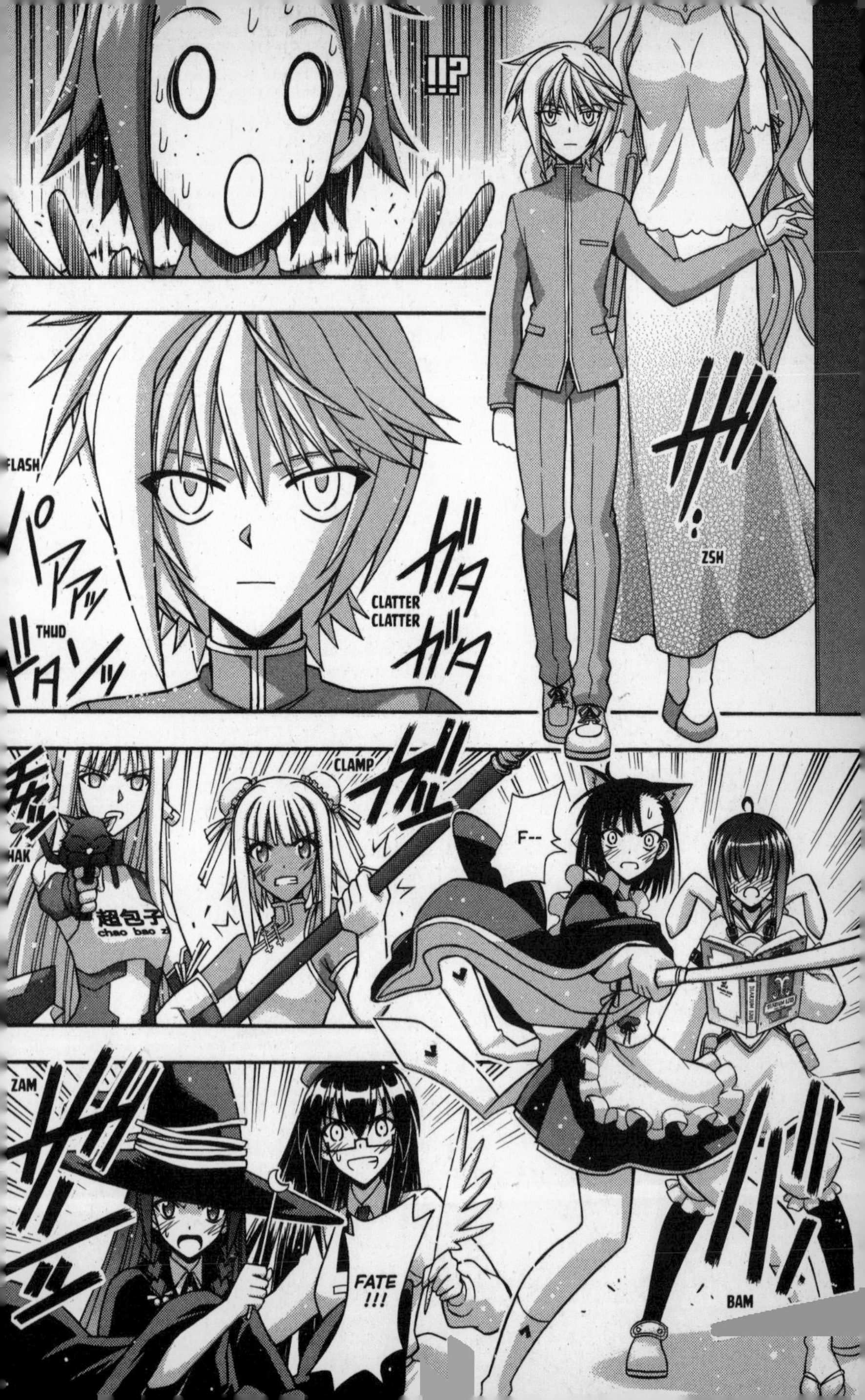
ZSH
!!?
CLATTER CLATTER
FLASH
THUD
F--
CLAMP
CHAK
超包子
chao bao z
BAM
FATE !!!
ZAM

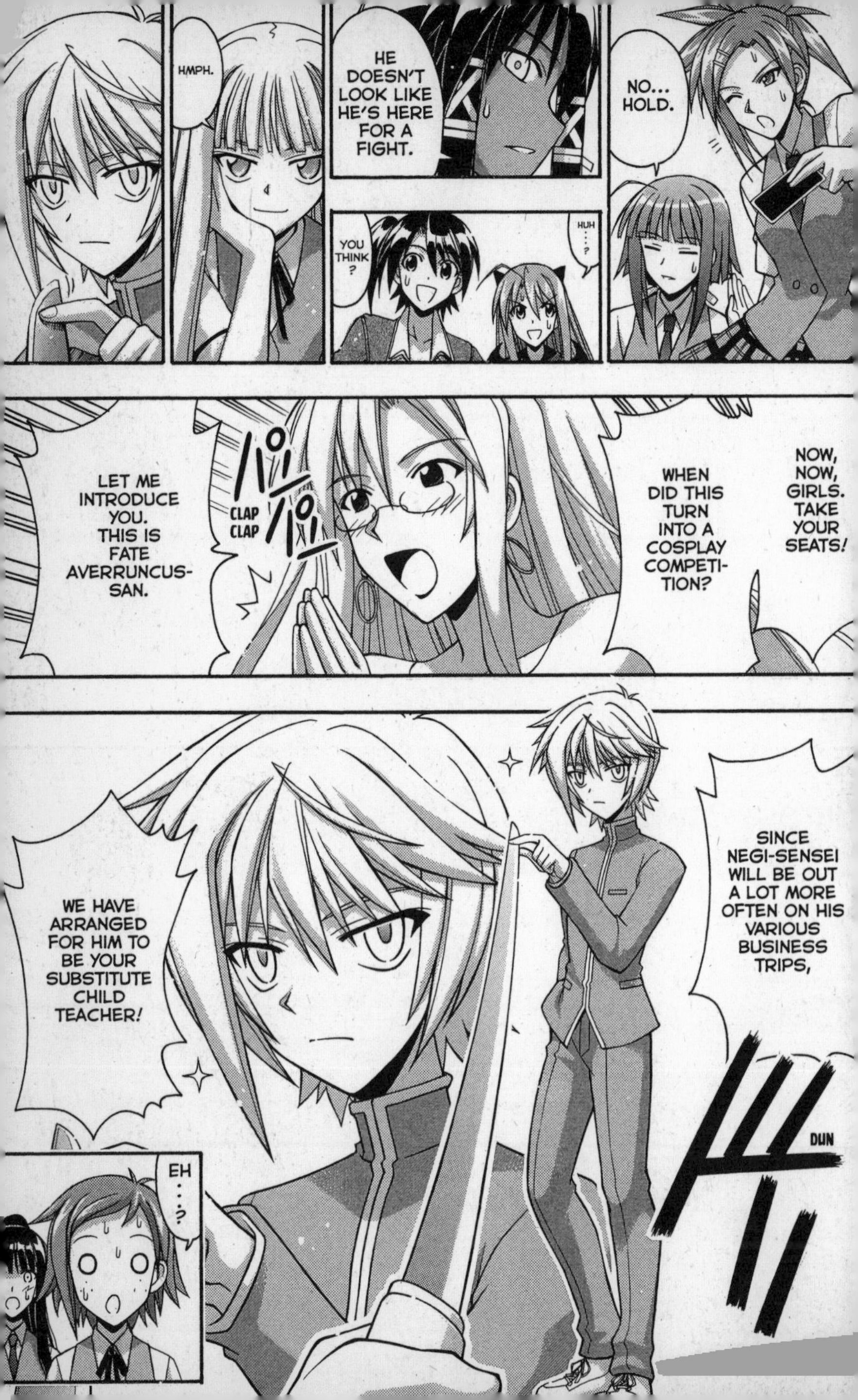
NO... HOLD.
HE DOESN'T LOOK LIKE HE'S HERE FOR A FIGHT.
HUH...?
YOU THINK?
HMPH.
NOW, NOW, GIRLS. TAKE YOUR SEATS!
WHEN DID THIS TURN INTO A COSPLAY COMPETITION?
CLAP CLAP
LET ME INTRODUCE YOU. THIS IS FATE AVERRUNCUS-SAN.
SINCE NEGI-SENSEI WILL BE OUT A LOT MORE OFTEN ON HIS VARIOUS BUSINESS TRIPS,
WE HAVE ARRANGED FOR HIM TO BE YOUR SUBSTITUTE CHILD TEACHER!
DUN
EH...?

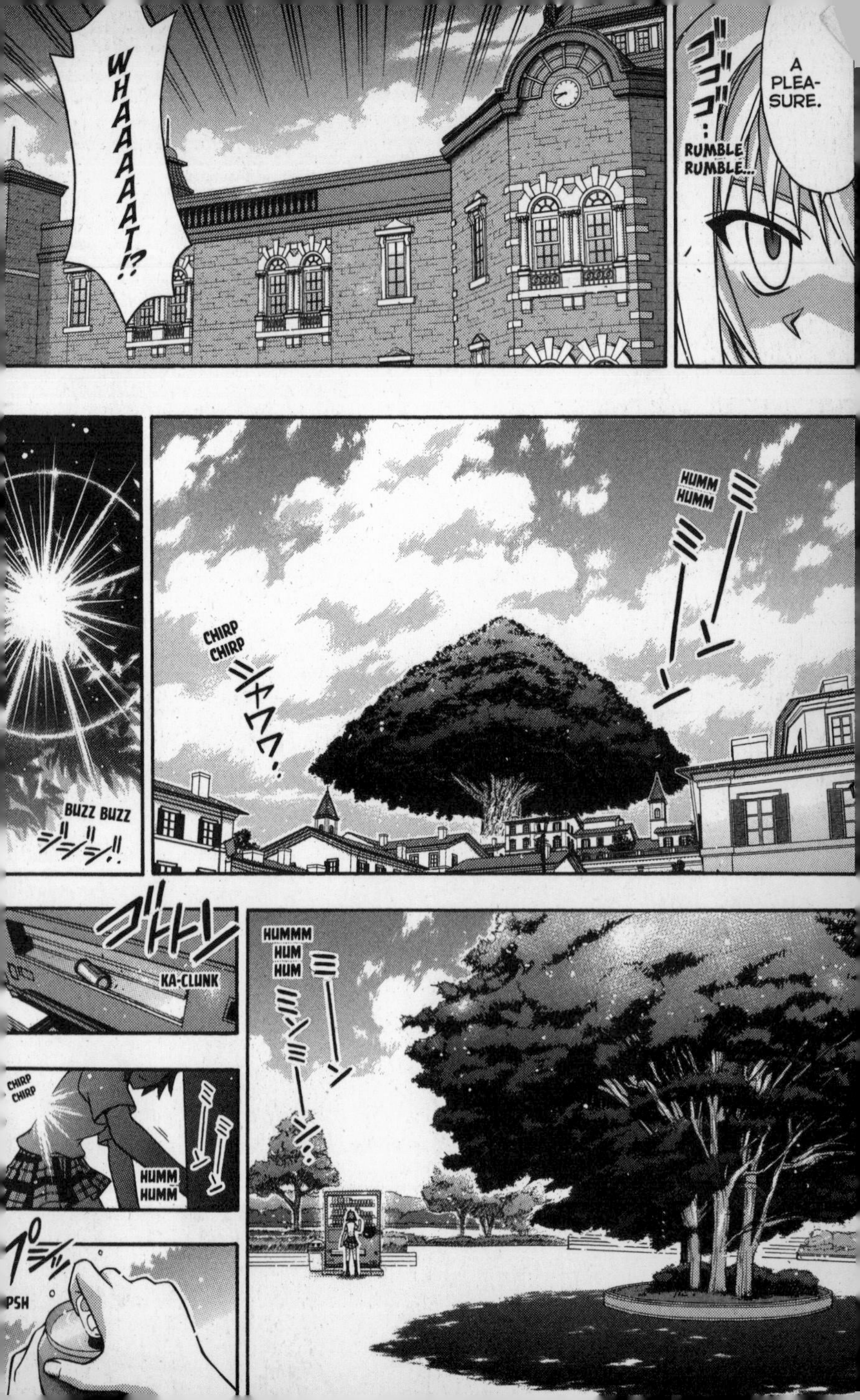
A PLEA-SURE.
ゴゴゴ…
RUMBLE RUMBLE...
WHAAAAAT!?
HUMM HUMM
CHIRP CHIRP
BUZZ BUZZ
HUMMM HUM HUM
KA-CLUNK
CHIRP CHIRP
HUMM HUMM
PSH

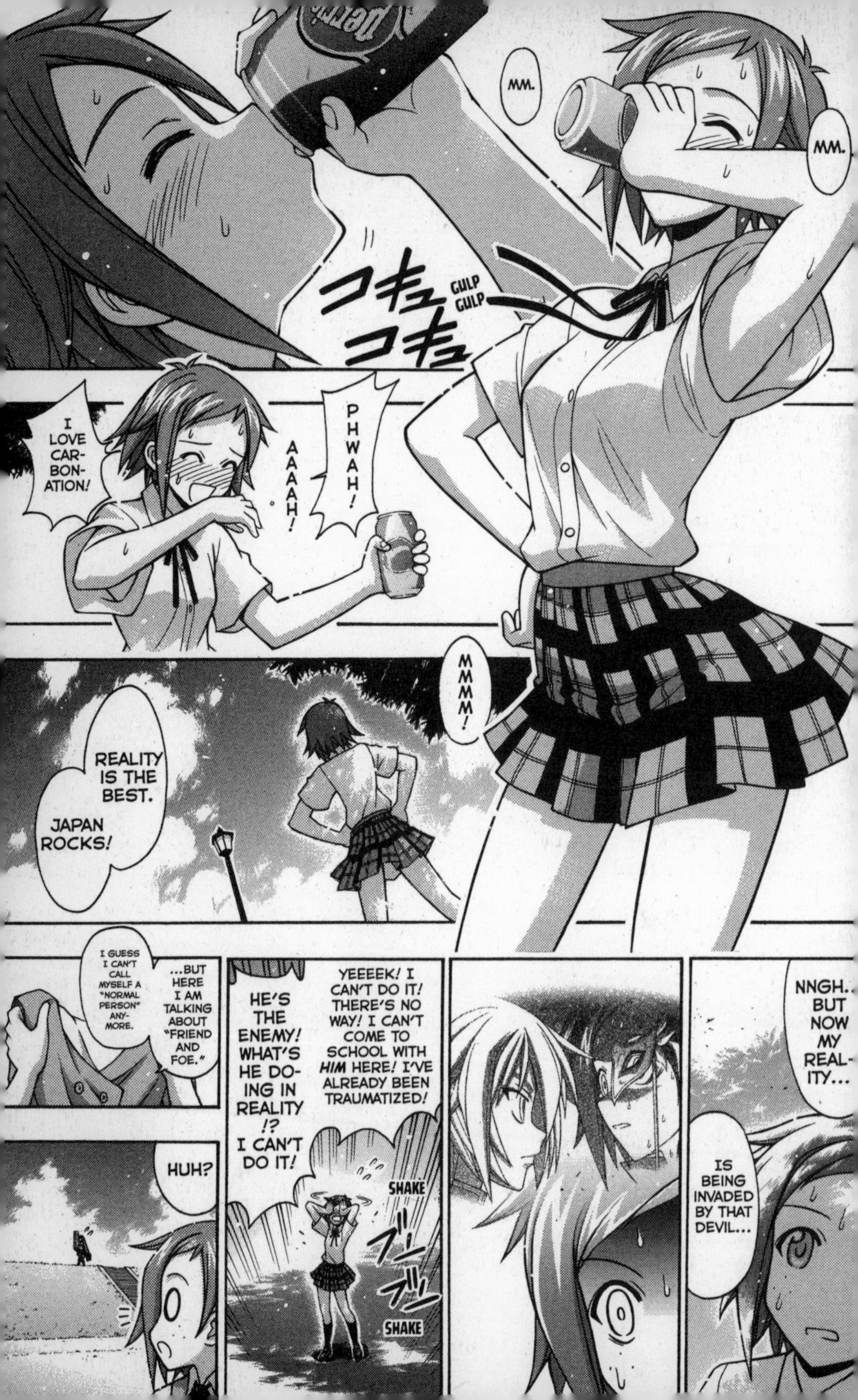
MM.
MM.
コキュ コキュ
GULP GULP
PHWAH! AAAAH!
I LOVE CAR-BON-ATION!
MMMM!
REALITY IS THE BEST.
JAPAN ROCKS!
NNGH.. BUT NOW MY REAL-ITY...
IS BEING INVADED BY THAT DEVIL...
YEEEEK! I CAN'T DO IT! THERE'S NO WAY! I CAN'T COME TO SCHOOL WITH HIM HERE! I'VE ALREADY BEEN TRAUMATIZED!
HE'S THE ENEMY! WHAT'S HE DO-ING IN REALITY!? I CAN'T DO IT!
SHAKE
SHAKE
...BUT HERE I AM TALKING ABOUT "FRIEND AND FOE."
I GUESS I CAN'T CALL MYSELF A "NORMAL PERSON" ANY-MORE.
HUH?

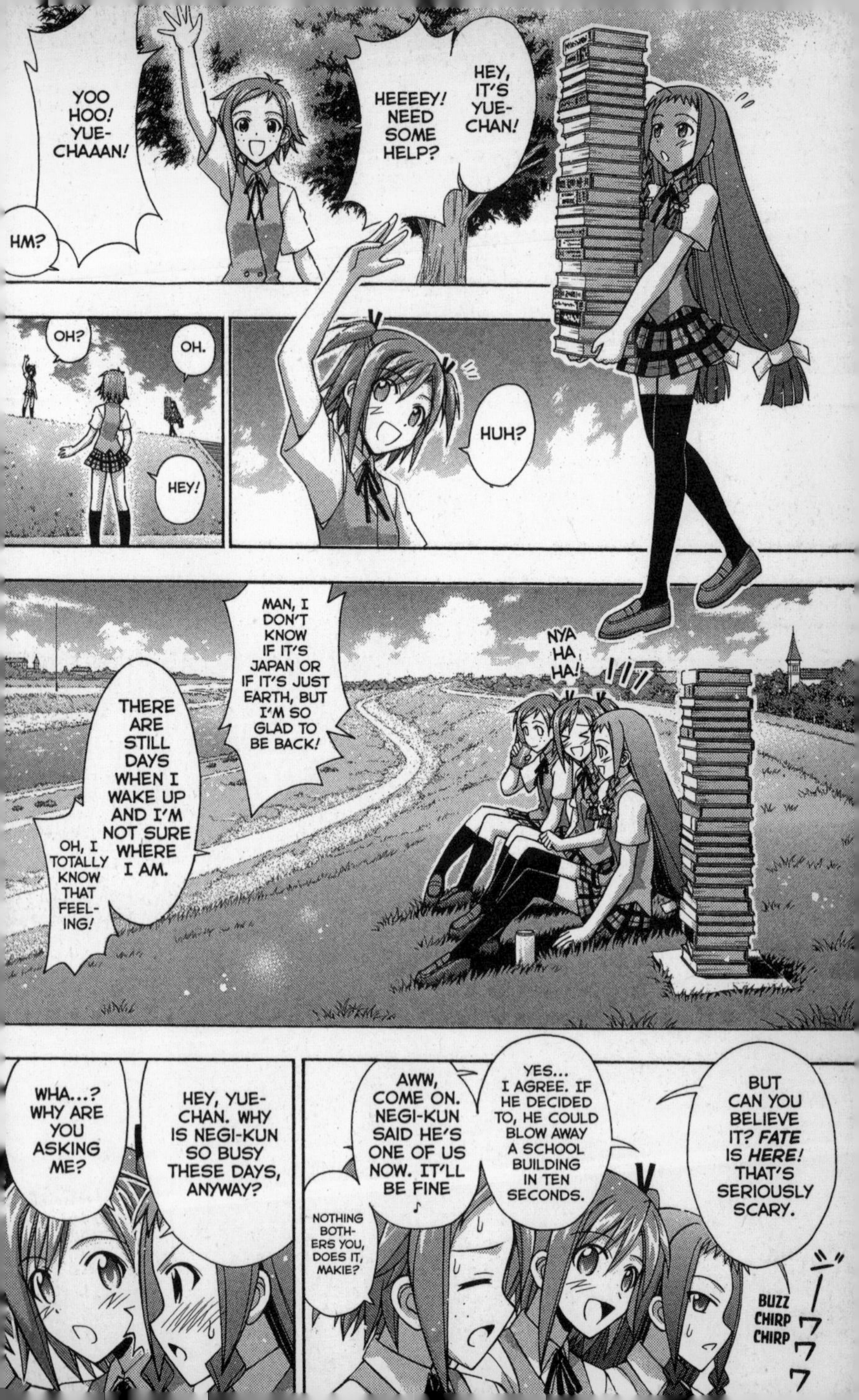
HEY, IT'S YUE-CHAN!
HEEEEY! NEED SOME HELP?
YOO HOO! YUE-CHAAAN!
HM?
HUH?
OH?
OH.
HEY!
NYA HA HA!
MAN, I DON'T KNOW IF IT'S JAPAN OR IF IT'S JUST EARTH, BUT I'M SO GLAD TO BE BACK!
THERE ARE STILL DAYS WHEN I WAKE UP AND I'M NOT SURE WHERE I AM.
OH, I TOTALLY KNOW THAT FEELING!
BUT CAN YOU BELIEVE IT? *FATE* IS *HERE!* THAT'S SERIOUSLY SCARY.
YES... I AGREE. IF HE DECIDED TO, HE COULD BLOW AWAY A SCHOOL BUILDING IN TEN SECONDS.
AWW, COME ON. NEGI-KUN SAID HE'S ONE OF US NOW. IT'LL BE FINE ♪
NOTHING BOTHERS YOU, DOES IT, MAKIE?
BUZZ CHIRP CHIRP
HEY, YUE-CHAN. WHY IS NEGI-KUN SO BUSY THESE DAYS, ANYWAY?
WHA...? WHY ARE YOU ASKING ME?

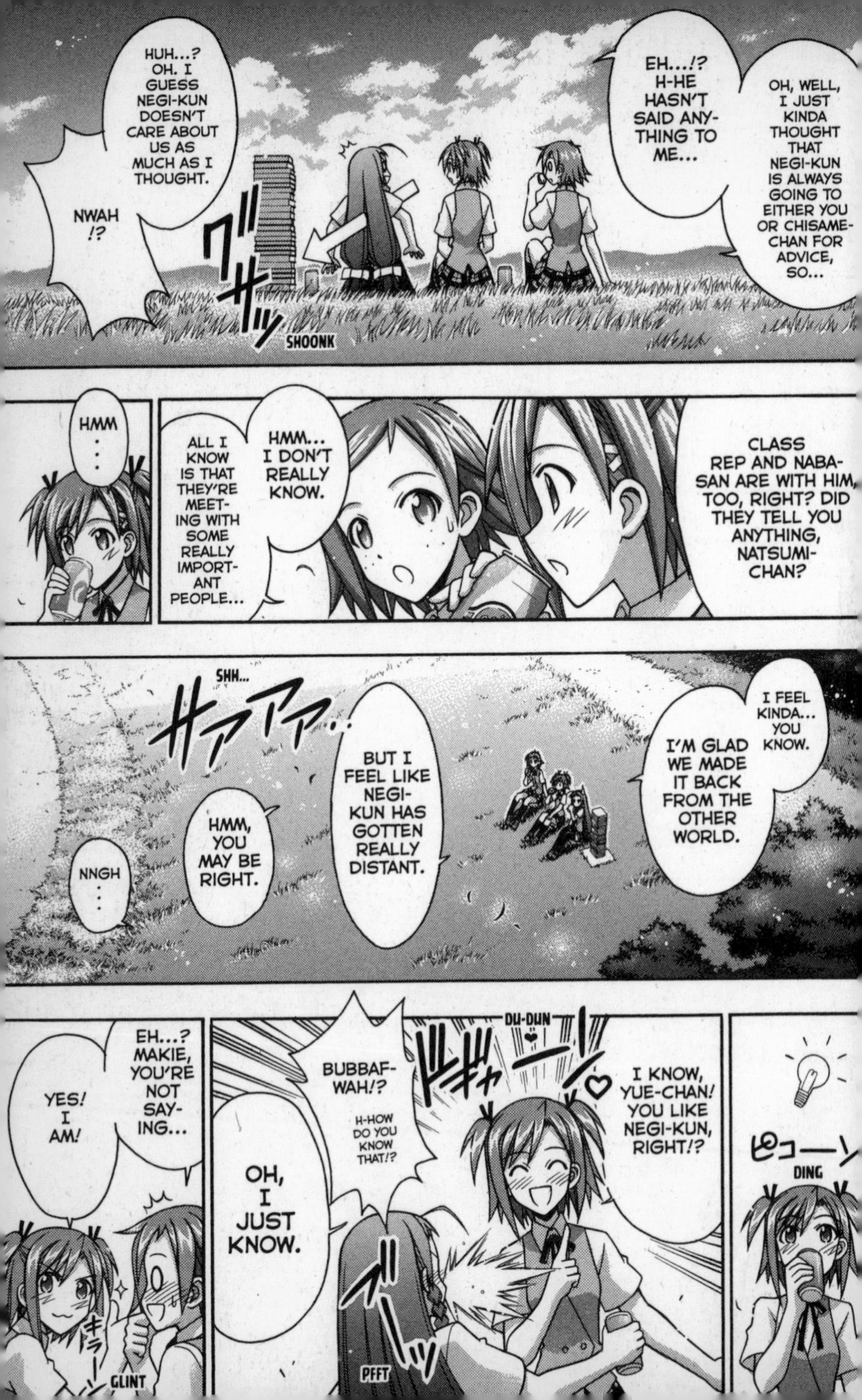
OH, WELL, I JUST KINDA THOUGHT THAT NEGI-KUN IS ALWAYS GOING TO EITHER YOU OR CHISAME-CHAN FOR ADVICE, SO...
EH...!? H-HE HASN'T SAID ANYTHING TO ME...
SHOONK
HUH...? OH. I GUESS NEGI-KUN DOESN'T CARE ABOUT US AS MUCH AS I THOUGHT.
NWAH !?
CLASS REP AND NABA-SAN ARE WITH HIM, TOO, RIGHT? DID THEY TELL YOU ANYTHING, NATSUMI-CHAN?
HMM... I DON'T REALLY KNOW.
ALL I KNOW IS THAT THEY'RE MEETING WITH SOME REALLY IMPORTANT PEOPLE...
HMM...
I FEEL KINDA... YOU KNOW.
I'M GLAD WE MADE IT BACK FROM THE OTHER WORLD.
BUT I FEEL LIKE NEGI-KUN HAS GOTTEN REALLY DISTANT.
SHH...
HMM, YOU MAY BE RIGHT.
NNGH...
DING
I KNOW, YUE-CHAN! YOU LIKE NEGI-KUN, RIGHT!?
DU-DUN
BUBBAFWAH!?
H-HOW DO YOU KNOW THAT!?
OH, I JUST KNOW.
PFFT
EH...? MAKIE, YOU'RE NOT SAYING...
YES! I AM!
GLINT

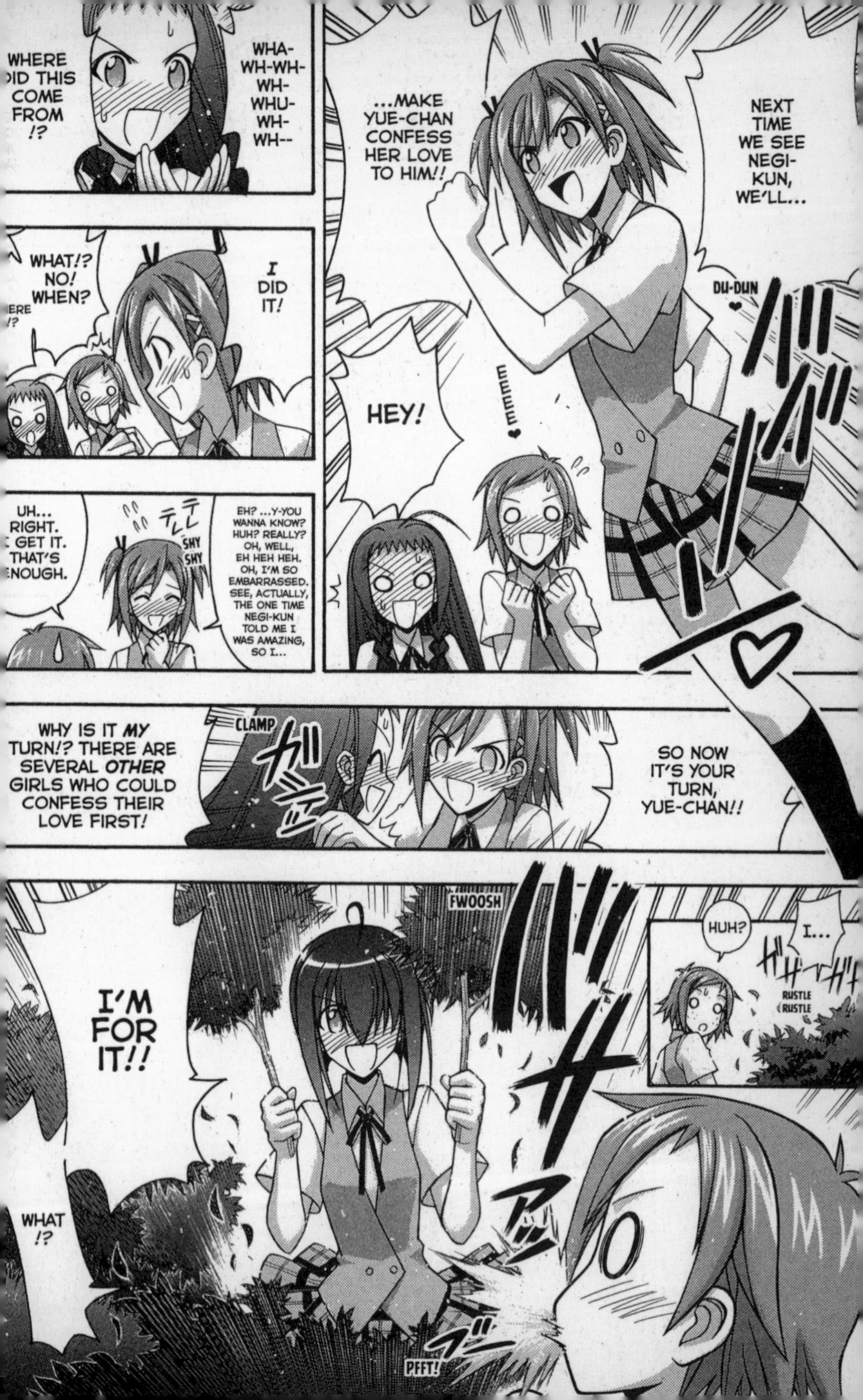

NEXT TIME WE SEE NEGI-KUN, WE'LL...
...MAKE YUE-CHAN CONFESS HER LOVE TO HIM!!
DU-DUN
HEY!
EEEE
WHA-WH-WH-WH-WHU-WH-WH--
WHERE DID THIS COME FROM !?
I DID IT!
WHAT!? NO! WHEN?
EH? ...Y-YOU WANNA KNOW? HUH? REALLY? OH, WELL, EH HEH HEH. OH, I'M SO EMBARRASSED. SEE, ACTUALLY, THE ONE TIME NEGI-KUN TOLD ME I WAS AMAZING, SO I...
SHY SHY
UH... RIGHT. I GET IT. THAT'S ENOUGH.
SO NOW IT'S YOUR TURN, YUE-CHAN!!
CLAMP
WHY IS IT MY TURN!? THERE ARE SEVERAL OTHER GIRLS WHO COULD CONFESS THEIR LOVE FIRST!
HUH?
I...
RUSTLE RUSTLE
FWOOSH
I'M FOR IT!!
WHAT !?
PFFT!

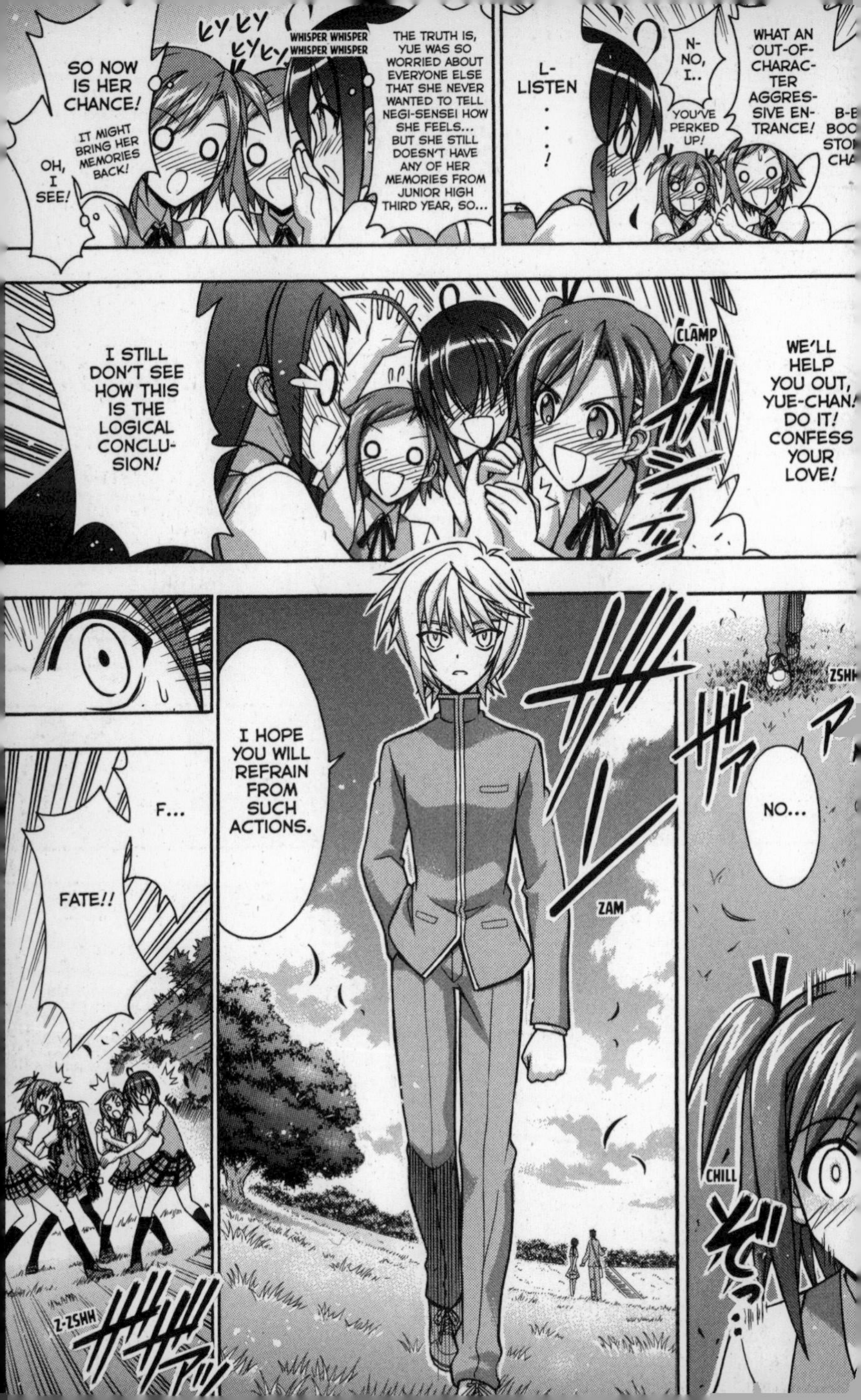
WHAT AN OUT-OF-CHARACTER AGGRESSIVE ENTRANCE!
B-B BOO STO CHA
N-NO, I..
YOU'VE PERKED UP!
L-LISTEN . . . . !
THE TRUTH IS, YUE WAS SO WORRIED ABOUT EVERYONE ELSE THAT SHE NEVER WANTED TO TELL NEGI-SENSEI HOW SHE FEELS... BUT SHE STILL DOESN'T HAVE ANY OF HER MEMORIES FROM JUNIOR HIGH THIRD YEAR, SO...
WHISPER WHISPER WHISPER WHISPER
SO NOW IS HER CHANCE!
IT MIGHT BRING HER MEMORIES BACK!
OH, I SEE!
WE'LL HELP YOU OUT, YUE-CHAN! DO IT! CONFESS YOUR LOVE!
CLAMP
I STILL DON'T SEE HOW THIS IS THE LOGICAL CONCLUSION!
ZSHH
NO...
CHILL
I HOPE YOU WILL REFRAIN FROM SUCH ACTIONS.
ZAM
F...
FATE!!
Z-ZSHH

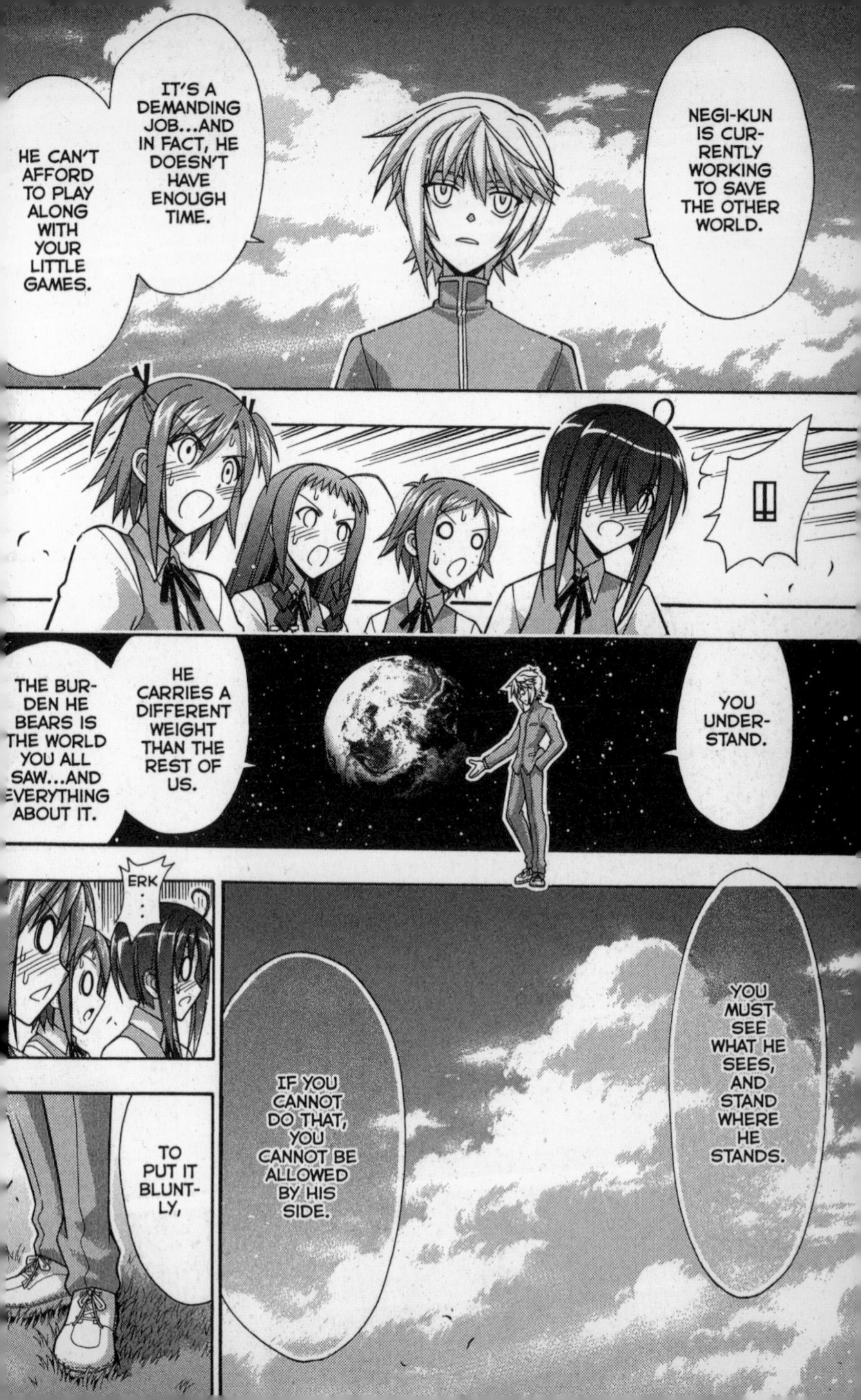
NEGI-KUN IS CURRENTLY WORKING TO SAVE THE OTHER WORLD.
IT'S A DEMANDING JOB...AND IN FACT, HE DOESN'T HAVE ENOUGH TIME.
HE CAN'T AFFORD TO PLAY ALONG WITH YOUR LITTLE GAMES.
!!
YOU UNDERSTAND.
HE CARRIES A DIFFERENT WEIGHT THAN THE REST OF US.
THE BURDEN HE BEARS IS THE WORLD YOU ALL SAW...AND EVERYTHING ABOUT IT.
YOU MUST SEE WHAT HE SEES, AND STAND WHERE HE STANDS.
IF YOU CANNOT DO THAT, YOU CANNOT BE ALLOWED BY HIS SIDE.
ERK...
TO PUT IT BLUNTLY,

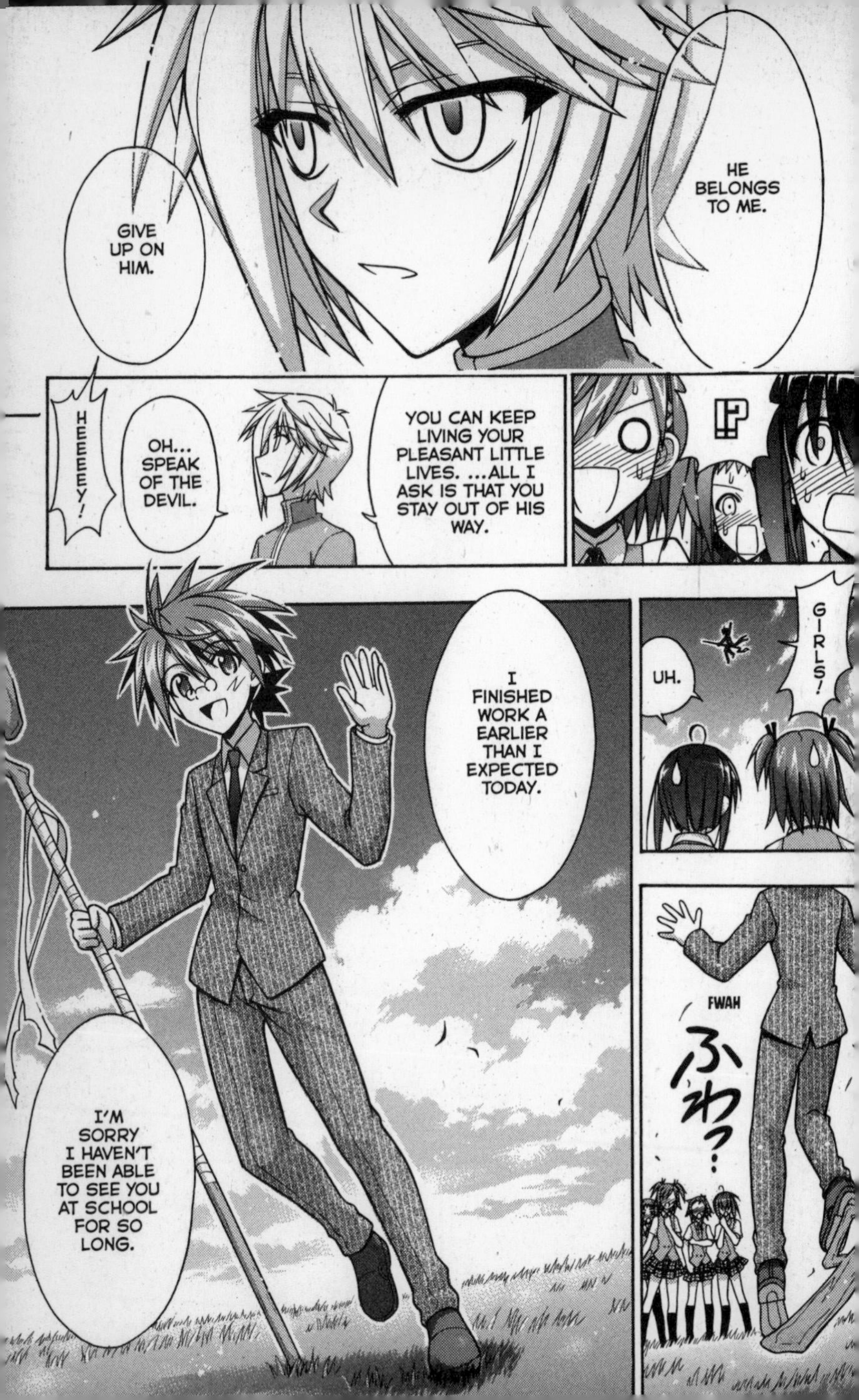
HE BELONGS TO ME.
GIVE UP ON HIM.
!?
YOU CAN KEEP LIVING YOUR PLEASANT LITTLE LIVES. ...ALL I ASK IS THAT YOU STAY OUT OF HIS WAY.
OH... SPEAK OF THE DEVIL.
HEEEEEY!
GIRLS!
UH.
FWAH
ふわっ
I FINISHED WORK A EARLIER THAN I EXPECTED TODAY.
I'M SORRY I HAVEN'T BEEN ABLE TO SEE YOU AT SCHOOL FOR SO LONG.

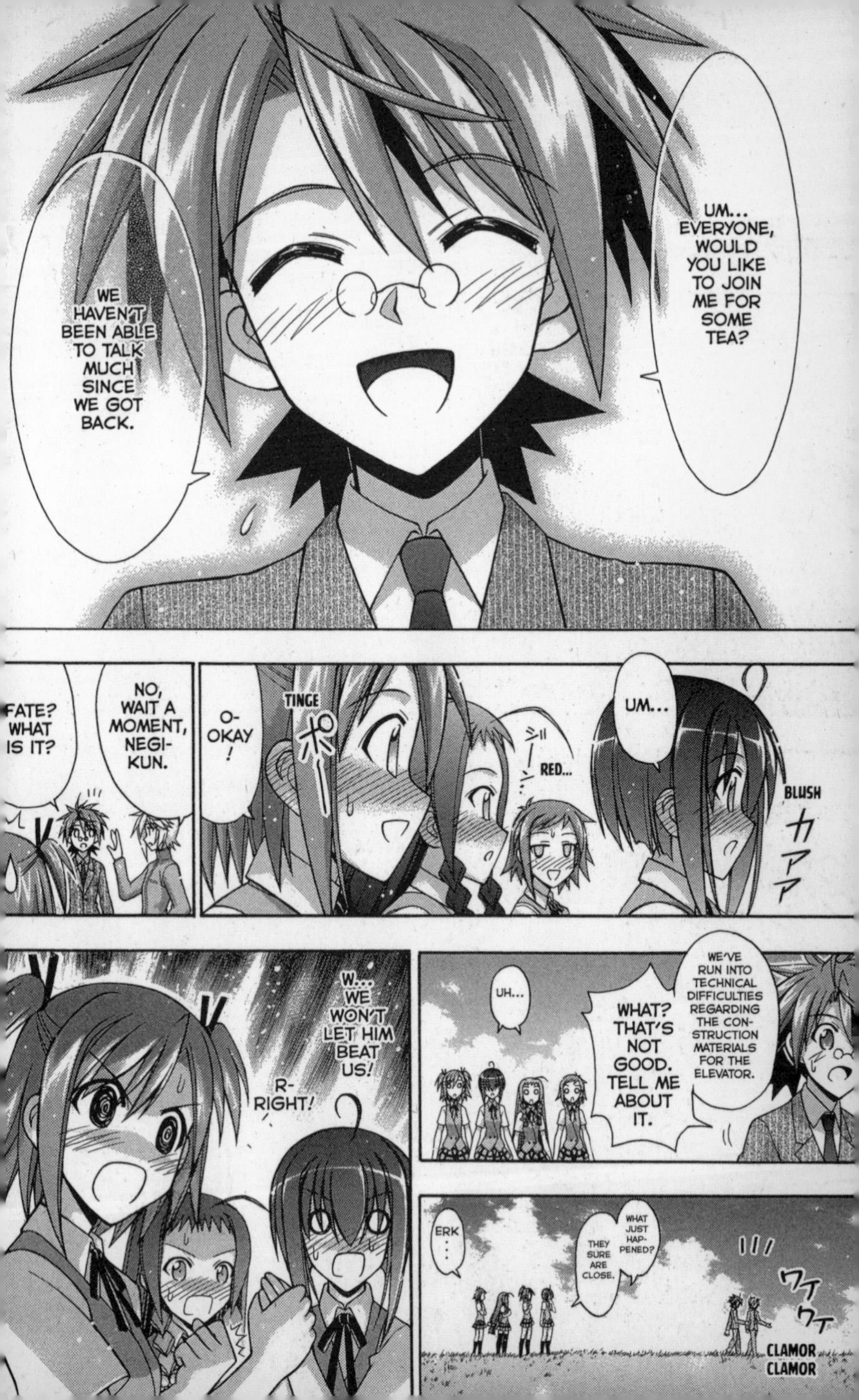
UM... EVERYONE, WOULD YOU LIKE TO JOIN ME FOR SOME TEA?
WE HAVEN'T BEEN ABLE TO TALK MUCH SINCE WE GOT BACK.
UM...
BLUSH
RED...
TINGE
O-OKAY!
NO, WAIT A MOMENT, NEGI-KUN.
FATE? WHAT IS IT?
WE'VE RUN INTO TECHNICAL DIFFICULTIES REGARDING THE CONSTRUCTION MATERIALS FOR THE ELEVATOR.
WHAT? THAT'S NOT GOOD. TELL ME ABOUT IT.
UH...
CLAMOR CLAMOR
WHAT JUST HAPPENED?
THEY SURE ARE CLOSE.
ERK...
W... WE WON'T LET HIM BEAT US!
R-RIGHT!

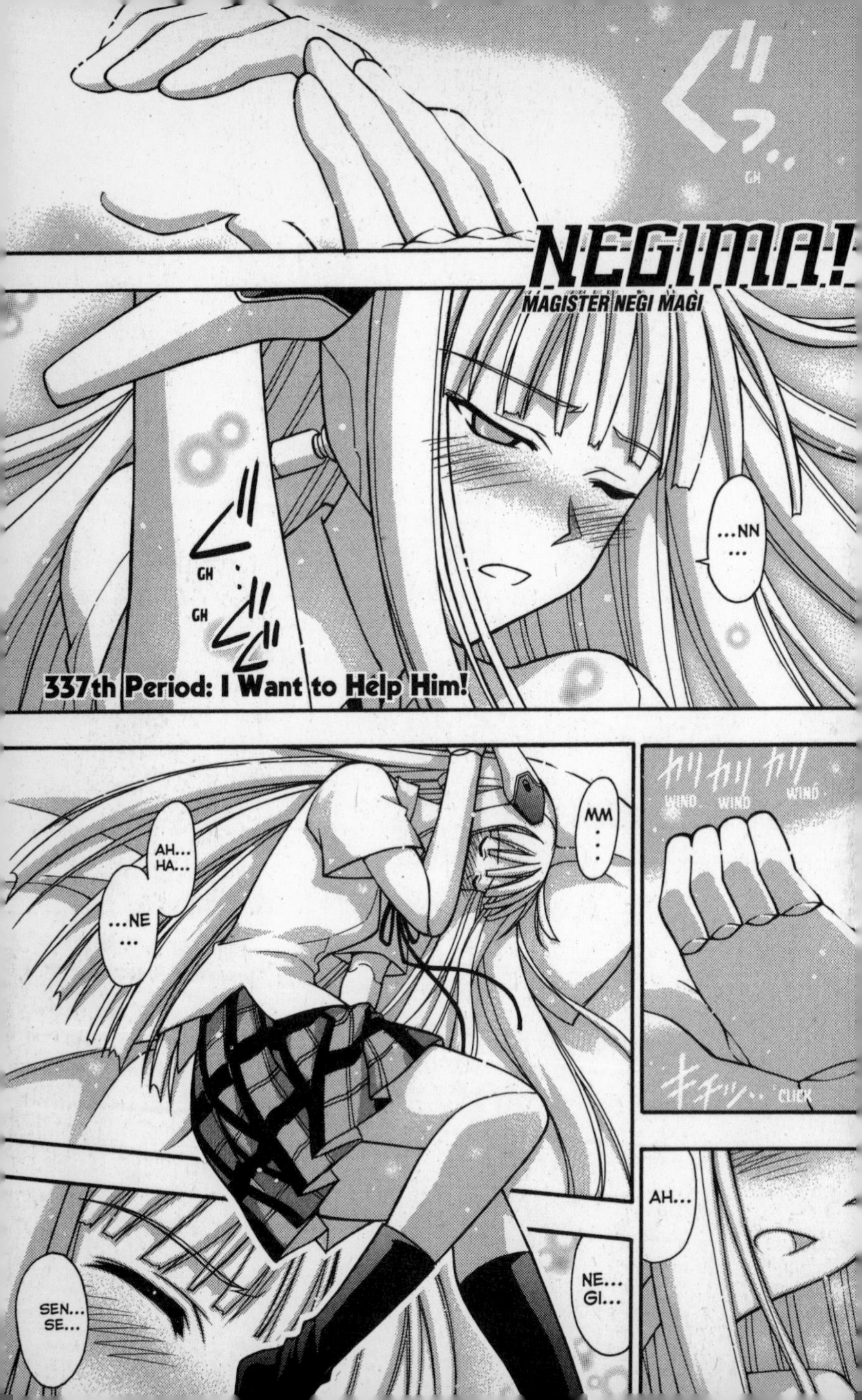
ぐっ..
GH
NEGIMA!
MAGISTER NEGI MAGI
...NN ...
GH
GH
337th Period: I Want to Help Him!
カリ カリ カリ
WIND WIND WIND
キチッ..
CLICK
MM ...
AH... HA...
...NE ...
AH...
NE... GI...
SEN... SE...

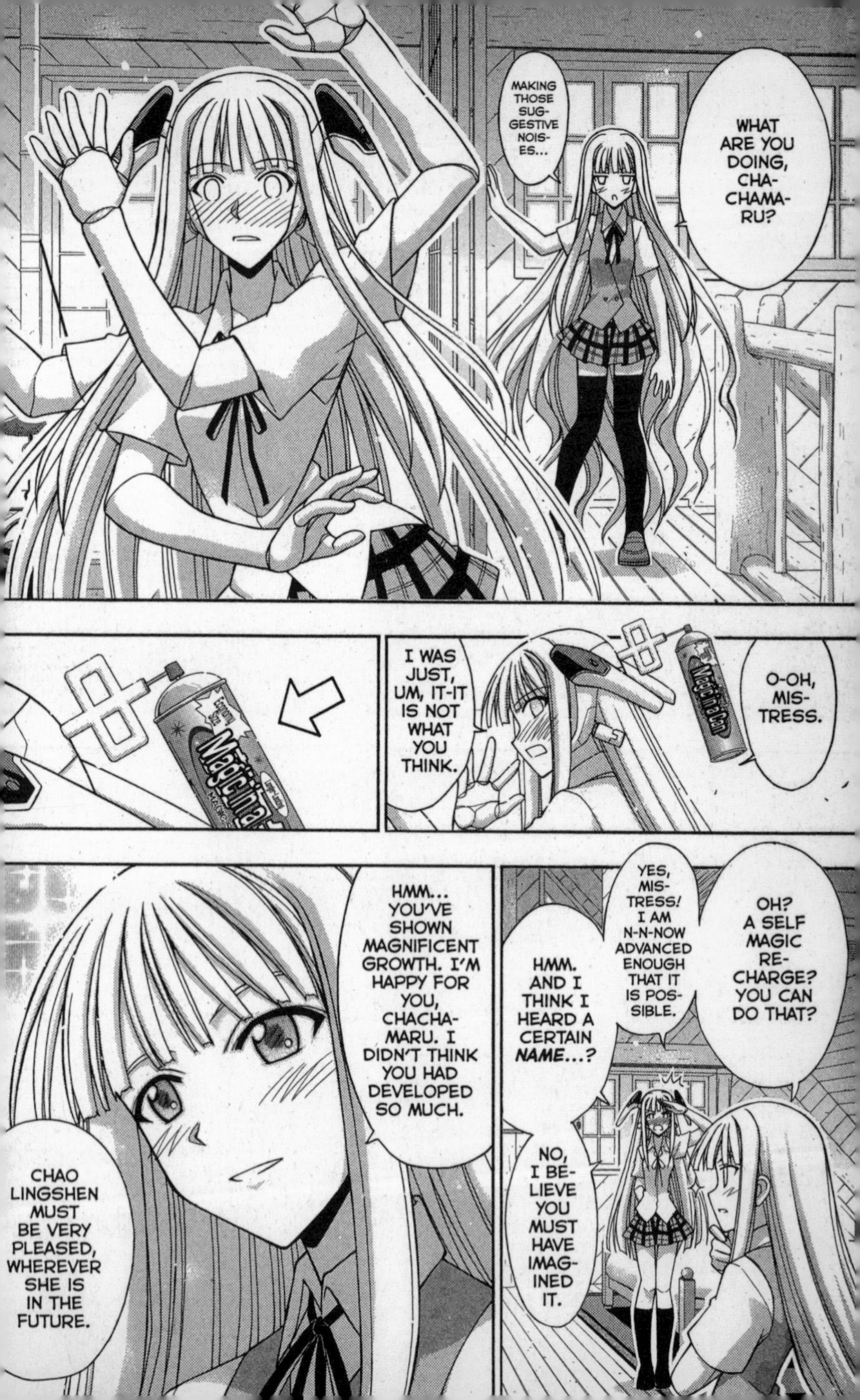
WHAT ARE YOU DOING, CHACHAMARU?
MAKING THOSE SUGGESTIVE NOISES...
O-OH, MISTRESS.
Magic in a Can
I WAS JUST, UM, IT-IT IS NOT WHAT YOU THINK.
OH? A SELF MAGIC RECHARGE? YOU CAN DO THAT?
YES, MISTRESS! I AM N-N-NOW ADVANCED ENOUGH THAT IT IS POSSIBLE.
HMM. AND I THINK I HEARD A CERTAIN *NAME...?*
NO, I BELIEVE YOU MUST HAVE IMAGINED IT.
HMM... YOU'VE SHOWN MAGNIFICENT GROWTH. I'M HAPPY FOR YOU, CHACHAMARU. I DIDN'T THINK YOU HAD DEVELOPED SO MUCH.
CHAO LINGSHEN MUST BE VERY PLEASED, WHEREVER SHE IS IN THE FUTURE.

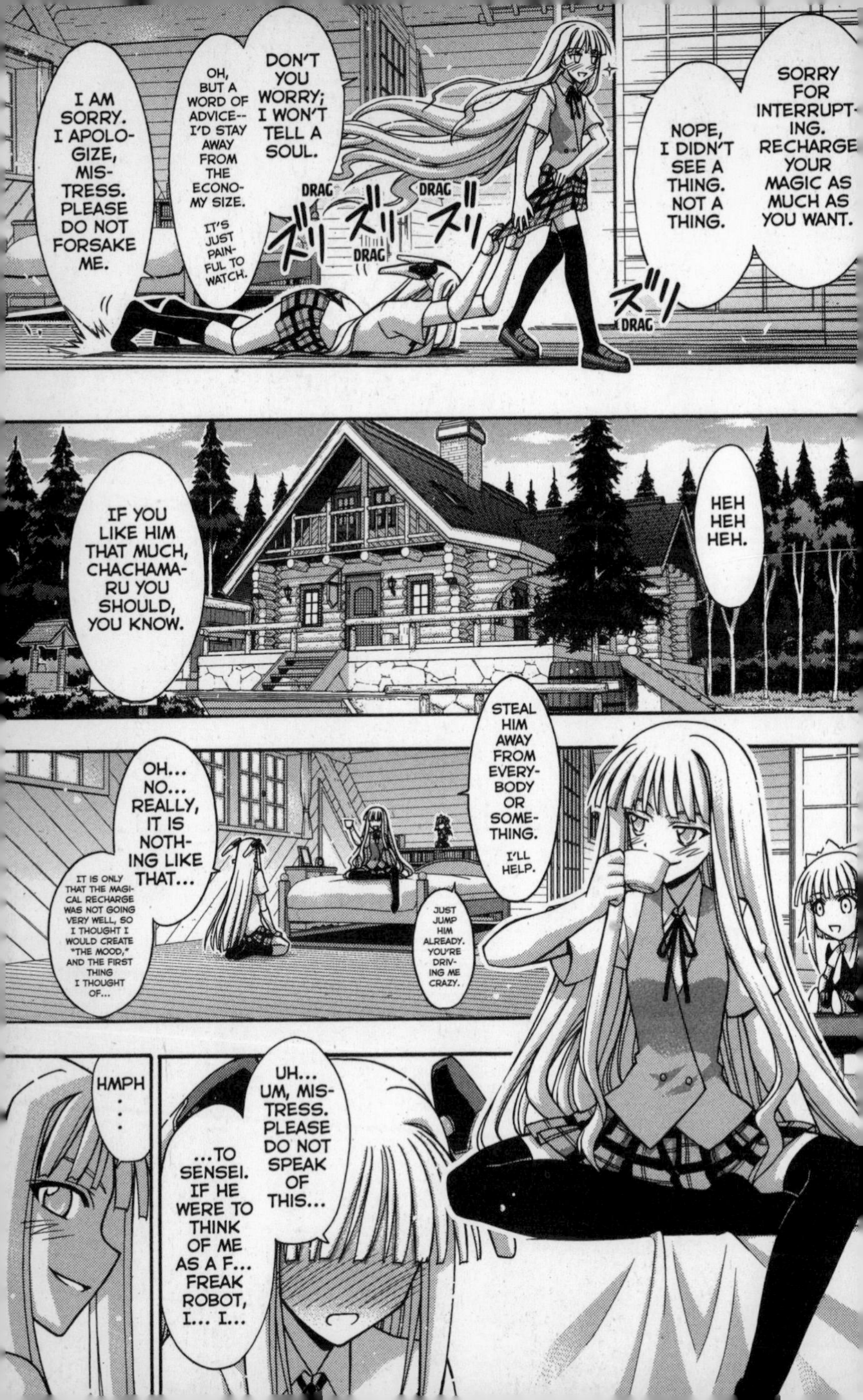
SORRY FOR INTERRUPTING. RECHARGE YOUR MAGIC AS MUCH AS YOU WANT.
NOPE, I DIDN'T SEE A THING. NOT A THING.
ズリ DRAG
ズリ DRAG
ズリ DRAG
ズリ DRAG
DON'T YOU WORRY; I WON'T TELL A SOUL.
OH, BUT A WORD OF ADVICE-- I'D STAY AWAY FROM THE ECONOMY SIZE.
IT'S JUST PAINFUL TO WATCH.
I AM SORRY. I APOLOGIZE, MISTRESS. PLEASE DO NOT FORSAKE ME.
HEH HEH HEH.
IF YOU LIKE HIM THAT MUCH, CHACHAMARU YOU SHOULD, YOU KNOW.
STEAL HIM AWAY FROM EVERYBODY OR SOMETHING.
I'LL HELP.
JUST JUMP HIM ALREADY. YOU'RE DRIVING ME CRAZY.
OH... NO... REALLY, IT IS NOTHING LIKE THAT...
IT IS ONLY THAT THE MAGICAL RECHARGE WAS NOT GOING VERY WELL, SO I THOUGHT I WOULD CREATE "THE MOOD," AND THE FIRST THING I THOUGHT OF...
UH... UM, MISTRESS. PLEASE DO NOT SPEAK OF THIS...
...TO SENSEI. IF HE WERE TO THINK OF ME AS A F... FREAK ROBOT, I... I...
HMPH . . .

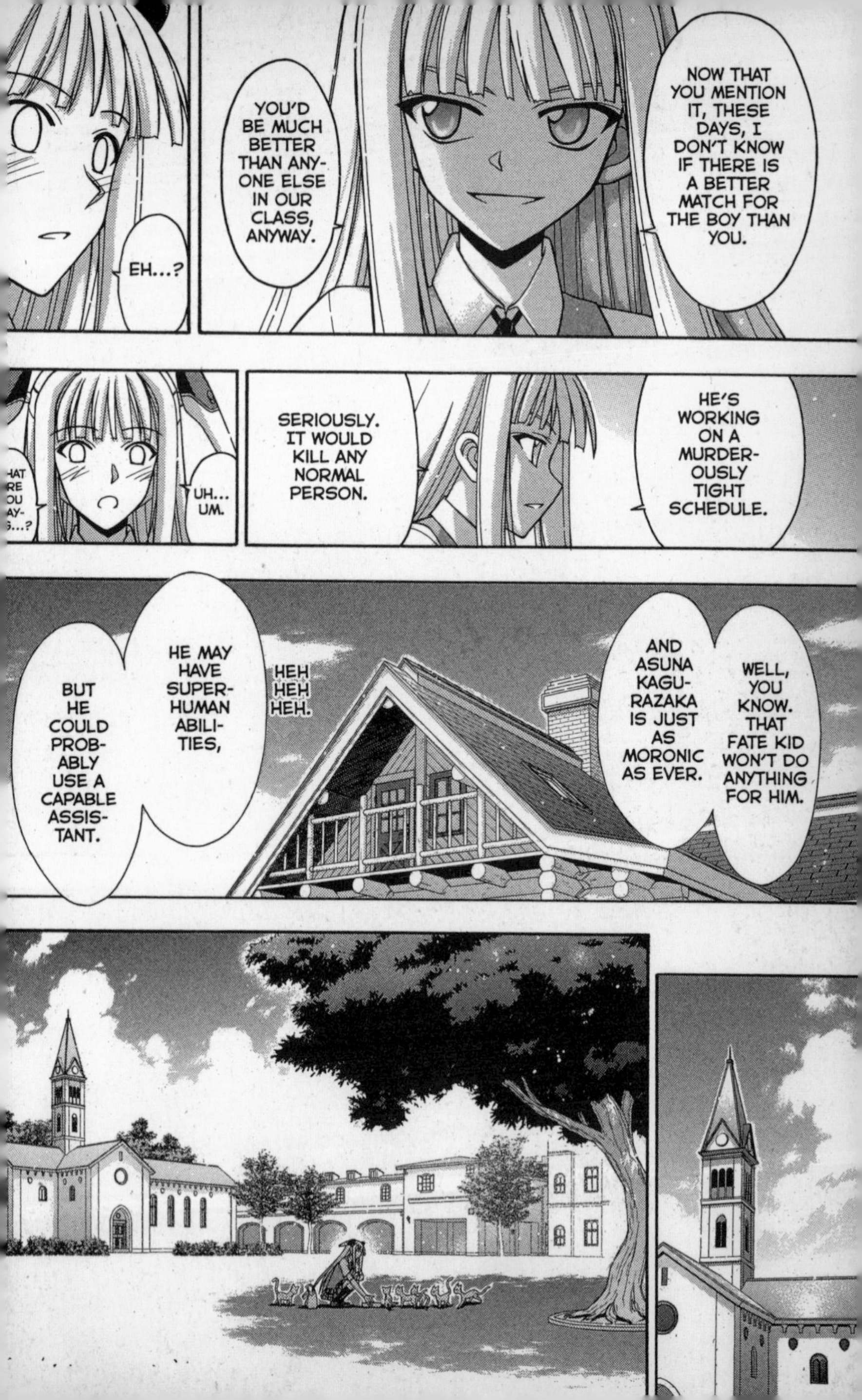
NOW THAT YOU MENTION IT, THESE DAYS, I DON'T KNOW IF THERE IS A BETTER MATCH FOR THE BOY THAN YOU.
YOU'D BE MUCH BETTER THAN ANY-ONE ELSE IN OUR CLASS, ANYWAY.
EH...?
HE'S WORKING ON A MURDER-OUSLY TIGHT SCHEDULE.
SERIOUSLY. IT WOULD KILL ANY NORMAL PERSON.
UH... UM.
WELL, YOU KNOW. THAT FATE KID WON'T DO ANYTHING FOR HIM.
AND ASUNA KAGU-RAZAKA IS JUST AS MORONIC AS EVER.
HEH HEH HEH.
HE MAY HAVE SUPER-HUMAN ABILI-TIES,
BUT HE COULD PROB-ABLY USE A CAPABLE ASSIS-TANT.

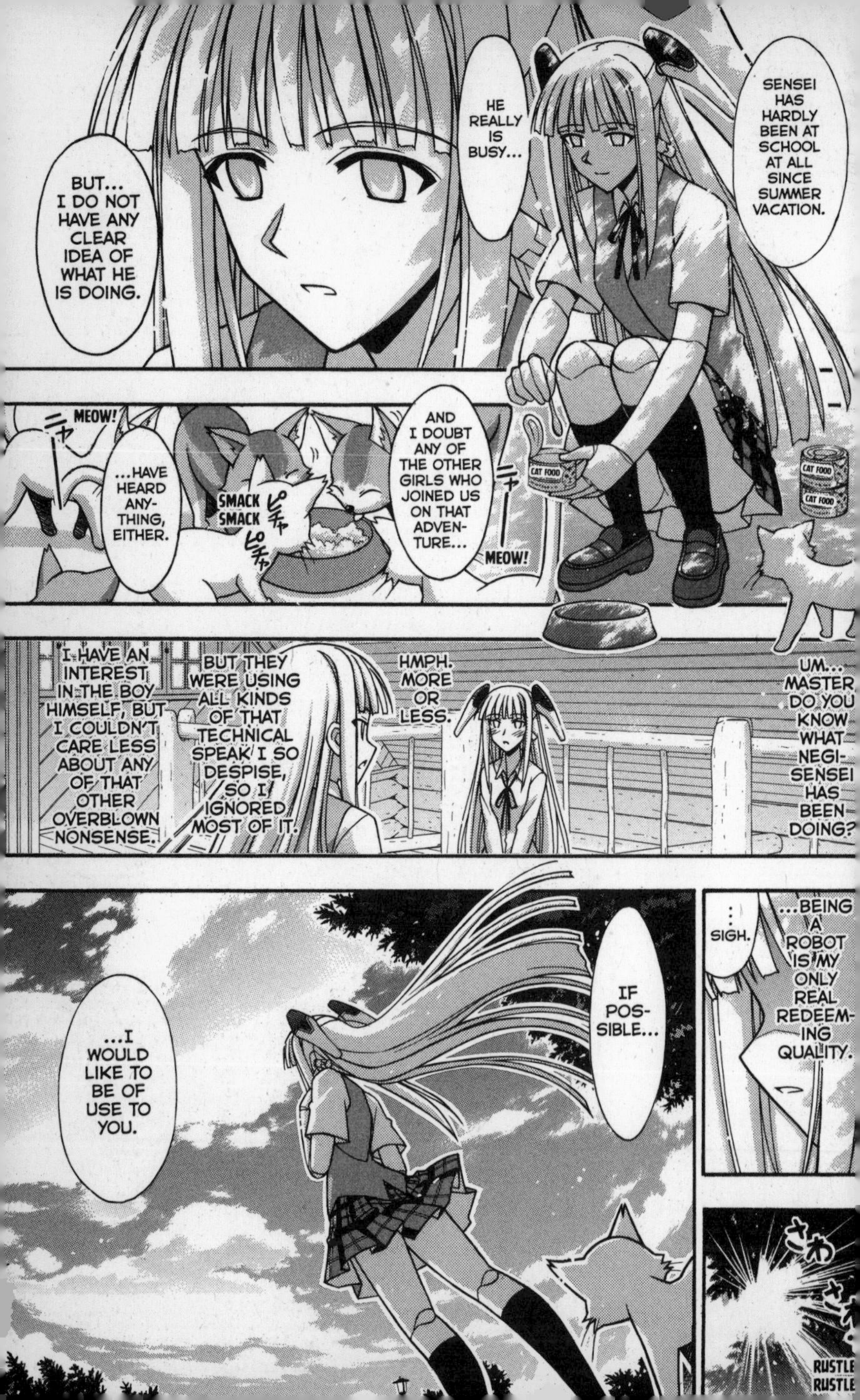
SENSEI HAS HARDLY BEEN AT SCHOOL AT ALL SINCE SUMMER VACATION.
HE REALLY IS BUSY...
BUT... I DO NOT HAVE ANY CLEAR IDEA OF WHAT HE IS DOING.
AND I DOUBT ANY OF THE OTHER GIRLS WHO JOINED US ON THAT ADVENTURE...
MEOW!
SMACK SMACK
...HAVE HEARD ANYTHING, EITHER.
MEOW!
UM... MASTER DO YOU KNOW WHAT NEGI-SENSEI HAS BEEN DOING?
HMPH. MORE OR LESS.
BUT THEY WERE USING ALL KINDS OF THAT TECHNICAL SPEAK I SO DESPISE, SO I IGNORED MOST OF IT.
I HAVE AN INTEREST IN THE BOY HIMSELF, BUT I COULDN'T CARE LESS ABOUT ANY OF THAT OTHER OVERBLOWN NONSENSE.
...BEING A ROBOT IS MY ONLY REAL REDEEMING QUALITY.
...SIGH.
RUSTLE RUSTLE
IF POSSIBLE...
...I WOULD LIKE TO BE OF USE TO YOU.

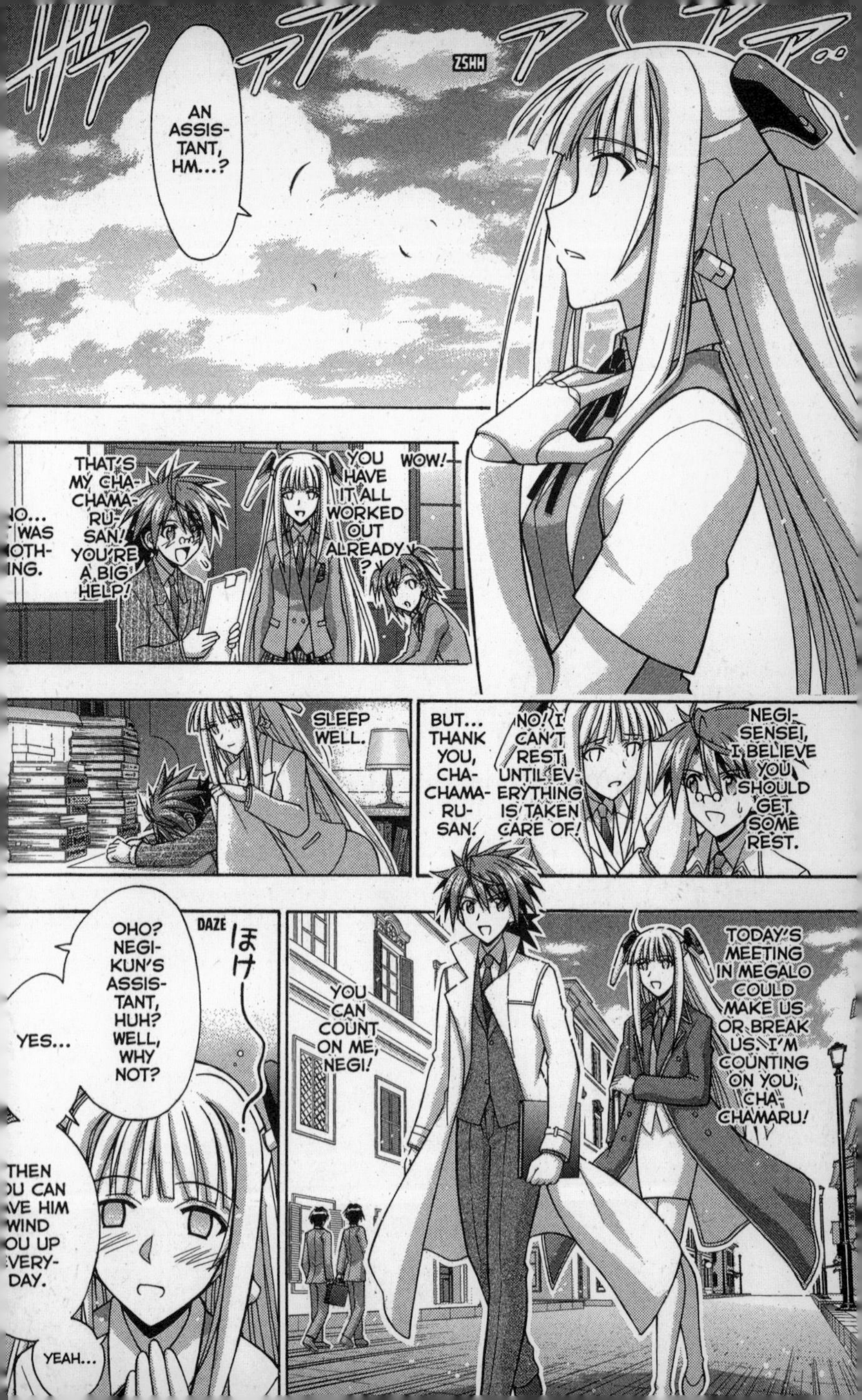
ZSHH
AN ASSISTANT, HM...?
WOW!
YOU HAVE IT ALL WORKED OUT ALREADY?
THAT'S MY CHACHAMARU-SAN! YOU'RE A BIG HELP!
NO... T WAS OTHING.
NEGI-SENSEI, I BELIEVE YOU SHOULD GET SOME REST.
NO! I CAN'T REST UNTIL EVERYTHING IS TAKEN CARE OF!
BUT... THANK YOU, CHACHAMARU-SAN.
SLEEP WELL.
TODAY'S MEETING IN MEGALO COULD MAKE US OR BREAK US. I'M COUNTING ON YOU, CHACHAMARU!
YOU CAN COUNT ON ME, NEGI!
DAZE
ほけ
OHO? NEGI-KUN'S ASSISTANT, HUH? WELL, WHY NOT?
YES...
THEN OU CAN AVE HIM WIND OU UP VERY-DAY.
YEAH...

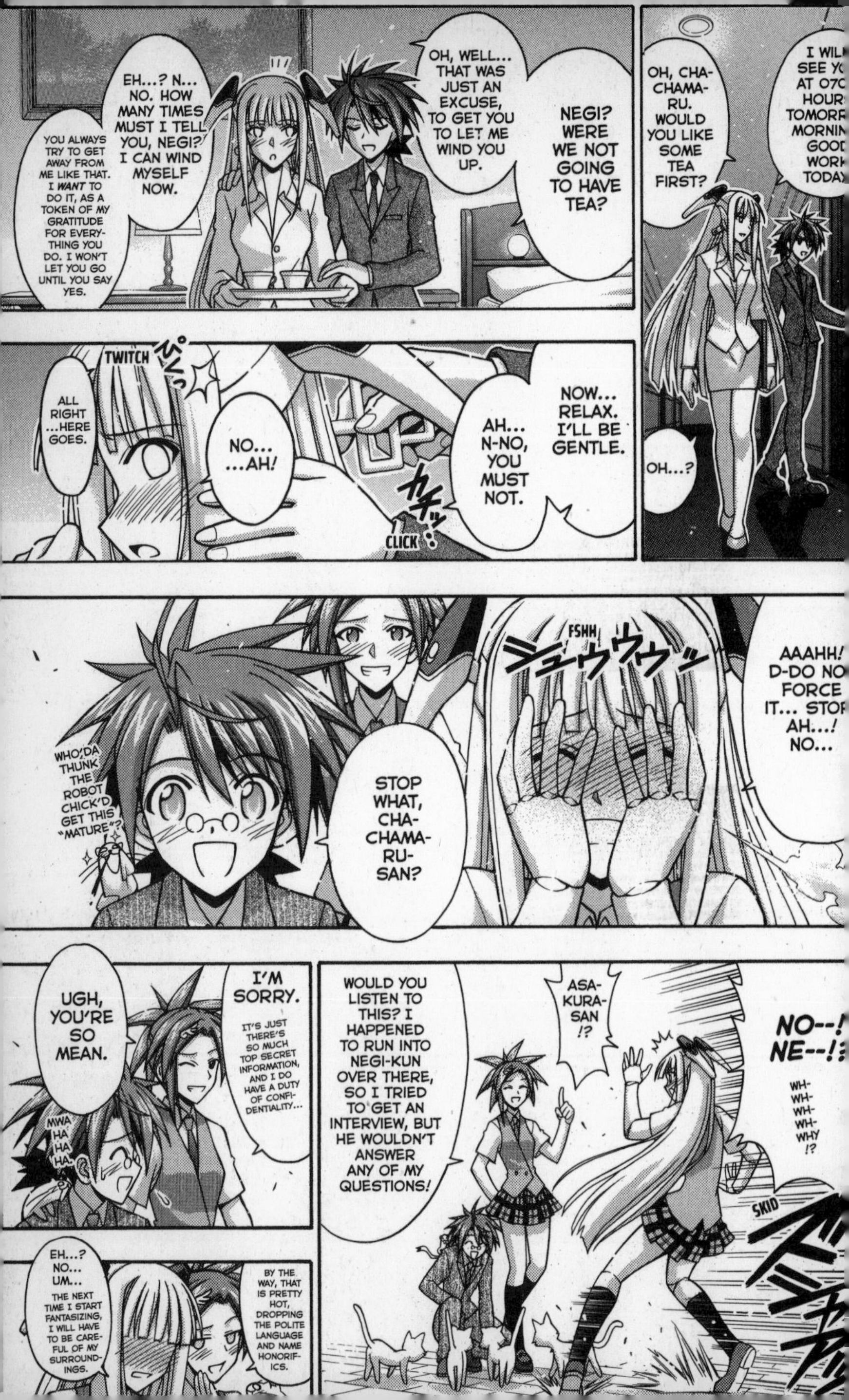
I WIL SEE YO AT 070 HOURS TOMORR MORNIN GOOD WORK TODAY
OH, CHA-CHAMA-RU. WOULD YOU LIKE SOME TEA FIRST?
OH...?
NEGI? WERE WE NOT GOING TO HAVE TEA?
OH, WELL... THAT WAS JUST AN EXCUSE, TO GET YOU TO LET ME WIND YOU UP.
EH...? N... NO. HOW MANY TIMES MUST I TELL YOU, NEGI? I CAN WIND MYSELF NOW.
YOU ALWAYS TRY TO GET AWAY FROM ME LIKE THAT. I *WANT* TO DO IT, AS A TOKEN OF MY GRATITUDE FOR EVERY-THING YOU DO. I WON'T LET YOU GO UNTIL YOU SAY YES.
NOW... RELAX. I'LL BE GENTLE.
AH... N-NO, YOU MUST NOT.
CLICK
NO... ...AH!
TWITCH
ALL RIGHT ...HERE GOES.
AAAHH! D-DO NO FORCE IT... STOP AH...! NO...
FSHH
STOP WHAT, CHA-CHAMA-RU-SAN?
WHO'DA THUNK THE ROBOT CHICK'D GET THIS "MATURE"?
NO--! NE--!?
WH-WH-WH-WH-WHY !?
ASA-KURA-SAN !?
WOULD YOU LISTEN TO THIS? I HAPPENED TO RUN INTO NEGI-KUN OVER THERE, SO I TRIED TO GET AN INTERVIEW, BUT HE WOULDN'T ANSWER ANY OF MY QUESTIONS!
SKID
I'M SORRY.
IT'S JUST THERE'S SO MUCH TOP SECRET INFORMATION, AND I DO HAVE A DUTY OF CONFI-DENTIALITY...
UGH, YOU'RE SO MEAN.
MWA HA HA HA.
BY THE WAY, THAT IS PRETTY HOT, DROPPING THE POLITE LANGUAGE AND NAME HONORIF-ICS.
EH...? NO... UM... THE NEXT TIME I START FANTASIZING, I WILL HAVE TO BE CARE-FUL OF MY SURROUND-INGS.

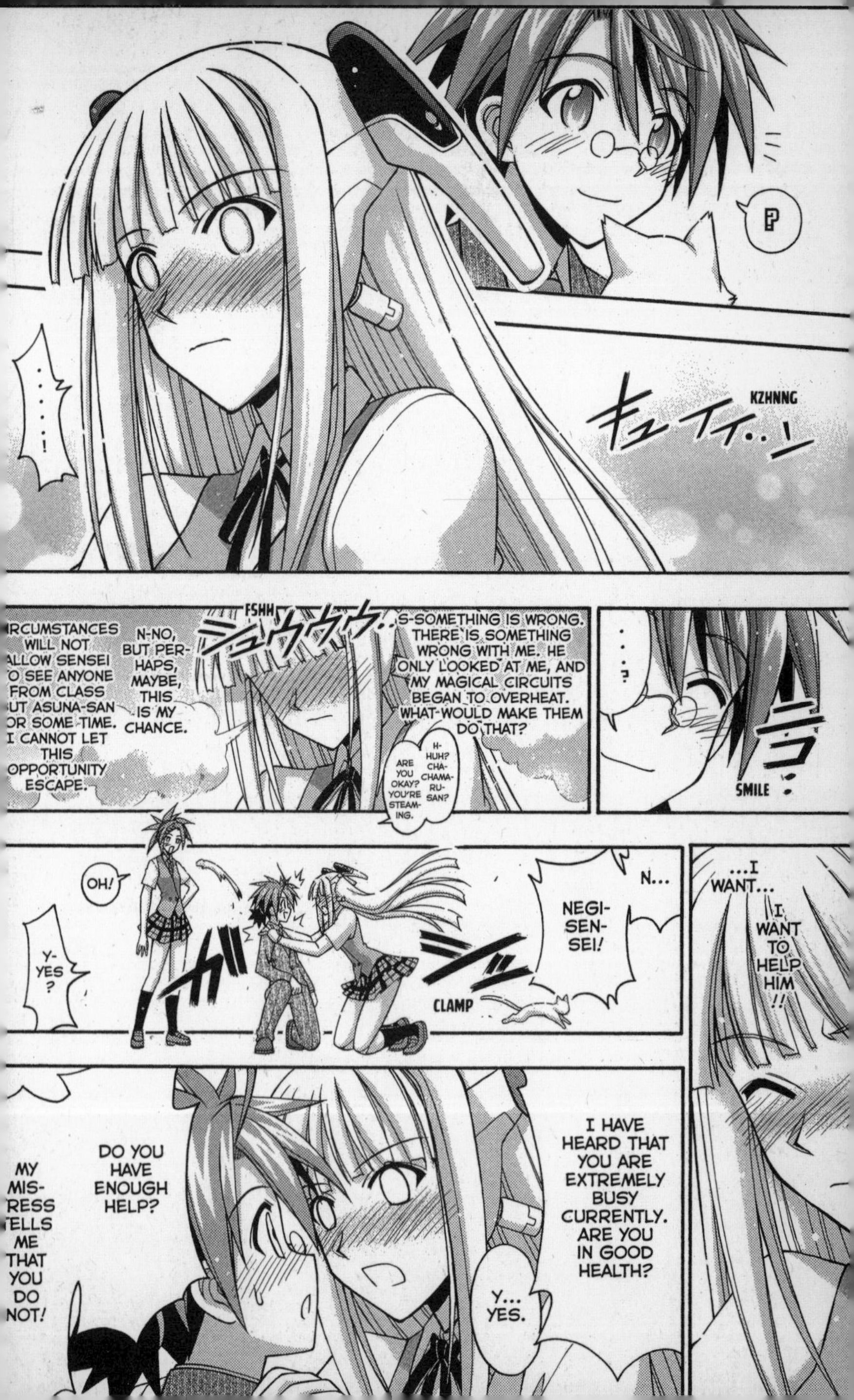
?
KZHNNG
......!
...?
SMILE
S-SOMETHING IS WRONG. THERE IS SOMETHING WRONG WITH ME. HE ONLY LOOKED AT ME, AND MY MAGICAL CIRCUITS BEGAN TO OVERHEAT. WHAT WOULD MAKE THEM DO THAT?
FSHH
N-NO, BUT PER-HAPS, MAYBE, THIS IS MY CHANCE.
RCUMSTANCES WILL NOT ALLOW SENSEI O SEE ANYONE FROM CLASS UT ASUNA-SAN OR SOME TIME. I CANNOT LET THIS OPPORTUNITY ESCAPE.
H-HUH? CHA-CHAMA-RU-SAN?
ARE YOU OKAY? YOU'RE STEAM-ING.
...I WANT...
I WANT TO HELP HIM!!
N...
NEGI-SEN-SEI!
CLAMP
OH!
Y-YES?
I HAVE HEARD THAT YOU ARE EXTREMELY BUSY CURRENTLY. ARE YOU IN GOOD HEALTH?
Y... YES.
DO YOU HAVE ENOUGH HELP?
MY MIS-RESS ELLS ME THAT YOU DO NOT!

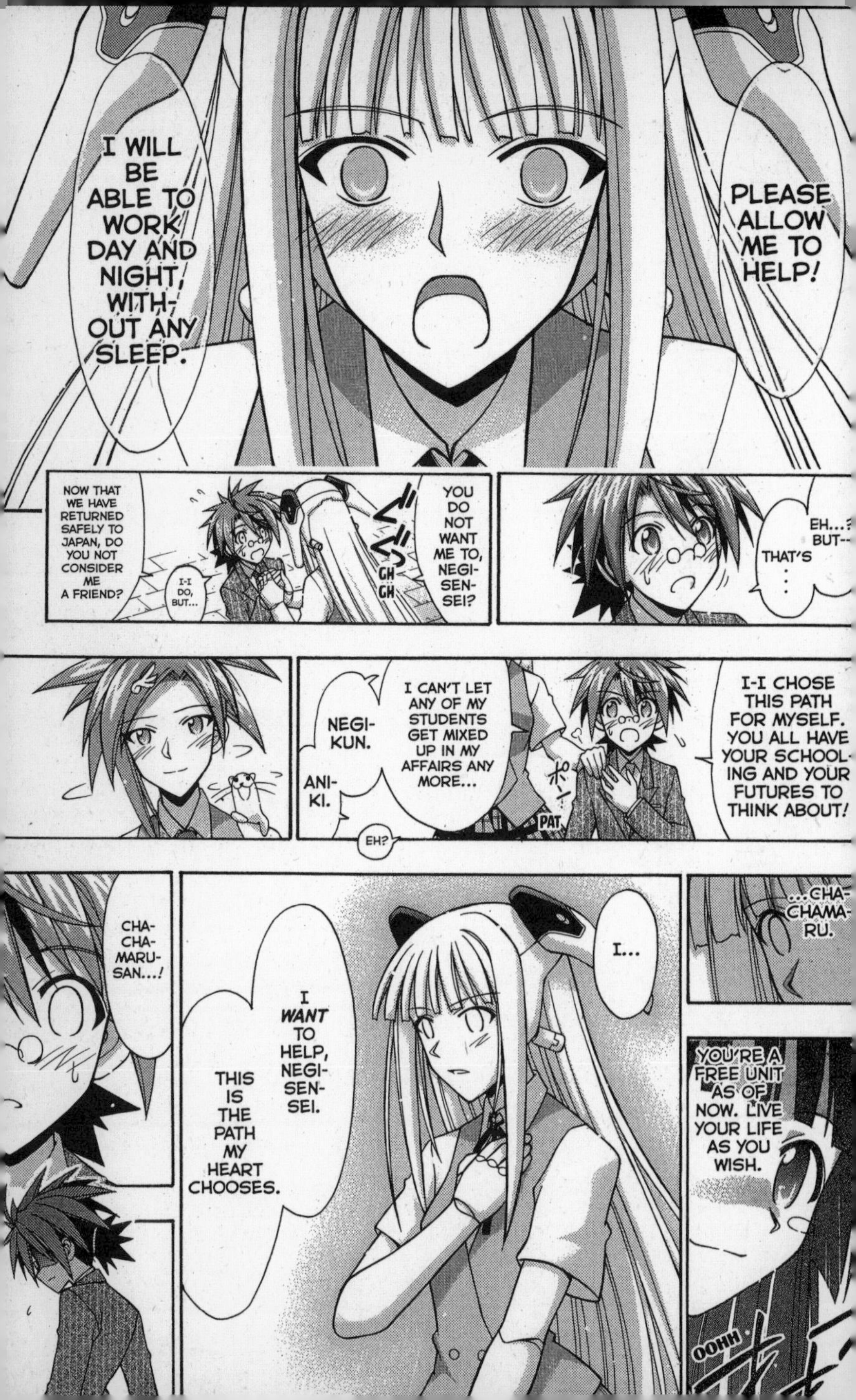
PLEASE ALLOW ME TO HELP!
I WILL BE ABLE TO WORK DAY AND NIGHT, WITHOUT ANY SLEEP.
EH...? BUT-- THAT'S ...
YOU DO NOT WANT ME TO, NEGI-SENSEI?
GH GH
NOW THAT WE HAVE RETURNED SAFELY TO JAPAN, DO YOU NOT CONSIDER ME A FRIEND?
I-I DO, BUT...
I-I CHOSE THIS PATH FOR MYSELF. YOU ALL HAVE YOUR SCHOOLING AND YOUR FUTURES TO THINK ABOUT!
PAT
I CAN'T LET ANY OF MY STUDENTS GET MIXED UP IN MY AFFAIRS ANY MORE...
NEGI-KUN.
ANI-KI.
EH?
...CHACHAMARU.
YOU'RE A FREE UNIT AS OF NOW. LIVE YOUR LIFE AS YOU WISH.
OOHH
I...
I *WANT* TO HELP, NEGI-SENSEI.
THIS IS THE PATH MY HEART CHOOSES.
CHACHAMARU-SAN...!

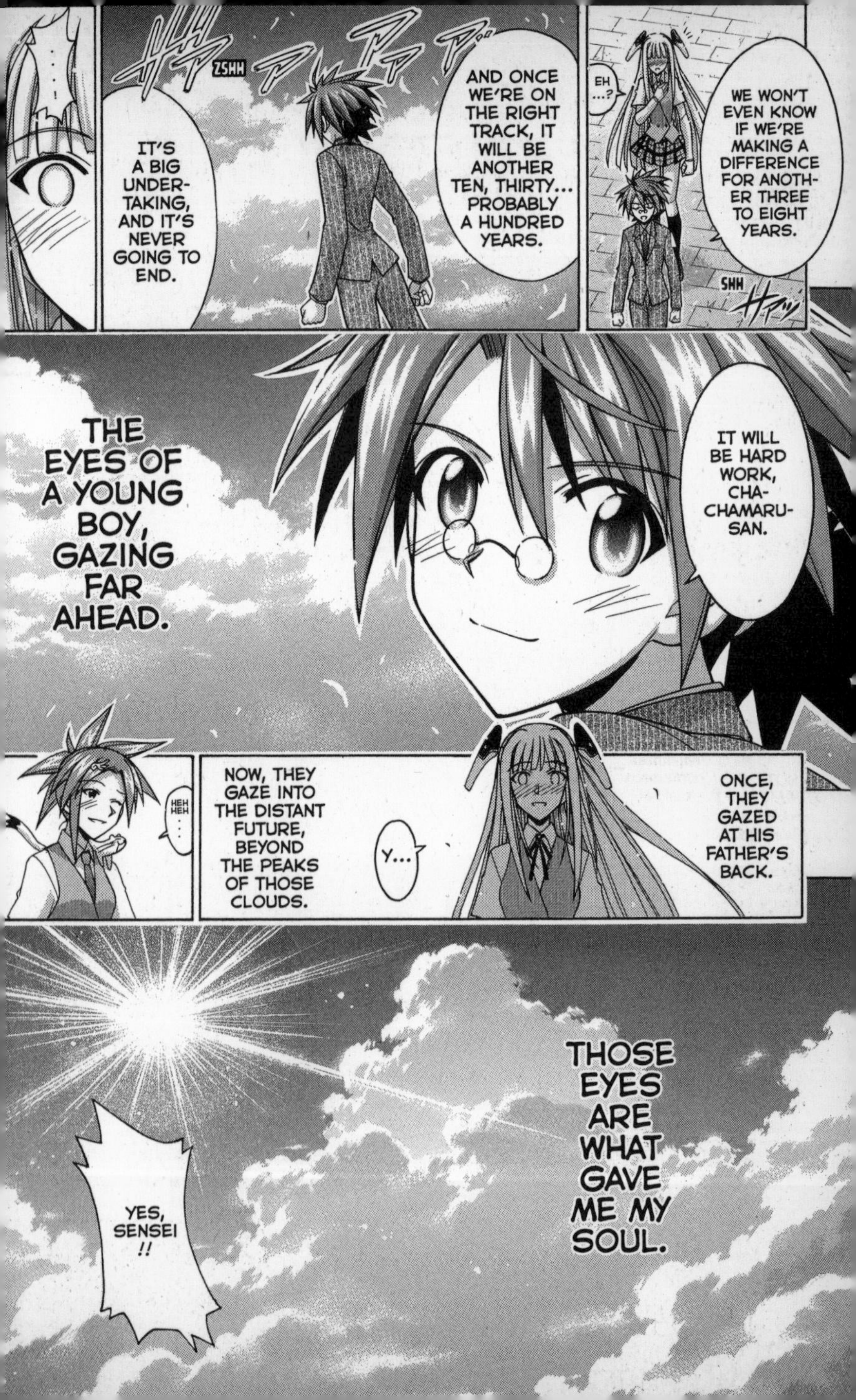

EH ...?
WE WON'T EVEN KNOW IF WE'RE MAKING A DIFFERENCE FOR ANOTHER THREE TO EIGHT YEARS.
SHH
AND ONCE WE'RE ON THE RIGHT TRACK, IT WILL BE ANOTHER TEN, THIRTY... PROBABLY A HUNDRED YEARS.
ZSHH
IT'S A BIG UNDERTAKING, AND IT'S NEVER GOING TO END.
...!
IT WILL BE HARD WORK, CHACHAMARU-SAN.
THE EYES OF A YOUNG BOY, GAZING FAR AHEAD.
ONCE, THEY GAZED AT HIS FATHER'S BACK.
Y...
NOW, THEY GAZE INTO THE DISTANT FUTURE, BEYOND THE PEAKS OF THOSE CLOUDS.
HEH HEH...
THOSE EYES ARE WHAT GAVE ME MY SOUL.
YES, SENSEI!!

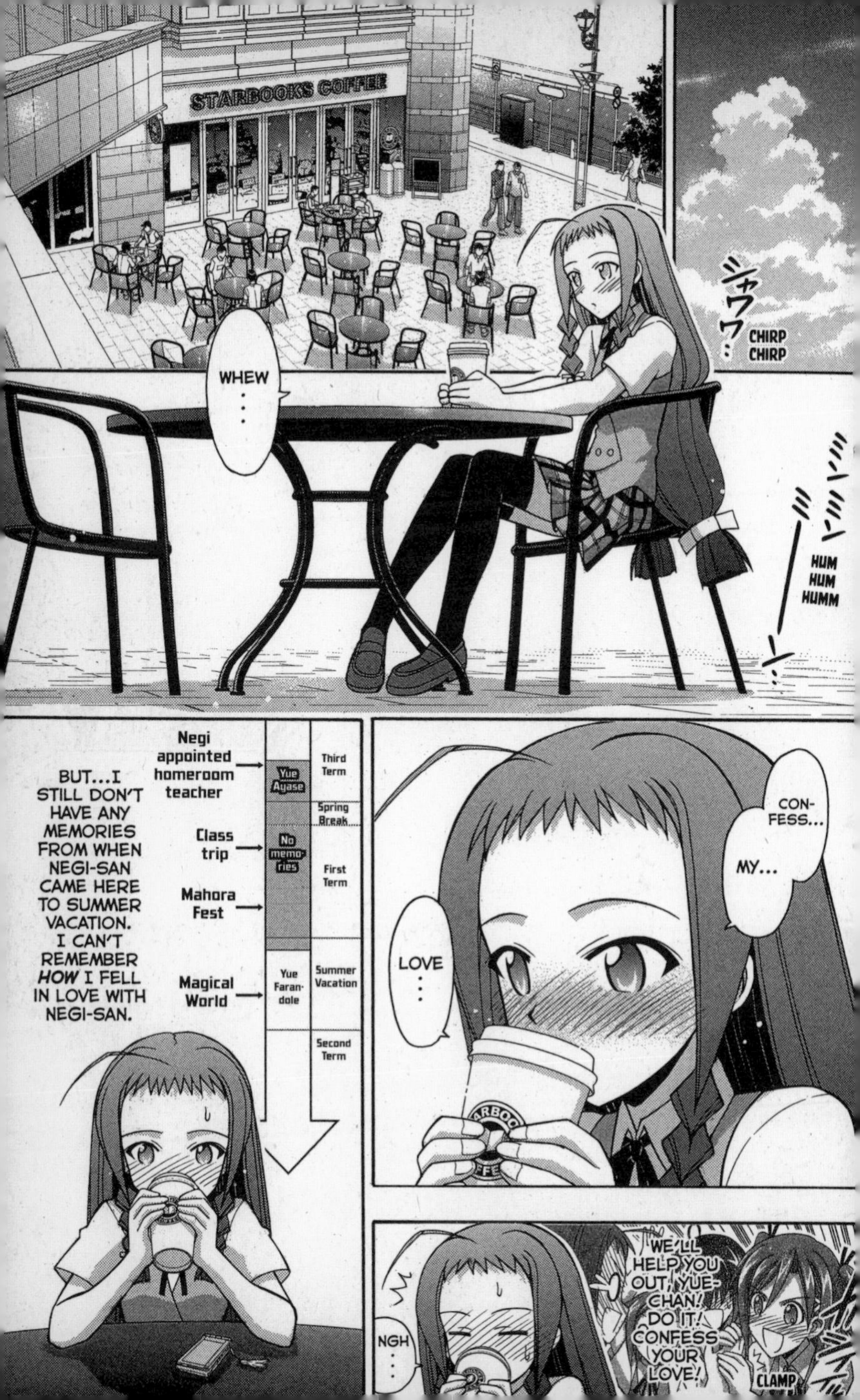
STARBOOKS COFFEE
シャワワ…
CHIRP CHIRP
WHEW…
ミンミンミーン
HUM HUM HUMM
CON-FESS…
MY…
LOVE…
NGH…
WE'LL HELP YOU OUT, YUE-CHAN! DO IT! CONFESS YOUR LOVE!
CLAMP
BUT…I STILL DON'T HAVE ANY MEMORIES FROM WHEN NEGI-SAN CAME HERE TO SUMMER VACATION. I CAN'T REMEMBER *HOW* I FELL IN LOVE WITH NEGI-SAN.
Negi appointed homeroom teacher
Class trip
Mahora Fest
Magical World
Yue Ayase
No memories
Yue Farandole
Third Term
Spring Break
First Term
Summer Vacation
Second Term

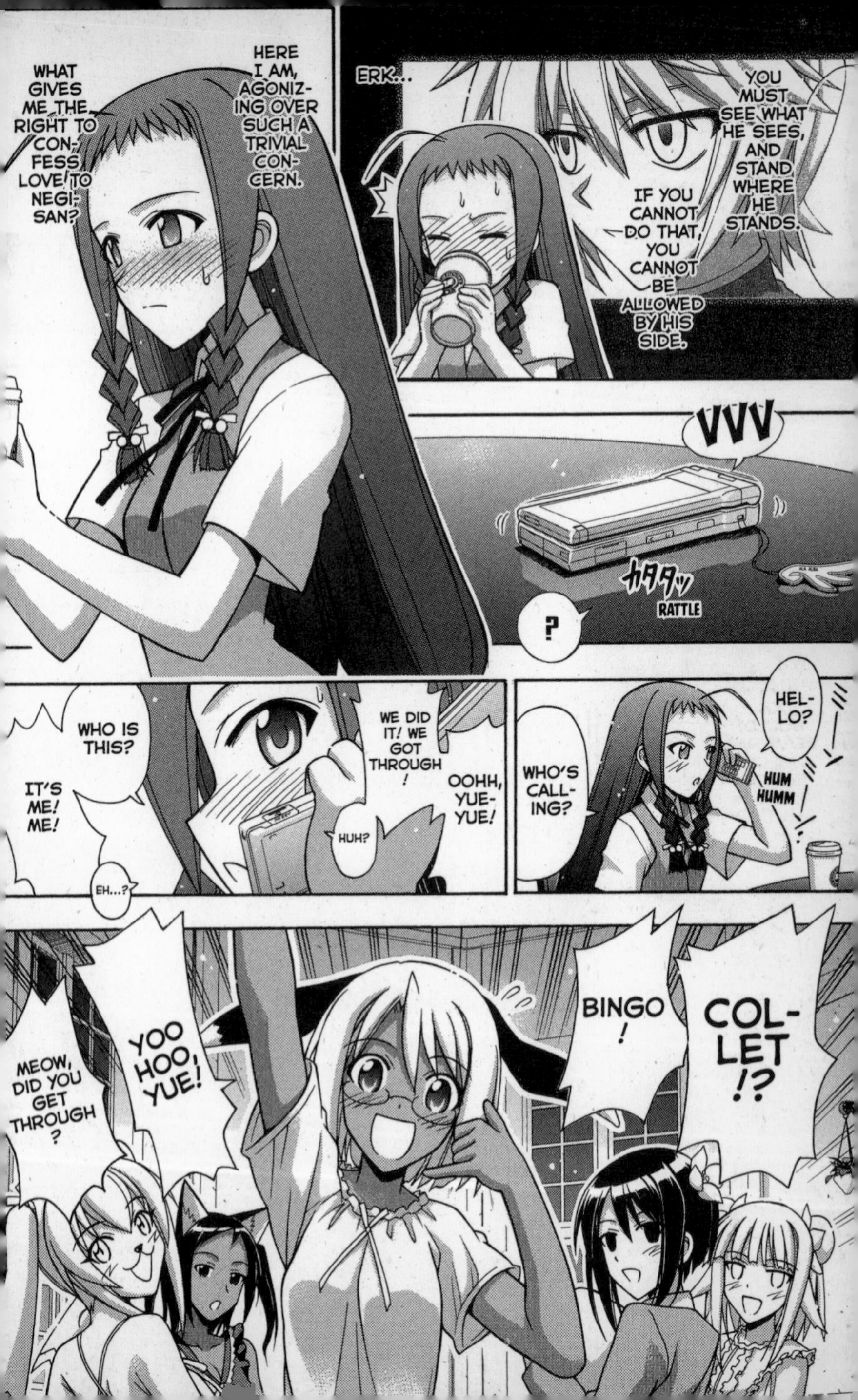
YOU MUST SEE WHAT HE SEES, AND STAND WHERE HE STANDS.
IF YOU CANNOT DO THAT, YOU CANNOT BE ALLOWED BY HIS SIDE.
ERK...
VVV
カタタッ
RATTLE
?
HERE I AM, AGONIZING OVER SUCH A TRIVIAL CONCERN.
WHAT GIVES ME THE RIGHT TO CONFESS LOVE TO NEGI-SAN?
HEL-LO?
HUM HUMM
WHO'S CALLING?
OOHH, YUE-YUE!
WE DID IT! WE GOT THROUGH!
HUH?
WHO IS THIS?
IT'S ME! ME!
EH...?
COL-LET!?
BINGO!
YOO HOO, YUE!
MEOW, DID YOU GET THROUGH?

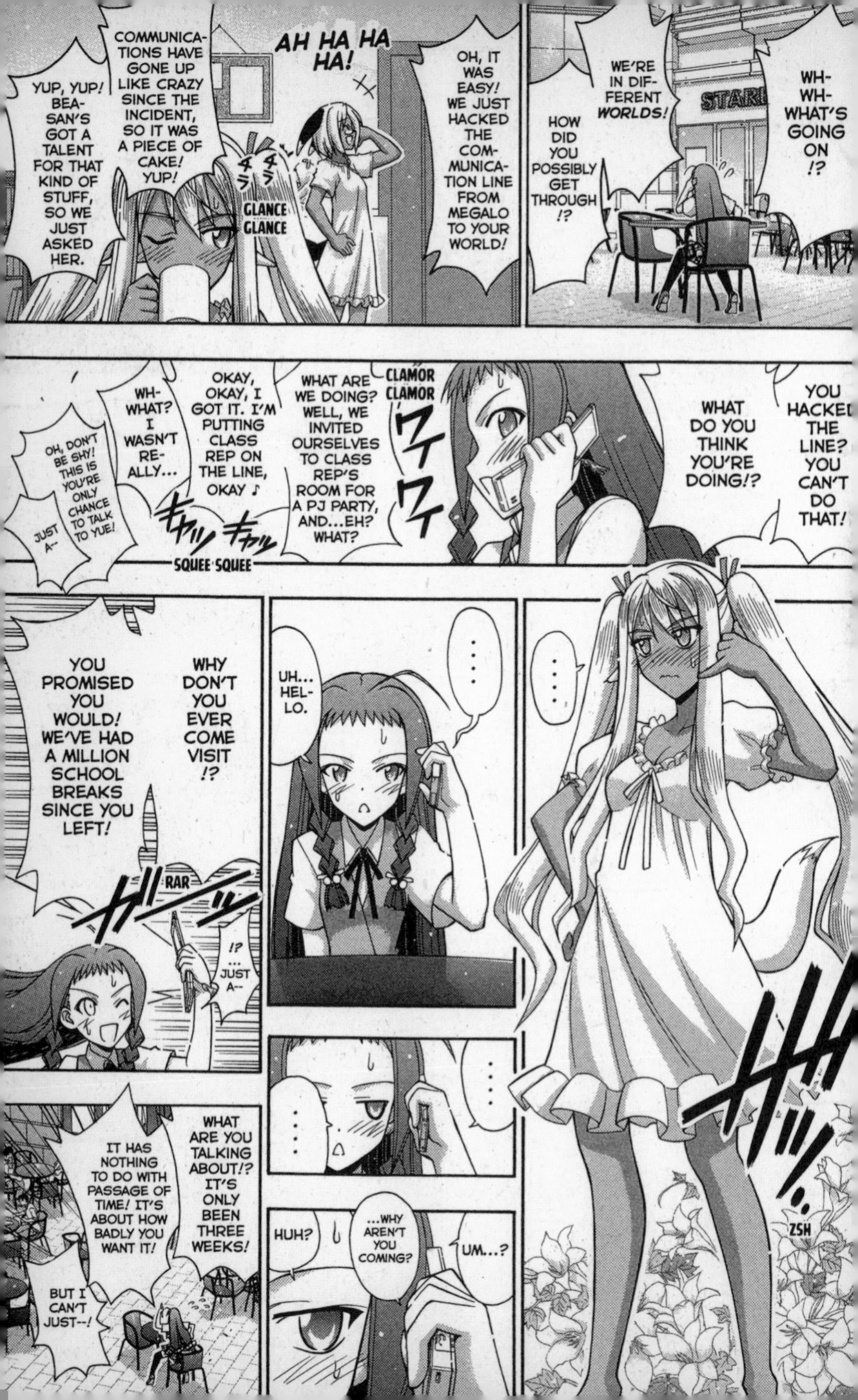
WH-WH-WHAT'S GOING ON !?
WE'RE IN DIF-FERENT WORLDS!
HOW DID YOU POSSIBLY GET THROUGH !?
OH, IT WAS EASY! WE JUST HACKED THE COM-MUNICA-TION LINE FROM MEGALO TO YOUR WORLD!
AH HA HA HA!
GLANCE GLANCE
COMMUNICA-TIONS HAVE GONE UP LIKE CRAZY SINCE THE INCIDENT, SO IT WAS A PIECE OF CAKE! YUP!
YUP, YUP! BEA-SAN'S GOT A TALENT FOR THAT KIND OF STUFF, SO WE JUST ASKED HER.
YOU HACKED THE LINE? YOU CAN'T DO THAT!
WHAT DO YOU THINK YOU'RE DOING!?
CLAMOR CLAMOR
WHAT ARE WE DOING? WELL, WE INVITED OURSELVES TO CLASS REP'S ROOM FOR A PJ PARTY, AND...EH? WHAT?
OKAY, OKAY, I GOT IT. I'M PUTTING CLASS REP ON THE LINE, OKAY ♪
SQUEE SQUEE
WH-WHAT? I WASN'T RE-ALLY...
OH, DON'T BE SHY! THIS IS YOU'RE ONLY CHANCE TO TALK TO YUE!
JUST A--
....
ZSH
....
UH... HEL-LO.
....
....
UM...?
...WHY AREN'T YOU COMING?
HUH?
WHY DON'T YOU EVER COME VISIT !?
YOU PROMISED YOU WOULD! WE'VE HAD A MILLION SCHOOL BREAKS SINCE YOU LEFT!
RAR
!? ... JUST A--
WHAT ARE YOU TALKING ABOUT!? IT'S ONLY BEEN THREE WEEKS!
IT HAS NOTHING TO DO WITH PASSAGE OF TIME! IT'S ABOUT HOW BADLY YOU WANT IT!
BUT I CAN'T JUST--!

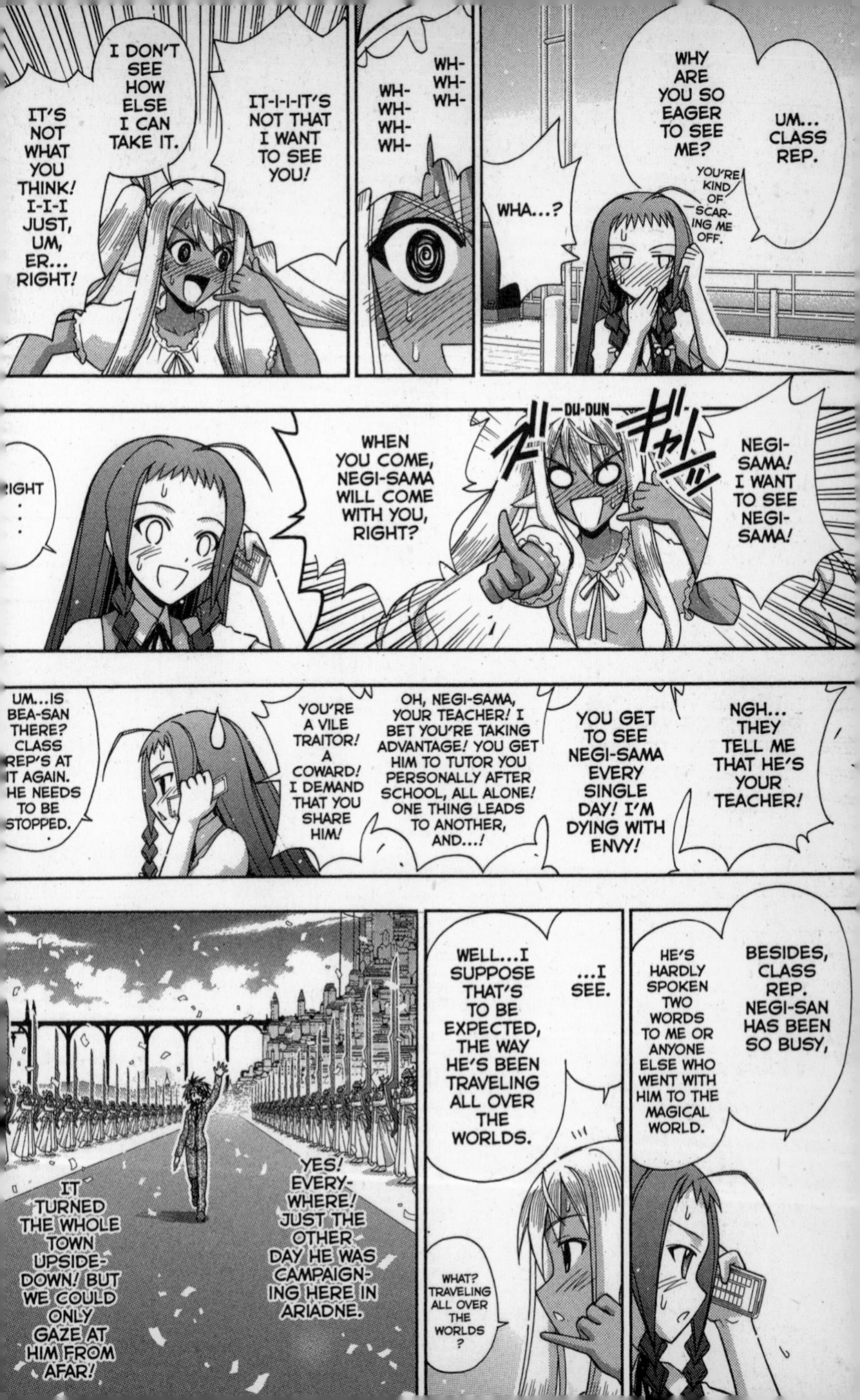

UM... CLASS REP.
WHY ARE YOU SO EAGER TO SEE ME?
YOU'RE KIND OF SCARING ME OFF.
WHA...?
WH- WH- WH-
WH- WH- WH- WH-
IT-I-I-IT'S NOT THAT I WANT TO SEE YOU!
I DON'T SEE HOW ELSE I CAN TAKE IT.
IT'S NOT WHAT YOU THINK! I-I-I JUST, UM, ER... RIGHT!
NEGI-SAMA! I WANT TO SEE NEGI-SAMA!
DU-DUN
WHEN YOU COME, NEGI-SAMA WILL COME WITH YOU, RIGHT?
RIGHT...
NGH... THEY TELL ME THAT HE'S YOUR TEACHER!
YOU GET TO SEE NEGI-SAMA EVERY SINGLE DAY! I'M DYING WITH ENVY!
OH, NEGI-SAMA, YOUR TEACHER! I BET YOU'RE TAKING ADVANTAGE! YOU GET HIM TO TUTOR YOU PERSONALLY AFTER SCHOOL, ALL ALONE! ONE THING LEADS TO ANOTHER, AND...!
YOU'RE A VILE TRAITOR! A COWARD! I DEMAND THAT YOU SHARE HIM!
UM...IS BEA-SAN THERE? CLASS REP'S AT IT AGAIN. HE NEEDS TO BE STOPPED.
BESIDES, CLASS REP. NEGI-SAN HAS BEEN SO BUSY,
HE'S HARDLY SPOKEN TWO WORDS TO ME OR ANYONE ELSE WHO WENT WITH HIM TO THE MAGICAL WORLD.
...I SEE.
WELL...I SUPPOSE THAT'S TO BE EXPECTED, THE WAY HE'S BEEN TRAVELING ALL OVER THE WORLDS.
WHAT? TRAVELING ALL OVER THE WORLDS?
YES! EVERYWHERE! JUST THE OTHER DAY HE WAS CAMPAIGNING HERE IN ARIADNE.
IT TURNED THE WHOLE TOWN UPSIDE-DOWN! BUT WE COULD ONLY GAZE AT HIM FROM AFAR!

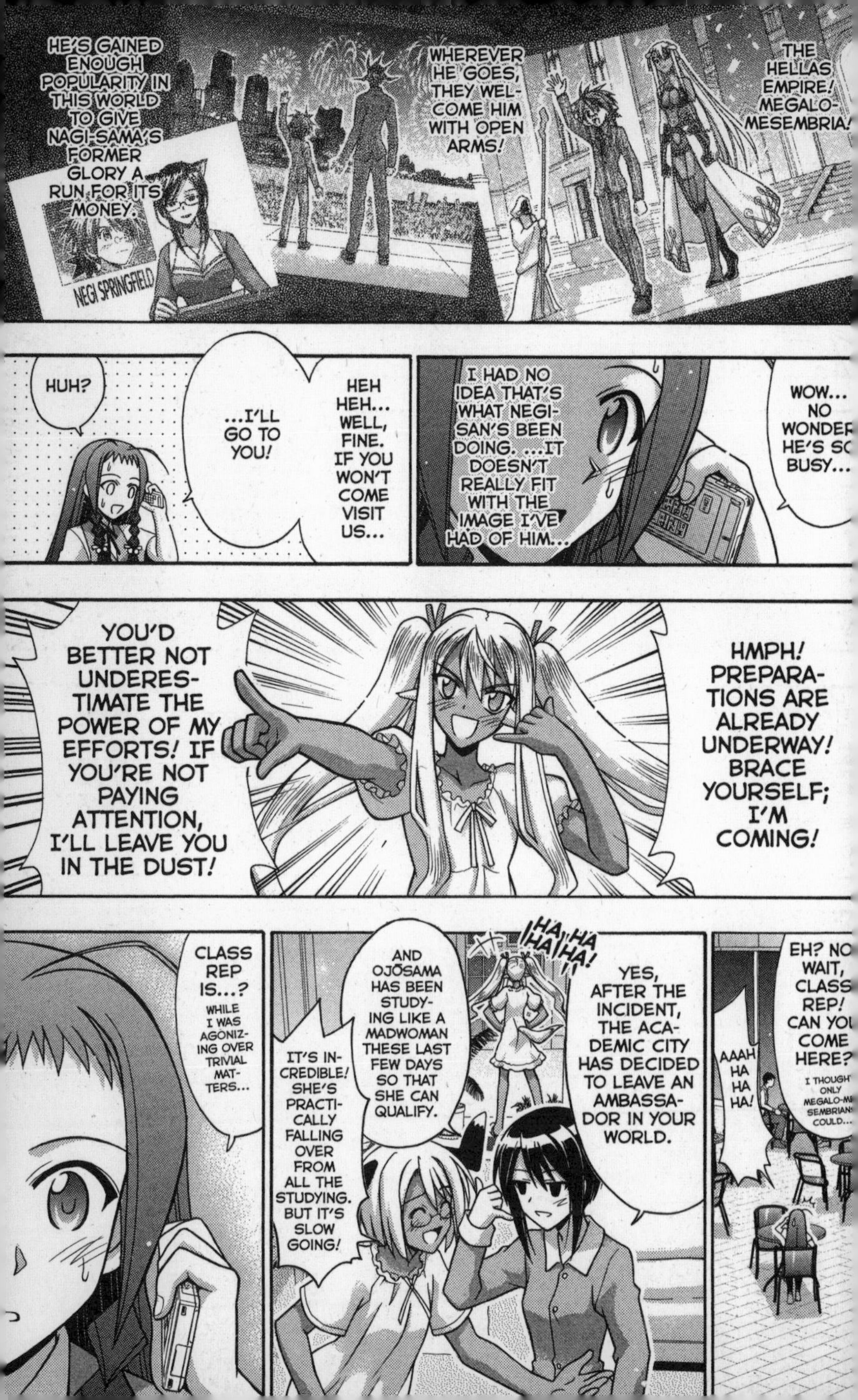
THE HELLAS EMPIRE! MEGALO-MESEMBRIA!
WHEREVER HE GOES, THEY WELCOME HIM WITH OPEN ARMS!
HE'S GAINED ENOUGH POPULARITY IN THIS WORLD TO GIVE NAGI-SAMA'S FORMER GLORY A RUN FOR ITS MONEY.
NEGI SPRINGFIELD
WOW... NO WONDER HE'S SO BUSY...
I HAD NO IDEA THAT'S WHAT NEGI-SAN'S BEEN DOING. ...IT DOESN'T REALLY FIT WITH THE IMAGE I'VE HAD OF HIM...
HEH HEH... WELL, FINE. IF YOU WON'T COME VISIT US...
...I'LL GO TO YOU!
HUH?
HMPH! PREPARATIONS ARE ALREADY UNDERWAY! BRACE YOURSELF; I'M COMING!
YOU'D BETTER NOT UNDERESTIMATE THE POWER OF MY EFFORTS! IF YOU'RE NOT PAYING ATTENTION, I'LL LEAVE YOU IN THE DUST!
EH? NO WAIT, CLASS REP! CAN YOU COME HERE?
I THOUGHT ONLY MEGALO-MESEMBRIANS COULD...
AAAH HA HA HA!
HA HA HA HA!
YES, AFTER THE INCIDENT, THE ACADEMIC CITY HAS DECIDED TO LEAVE AN AMBASSADOR IN YOUR WORLD.
AND OJŌSAMA HAS BEEN STUDYING LIKE A MADWOMAN THESE LAST FEW DAYS SO THAT SHE CAN QUALIFY.
IT'S INCREDIBLE! SHE'S PRACTICALLY FALLING OVER FROM ALL THE STUDYING. BUT IT'S SLOW GOING!
CLASS REP IS...?
WHILE I WAS AGONIZING OVER TRIVIAL MATTERS...

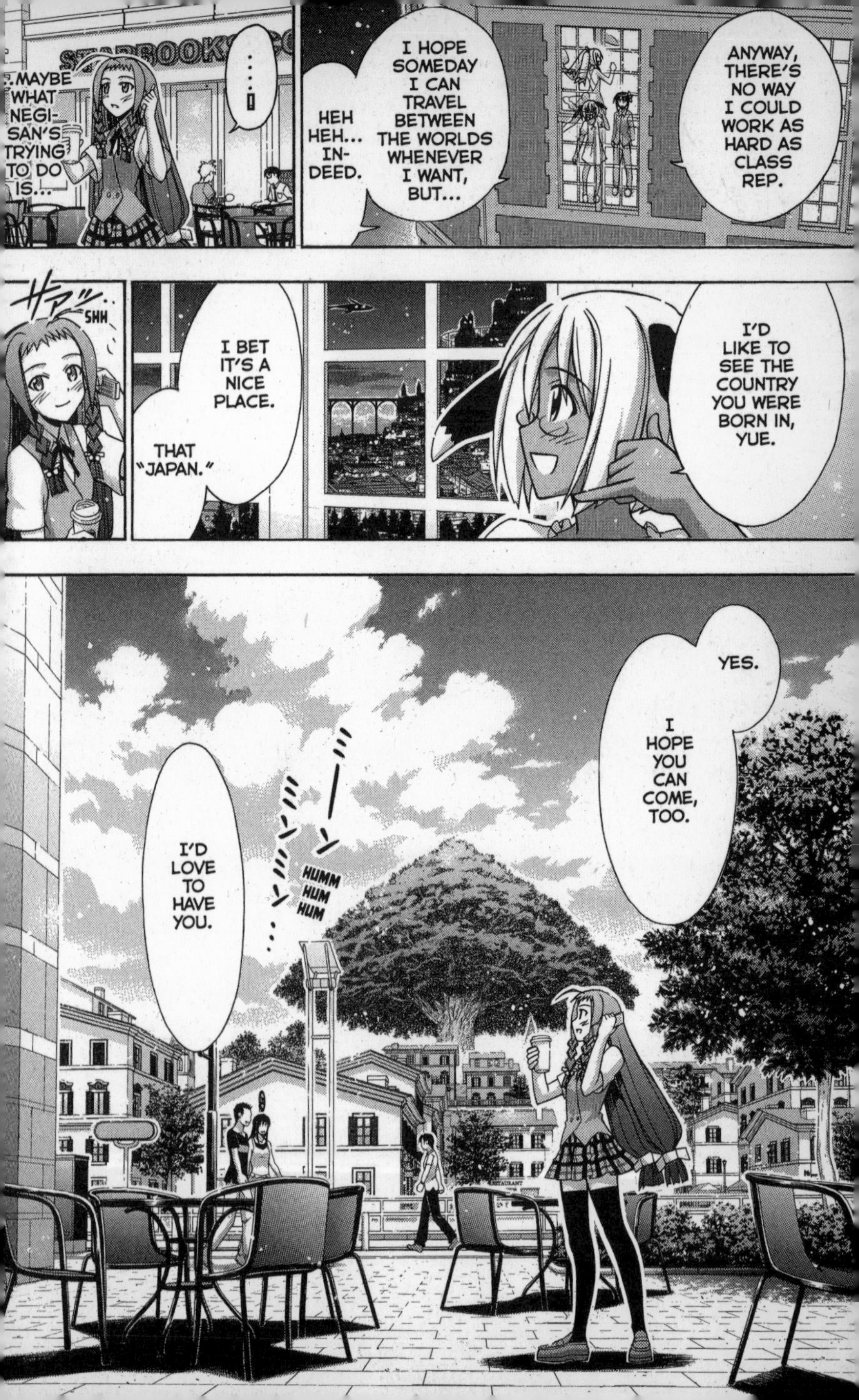
ANYWAY, THERE'S NO WAY I COULD WORK AS HARD AS CLASS REP.
I HOPE SOMEDAY I CAN TRAVEL BETWEEN THE WORLDS WHENEVER I WANT, BUT...
HEH HEH... IN-DEED.
....!
...MAYBE WHAT NEGI-SAN'S TRYING TO DO IS...
I'D LIKE TO SEE THE COUNTRY YOU WERE BORN IN, YUE.
I BET IT'S A NICE PLACE.
THAT "JAPAN."
SHH
YES.
I HOPE YOU CAN COME, TOO.
HUMM HUM HUM
I'D LOVE TO HAVE YOU.

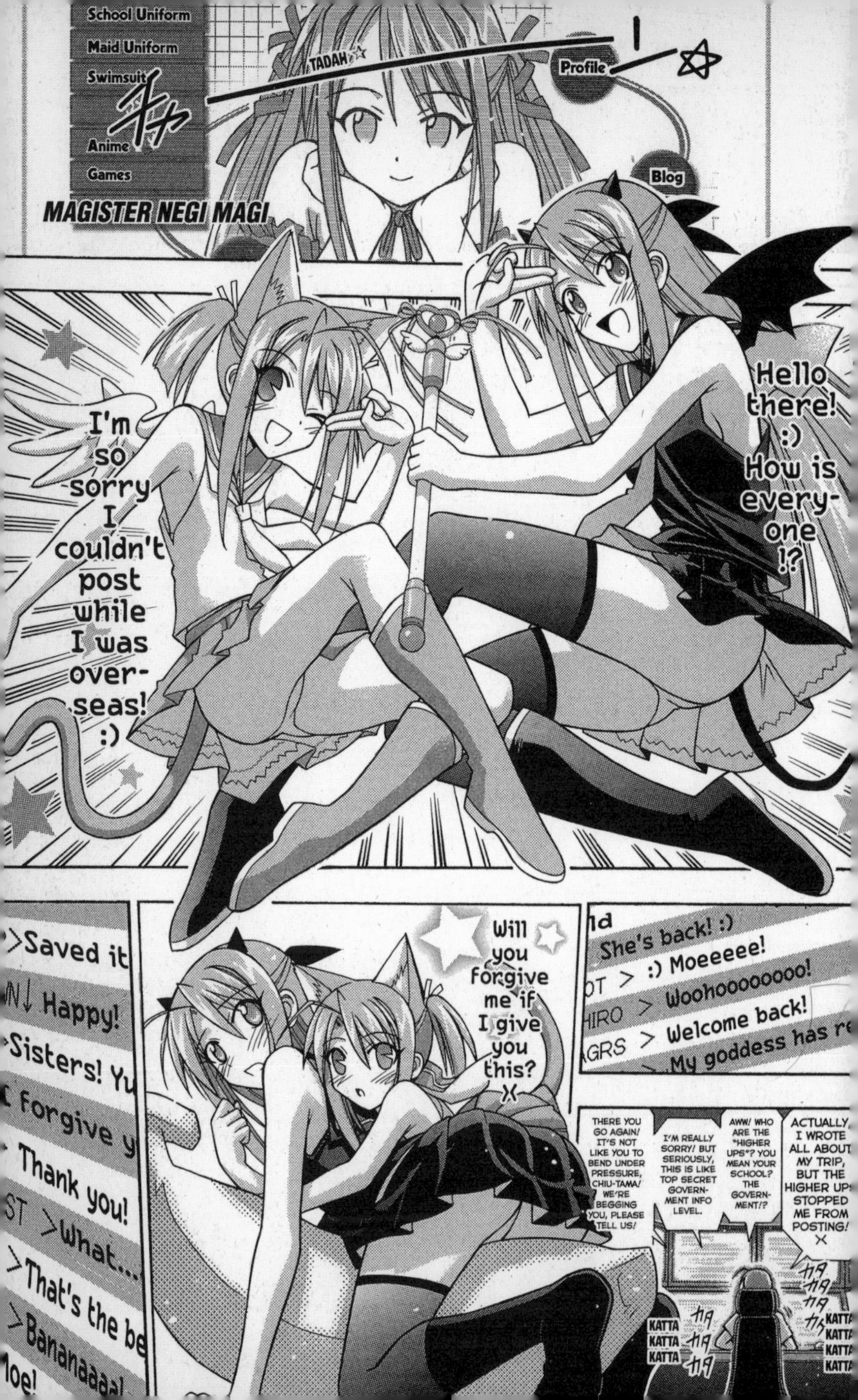
School Uniform
Maid Uniform
Swimsuit
Anime
Games
TADAH☆
Profile
Blog
MAGISTER NEGI MAGI
Hello there! :) How is every-one !?
I'm so sorry I couldn't post while I was over-seas! :)
ld
She's back! :)
OT > :) Moeeeee!
HIRO > Woohoooooooo!
AGRS > Welcome back!
My goddess has r
ACTUALLY, I WROTE ALL ABOUT MY TRIP, BUT THE HIGHER UPS STOPPED ME FROM POSTING! ✕
AWW! WHO ARE THE "HIGHER UPS"? YOU MEAN YOUR SCHOOL? THE GOVERNMENT!?
I'M REALLY SORRY! BUT SERIOUSLY, THIS IS LIKE TOP SECRET GOVERNMENT INFO LEVEL.
THERE YOU GO AGAIN! IT'S NOT LIKE YOU TO BEND UNDER PRESSURE, CHIU-TAMA! WE'RE BEGGING YOU, PLEASE TELL US!
KATTA KATTA KATTA KATTA
KATTA KATTA KATTA
Will you forgive me if I give you this? ✕
>Saved it
N↓ Happy!
Sisters! Yu
forgive y
Thank you!
ST >What...
>That's the be
>Bananaaaa!
loe!

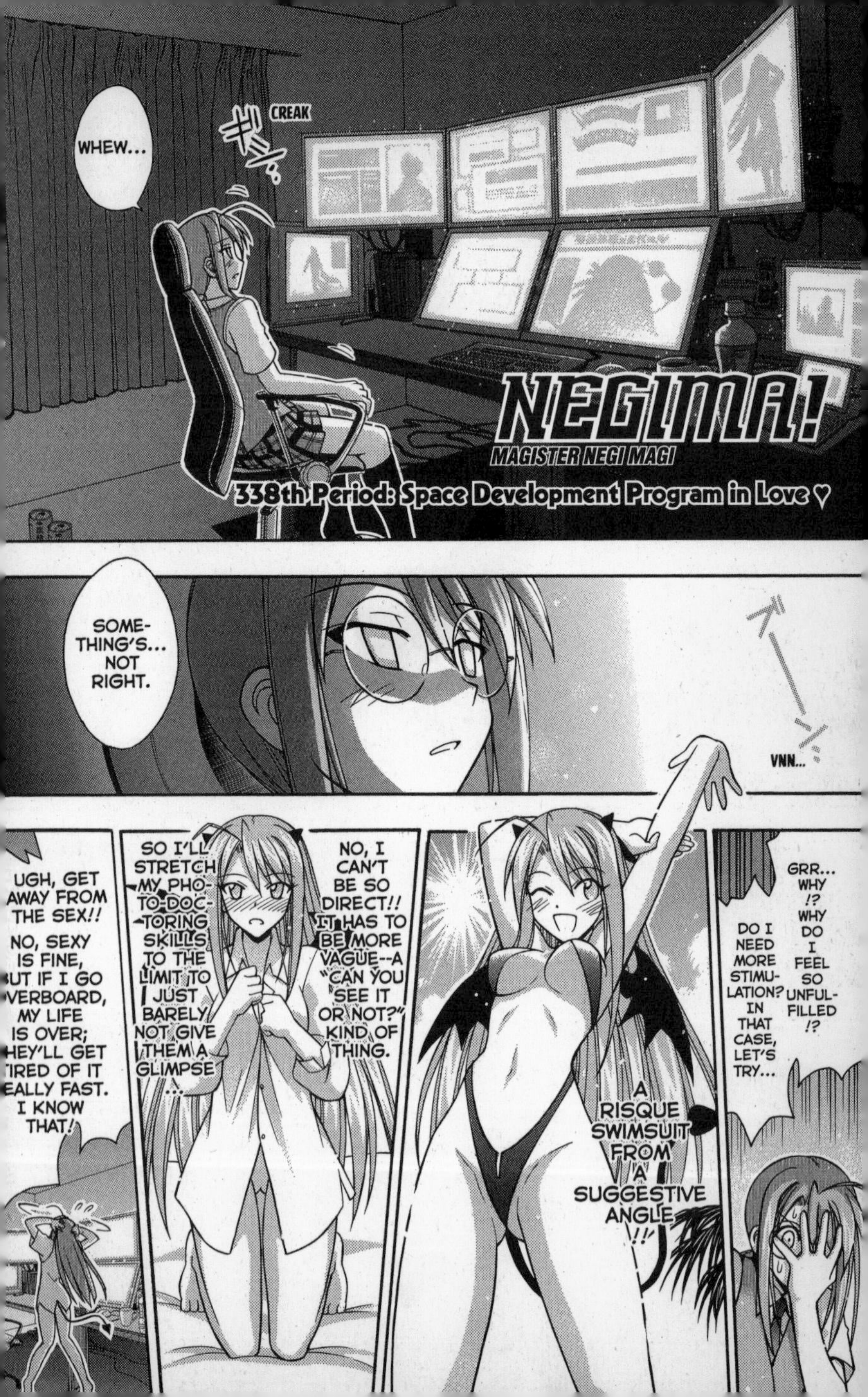
NEGIMA!
MAGISTER NEGI MAGI
338th Period: Space Development Program in Love ♥
CREAK
WHEW...
VNN...
SOME-THING'S... NOT RIGHT.
GRR... WHY !? WHY DO I FEEL SO UNFUL-FILLED !?
DO I NEED MORE STIMU-LATION? IN THAT CASE, LET'S TRY...
A RISQUE SWIMSUIT FROM A SUGGESTIVE ANGLE !!
NO, I CAN'T BE SO DIRECT!! IT HAS TO BE MORE VAGUE--A "CAN YOU SEE IT OR NOT?" KIND OF THING.
SO I'LL STRETCH MY PHO-TO-DOC-TORING SKILLS TO THE LIMIT TO JUST BARELY NOT GIVE THEM A GLIMPSE ...
UGH, GET AWAY FROM THE SEX!!
NO, SEXY IS FINE, UT IF I GO VERBOARD, MY LIFE IS OVER; HEY'LL GET IRED OF IT EALLY FAST. I KNOW THAT!

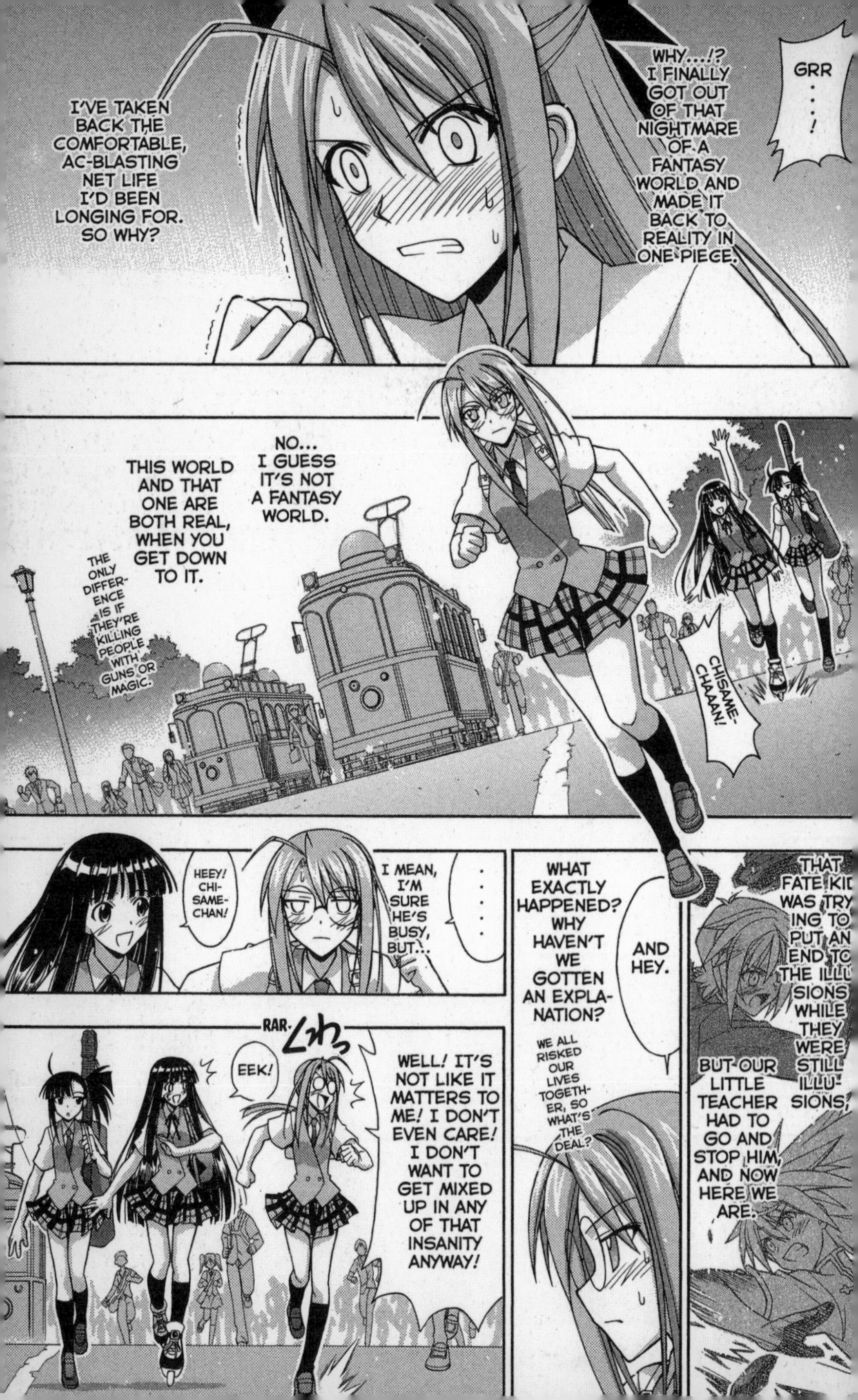
GRR...!
WHY...!? I FINALLY GOT OUT OF THAT NIGHTMARE OF A FANTASY WORLD AND MADE IT BACK TO REALITY IN ONE PIECE.
I'VE TAKEN BACK THE COMFORTABLE, AC-BLASTING NET LIFE I'D BEEN LONGING FOR. SO WHY?
CHISAME-CHAAAN!
NO... I GUESS IT'S NOT A FANTASY WORLD.
THIS WORLD AND THAT ONE ARE BOTH REAL, WHEN YOU GET DOWN TO IT.
THE ONLY DIFFERENCE IS IF THEY'RE KILLING PEOPLE WITH GUNS OR MAGIC.
THAT FATE KID WAS TRYING TO PUT AN END TO THE ILLUSIONS WHILE THEY WERE STILL ILLUSIONS,
BUT OUR LITTLE TEACHER HAD TO GO AND STOP HIM, AND NOW HERE WE ARE.
AND HEY.
WHAT EXACTLY HAPPENED? WHY HAVEN'T WE GOTTEN AN EXPLANATION?
WE ALL RISKED OUR LIVES TOGETHER, SO WHAT'S THE DEAL?
......
I MEAN, I'M SURE HE'S BUSY, BUT...
HEEY! CHI-SAME-CHAN!
RAR. くわっ
WELL! IT'S NOT LIKE IT MATTERS TO ME! I DON'T EVEN CARE! I DON'T WANT TO GET MIXED UP IN ANY OF THAT INSANITY ANYWAY!
EEK!

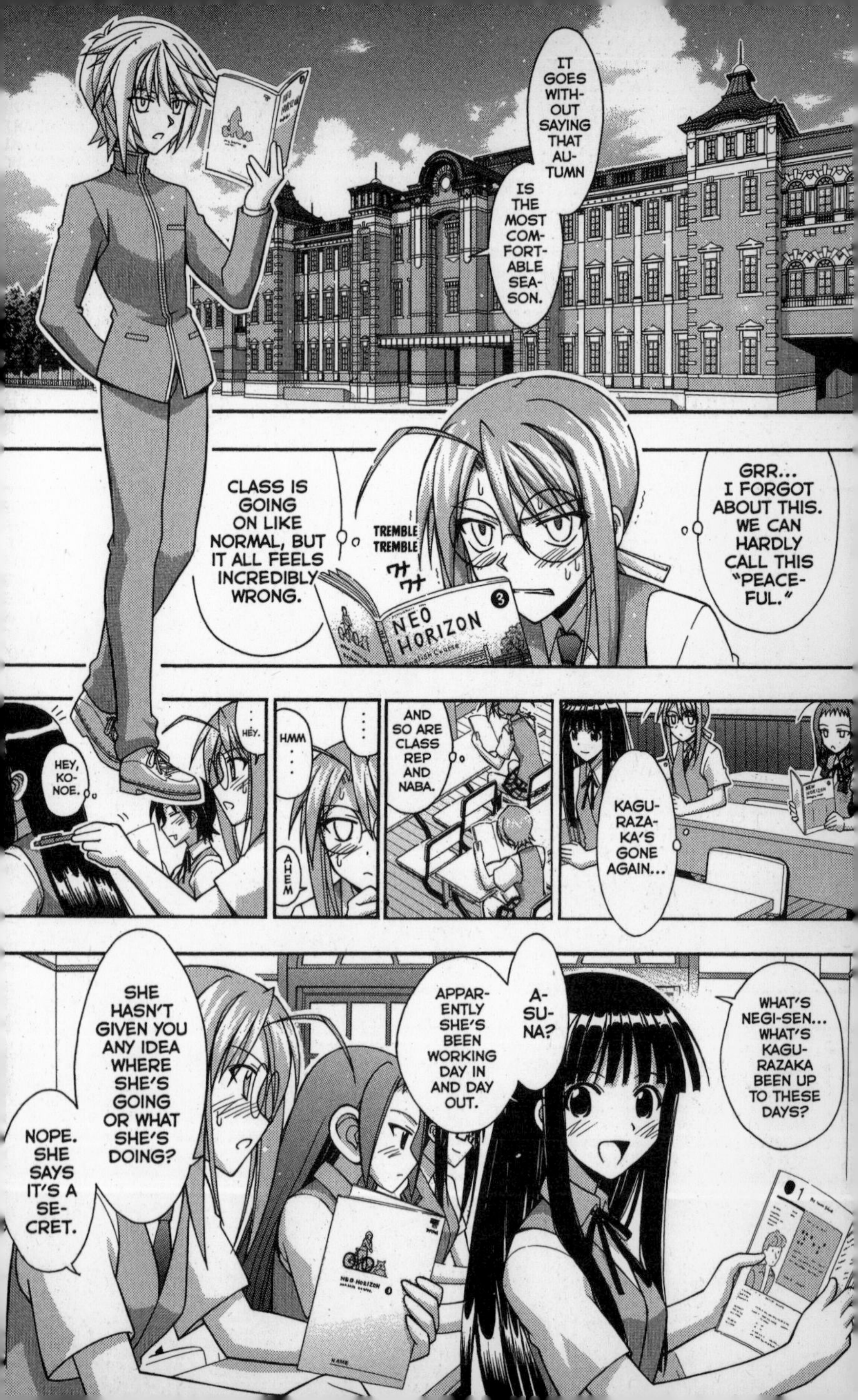
IT GOES WITHOUT SAYING THAT AUTUMN
IS THE MOST COMFORTABLE SEASON.
GRR... I FORGOT ABOUT THIS. WE CAN HARDLY CALL THIS "PEACEFUL."
NEO HORIZON
TREMBLE TREMBLE
CLASS IS GOING ON LIKE NORMAL, BUT IT ALL FEELS INCREDIBLY WRONG.
KAGURAZAKA'S GONE AGAIN...
AND SO ARE CLASS REP AND NABA.
......
HMM...
AHEM
...HEY.
HEY, KONOE.
WHAT'S NEGI-SEN... WHAT'S KAGURAZAKA BEEN UP TO THESE DAYS?
A-SUNA?
APPARENTLY SHE'S BEEN WORKING DAY IN AND DAY OUT.
SHE HASN'T GIVEN YOU ANY IDEA WHERE SHE'S GOING OR WHAT SHE'S DOING?
NOPE. SHE SAYS IT'S A SECRET.

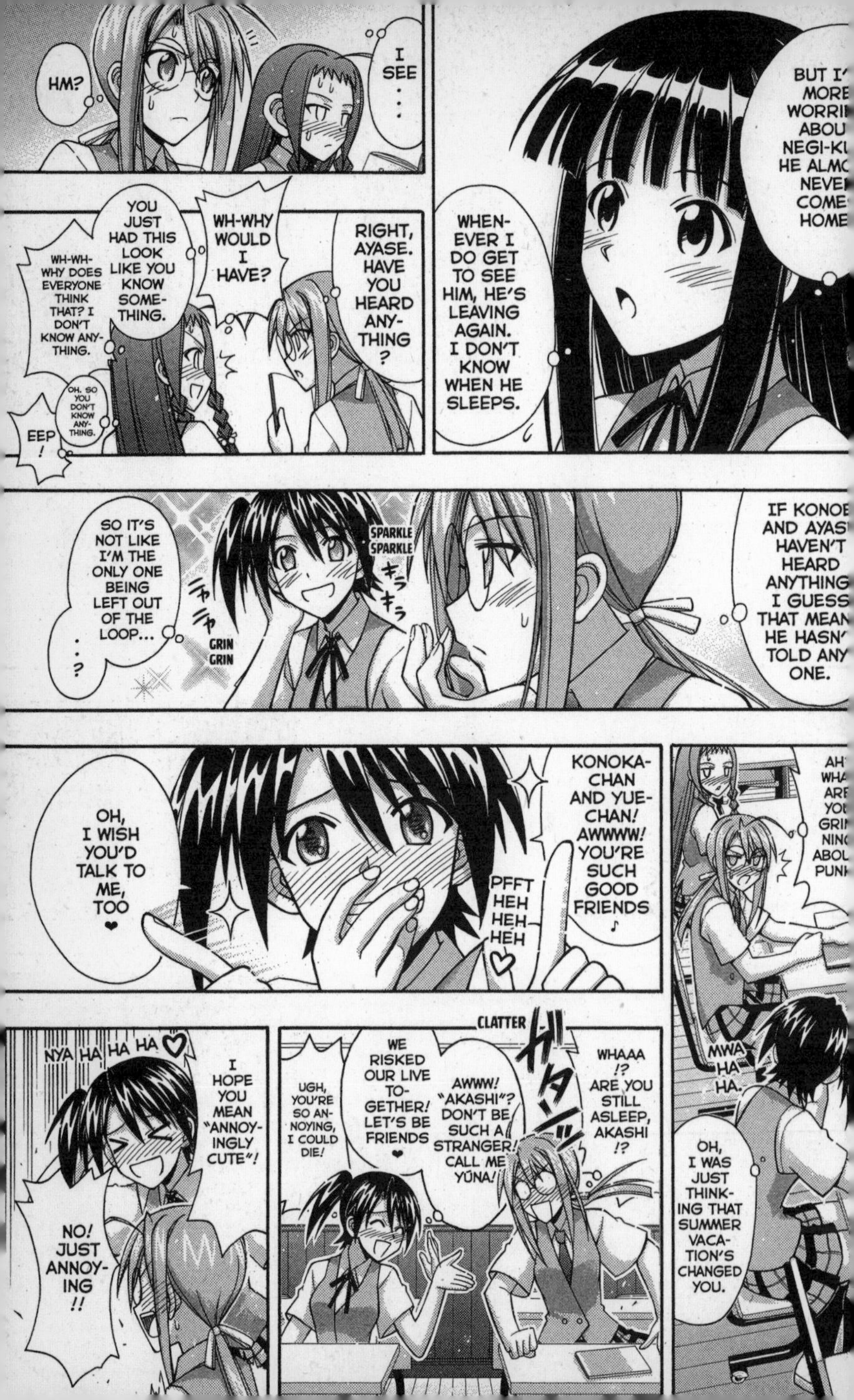
BUT I' MORE WORRI ABOU NEGI-KU HE ALMO NEVER COME HOME
WHEN-EVER I DO GET TO SEE HIM, HE'S LEAVING AGAIN. I DON'T KNOW WHEN HE SLEEPS.
I SEE . . .
HM?
RIGHT, AYASE. HAVE YOU HEARD ANY-THING?
WH-WHY WOULD I HAVE?
YOU JUST HAD THIS LOOK LIKE YOU KNOW SOME-THING.
WH-WH-WHY DOES EVERYONE THINK THAT? I DON'T KNOW ANY-THING.
OH, SO YOU DON'T KNOW ANY-THING.
EEP!
IF KONOE AND AYAS HAVEN'T HEARD ANYTHING I GUESS THAT MEAN HE HASN' TOLD ANY ONE.
SPARKLE SPARKLE
SO IT'S NOT LIKE I'M THE ONLY ONE BEING LEFT OUT OF THE LOOP...
GRIN GRIN
. . ?
AH WHA ARE YO GRIN-NING ABOU PUNK
MWA HA HA HA.
OH, I WAS JUST THINK-ING THAT SUMMER VACA-TION'S CHANGED YOU.
KONOKA-CHAN AND YUE-CHAN! AWWWW! YOU'RE SUCH GOOD FRIENDS ♪
PFFT HEH HEH HEH ♡
OH, I WISH YOU'D TALK TO ME, TOO ❤
CLATTER
WHAAA!? ARE YOU STILL ASLEEP, AKASHI!?
AWWW! "AKASHI"? DON'T BE SUCH A STRANGER! CALL ME YŪNA!
WE RISKED OUR LIVE TO-GETHER! LET'S BE FRIENDS ❤
UGH, YOU'RE SO AN-NOYING, I COULD DIE!
NYA HA HA HA ♡
I HOPE YOU MEAN "ANNOY-INGLY CUTE"!
NO! JUST ANNOY-ING!!

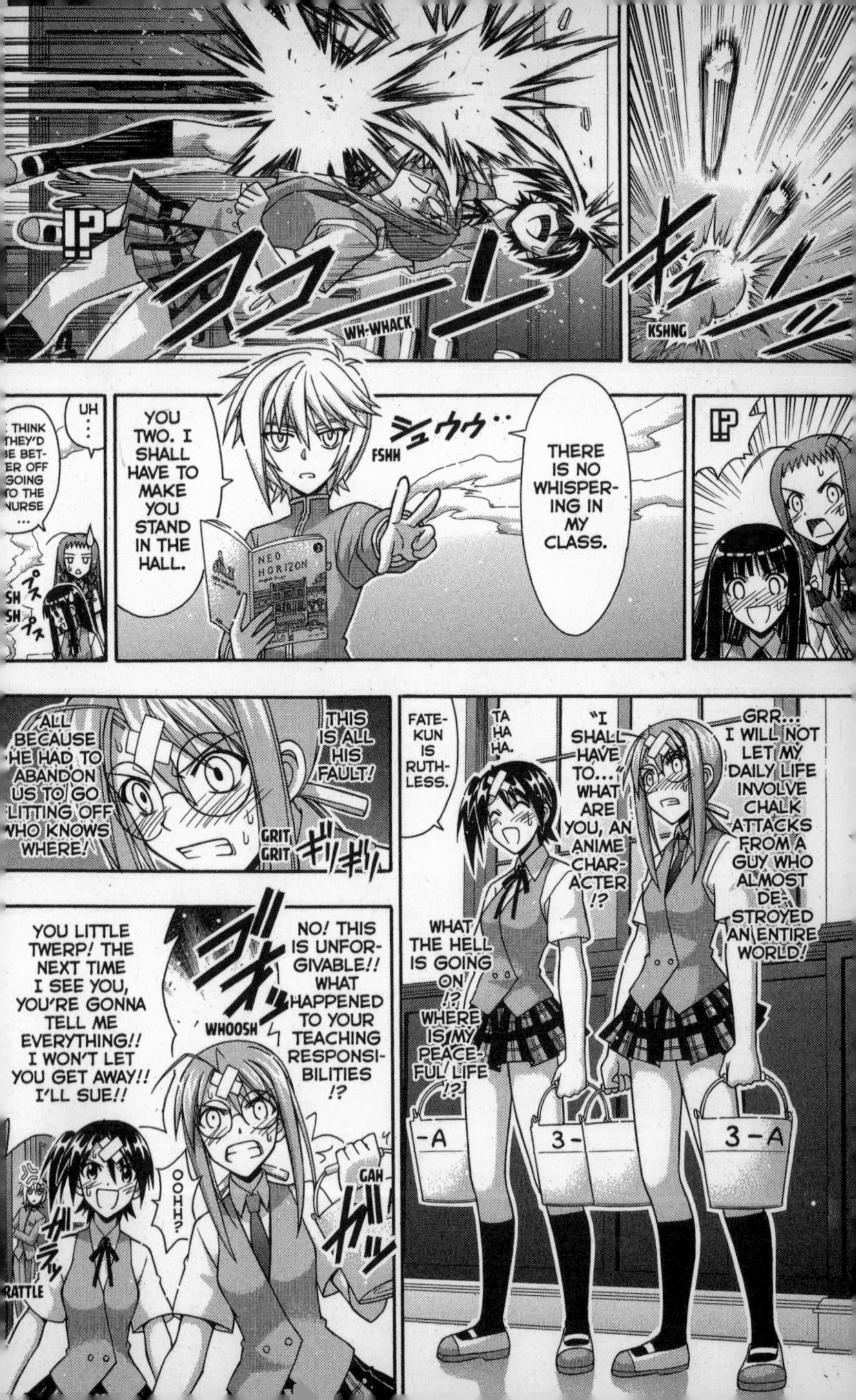
KSHNG
!?
WH-WHACK
!?
THERE IS NO WHISPERING IN MY CLASS.
シュウウ‥
FSHH
YOU TWO. I SHALL HAVE TO MAKE YOU STAND IN THE HALL.
UH ...
I THINK THEY'D BE BETTER OFF GOING TO THE NURSE ...
SH SH
GRR... I WILL NOT LET MY DAILY LIFE INVOLVE CHALK ATTACKS FROM A GUY WHO ALMOST DESTROYED AN ENTIRE WORLD!
"I SHALL HAVE TO..." WHAT ARE YOU, AN ANIME CHARACTER!?
TA HA HA.
FATE-KUN IS RUTHLESS.
WHAT THE HELL IS GOING ON!? WHERE IS MY PEACEFUL LIFE!?
3-A
3-
-A
THIS IS ALL HIS FAULT!
ALL BECAUSE HE HAD TO ABANDON US TO GO FLITTING OFF WHO KNOWS WHERE!
GRIT GRIT
NO! THIS IS UNFORGIVABLE!! WHAT HAPPENED TO YOUR TEACHING RESPONSIBILITIES!?
WHOOSH
YOU LITTLE TWERP! THE NEXT TIME I SEE YOU, YOU'RE GONNA TELL ME EVERYTHING!! I WON'T LET YOU GET AWAY!! I'LL SUE!!
GAH
OOHH?
RATTLE

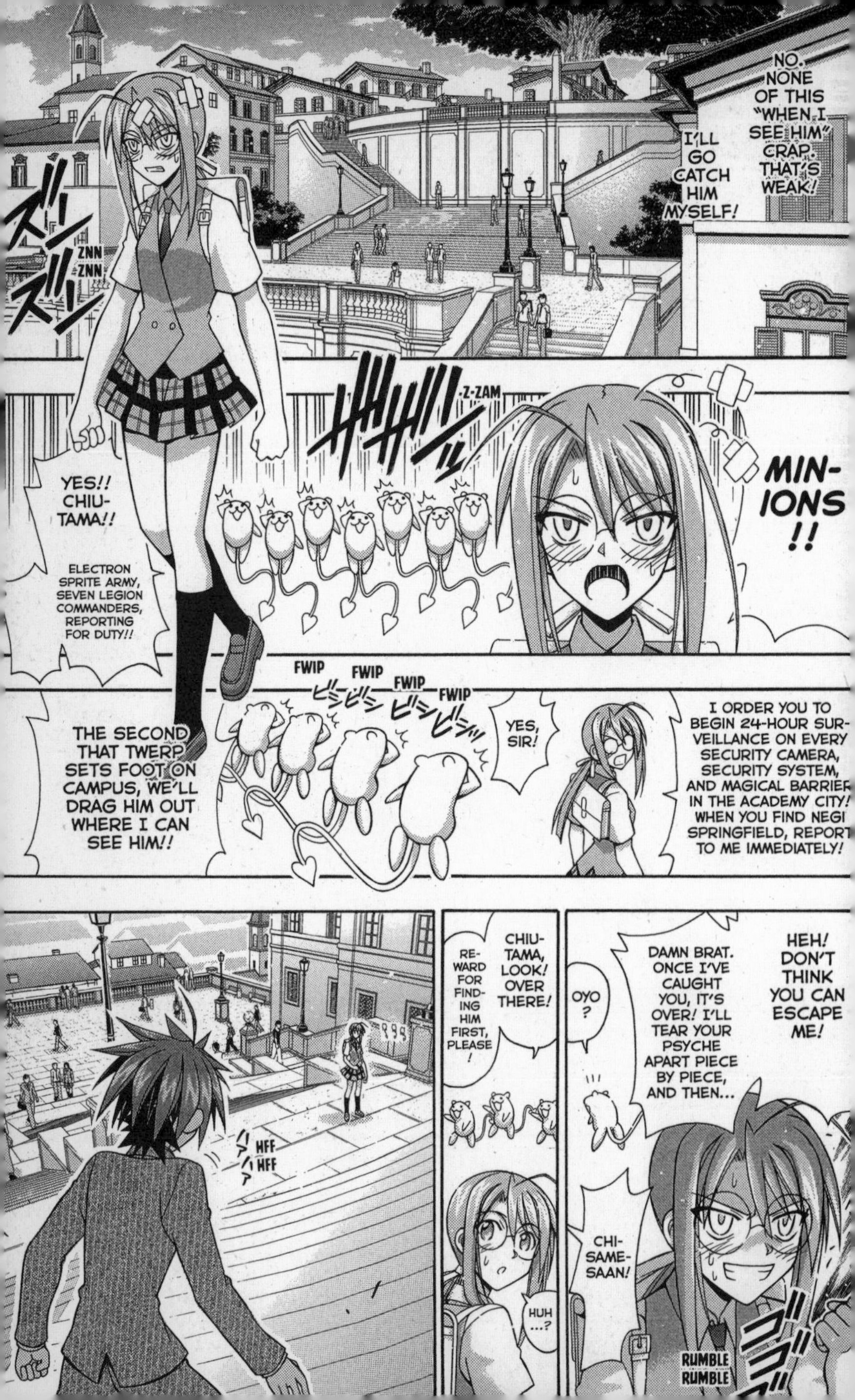

NO. NONE OF THIS "WHEN I SEE HIM" CRAP. THAT'S WEAK!
I'LL GO CATCH HIM MYSELF!
ZNN ZNN
MIN-IONS!!
Z-ZAM
YES!! CHIU-TAMA!!
ELECTRON SPRITE ARMY, SEVEN LEGION COMMANDERS, REPORTING FOR DUTY!!
I ORDER YOU TO BEGIN 24-HOUR SURVEILLANCE ON EVERY SECURITY CAMERA, SECURITY SYSTEM, AND MAGICAL BARRIER IN THE ACADEMY CITY! WHEN YOU FIND NEGI SPRINGFIELD, REPORT TO ME IMMEDIATELY!
YES, SIR!
FWIP FWIP FWIP FWIP
THE SECOND THAT TWERP SETS FOOT ON CAMPUS, WE'LL DRAG HIM OUT WHERE I CAN SEE HIM!!
HEH! DON'T THINK YOU CAN ESCAPE ME!
DAMN BRAT. ONCE I'VE CAUGHT YOU, IT'S OVER! I'LL TEAR YOUR PSYCHE APART PIECE BY PIECE, AND THEN...
OYO?
RUMBLE RUMBLE
CHIU-TAMA, LOOK! OVER THERE!
REWARD FOR FINDING HIM FIRST, PLEASE!
CHI-SAME-SAAN!
HUH...?
HFF HFF

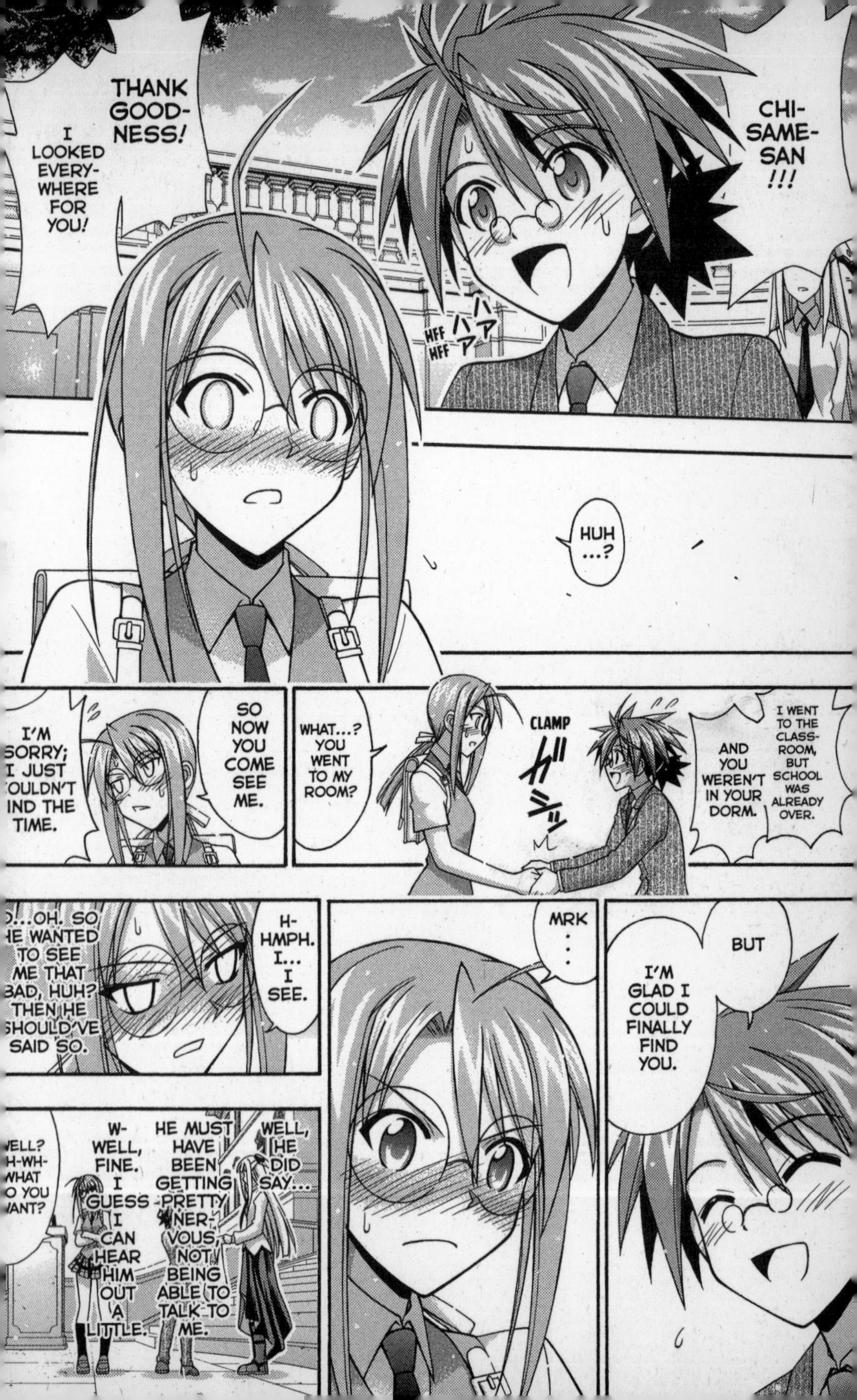
CHI-SAME-SAN!!!
HFF HFF
ハァハァ
THANK GOODNESS!
I LOOKED EVERYWHERE FOR YOU!
HUH...?
I WENT TO THE CLASSROOM, BUT SCHOOL WAS ALREADY OVER.
AND YOU WEREN'T IN YOUR DORM.
CLAMP
WHAT...? YOU WENT TO MY ROOM?
SO NOW YOU COME SEE ME.
I'M SORRY; I JUST COULDN'T FIND THE TIME.
BUT
I'M GLAD I COULD FINALLY FIND YOU.
MRK...
H-HMPH. I... I SEE.
...OH. SO HE WANTED TO SEE ME THAT BAD, HUH? THEN HE SHOULD'VE SAID SO.
WELL, HE DID SAY...
HE MUST HAVE BEEN GETTING PRETTY NERVOUS, NOT BEING ABLE TO TALK TO ME.
W-WELL, FINE. I GUESS I CAN HEAR HIM OUT A LITTLE.
WELL? WH-WHAT DO YOU WANT?

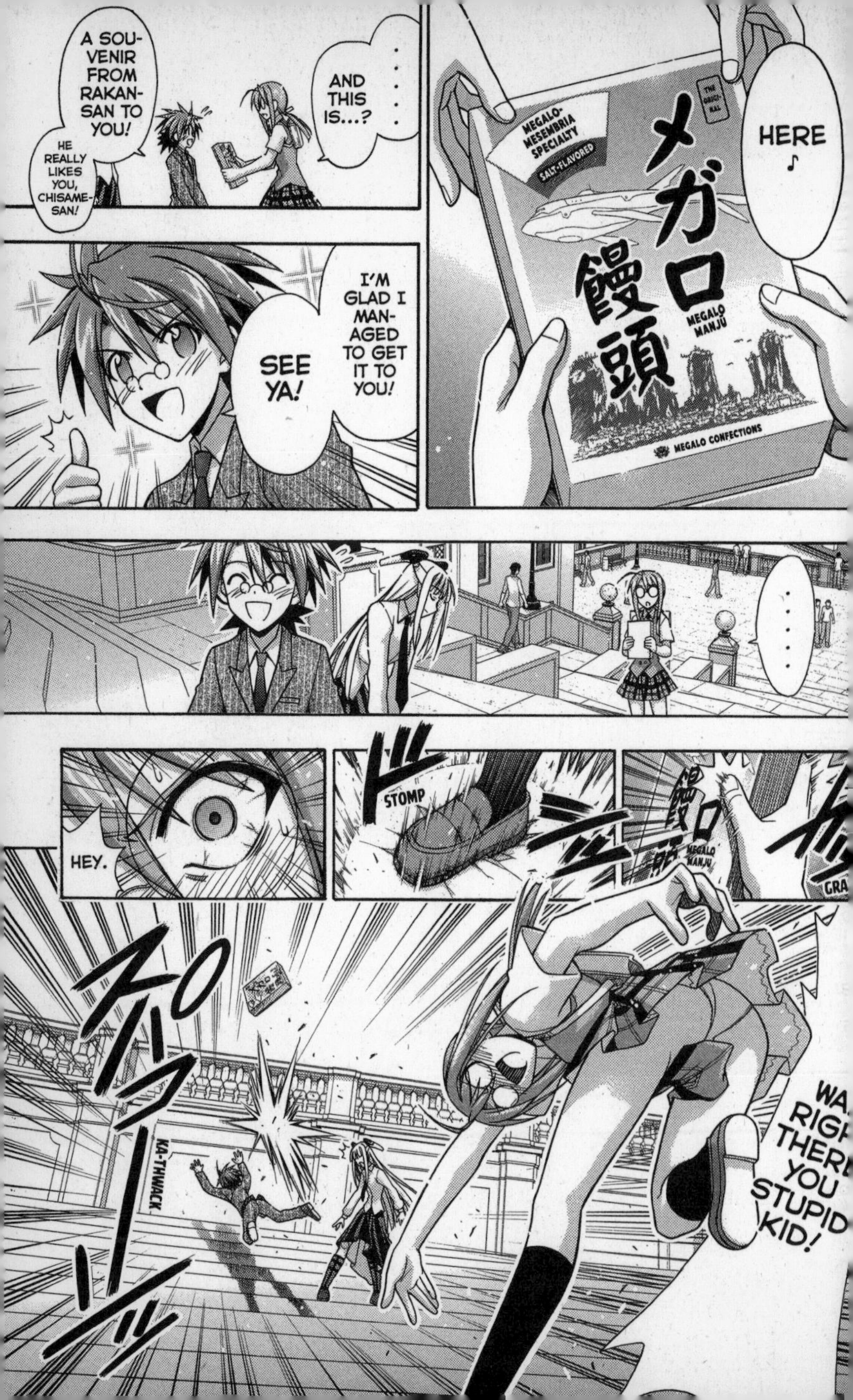
HERE ♪
THE ORIGINAL
MEGALO-MESEMBRIA SPECIALTY
SALT-FLAVORED
メガロ饅頭
MEGALO MANJU
MEGALO CONFECTIONS
. . . . .
AND THIS IS...?
A SOUVENIR FROM RAKAN-SAN TO YOU!
HE REALLY LIKES YOU, CHISAME-SAN!
I'M GLAD I MANAGED TO GET IT TO YOU!
SEE YA!
. . . . .
GRA
饅ロ頭
MEGALO MANJU
STOMP
HEY.
WAI RIGH THERE YOU STUPID KID!
KA-THWACK

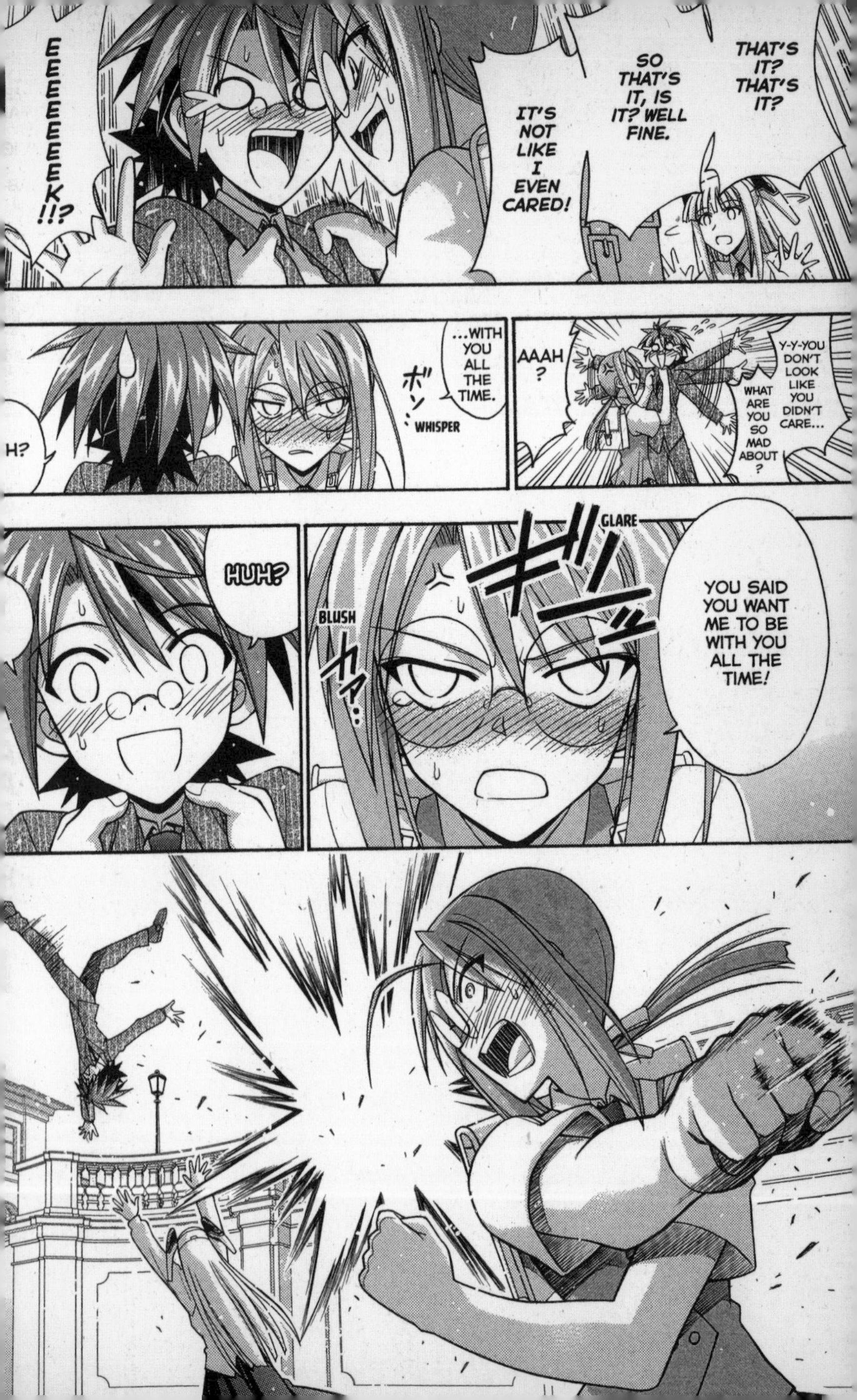
THAT'S IT? THAT'S IT?
SO THAT'S IT, IS IT? WELL FINE.
IT'S NOT LIKE I EVEN CARED!
EEEEEEEEEK!!?
Y-Y-YOU DON'T LOOK LIKE YOU DIDN'T CARE...
WHAT ARE YOU SO MAD ABOUT?
AAAH?
...WITH YOU ALL THE TIME.
WHISPER
H?
YOU SAID YOU WANT ME TO BE WITH YOU ALL THE TIME!
GLARE
BLUSH
HUH?

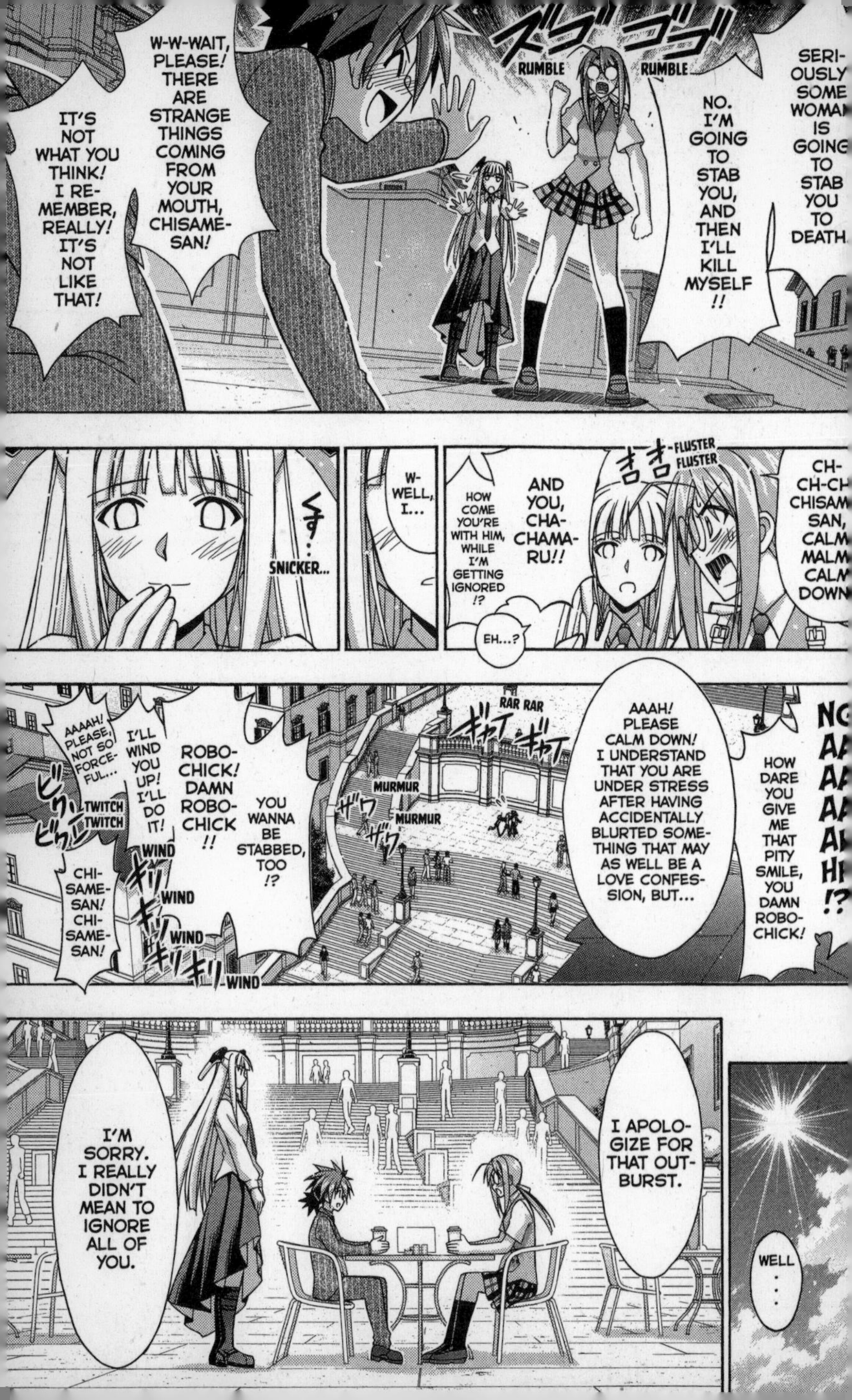
RUMBLE RUMBLE
SERIOUSLY SOME WOMAN IS GOING TO STAB YOU TO DEATH.
NO. I'M GOING TO STAB YOU, AND THEN I'LL KILL MYSELF!!
W-W-WAIT, PLEASE! THERE ARE STRANGE THINGS COMING FROM YOUR MOUTH, CHISAME-SAN!
IT'S NOT WHAT YOU THINK! I RE-MEMBER, REALLY! IT'S NOT LIKE THAT!
CH-CH-CH CHISAME-SAN, CALM MALM CALM DOWN
FLUSTER FLUSTER
AND YOU, CHA-CHAMA-RU!!
HOW COME YOU'RE WITH HIM, WHILE I'M GETTING IGNORED!?
EH...?
W-WELL, I...
SNICKER...
NOAAAAAH!?
HOW DARE YOU GIVE ME THAT PITY SMILE, YOU DAMN ROBO-CHICK!
AAAH! PLEASE CALM DOWN! I UNDERSTAND THAT YOU ARE UNDER STRESS AFTER HAVING ACCIDENTALLY BLURTED SOME-THING THAT MAY AS WELL BE A LOVE CONFES-SION, BUT...
RAR RAR
MURMUR MURMUR
YOU WANNA BE STABBED, TOO!?
ROBO-CHICK! DAMN ROBO-CHICK!!
I'LL WIND YOU UP! I'LL DO IT!
WIND WIND WIND WIND
AAAAH! PLEASE, NOT SO FORCE-FUL...
TWITCH TWITCH
CHI-SAME-SAN! CHI-SAME-SAN!
WELL...
I APOLO-GIZE FOR THAT OUT-BURST.
I'M SORRY. I REALLY DIDN'T MEAN TO IGNORE ALL OF YOU.

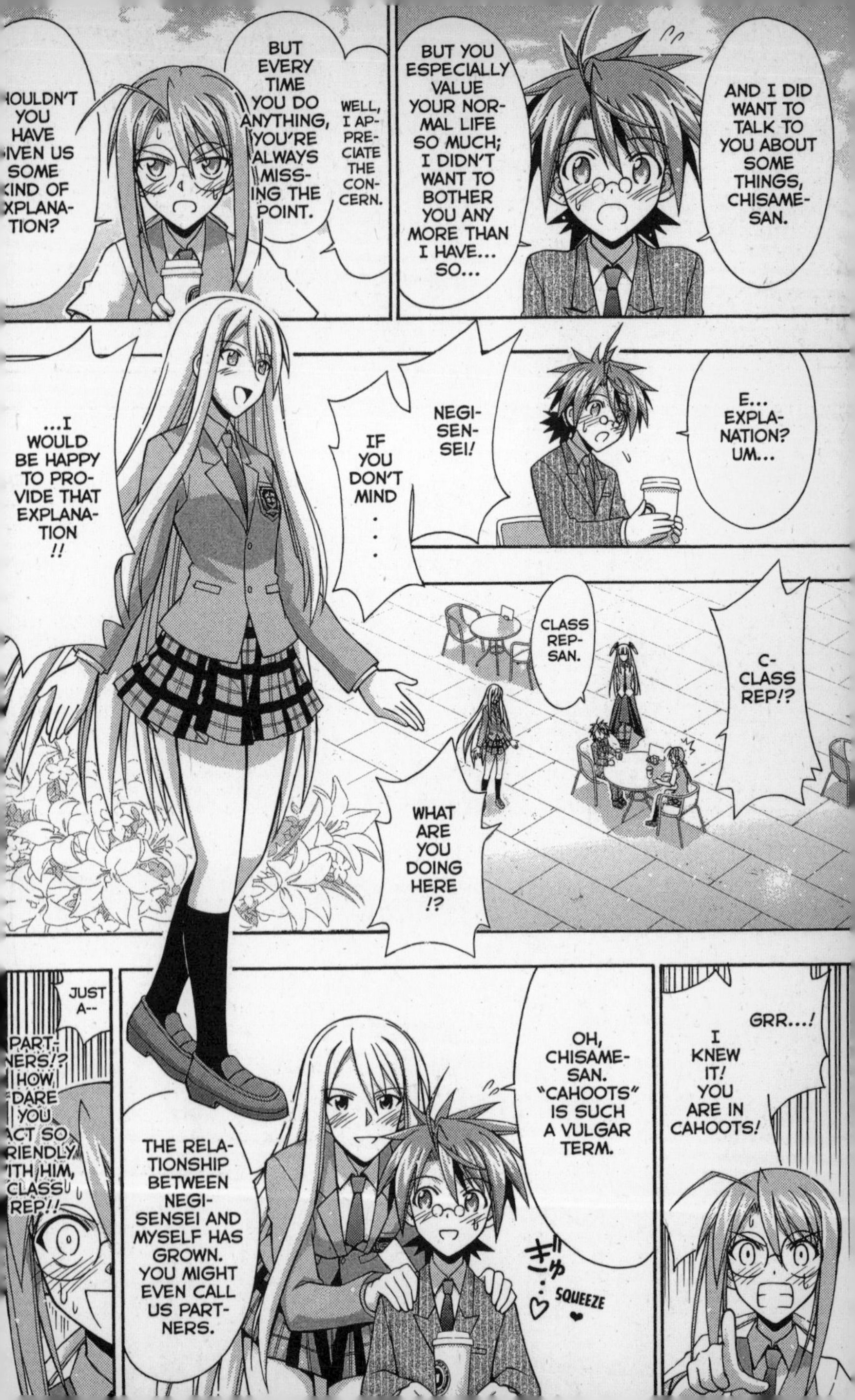

AND I DID WANT TO TALK TO YOU ABOUT SOME THINGS, CHISAME-SAN.
BUT YOU ESPECIALLY VALUE YOUR NORMAL LIFE SO MUCH; I DIDN'T WANT TO BOTHER YOU ANY MORE THAN I HAVE... SO...
WELL, I APPRECIATE THE CONCERN.
BUT EVERY TIME YOU DO ANYTHING, YOU'RE ALWAYS MISSING THE POINT.
HOULDN'T YOU HAVE IVEN US SOME KIND OF XPLANATION?
E... EXPLANATION? UM...
NEGI-SENSEI!
IF YOU DON'T MIND...
...I WOULD BE HAPPY TO PROVIDE THAT EXPLANATION!!
C-CLASS REP!?
CLASS REP-SAN.
WHAT ARE YOU DOING HERE!?
GRR...!
I KNEW IT! YOU ARE IN CAHOOTS!
OH, CHISAME-SAN. "CAHOOTS" IS SUCH A VULGAR TERM.
THE RELATIONSHIP BETWEEN NEGI-SENSEI AND MYSELF HAS GROWN. YOU MIGHT EVEN CALL US PARTNERS.
SQUEEZE
JUST A--
PARTNERS!? HOW DARE YOU ACT SO RIENDLY ITH HIM, CLASS REP!!

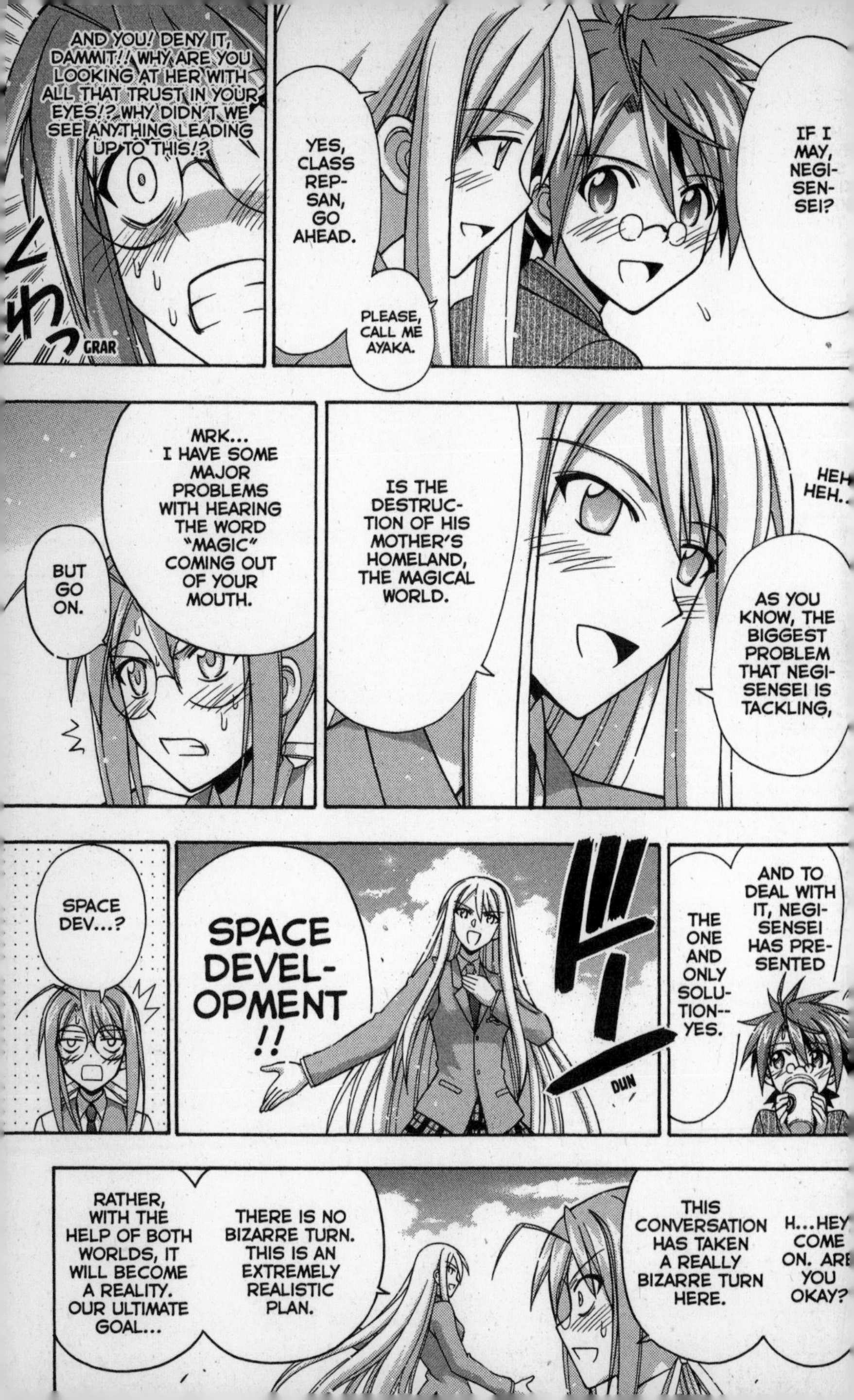
IF I MAY, NEGI-SENSEI?
YES, CLASS REP-SAN, GO AHEAD.
PLEASE, CALL ME AYAKA.
AND YOU! DENY IT, DAMMIT!! WHY ARE YOU LOOKING AT HER WITH ALL THAT TRUST IN YOUR EYES!? WHY DIDN'T WE SEE ANYTHING LEADING UP TO THIS!?
GRAR
HEH HEH...
AS YOU KNOW, THE BIGGEST PROBLEM THAT NEGI-SENSEI IS TACKLING,
IS THE DESTRUCTION OF HIS MOTHER'S HOMELAND, THE MAGICAL WORLD.
MRK... I HAVE SOME MAJOR PROBLEMS WITH HEARING THE WORD "MAGIC" COMING OUT OF YOUR MOUTH.
BUT GO ON.
AND TO DEAL WITH IT, NEGI-SENSEI HAS PRESENTED
THE ONE AND ONLY SOLUTION-- YES.
DUN
SPACE DEVELOPMENT!!
SPACE DEV...?
H...HEY COME ON. ARE YOU OKAY?
THIS CONVERSATION HAS TAKEN A REALLY BIZARRE TURN HERE.
THERE IS NO BIZARRE TURN. THIS IS AN EXTREMELY REALISTIC PLAN.
RATHER, WITH THE HELP OF BOTH WORLDS, IT WILL BECOME A REALITY. OUR ULTIMATE GOAL...

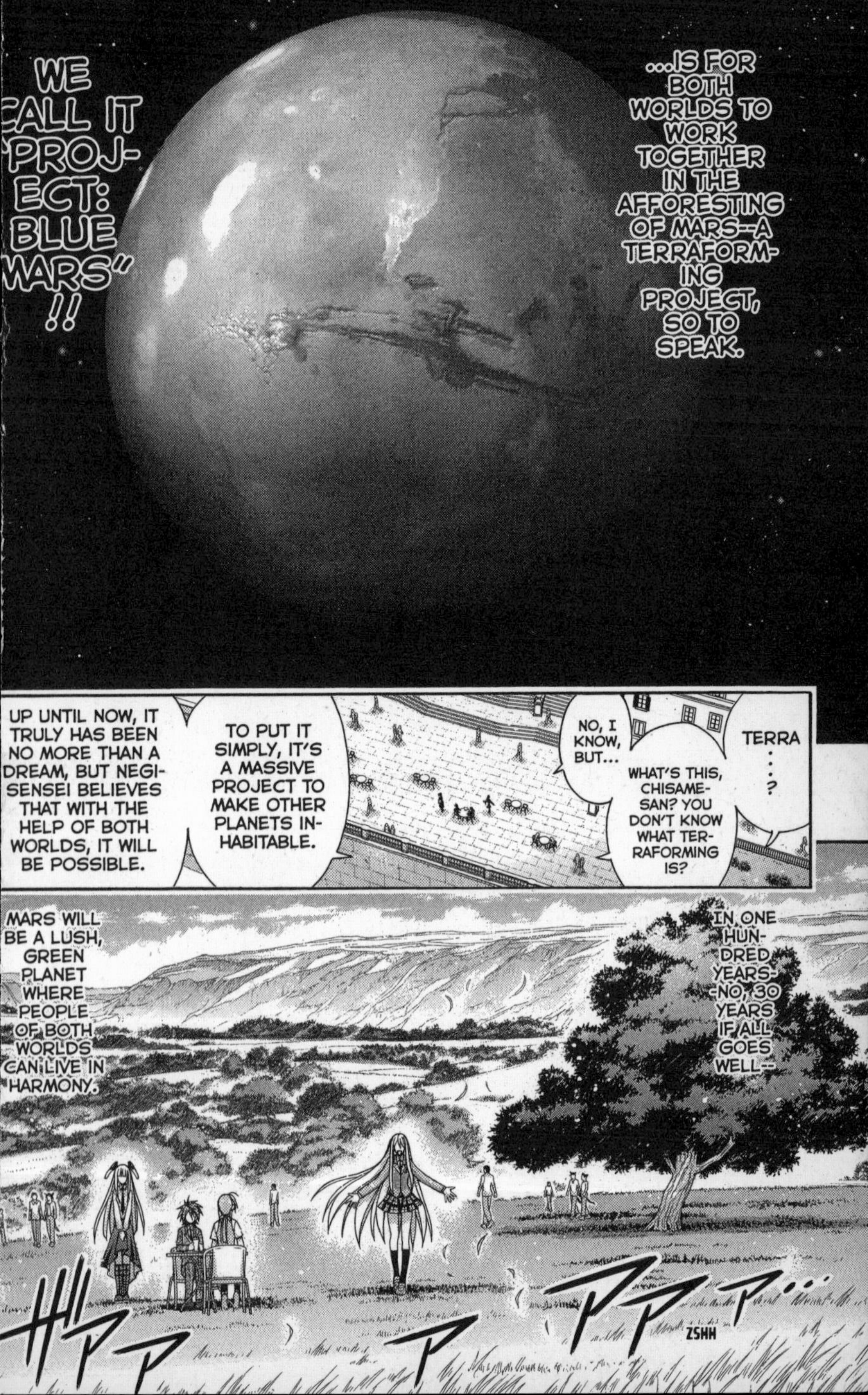
...IS FOR BOTH WORLDS TO WORK TOGETHER IN THE AFFORESTING OF MARS--A TERRAFORMING PROJECT, SO TO SPEAK.
WE CALL IT "PROJECT: BLUE MARS"!!
TERRA...?
WHAT'S THIS, CHISAME-SAN? YOU DON'T KNOW WHAT TERRAFORMING IS?
NO, I KNOW, BUT...
TO PUT IT SIMPLY, IT'S A MASSIVE PROJECT TO MAKE OTHER PLANETS INHABITABLE.
UP UNTIL NOW, IT TRULY HAS BEEN NO MORE THAN A DREAM, BUT NEGI-SENSEI BELIEVES THAT WITH THE HELP OF BOTH WORLDS, IT WILL BE POSSIBLE.
IN ONE HUNDRED YEARS-NO, 30 YEARS IF ALL GOES WELL--
MARS WILL BE A LUSH, GREEN PLANET WHERE PEOPLE OF BOTH WORLDS CAN LIVE IN HARMONY.
ZSHH

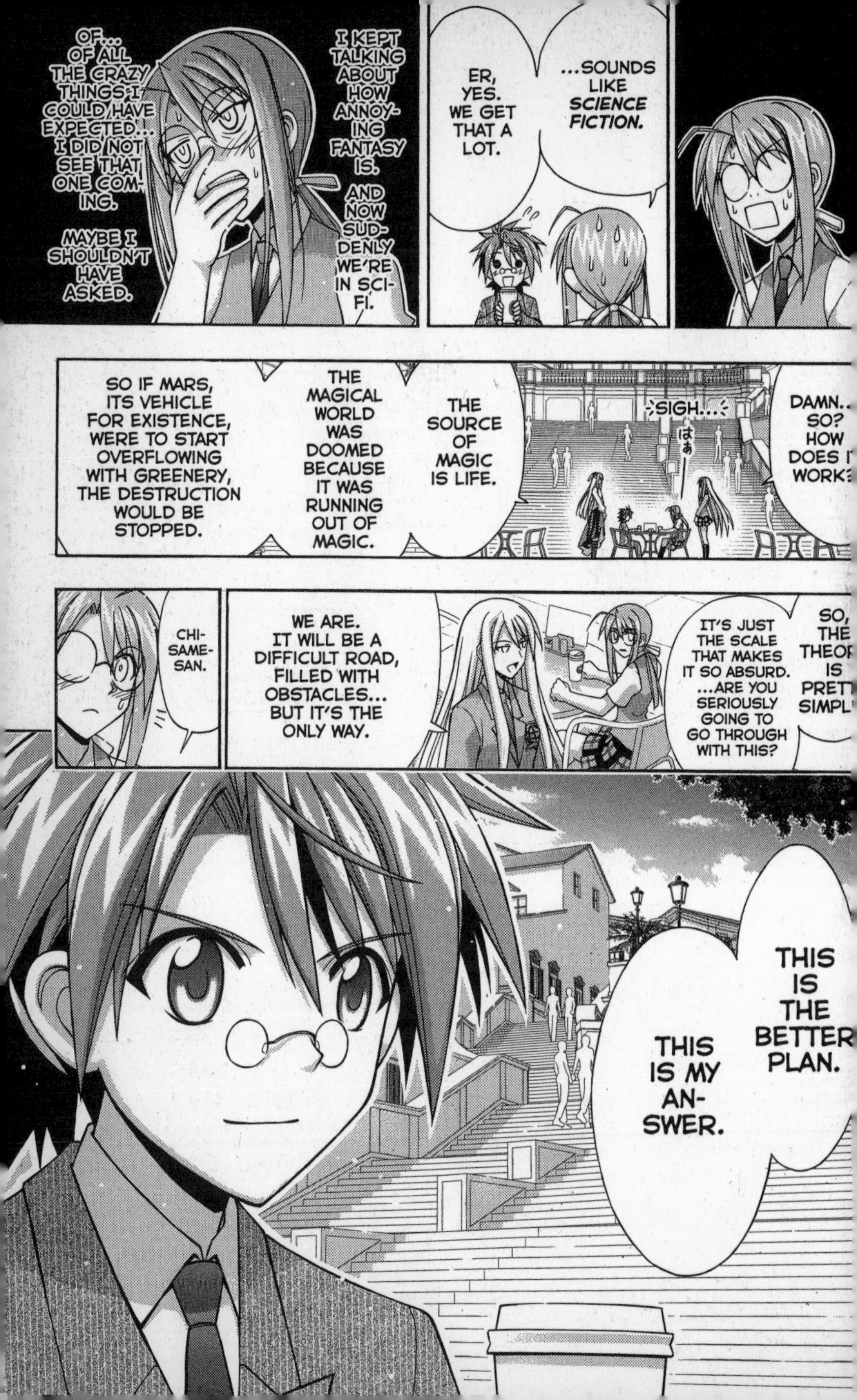
...SOUNDS LIKE SCIENCE FICTION.
ER, YES. WE GET THAT A LOT.
I KEPT TALKING ABOUT HOW ANNOYING FANTASY IS.
AND NOW SUDDENLY WE'RE IN SCI-FI.
OF... OF ALL THE CRAZY THINGS I COULD HAVE EXPECTED... I DID NOT SEE THAT ONE COMING.
MAYBE I SHOULDN'T HAVE ASKED.
DAMN... SO? HOW DOES IT WORK?
SIGH...
はぁ
THE SOURCE OF MAGIC IS LIFE.
THE MAGICAL WORLD WAS DOOMED BECAUSE IT WAS RUNNING OUT OF MAGIC.
SO IF MARS, ITS VEHICLE FOR EXISTENCE, WERE TO START OVERFLOWING WITH GREENERY, THE DESTRUCTION WOULD BE STOPPED.
SO, THE THEOR IS PRETT SIMPL
IT'S JUST THE SCALE THAT MAKES IT SO ABSURD. ...ARE YOU SERIOUSLY GOING TO GO THROUGH WITH THIS?
WE ARE. IT WILL BE A DIFFICULT ROAD, FILLED WITH OBSTACLES... BUT IT'S THE ONLY WAY.
CHISAME-SAN.
THIS IS THE BETTER PLAN.
THIS IS MY ANSWER.

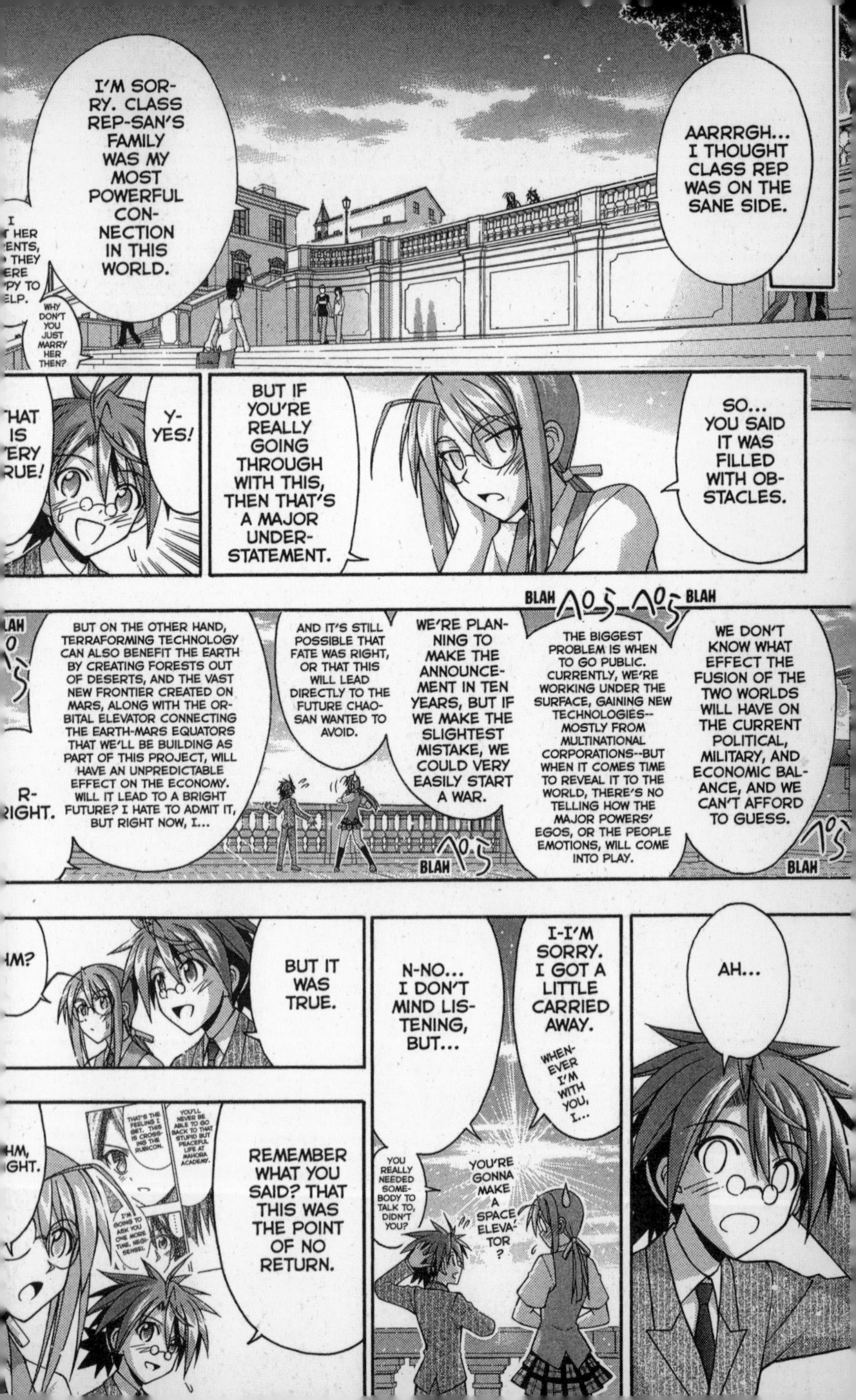
AARRRGH... I THOUGHT CLASS REP WAS ON THE SANE SIDE.
I'M SORRY. CLASS REP-SAN'S FAMILY WAS MY MOST POWERFUL CONNECTION IN THIS WORLD.
I T HER ENTS, THEY ERE PPY TO ELP.
WHY DON'T YOU JUST MARRY HER THEN?
SO... YOU SAID IT WAS FILLED WITH OBSTACLES.
BUT IF YOU'RE REALLY GOING THROUGH WITH THIS, THEN THAT'S A MAJOR UNDERSTATEMENT.
Y-YES!
HAT IS ERY RUE!
BLAH
BLAH
WE DON'T KNOW WHAT EFFECT THE FUSION OF THE TWO WORLDS WILL HAVE ON THE CURRENT POLITICAL, MILITARY, AND ECONOMIC BALANCE, AND WE CAN'T AFFORD TO GUESS.
BLAH
THE BIGGEST PROBLEM IS WHEN TO GO PUBLIC. CURRENTLY, WE'RE WORKING UNDER THE SURFACE, GAINING NEW TECHNOLOGIES--MOSTLY FROM MULTINATIONAL CORPORATIONS--BUT WHEN IT COMES TIME TO REVEAL IT TO THE WORLD, THERE'S NO TELLING HOW THE MAJOR POWERS' EGOS, OR THE PEOPLE EMOTIONS, WILL COME INTO PLAY.
WE'RE PLANNING TO MAKE THE ANNOUNCEMENT IN TEN YEARS, BUT IF WE MAKE THE SLIGHTEST MISTAKE, WE COULD VERY EASILY START A WAR.
AND IT'S STILL POSSIBLE THAT FATE WAS RIGHT, OR THAT THIS WILL LEAD DIRECTLY TO THE FUTURE CHAO-SAN WANTED TO AVOID.
BLAH
BUT ON THE OTHER HAND, TERRAFORMING TECHNOLOGY CAN ALSO BENEFIT THE EARTH BY CREATING FORESTS OUT OF DESERTS, AND THE VAST NEW FRONTIER CREATED ON MARS, ALONG WITH THE ORBITAL ELEVATOR CONNECTING THE EARTH-MARS EQUATORS THAT WE'LL BE BUILDING AS PART OF THIS PROJECT, WILL HAVE AN UNPREDICTABLE EFFECT ON THE ECONOMY. WILL IT LEAD TO A BRIGHT FUTURE? I HATE TO ADMIT IT, BUT RIGHT NOW, I...
R-RIGHT.
LAH
AH...
I-I'M SORRY. I GOT A LITTLE CARRIED AWAY.
N-NO... I DON'T MIND LISTENING, BUT...
WHENEVER I'M WITH YOU, I...
YOU'RE GONNA MAKE A SPACE ELEVATOR?
YOU REALLY NEEDED SOMEBODY TO TALK TO, DIDN'T YOU?
BUT IT WAS TRUE.
HM?
REMEMBER WHAT YOU SAID? THAT THIS WAS THE POINT OF NO RETURN.
YOU'LL NEVER BE ABLE TO GO BACK TO THAT STUPID BUT PEACEFUL LIFE AT MAHORA ACADEMY.
THAT'S THE FEELING I GET. THIS IS CROSSING THE RUBICON.
I'M GOING TO ASK YOU ONE MORE TIME, NEGI-SENSEI.
HM, IGHT.

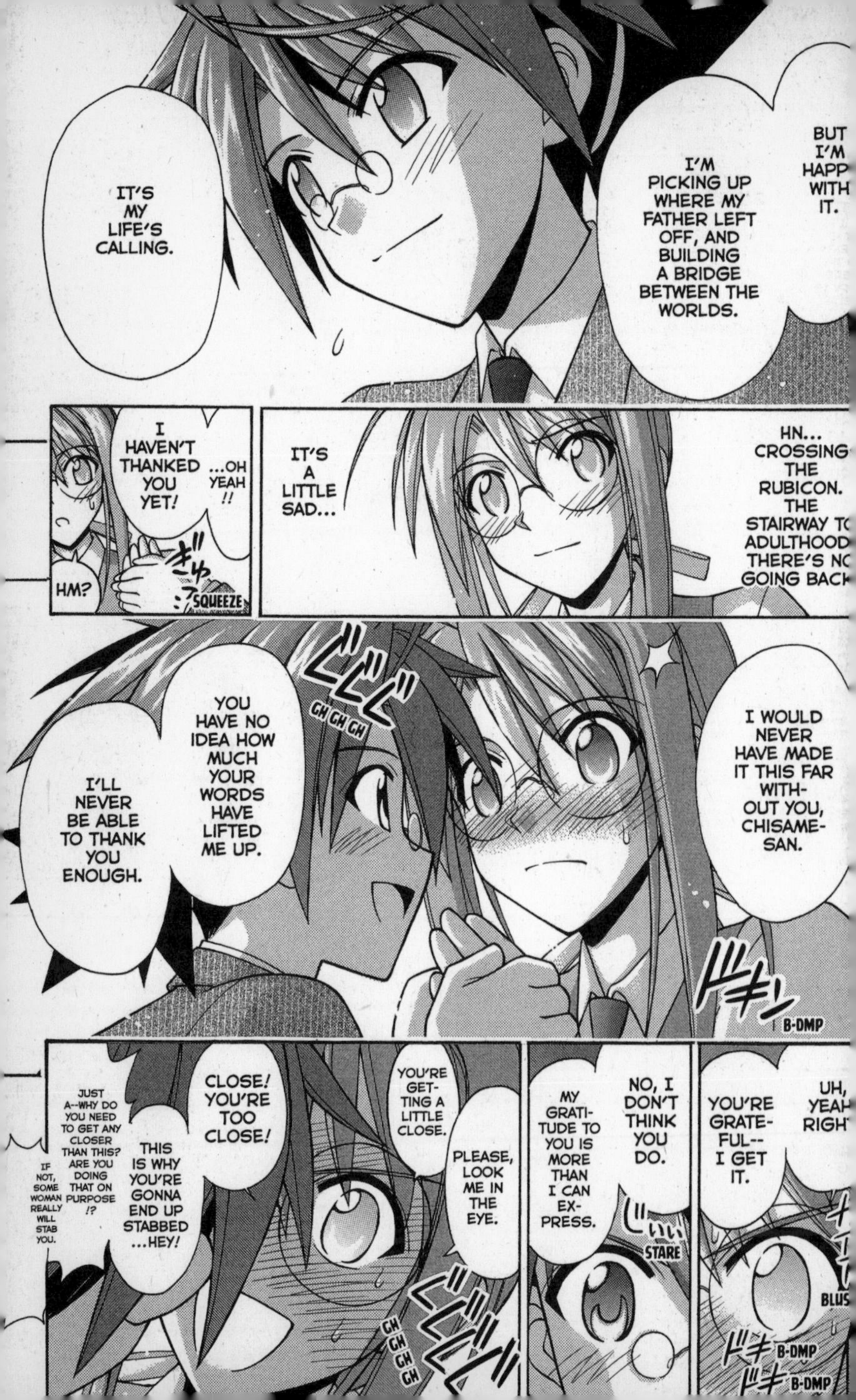
BUT I'M HAPP WITH IT.
I'M PICKING UP WHERE MY FATHER LEFT OFF, AND BUILDING A BRIDGE BETWEEN THE WORLDS.
IT'S MY LIFE'S CALLING.
HN... CROSSING THE RUBICON. THE STAIRWAY TC ADULTHOOD THERE'S NC GOING BACK
IT'S A LITTLE SAD...
...OH YEAH!!
I HAVEN'T THANKED YOU YET!
SQUEEZE
HM?
I WOULD NEVER HAVE MADE IT THIS FAR WITHOUT YOU, CHISAME-SAN.
B-DMP
GH GH GH
YOU HAVE NO IDEA HOW MUCH YOUR WORDS HAVE LIFTED ME UP.
I'LL NEVER BE ABLE TO THANK YOU ENOUGH.
UH, YEAH RIGHT
YOU'RE GRATEFUL-- I GET IT.
BLUS
B-DMP
B-DMP
NO, I DON'T THINK YOU DO.
MY GRATITUDE TO YOU IS MORE THAN I CAN EXPRESS.
STARE
YOU'RE GETTING A LITTLE CLOSE.
PLEASE, LOOK ME IN THE EYE.
CLOSE! YOU'RE TOO CLOSE!
THIS IS WHY YOU'RE GONNA END UP STABBED ...HEY!
JUST A--WHY DO YOU NEED TO GET ANY CLOSER THAN THIS? ARE YOU DOING THAT ON PURPOSE!?
IF NOT, SOME WOMAN REALLY WILL STAB YOU.
GH GH GH GH

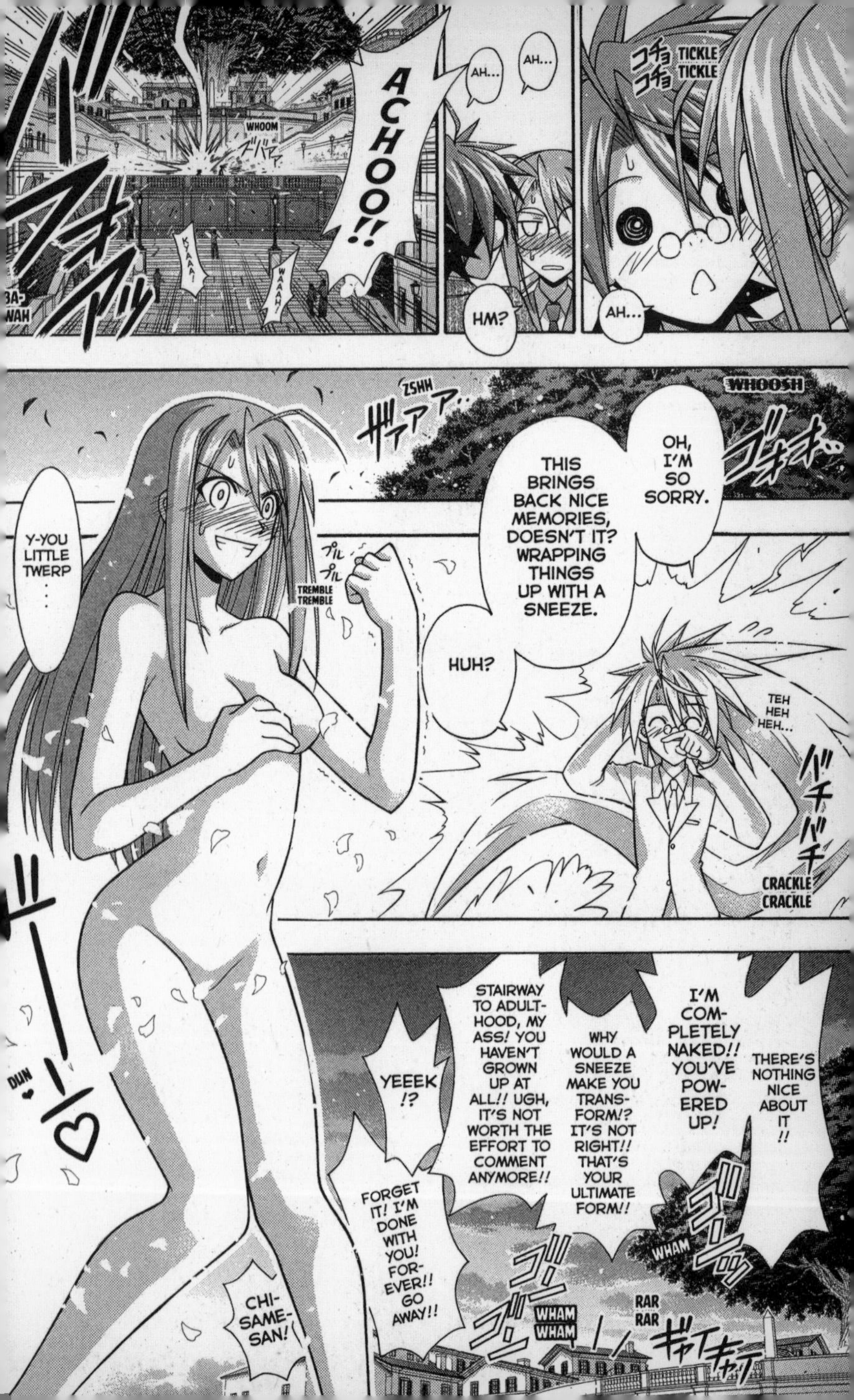

コチョコチョ TICKLE TICKLE
AH...
AH...
AH...
ACHOO!!
HM?
WHOOM
ズバァア
KYAAA!
WAAAH!
BA-WAH
WHOOSH
OH, I'M SO SORRY.
THIS BRINGS BACK NICE MEMORIES, DOESN'T IT? WRAPPING THINGS UP WITH A SNEEZE.
HUH?
TEH HEH HEH...
CRACKLE CRACKLE
ZSHH
Y-YOU LITTLE TWERP...
TREMBLE TREMBLE
DUN
THERE'S NOTHING NICE ABOUT IT!!
I'M COMPLETELY NAKED!! YOU'VE POWERED UP!
WHY WOULD A SNEEZE MAKE YOU TRANSFORM!? IT'S NOT RIGHT!! THAT'S YOUR ULTIMATE FORM!!
STAIRWAY TO ADULTHOOD, MY ASS! YOU HAVEN'T GROWN UP AT ALL!! UGH, IT'S NOT WORTH THE EFFORT TO COMMENT ANYMORE!!
YEEEK!?
WHAM
FORGET IT! I'M DONE WITH YOU! FOREVER!! GO AWAY!!
RAR RAR
WHAM WHAM
CHISAME-SAN!

NEGIMA!

MAGISTER NEGI MAGI

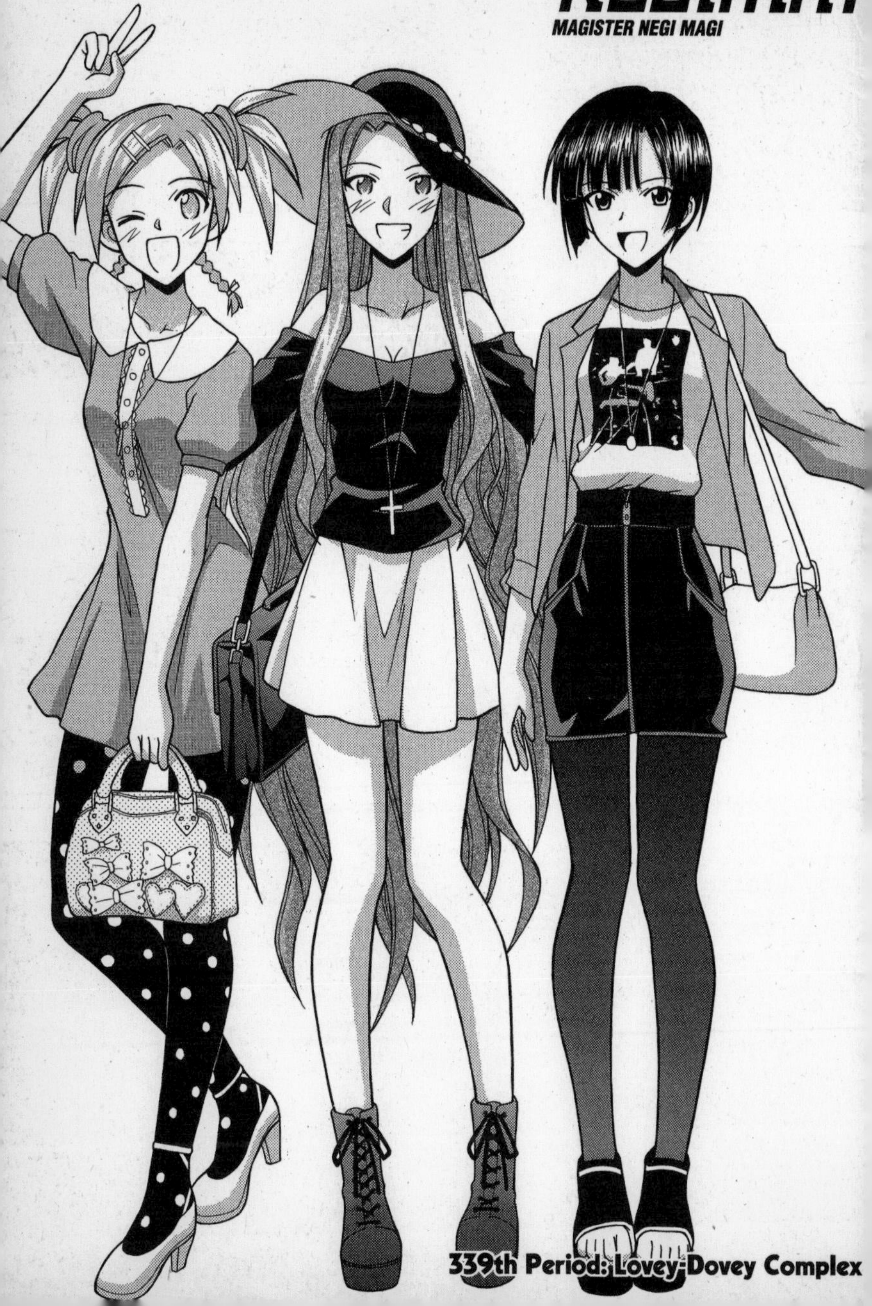

339th Period: Lovey-Dovey Complex

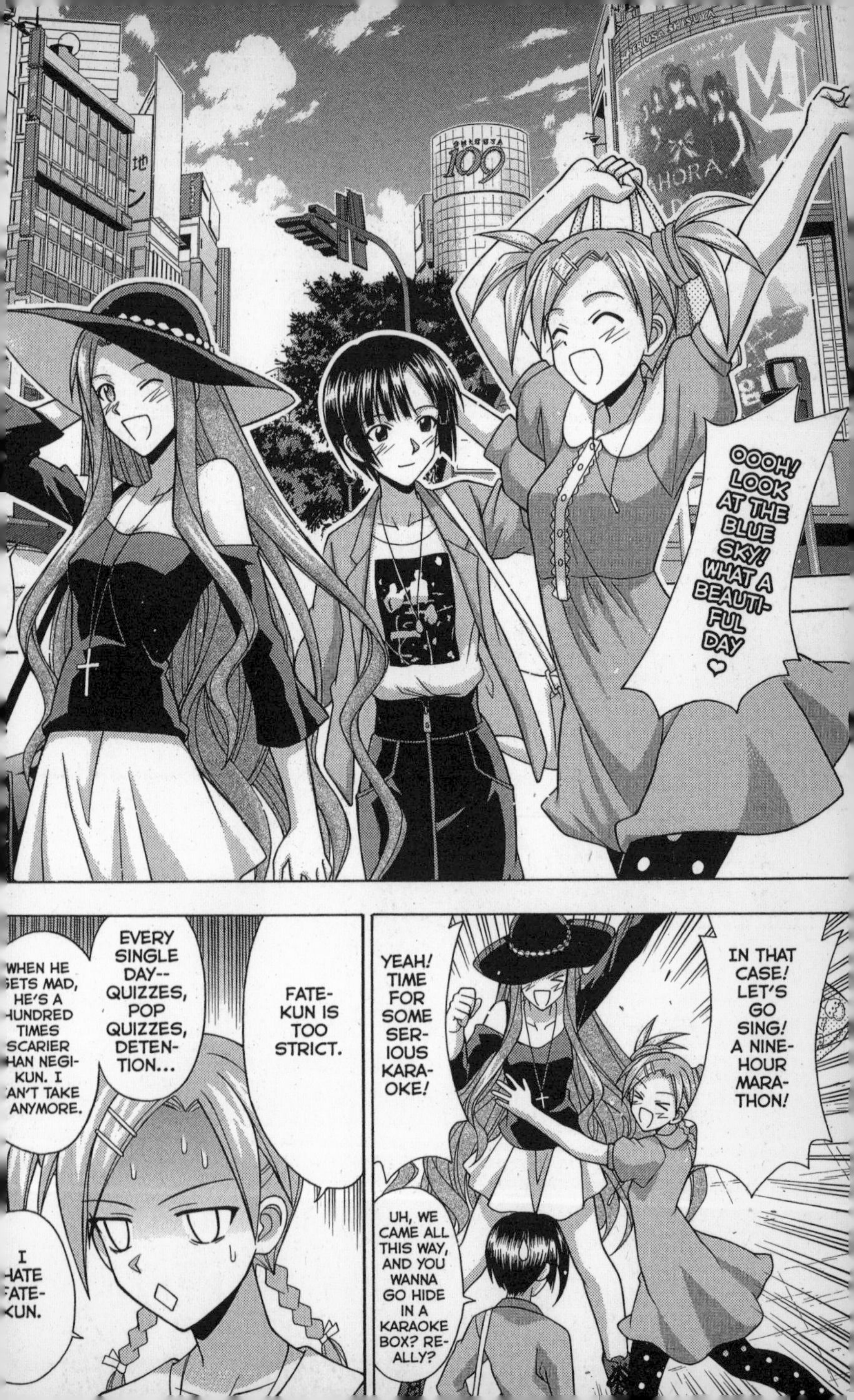
109
OOOH! LOOK AT THE BLUE SKY! WHAT A BEAUTI-FUL DAY ♡
IN THAT CASE! LET'S GO SING! A NINE-HOUR MARA-THON!
YEAH! TIME FOR SOME SER-IOUS KARA-OKE!
UH, WE CAME ALL THIS WAY, AND YOU WANNA GO HIDE IN A KARAOKE BOX? RE-ALLY?
FATE-KUN IS TOO STRICT.
EVERY SINGLE DAY-- QUIZZES, POP QUIZZES, DETEN-TION...
WHEN HE ETS MAD, HE'S A HUNDRED TIMES SCARIER HAN NEGI-KUN. I AN'T TAKE ANYMORE.
I HATE ATE-KUN.

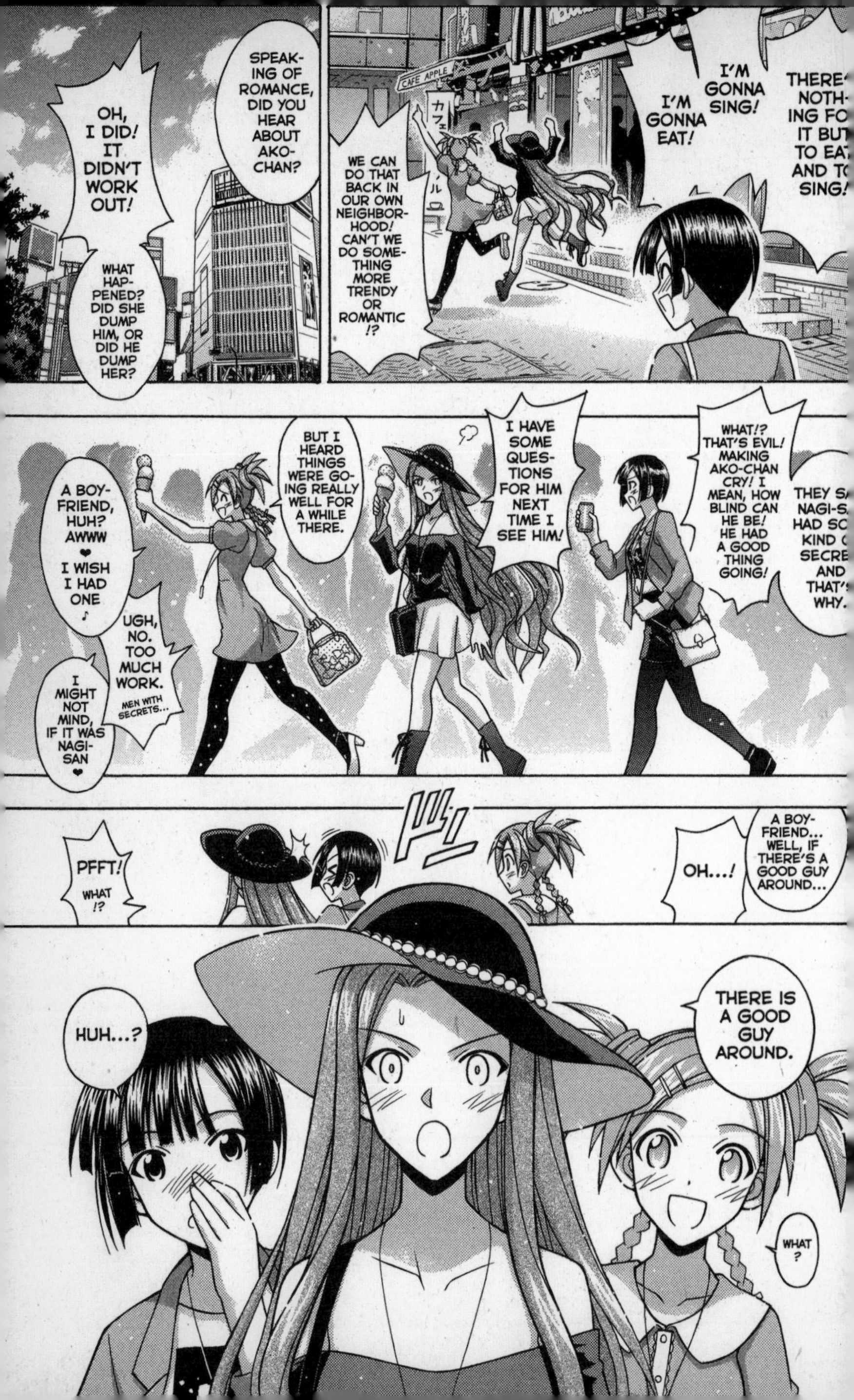
THERE' NOTH- ING FO IT BUT TO EA AND TO SING!
I'M GONNA SING!
I'M GONNA EAT!
WE CAN DO THAT BACK IN OUR OWN NEIGHBOR-HOOD! CAN'T WE DO SOME-THING MORE TRENDY OR ROMANTIC !?
CAFE APPLE
SPEAK-ING OF ROMANCE, DID YOU HEAR ABOUT AKO-CHAN?
OH, I DID! IT DIDN'T WORK OUT!
WHAT HAP-PENED? DID SHE DUMP HIM, OR DID HE DUMP HER?
THEY S NAGI-S HAD SO KIND SECRE AND THAT'S WHY.
WHAT!? THAT'S EVIL! MAKING AKO-CHAN CRY! I MEAN, HOW BLIND CAN HE BE! HE HAD A GOOD THING GOING!
I HAVE SOME QUES-TIONS FOR HIM NEXT TIME I SEE HIM!
BUT I HEARD THINGS WERE GO-ING REALLY WELL FOR A WHILE THERE.
A BOY-FRIEND, HUH? AWWW ❤ I WISH I HAD ONE ♪
UGH, NO. TOO MUCH WORK.
MEN WITH SECRETS...
I MIGHT NOT MIND, IF IT WAS NAGI-SAN ❤
A BOY-FRIEND... WELL, IF THERE'S A GOOD GUY AROUND...
OH...!
PFFT!
WHAT !?
THERE IS A GOOD GUY AROUND.
WHAT ?
HUH...?

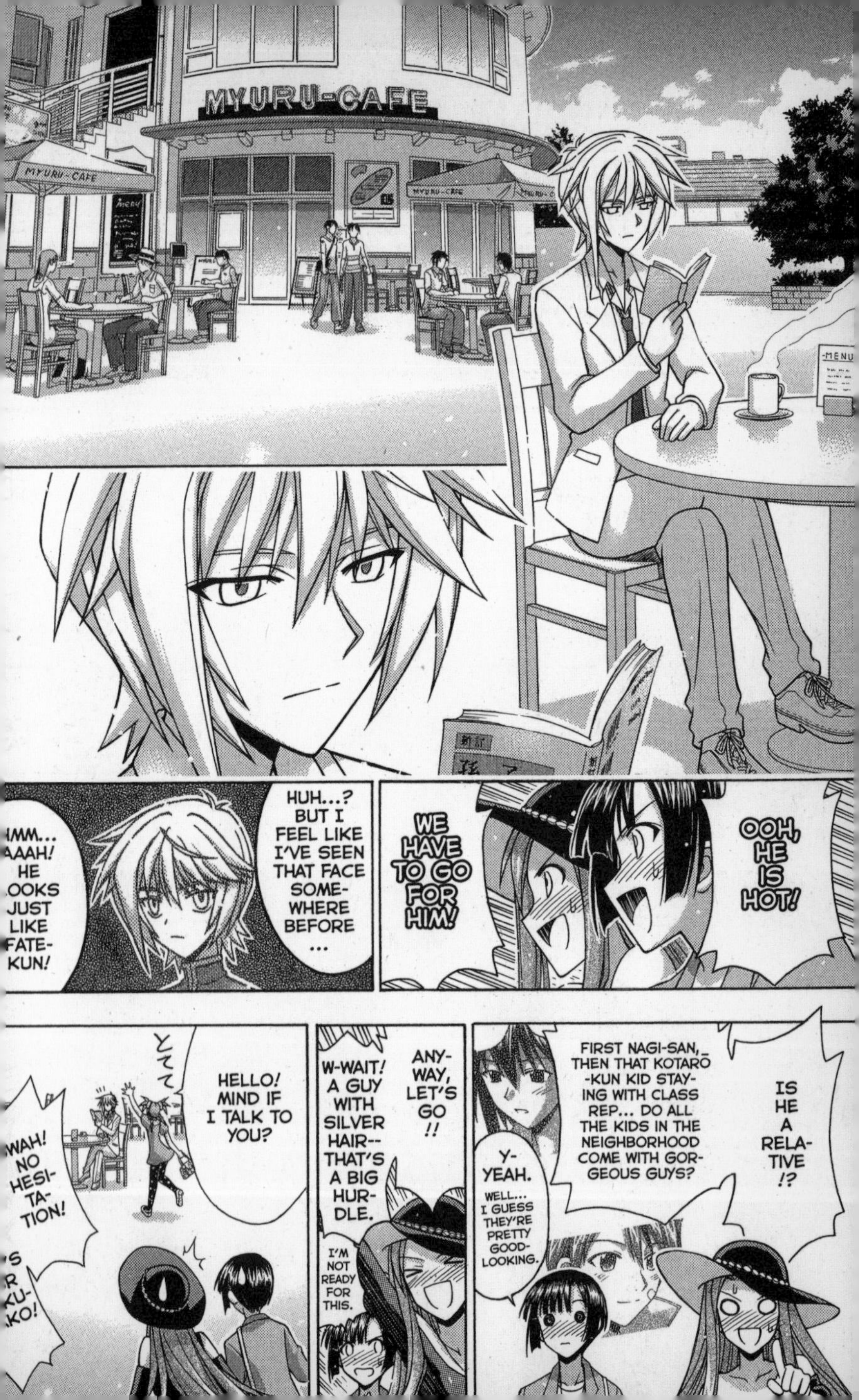
MYURU-CAFE
MENU
OOH, HE IS HOT!
WE HAVE TO GO FOR HIM!
HUH...? BUT I FEEL LIKE I'VE SEEN THAT FACE SOMEWHERE BEFORE...
MM... AAAH! HE OOKS JUST LIKE FATE-KUN!
IS HE A RELATIVE!?
FIRST NAGI-SAN, THEN THAT KOTARO-KUN KID STAYING WITH CLASS REP... DO ALL THE KIDS IN THE NEIGHBORHOOD COME WITH GORGEOUS GUYS?
Y-YEAH.
WELL... I GUESS THEY'RE PRETTY GOOD-LOOKING.
ANYWAY, LET'S GO!!
W-WAIT! A GUY WITH SILVER HAIR--THAT'S A BIG HURDLE.
I'M NOT READY FOR THIS.
とてて
HELLO! MIND IF I TALK TO YOU?
WAH! NO HESITATION!

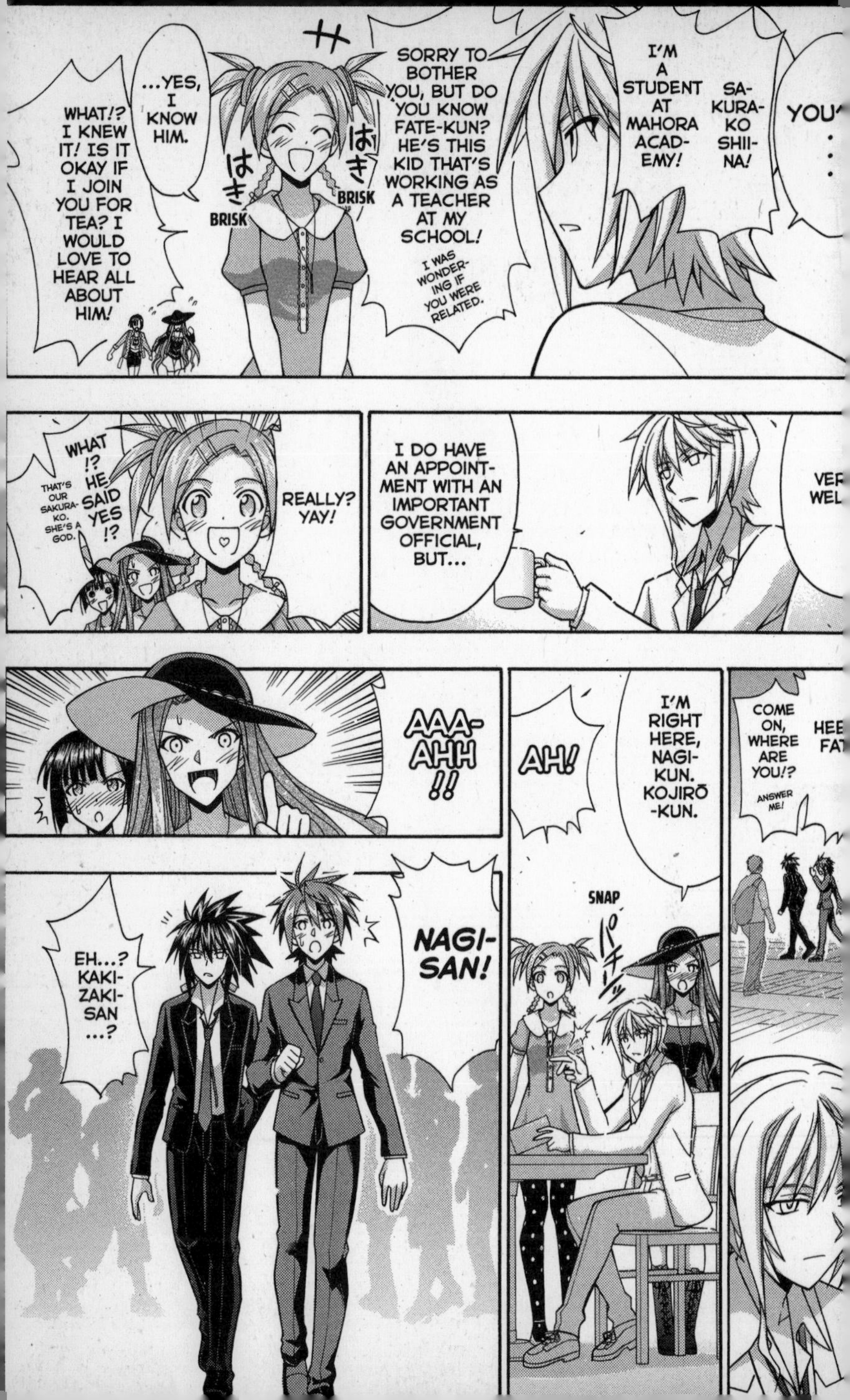

YOU...
SAKURAKO SHIINA!
I'M A STUDENT AT MAHORA ACADEMY!
SORRY TO BOTHER YOU, BUT DO YOU KNOW FATE-KUN? HE'S THIS KID THAT'S WORKING AS A TEACHER AT MY SCHOOL!
I WAS WONDERING IF YOU WERE RELATED.
はき BRISK
はき BRISK
...YES, I KNOW HIM.
WHAT!? I KNEW IT! IS IT OKAY IF I JOIN YOU FOR TEA? I WOULD LOVE TO HEAR ALL ABOUT HIM!
VER WEL
I DO HAVE AN APPOINTMENT WITH AN IMPORTANT GOVERNMENT OFFICIAL, BUT...
REALLY? YAY!
WHAT!? HE SAID YES!?
THAT'S OUR SAKURAKO. SHE'S A GOD.
HEE FAT
COME ON, WHERE ARE YOU!?
ANSWER ME!
I'M RIGHT HERE, NAGI-KUN. KOJIRŌ-KUN.
AH!
パチッ SNAP
AAA-AHH!!
NAGI-SAN!
EH...? KAKIZAKI-SAN...?

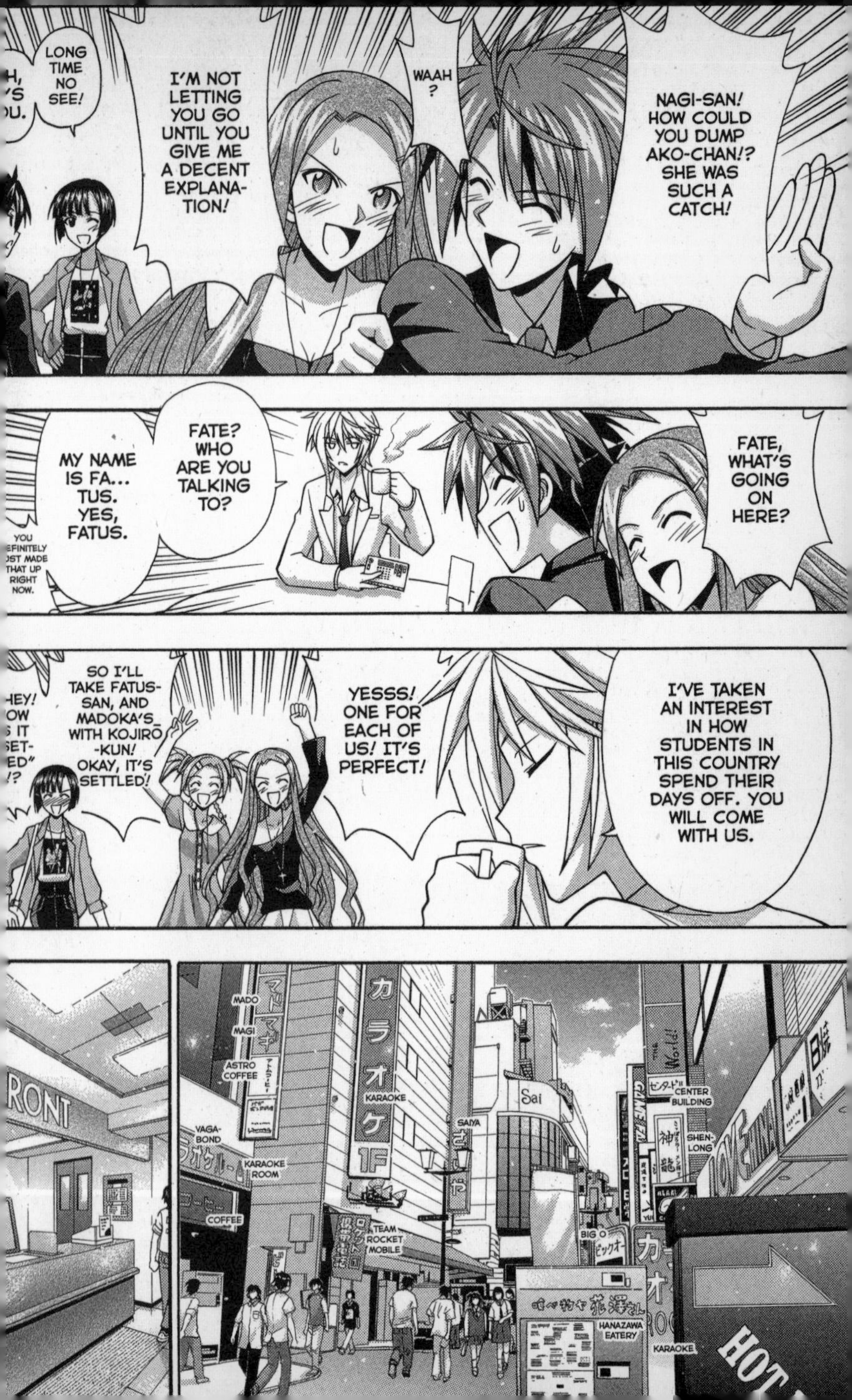
NAGI-SAN! HOW COULD YOU DUMP AKO-CHAN!? SHE WAS SUCH A CATCH!
WAAH?
I'M NOT LETTING YOU GO UNTIL YOU GIVE ME A DECENT EXPLANATION!
LONG TIME NO SEE!
FATE, WHAT'S GOING ON HERE?
FATE? WHO ARE YOU TALKING TO?
MY NAME IS FA... TUS. YES, FATUS.
THAT UP RIGHT NOW.
I'VE TAKEN AN INTEREST IN HOW STUDENTS IN THIS COUNTRY SPEND THEIR DAYS OFF. YOU WILL COME WITH US.
YESSS! ONE FOR EACH OF US! IT'S PERFECT!
SO I'LL TAKE FATUS-SAN, AND MADOKA'S WITH KOJIRŌ-KUN! OKAY, IT'S SETTLED!
HOT
KARAOKE
HANAZAWA EATERY
BIG O
SHEN-LONG
CENTER BUILDING
SAIYA
Sai
カラオケ
KARAOKE
1F
TEAM ROCKET MOBILE
COFFEE
KARAOKE ROOM
VAGA-BOND
ASTRO COFFEE
MAGI
MADO
RONT

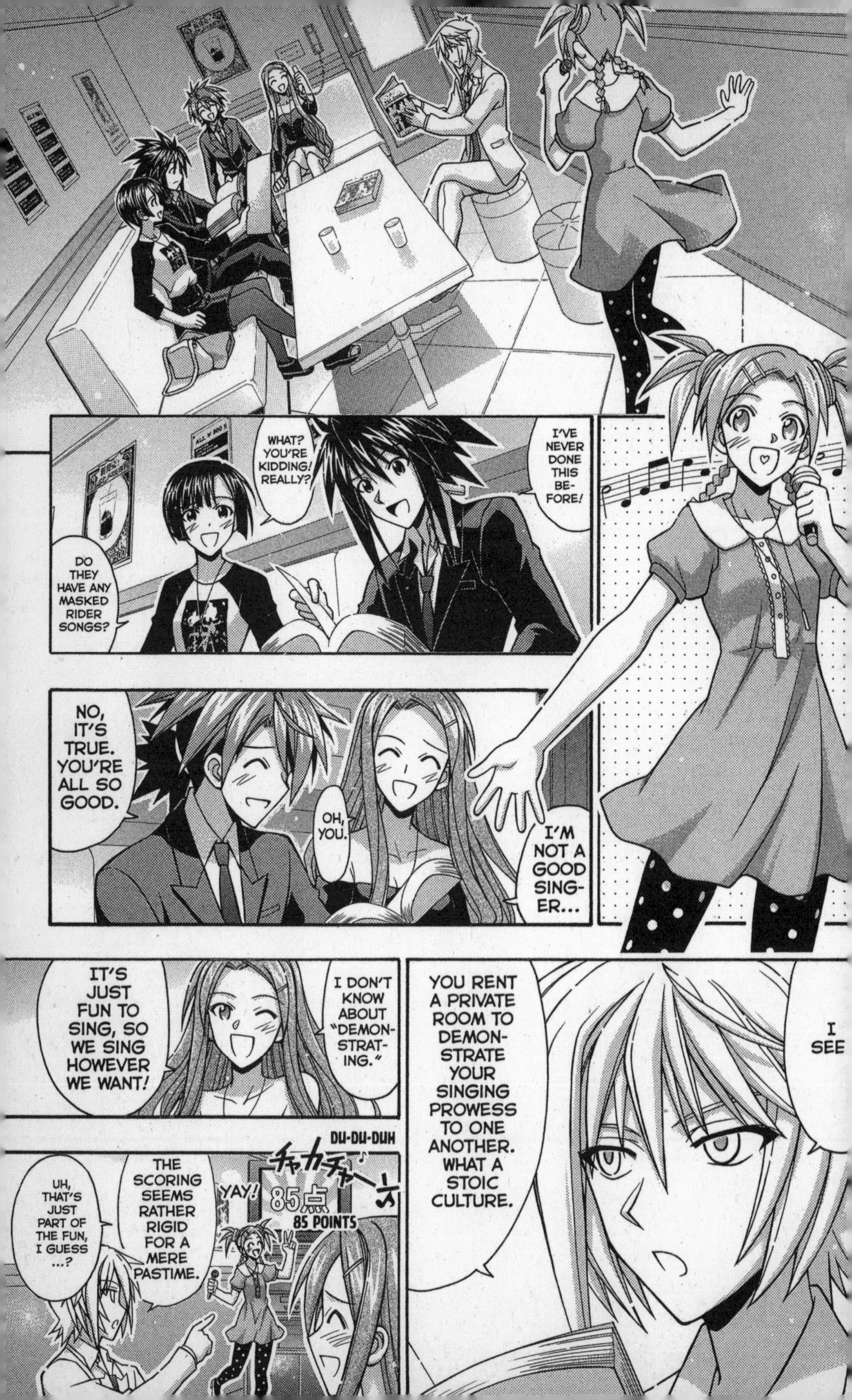

I'VE NEVER DONE THIS BE-FORE!
WHAT? YOU'RE KIDDING! REALLY?
DO THEY HAVE ANY MASKED RIDER SONGS?
I'M NOT A GOOD SING-ER...
NO, IT'S TRUE. YOU'RE ALL SO GOOD.
OH, YOU.
I SEE
YOU RENT A PRIVATE ROOM TO DEMON-STRATE YOUR SINGING PROWESS TO ONE ANOTHER. WHAT A STOIC CULTURE.
I DON'T KNOW ABOUT "DEMON-STRAT-ING."
IT'S JUST FUN TO SING, SO WE SING HOWEVER WE WANT!
チャカチャーン♪
DU-DU-DUH
85点
85 POINTS
YAY!
THE SCORING SEEMS RATHER RIGID FOR A MERE PASTIME.
UH, THAT'S JUST PART OF THE FUN, I GUESS ...?

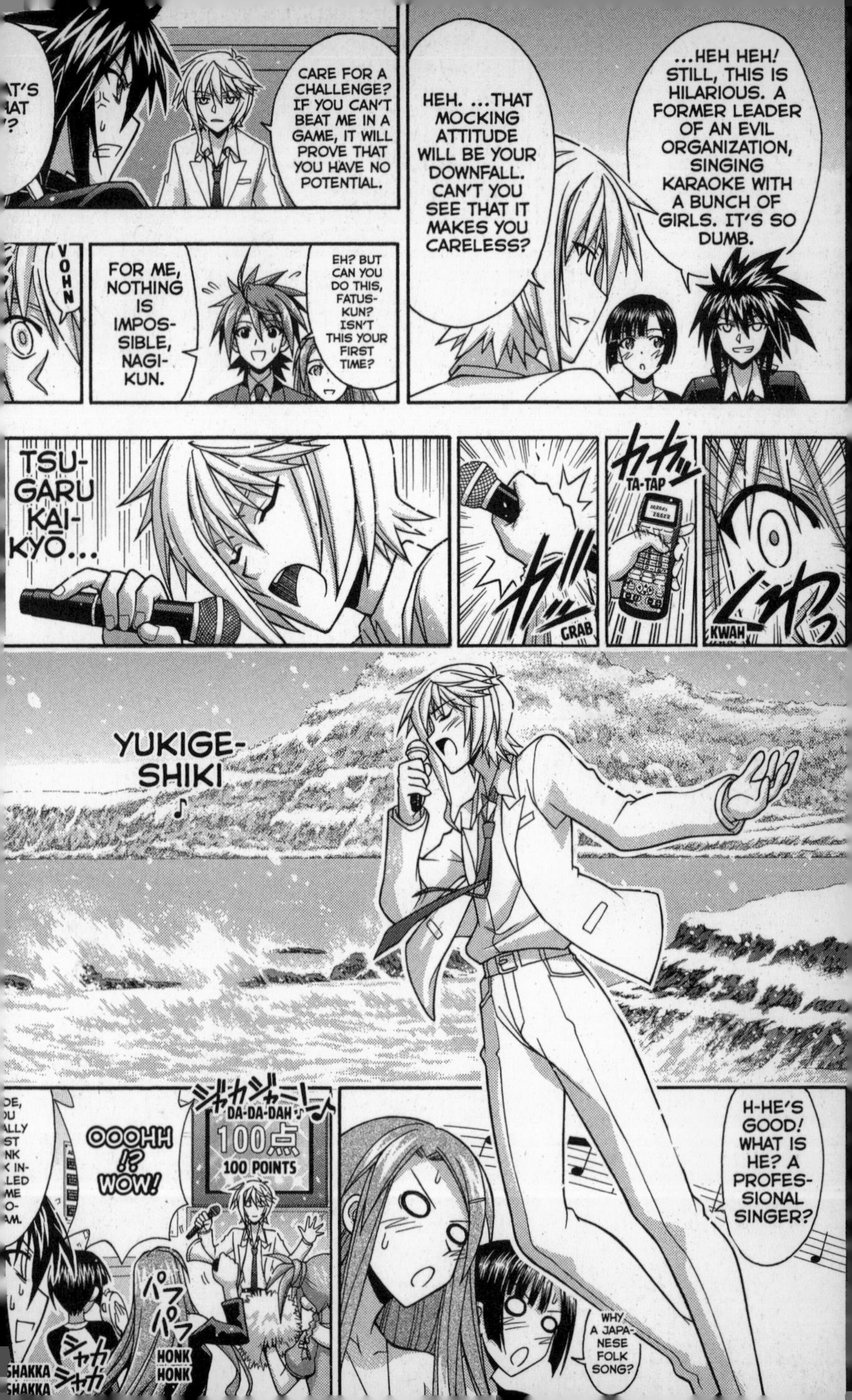
...HEH HEH! STILL, THIS IS HILARIOUS. A FORMER LEADER OF AN EVIL ORGANIZATION, SINGING KARAOKE WITH A BUNCH OF GIRLS. IT'S SO DUMB.
HEH. ...THAT MOCKING ATTITUDE WILL BE YOUR DOWNFALL. CAN'T YOU SEE THAT IT MAKES YOU CARELESS?
CARE FOR A CHALLENGE? IF YOU CAN'T BEAT ME IN A GAME, IT WILL PROVE THAT YOU HAVE NO POTENTIAL.
EH? BUT CAN YOU DO THIS, FATUS-KUN? ISN'T THIS YOUR FIRST TIME?
FOR ME, NOTHING IS IMPOS-SIBLE, NAGI-KUN.
VOHN
KWAH
TA-TAP
GRAB
TSU-GARU KAI-KYŌ...
YUKIGE-SHIKI ♪
H-HE'S GOOD! WHAT IS HE? A PROFES-SIONAL SINGER?
WHY A JAPA-NESE FOLK SONG?
DA-DA-DAH♪
100点
100 POINTS
OOOHH !? WOW!
HONK HONK
SHAKKA SHAKKA

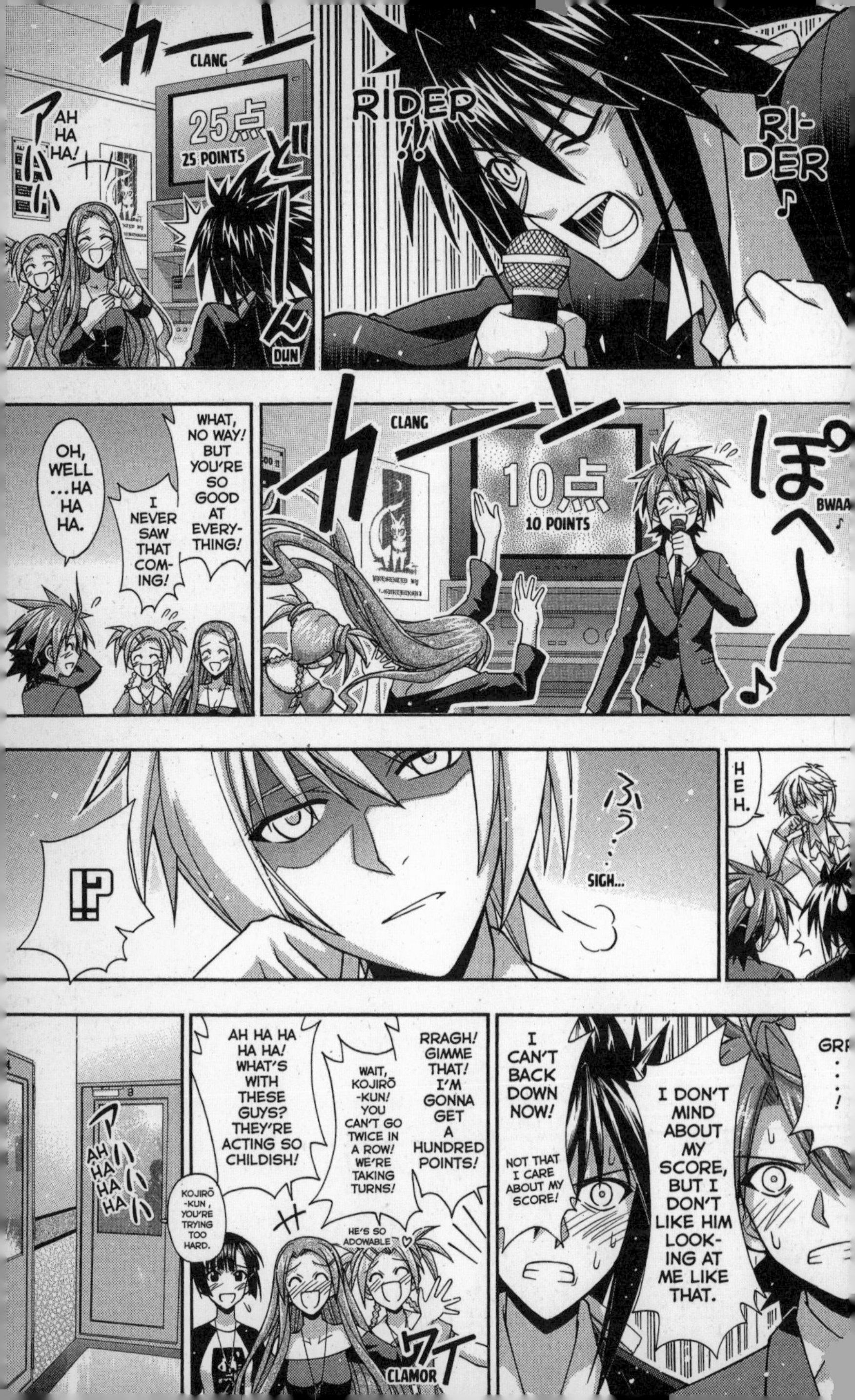
RI-DER ♪
RIDER!!
CLANG
25点
25 POINTS
DUN
AH HA HA!
BWAA ♪
CLANG
10点
10 POINTS
WHAT, NO WAY! BUT YOU'RE SO GOOD AT EVERYTHING!
I NEVER SAW THAT COMING!
OH, WELL ...HA HA HA.
HEH.
SIGH...
!?
GRR...!
I DON'T MIND ABOUT MY SCORE, BUT I DON'T LIKE HIM LOOKING AT ME LIKE THAT.
I CAN'T BACK DOWN NOW!
NOT THAT I CARE ABOUT MY SCORE!
RRAGH! GIMME THAT! I'M GONNA GET A HUNDRED POINTS!
WAIT, KOJIRŌ-KUN! YOU CAN'T GO TWICE IN A ROW! WE'RE TAKING TURNS!
AH HA HA HA HA! WHAT'S WITH THESE GUYS? THEY'RE ACTING SO CHILDISH!
HE'S SO ADOWABLE
KOJIRŌ-KUN, YOU'RE TRYING TOO HARD.
CLAMOR
AH HA HA HA

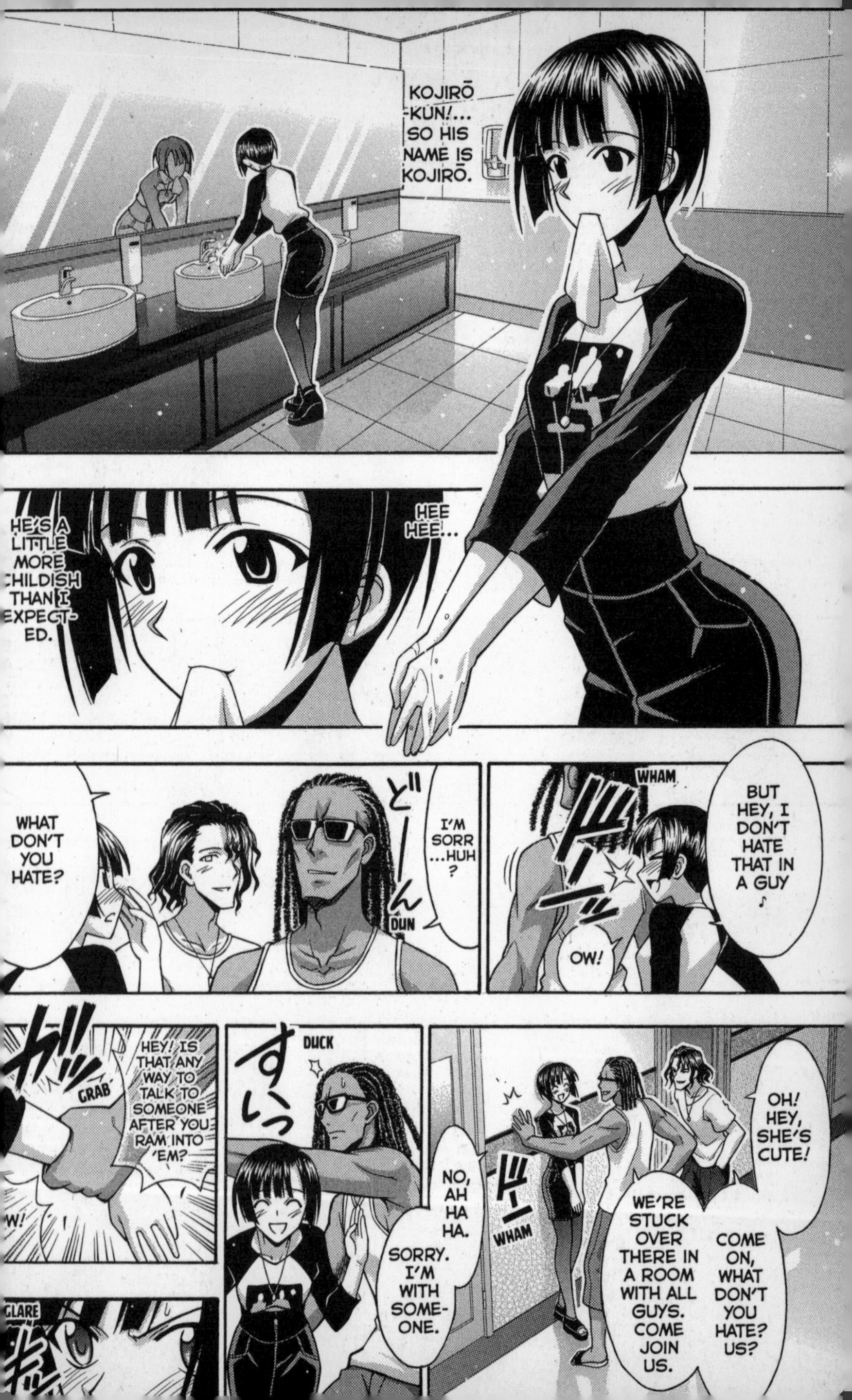
KOJIRŌ-KUN!... SO HIS NAME IS KOJIRŌ.
HEE HEE...
HE'S A LITTLE MORE CHILDISH THAN I EXPECTED.
WHAM
BUT HEY, I DON'T HATE THAT IN A GUY ♪
OW!
I'M SORR ...HUH?
DUN
WHAT DON'T YOU HATE?
OH! HEY, SHE'S CUTE!
COME ON, WHAT DON'T YOU HATE? US?
WE'RE STUCK OVER THERE IN A ROOM WITH ALL GUYS. COME JOIN US.
WHAM
DUCK
NO, AH HA HA.
SORRY. I'M WITH SOMEONE.
HEY! IS THAT ANY WAY TO TALK TO SOMEONE AFTER YOU RAM INTO 'EM?
GRAB
GLARE

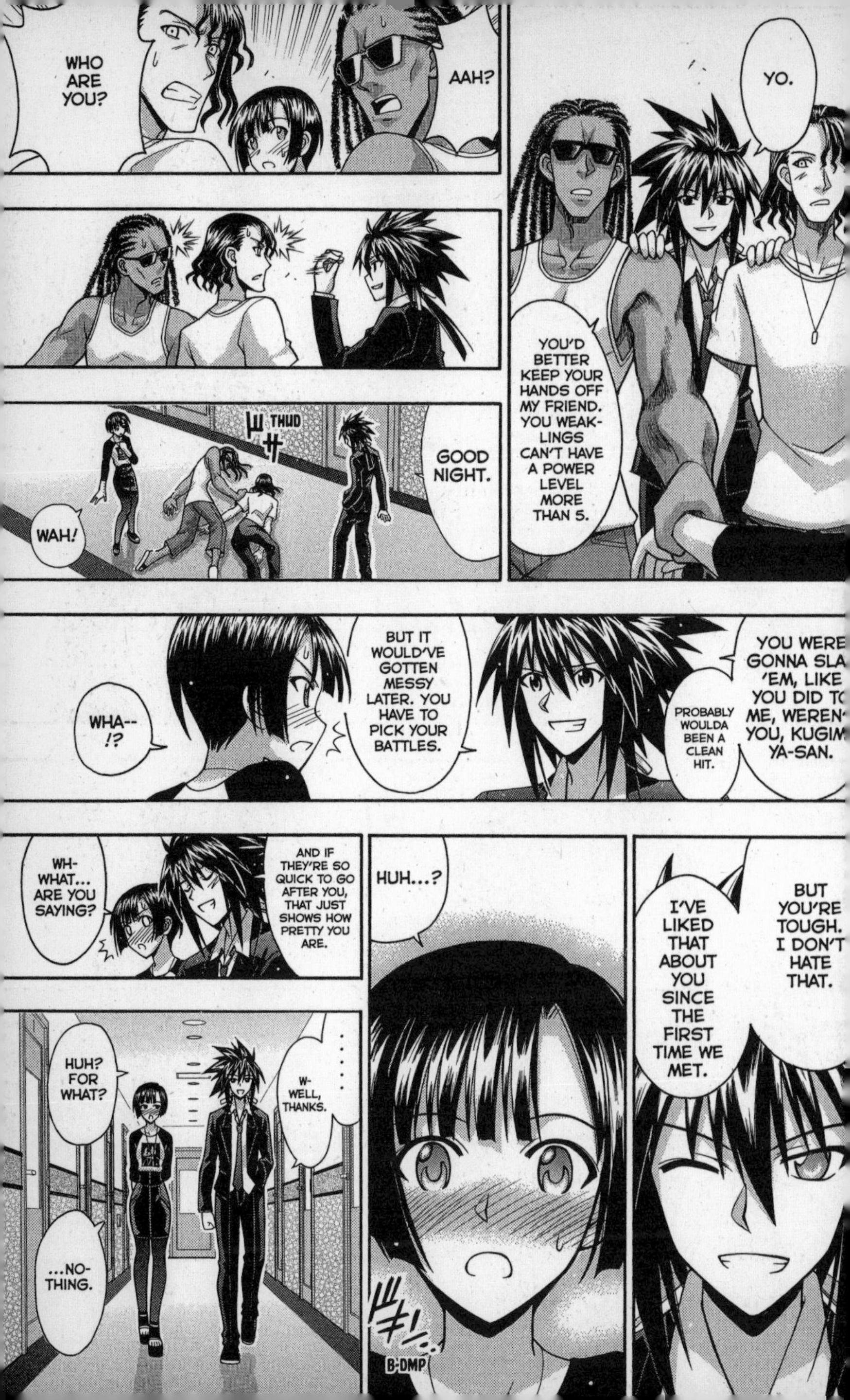

YO.
YOU'D BETTER KEEP YOUR HANDS OFF MY FRIEND. YOU WEAKLINGS CAN'T HAVE A POWER LEVEL MORE THAN 5.
AAH?
WHO ARE YOU?
THUD
GOOD NIGHT.
WAH!
YOU WERE GONNA SLA 'EM, LIKE YOU DID TO ME, WEREN' YOU, KUGIM YA-SAN.
PROBABLY WOULDA BEEN A CLEAN HIT.
BUT IT WOULD'VE GOTTEN MESSY LATER. YOU HAVE TO PICK YOUR BATTLES.
WHA-- !?
BUT YOU'RE TOUGH. I DON'T HATE THAT.
I'VE LIKED THAT ABOUT YOU SINCE THE FIRST TIME WE MET.
HUH...?
B-DMP
AND IF THEY'RE SO QUICK TO GO AFTER YOU, THAT JUST SHOWS HOW PRETTY YOU ARE.
WH- WHAT... ARE YOU SAYING?
W- WELL, THANKS.
HUH? FOR WHAT?
...NO- THING.

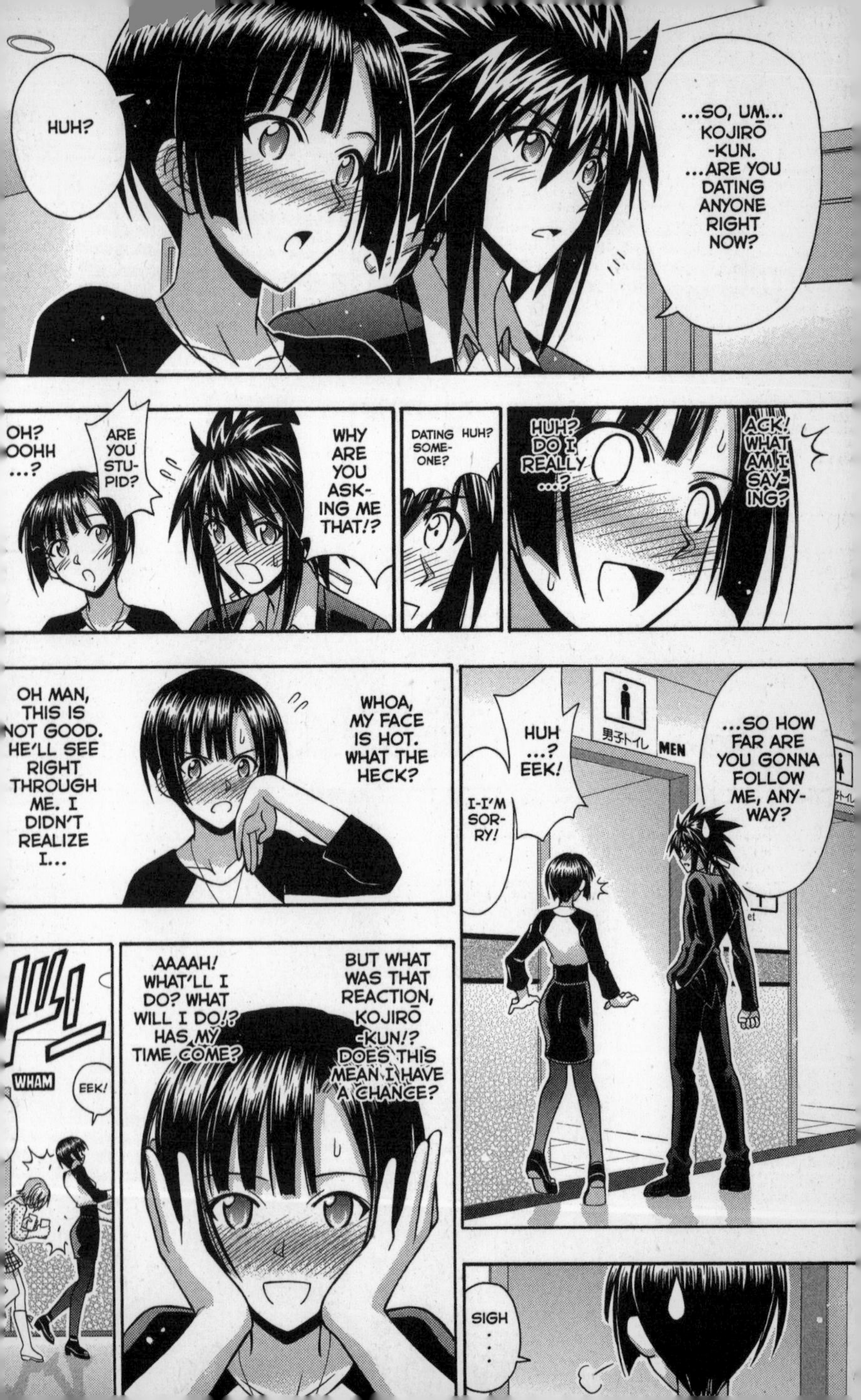
...SO, UM... KOJIRŌ -KUN. ...ARE YOU DATING ANYONE RIGHT NOW?
HUH?
ACK! WHAT AM I SAYING?
HUH? DO I REALLY ...?
HUH?
DATING SOME-ONE?
WHY ARE YOU ASK-ING ME THAT!?
ARE YOU STU-PID?
OH? OOHH ...?
...SO HOW FAR ARE YOU GONNA FOLLOW ME, ANY-WAY?
男子トイレ
MEN
HUH ...? EEK!
I-I'M SOR-RY!
SIGH . . .
WHOA, MY FACE IS HOT. WHAT THE HECK?
OH MAN, THIS IS NOT GOOD. HE'LL SEE RIGHT THROUGH ME. I DIDN'T REALIZE I...
BUT WHAT WAS THAT REACTION, KOJIRŌ -KUN!? DOES THIS MEAN I HAVE A CHANCE?
AAAAH! WHAT'LL I DO? WHAT WILL I DO!? HAS MY TIME COME?
WHAM
EEK!

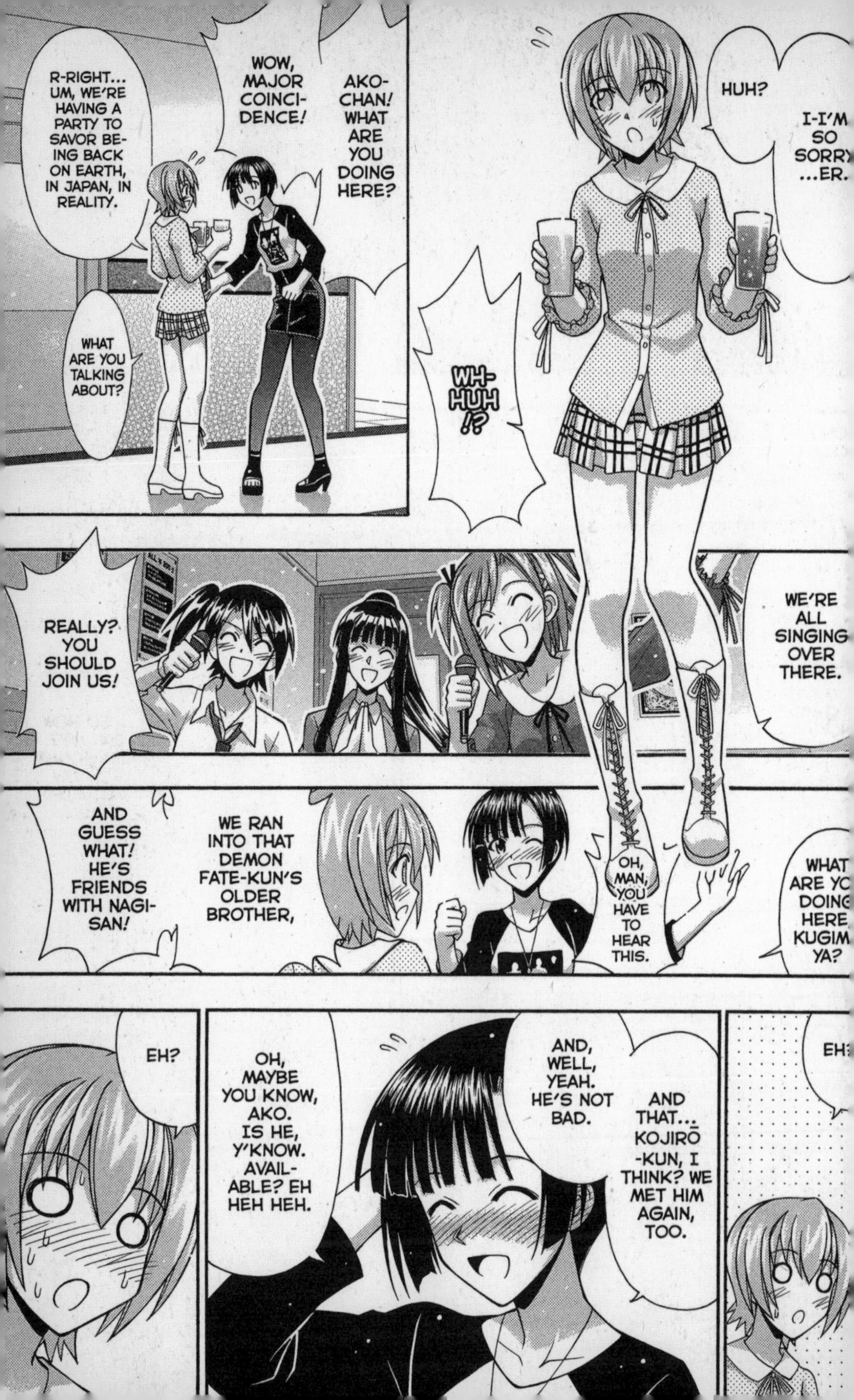
HUH?
I-I'M SO SORRY ...ER.
WH-HUH!?
AKO-CHAN! WHAT ARE YOU DOING HERE?
WOW, MAJOR COINCIDENCE!
R-RIGHT... UM, WE'RE HAVING A PARTY TO SAVOR BEING BACK ON EARTH, IN JAPAN, IN REALITY.
WHAT ARE YOU TALKING ABOUT?
WE'RE ALL SINGING OVER THERE.
REALLY? YOU SHOULD JOIN US!
WHAT ARE YO DOING HERE, KUGIM YA?
OH, MAN, YOU HAVE TO HEAR THIS.
WE RAN INTO THAT DEMON FATE-KUN'S OLDER BROTHER,
AND GUESS WHAT! HE'S FRIENDS WITH NAGI-SAN!
EH
AND THAT... KOJIRŌ-KUN, I THINK? WE MET HIM AGAIN, TOO.
AND, WELL, YEAH. HE'S NOT BAD.
OH, MAYBE YOU KNOW, AKO. IS HE, Y'KNOW. AVAILABLE? EH HEH HEH.
EH?

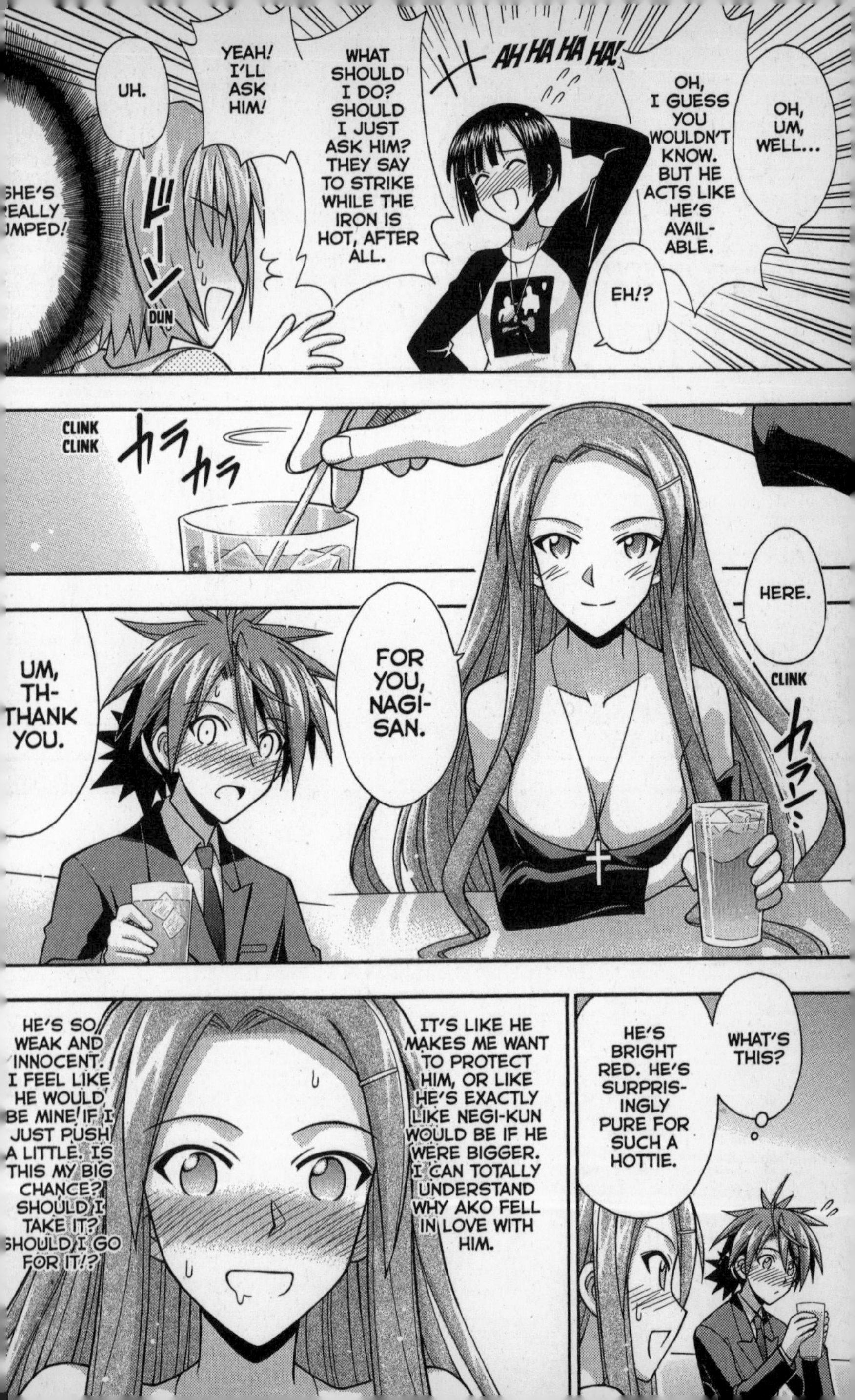
OH, UM, WELL...
OH, I GUESS YOU WOULDN'T KNOW. BUT HE ACTS LIKE HE'S AVAIL-ABLE.
EH!?
AH HA HA HA!
WHAT SHOULD I DO? SHOULD I JUST ASK HIM? THEY SAY TO STRIKE WHILE THE IRON IS HOT, AFTER ALL.
YEAH! I'LL ASK HIM!
UH.
ドーン
DUN
HE'S EALLY UMPED!
カラ カラ
CLINK CLINK
HERE.
カラーン
CLINK
FOR YOU, NAGI-SAN.
UM, TH-THANK YOU.
WHAT'S THIS?
HE'S BRIGHT RED. HE'S SURPRIS-INGLY PURE FOR SUCH A HOTTIE.
IT'S LIKE HE MAKES ME WANT TO PROTECT HIM, OR LIKE HE'S EXACTLY LIKE NEGI-KUN WOULD BE IF HE WERE BIGGER. I CAN TOTALLY UNDERSTAND WHY AKO FELL IN LOVE WITH HIM.
HE'S SO WEAK AND INNOCENT. I FEEL LIKE HE WOULD BE MINE IF I JUST PUSH A LITTLE. IS THIS MY BIG CHANCE? SHOULD I TAKE IT? SHOULD I GO FOR IT!?

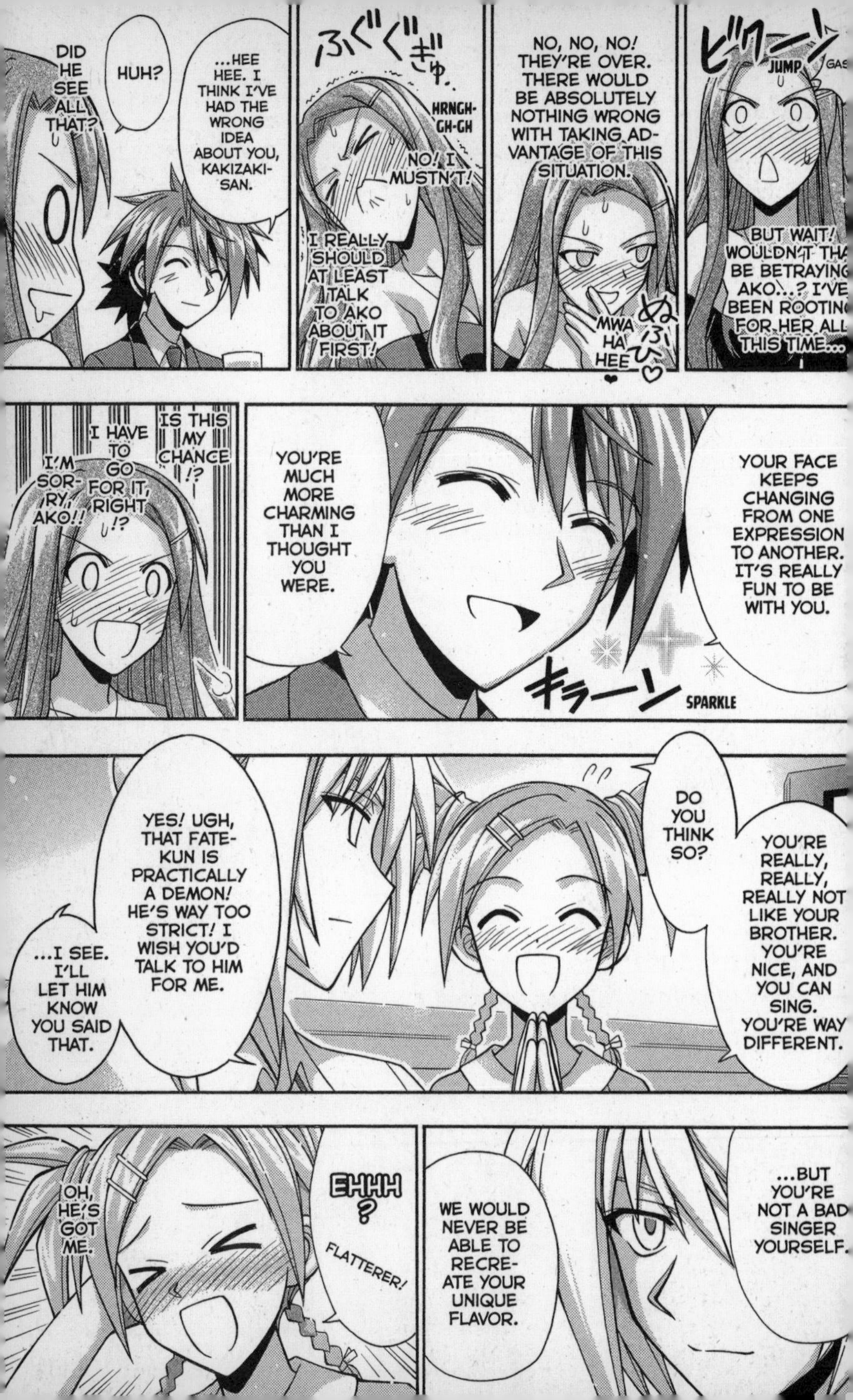
ビクーッ
JUMP
BUT WAIT! WOULDN'T THA BE BETRAYING AKO...? I'VE BEEN ROOTIN FOR HER ALL THIS TIME...
NO, NO, NO! THEY'RE OVER. THERE WOULD BE ABSOLUTELY NOTHING WRONG WITH TAKING ADVANTAGE OF THIS SITUATION.
ぬふひ♡
MWA HA HEE
ふぐぎゅ
HRNGH-GH-GH
NO! I MUSTN'T!
I REALLY SHOULD AT LEAST TALK TO AKO ABOUT IT FIRST!
...HEE HEE. I THINK I'VE HAD THE WRONG IDEA ABOUT YOU, KAKIZAKI-SAN.
HUH?
DID HE SEE ALL THAT?
YOUR FACE KEEPS CHANGING FROM ONE EXPRESSION TO ANOTHER. IT'S REALLY FUN TO BE WITH YOU.
YOU'RE MUCH MORE CHARMING THAN I THOUGHT YOU WERE.
キラーン
SPARKLE
IS THIS MY CHANCE!?
I HAVE TO GO FOR IT, RIGHT!?
I'M SORRY, AKO!!
DO YOU THINK SO?
YOU'RE REALLY, REALLY, REALLY NOT LIKE YOUR BROTHER. YOU'RE NICE, AND YOU CAN SING. YOU'RE WAY DIFFERENT.
YES! UGH, THAT FATE-KUN IS PRACTICALLY A DEMON! HE'S WAY TOO STRICT! I WISH YOU'D TALK TO HIM FOR ME.
...I SEE. I'LL LET HIM KNOW YOU SAID THAT.
...BUT YOU'RE NOT A BAD SINGER YOURSELF.
WE WOULD NEVER BE ABLE TO RECREATE YOUR UNIQUE FLAVOR.
EHHH?
FLATTERER!
OH, HE'S GOT ME.

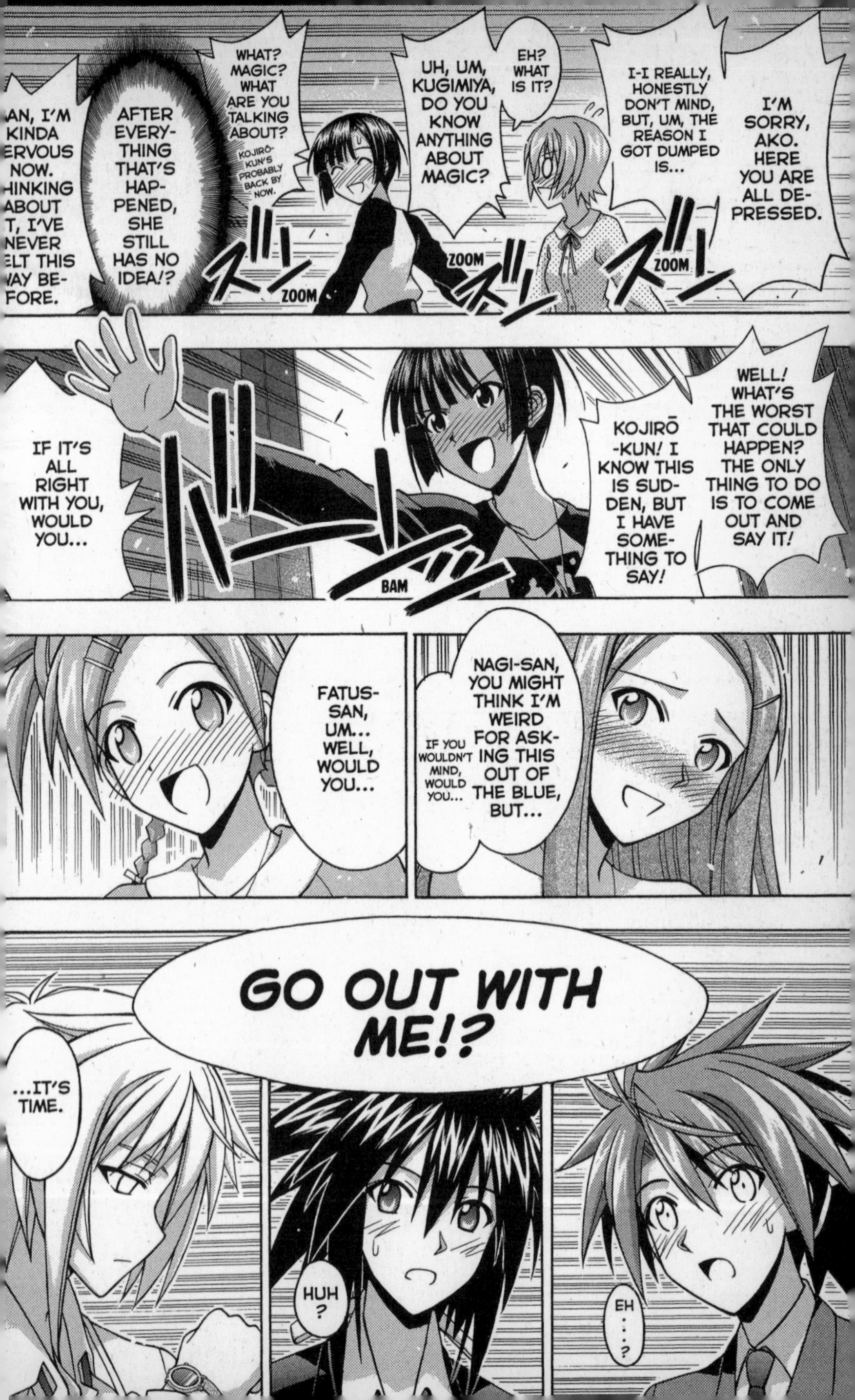
I'M SORRY, AKO. HERE YOU ARE ALL DEPRESSED.
I-I REALLY, HONESTLY DON'T MIND, BUT, UM, THE REASON I GOT DUMPED IS...
ZOOM
EH? WHAT IS IT?
UH, UM, KUGIMIYA, DO YOU KNOW ANYTHING ABOUT MAGIC?
ZOOM
WHAT? MAGIC? WHAT ARE YOU TALKING ABOUT?
KOJIRŌ-KUN'S PROBABLY BACK BY NOW.
ZOOM
AFTER EVERYTHING THAT'S HAPPENED, SHE STILL HAS NO IDEA!?
AN, I'M KINDA ERVOUS NOW. HINKING ABOUT T, I'VE NEVER ELT THIS AY BEFORE.
WELL! WHAT'S THE WORST THAT COULD HAPPEN? THE ONLY THING TO DO IS TO COME OUT AND SAY IT!
KOJIRŌ-KUN! I KNOW THIS IS SUDDEN, BUT I HAVE SOMETHING TO SAY!
BAM
IF IT'S ALL RIGHT WITH YOU, WOULD YOU...
NAGI-SAN, YOU MIGHT THINK I'M WEIRD FOR ASKING THIS OUT OF THE BLUE, BUT...
IF YOU WOULDN'T MIND, WOULD YOU...
FATUS-SAN, UM... WELL, WOULD YOU...
GO OUT WITH ME!?
EH...?
HUH?
...IT'S TIME.

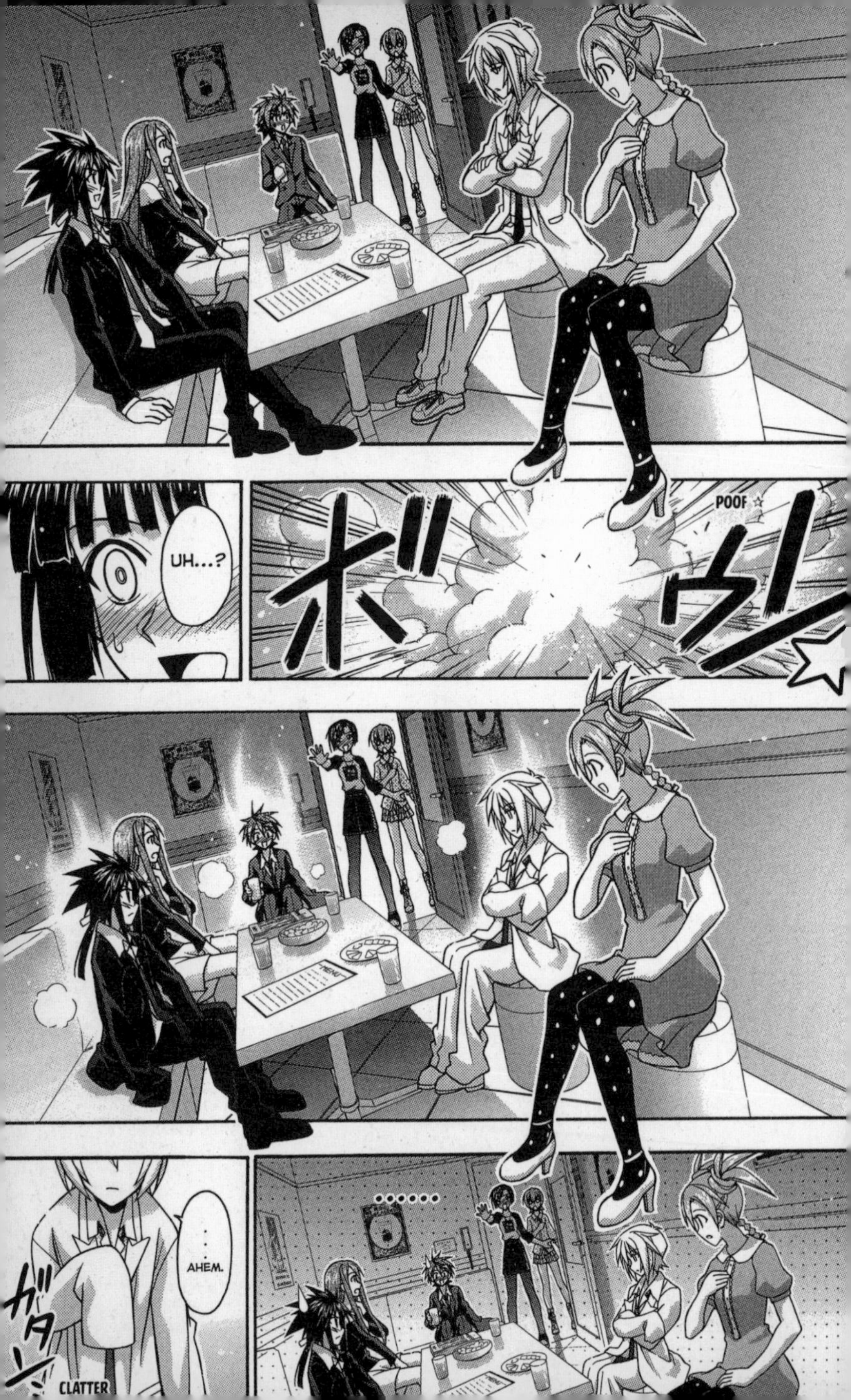
POOF ☆
UH...?
......
... AHEM.
CLATTER

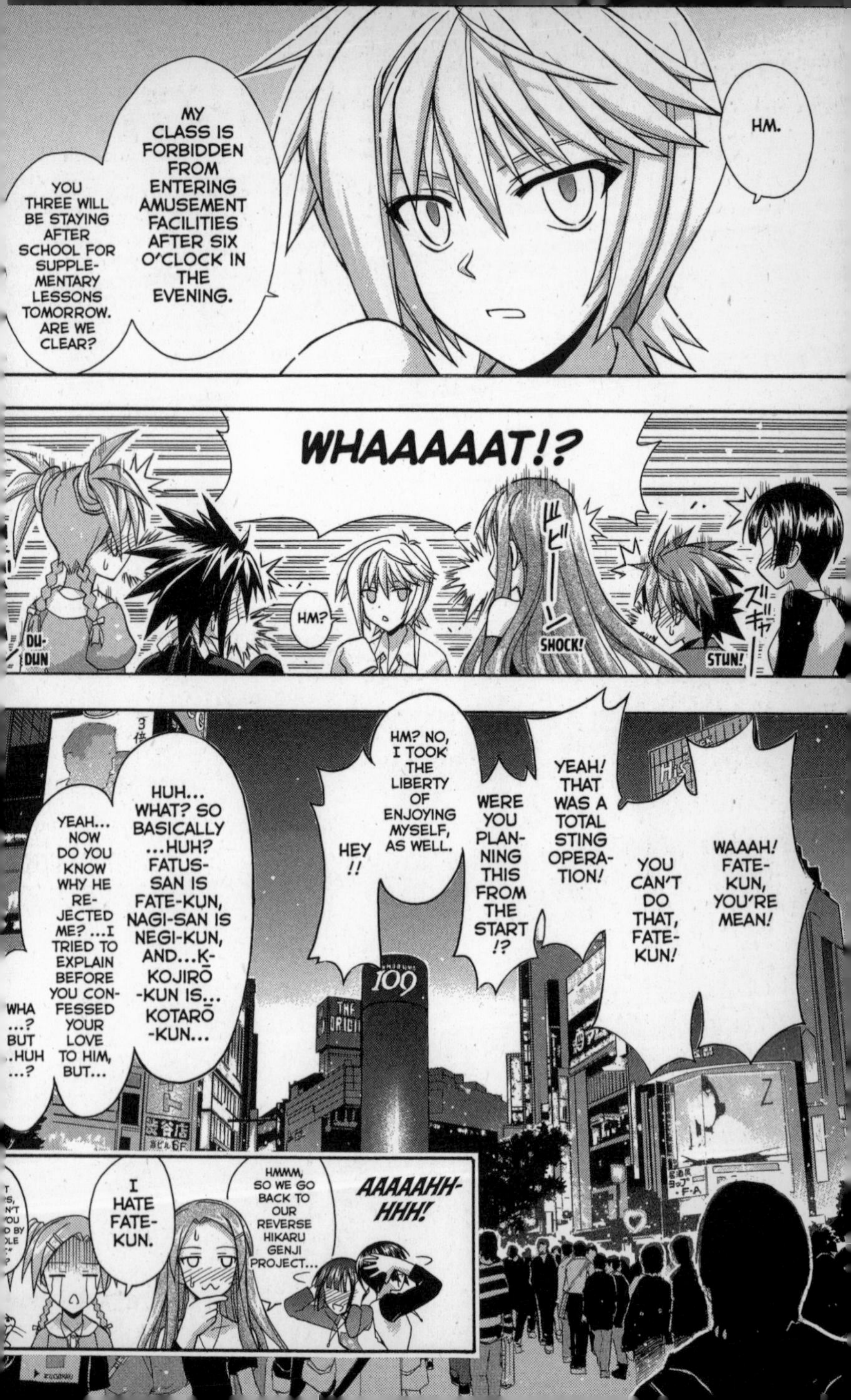
HM.
MY CLASS IS FORBIDDEN FROM ENTERING AMUSEMENT FACILITIES AFTER SIX O'CLOCK IN THE EVENING.
YOU THREE WILL BE STAYING AFTER SCHOOL FOR SUPPLEMENTARY LESSONS TOMORROW. ARE WE CLEAR?
WHAAAAAT!?
STUN!
SHOCK!
HM?
DU-DUN
WAAAH! FATE-KUN, YOU'RE MEAN!
YOU CAN'T DO THAT, FATE-KUN!
YEAH! THAT WAS A TOTAL STING OPERATION!
WERE YOU PLANNING THIS FROM THE START!?
HM? NO, I TOOK THE LIBERTY OF ENJOYING MYSELF, AS WELL.
HEY!!
HUH... WHAT? SO BASICALLY ...HUH? FATUS-SAN IS FATE-KUN, NAGI-SAN IS NEGI-KUN, AND...K-KOJIRŌ-KUN IS... KOTARŌ-KUN...
YEAH... NOW DO YOU KNOW WHY HE REJECTED ME? ...I TRIED TO EXPLAIN BEFORE YOU CONFESSED YOUR LOVE TO HIM, BUT...
WHA...? BUT ..HUH...?
AAAAAHH-HHH!
HMMM, SO WE GO BACK TO OUR REVERSE HIKARU GENJI PROJECT...
I HATE FATE-KUN.

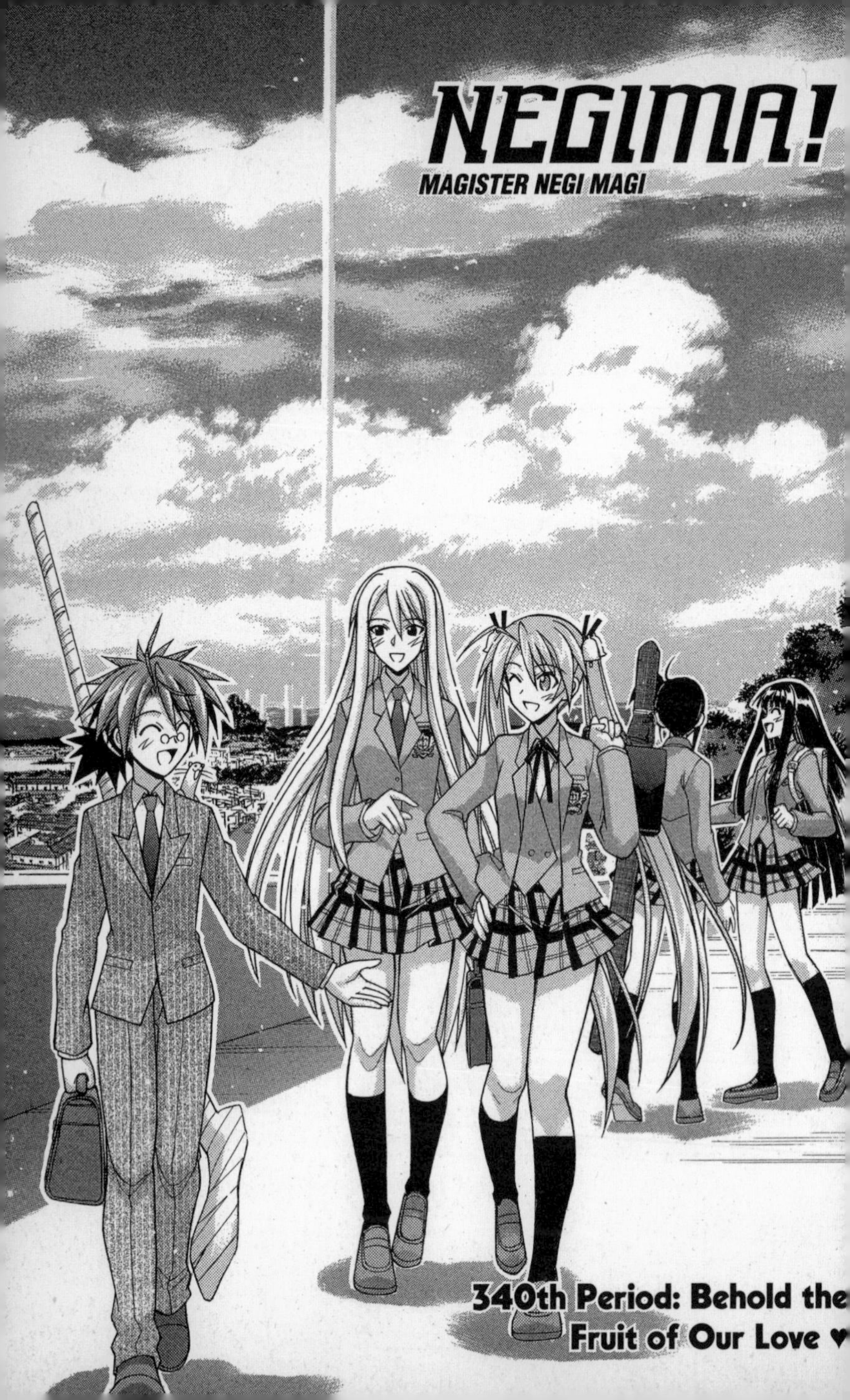
NEGIMA!
MAGISTER NEGI MAGI
340th Period: Behold the Fruit of Our Love ♥

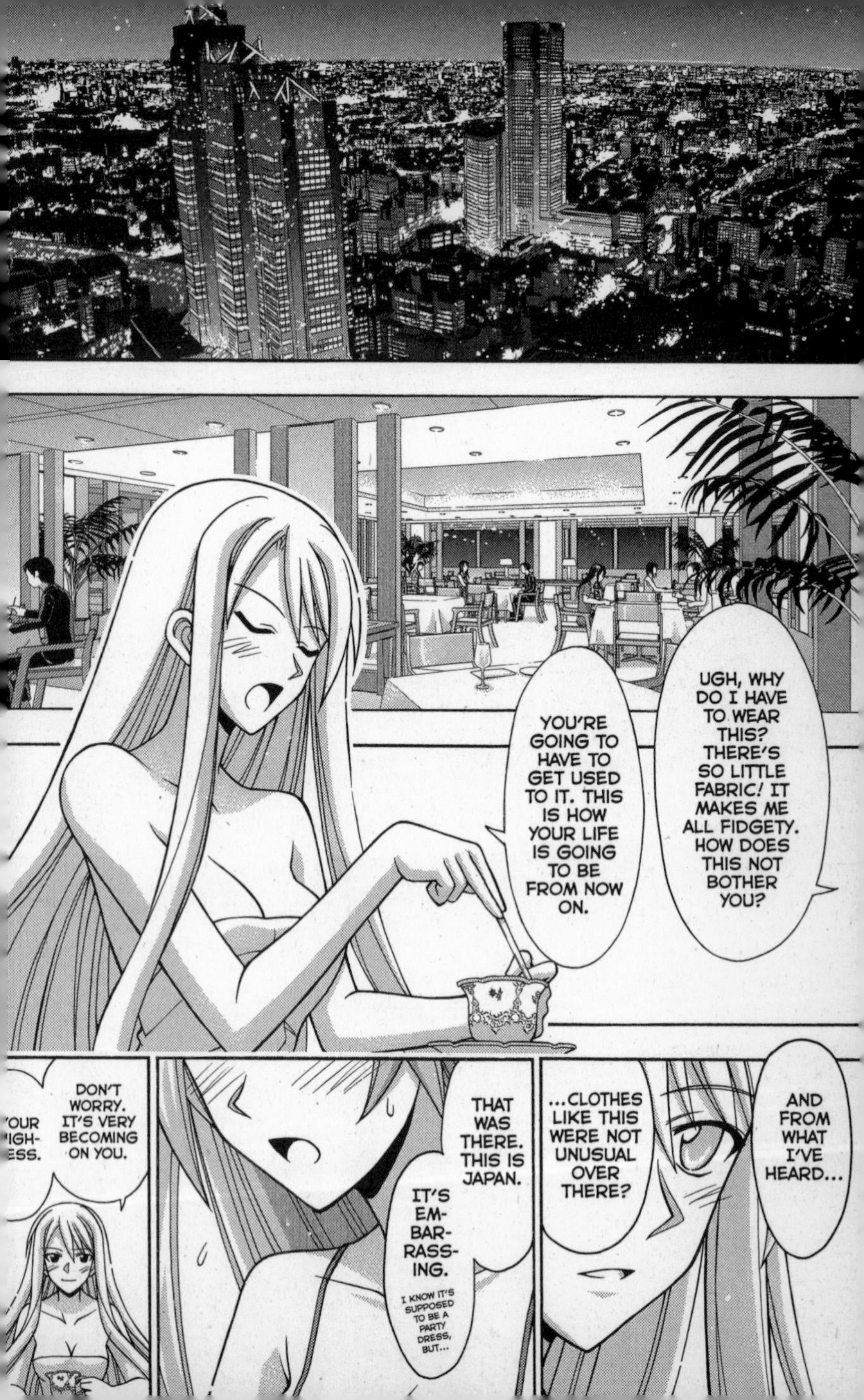
UGH, WHY DO I HAVE TO WEAR THIS? THERE'S SO LITTLE FABRIC! IT MAKES ME ALL FIDGETY. HOW DOES THIS NOT BOTHER YOU?
YOU'RE GOING TO HAVE TO GET USED TO IT. THIS IS HOW YOUR LIFE IS GOING TO BE FROM NOW ON.
AND FROM WHAT I'VE HEARD...
...CLOTHES LIKE THIS WERE NOT UNUSUAL OVER THERE?
THAT WAS THERE. THIS IS JAPAN.
IT'S EM-BAR-RASS-ING.
I KNOW IT'S SUPPOSED TO BE A PARTY DRESS, BUT...
DON'T WORRY. IT'S VERY BECOMING ON YOU.

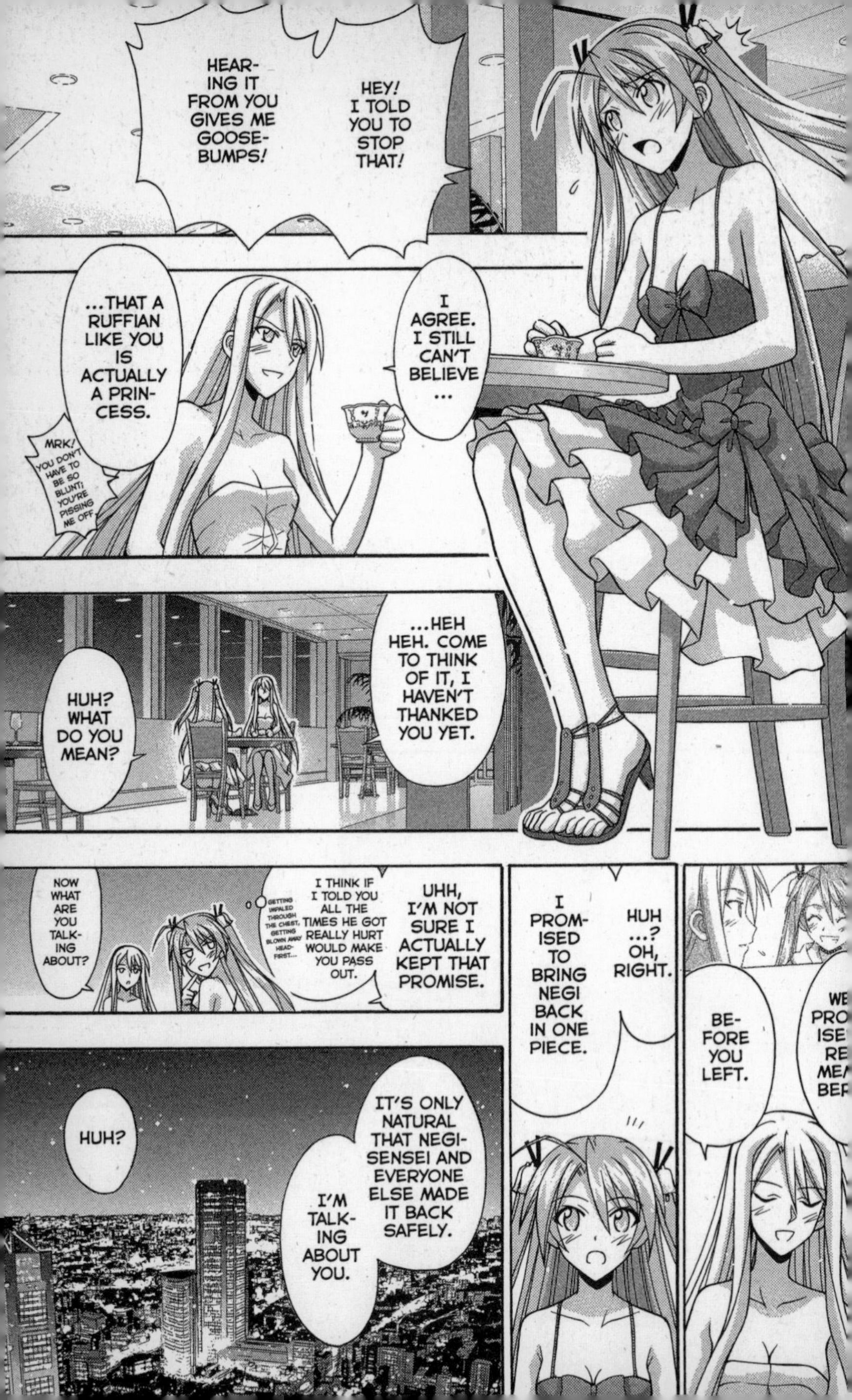
HEY! I TOLD YOU TO STOP THAT!
HEARING IT FROM YOU GIVES ME GOOSEBUMPS!
I AGREE. I STILL CAN'T BELIEVE ...
...THAT A RUFFIAN LIKE YOU IS ACTUALLY A PRINCESS.
MRK! YOU DON'T HAVE TO BE SO BLUNT; YOU'RE PISSING ME OFF.
...HEH HEH. COME TO THINK OF IT, I HAVEN'T THANKED YOU YET.
HUH? WHAT DO YOU MEAN?
WE PRO ISE RE MEM BER
BEFORE YOU LEFT.
HUH ...? OH, RIGHT.
I PROMISED TO BRING NEGI BACK IN ONE PIECE.
UHH, I'M NOT SURE I ACTUALLY KEPT THAT PROMISE.
I THINK IF I TOLD YOU ALL THE TIMES HE GOT REALLY HURT WOULD MAKE YOU PASS OUT.
GETTING IMPALED THROUGH THE CHEST, GETTING BLOWN AWAY HEAD-FIRST...
NOW WHAT ARE YOU TALKING ABOUT?
IT'S ONLY NATURAL THAT NEGI-SENSEI AND EVERYONE ELSE MADE IT BACK SAFELY.
I'M TALKING ABOUT YOU.
HUH?

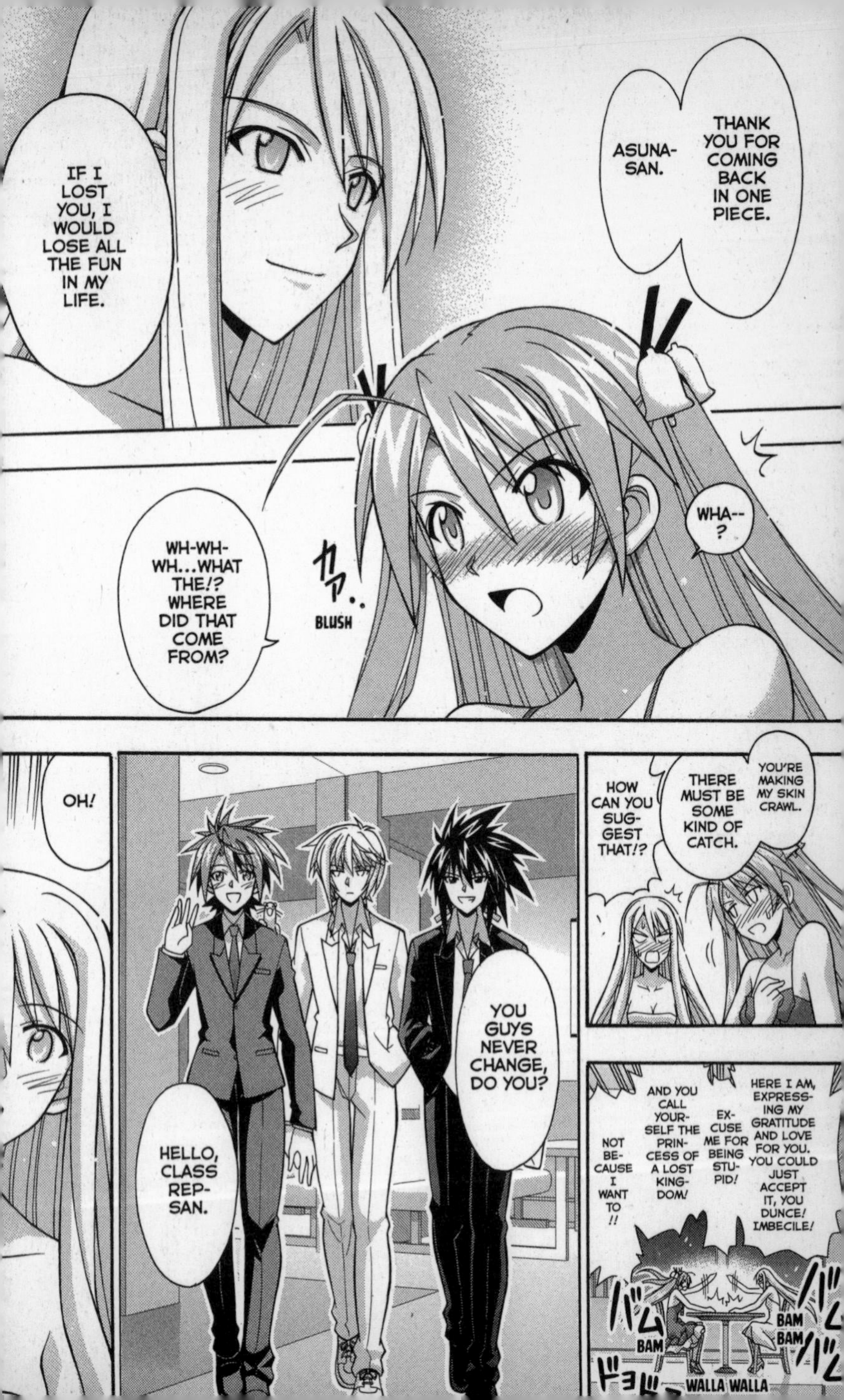

ASUNA-SAN.
THANK YOU FOR COMING BACK IN ONE PIECE.
IF I LOST YOU, I WOULD LOSE ALL THE FUN IN MY LIFE.
WHA--?
BLUSH
WH-WH-WH...WHAT THE!? WHERE DID THAT COME FROM?
YOU'RE MAKING MY SKIN CRAWL.
THERE MUST BE SOME KIND OF CATCH.
HOW CAN YOU SUGGEST THAT!?
HERE I AM, EXPRESSING MY GRATITUDE AND LOVE FOR YOU. YOU COULD JUST ACCEPT IT, YOU DUNCE! IMBECILE!
EXCUSE ME FOR BEING STUPID!
AND YOU CALL YOURSELF THE PRINCESS OF A LOST KINGDOM!
NOT BECAUSE I WANT TO!!
BAM BAM
BAM
WALLA WALLA
YOU GUYS NEVER CHANGE, DO YOU?
HELLO, CLASS REP-SAN.
OH!

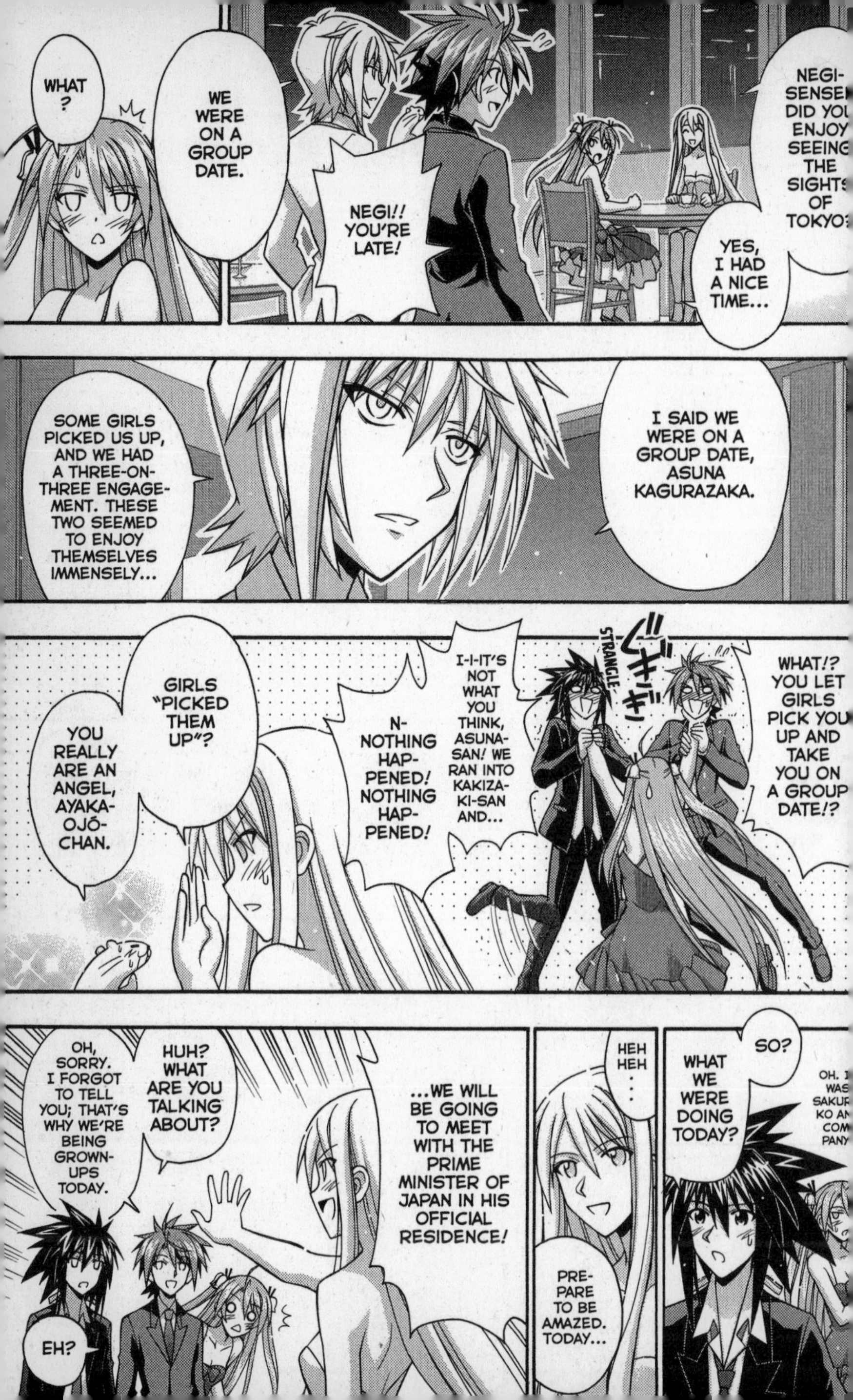
NEGI-SENSEI DID YOU ENJOY SEEING THE SIGHTS OF TOKYO?
YES, I HAD A NICE TIME...
NEGI!! YOU'RE LATE!
WE WERE ON A GROUP DATE.
WHAT?
I SAID WE WERE ON A GROUP DATE, ASUNA KAGURAZAKA.
SOME GIRLS PICKED US UP, AND WE HAD A THREE-ON-THREE ENGAGEMENT. THESE TWO SEEMED TO ENJOY THEMSELVES IMMENSELY...
WHAT!? YOU LET GIRLS PICK YOU UP AND TAKE YOU ON A GROUP DATE!?
STRANGLE
I-I-IT'S NOT WHAT YOU THINK, ASUNA-SAN! WE RAN INTO KAKIZAKI-SAN AND...
N-NOTHING HAPPENED! NOTHING HAPPENED!
GIRLS "PICKED THEM UP"?
YOU REALLY ARE AN ANGEL, AYAKA-OJŌ-CHAN.
SO?
WHAT WE WERE DOING TODAY?
HEH HEH...
PREPARE TO BE AMAZED. TODAY...
...WE WILL BE GOING TO MEET WITH THE PRIME MINISTER OF JAPAN IN HIS OFFICIAL RESIDENCE!
HUH? WHAT ARE YOU TALKING ABOUT?
OH, SORRY. I FORGOT TO TELL YOU; THAT'S WHY WE'RE BEING GROWN-UPS TODAY.
EH?

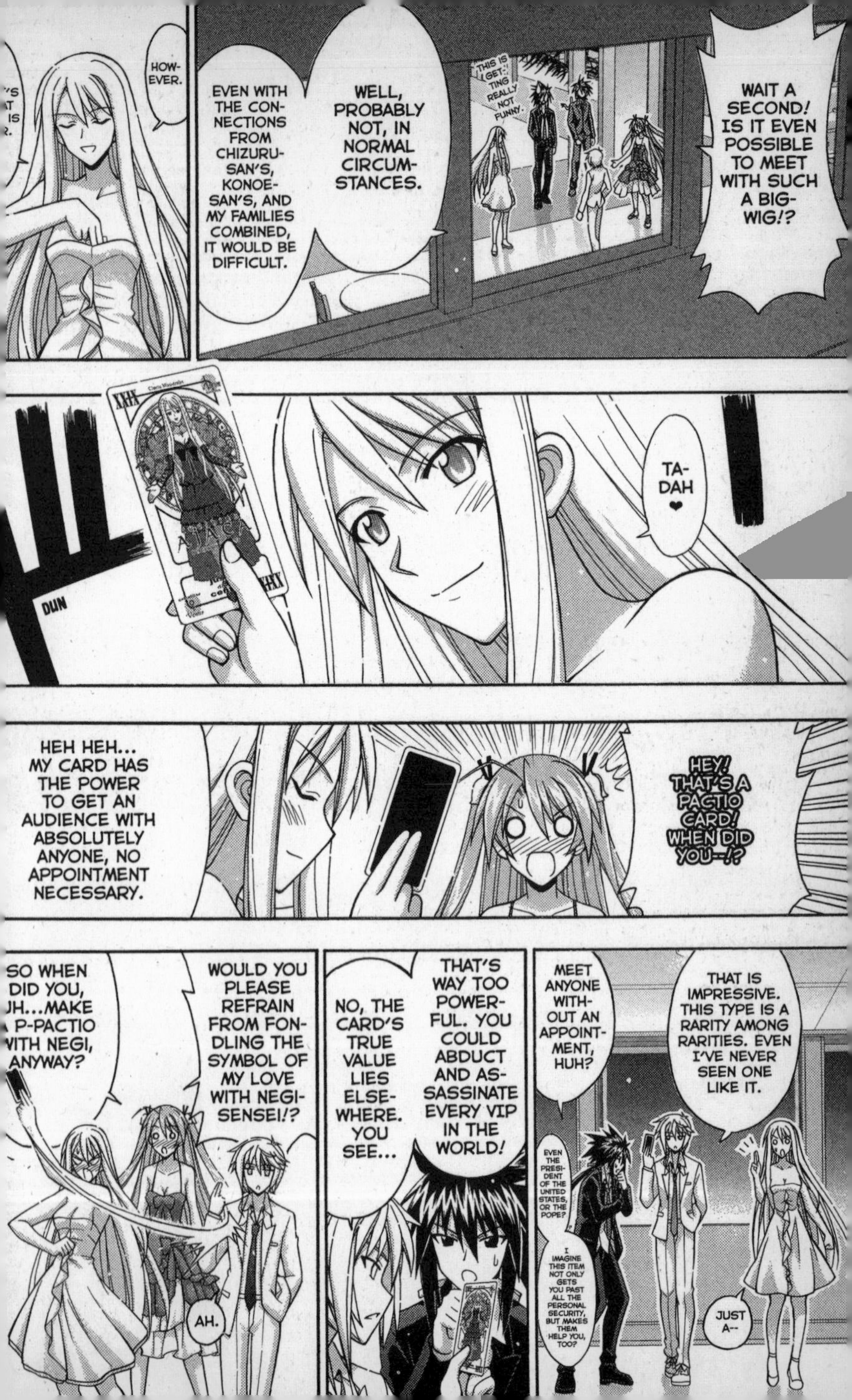
WAIT A SECOND! IS IT EVEN POSSIBLE TO MEET WITH SUCH A BIG-WIG!?
THIS IS GETTING REALLY NOT FUNNY.
WELL, PROBABLY NOT, IN NORMAL CIRCUMSTANCES.
EVEN WITH THE CONNECTIONS FROM CHIZURU-SAN'S, KONOE-SAN'S, AND MY FAMILIES COMBINED, IT WOULD BE DIFFICULT.
HOW-EVER.
TA-DAH ❤
DUN
HEY! THAT'S A PACTIO CARD! WHEN DID YOU--!?
HEH HEH... MY CARD HAS THE POWER TO GET AN AUDIENCE WITH ABSOLUTELY ANYONE, NO APPOINTMENT NECESSARY.
THAT IS IMPRESSIVE. THIS TYPE IS A RARITY AMONG RARITIES. EVEN I'VE NEVER SEEN ONE LIKE IT.
MEET ANYONE WITHOUT AN APPOINTMENT, HUH?
EVEN THE PRESIDENT OF THE UNITED STATES, OR THE POPE?
I IMAGINE THIS ITEM NOT ONLY GETS YOU PAST ALL THE PERSONAL SECURITY, BUT MAKES THEM HELP YOU, TOO?
JUST A--
THAT'S WAY TOO POWERFUL. YOU COULD ABDUCT AND ASSASSINATE EVERY VIP IN THE WORLD!
NO, THE CARD'S TRUE VALUE LIES ELSEWHERE. YOU SEE...
WOULD YOU PLEASE REFRAIN FROM FONDLING THE SYMBOL OF MY LOVE WITH NEGI-SENSEI!?
SO WHEN DID YOU, ...MAKE P-PACTIO WITH NEGI, ANYWAY?
AH.

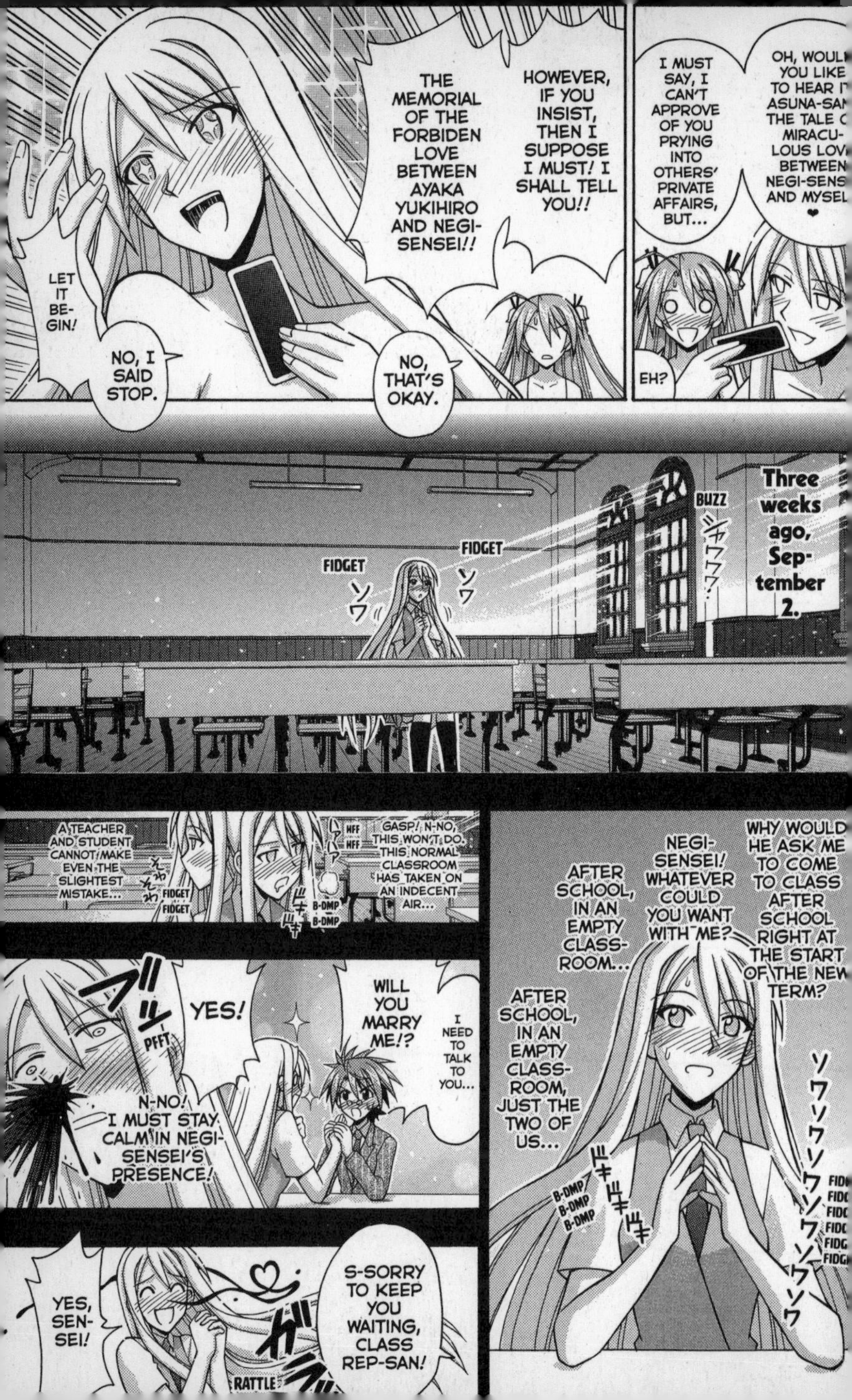
OH, WOUL YOU LIKE TO HEAR IT ASUNA-SAN THE TALE C MIRACU-LOUS LOV BETWEEN NEGI-SENS AND MYSEL ❤
I MUST SAY, I CAN'T APPROVE OF YOU PRYING INTO OTHERS' PRIVATE AFFAIRS, BUT...
EH?
HOWEVER, IF YOU INSIST, THEN I SUPPOSE I MUST! I SHALL TELL YOU!!
THE MEMORIAL OF THE FORBIDEN LOVE BETWEEN AYAKA YUKIHIRO AND NEGI-SENSEI!!
NO, THAT'S OKAY.
LET IT BE-GIN!
NO, I SAID STOP.
Three weeks ago, Sep-tember 2.
BUZZ
FIDGET
FIDGET
WHY WOULD HE ASK ME TO COME TO CLASS AFTER SCHOOL RIGHT AT THE START OF THE NEW TERM?
NEGI-SENSEI! WHATEVER COULD YOU WANT WITH ME?
AFTER SCHOOL, IN AN EMPTY CLASS-ROOM...
AFTER SCHOOL, IN AN EMPTY CLASS-ROOM, JUST THE TWO OF US...
B-DMP B-DMP B-DMP
GASP! N-NO, THIS WON'T DO. THIS NORMAL CLASSROOM HAS TAKEN ON AN INDECENT AIR...
HFF HFF
B-DMP B-DMP
A TEACHER AND STUDENT CANNOT MAKE EVEN THE SLIGHTEST MISTAKE...
FIDGET FIDGET
I NEED TO TALK TO YOU...
WILL YOU MARRY ME!?
YES!
PFFT
N-NO! I MUST STAY CALM IN NEGI-SENSEI'S PRESENCE!
S-SORRY TO KEEP YOU WAITING, CLASS REP-SAN!
RATTLE
YES, SEN-SEI!

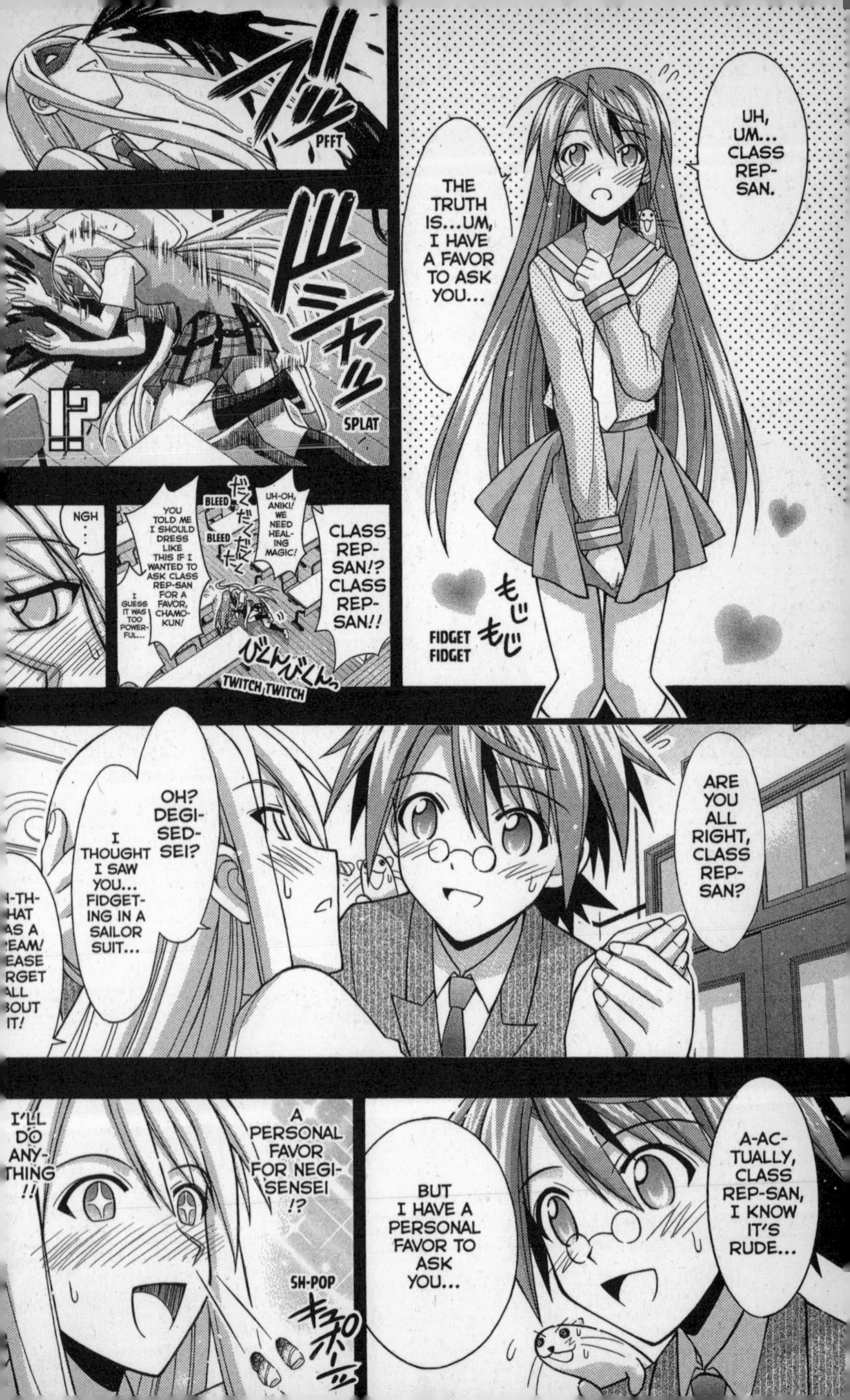
UH, UM... CLASS REP-SAN.
THE TRUTH IS...UM, I HAVE A FAVOR TO ASK YOU...
もじもじ
FIDGET FIDGET
PFFT
SPLAT
!?
CLASS REP-SAN!? CLASS REP-SAN!!
UH-OH, ANIKI! WE NEED HEALING MAGIC!
BLEED
BLEED
YOU TOLD ME I SHOULD DRESS LIKE THIS IF I WANTED TO ASK CLASS REP-SAN FOR A FAVOR, CHAMO-KUN!
I GUESS IT WAS TOO POWERFUL...
TWITCH TWITCH
NGH...
ARE YOU ALL RIGHT, CLASS REP-SAN?
OH? DEGI-SED-SEI?
I THOUGHT I SAW YOU... FIDGETING IN A SAILOR SUIT...
H-TH- HAT AS A REAM! EASE RGET ALL BOUT IT!
A-ACTUALLY, CLASS REP-SAN, I KNOW IT'S RUDE...
BUT I HAVE A PERSONAL FAVOR TO ASK YOU...
A PERSONAL FAVOR FOR NEGI-SENSEI!?
SH-POP
I'LL DO ANYTHING!!

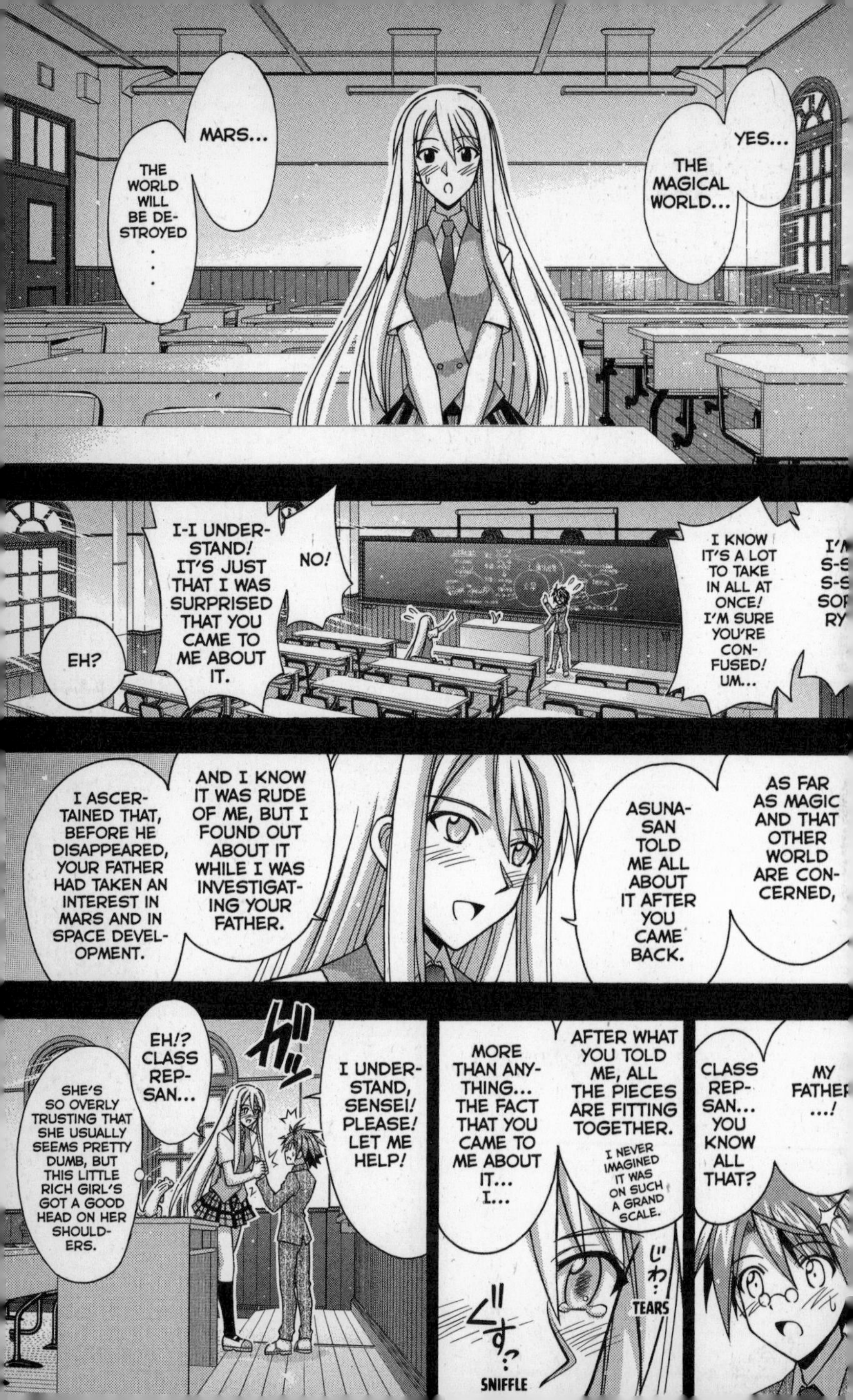
YES... THE MAGICAL WORLD...
MARS... THE WORLD WILL BE DESTROYED . . .
I'M S-S S-S SORRY
I KNOW IT'S A LOT TO TAKE IN ALL AT ONCE! I'M SURE YOU'RE CONFUSED! UM...
NO!
I-I UNDERSTAND! IT'S JUST THAT I WAS SURPRISED THAT YOU CAME TO ME ABOUT IT.
EH?
AS FAR AS MAGIC AND THAT OTHER WORLD ARE CONCERNED,
ASUNA-SAN TOLD ME ALL ABOUT IT AFTER YOU CAME BACK.
AND I KNOW IT WAS RUDE OF ME, BUT I FOUND OUT ABOUT IT WHILE I WAS INVESTIGATING YOUR FATHER.
I ASCERTAINED THAT, BEFORE HE DISAPPEARED, YOUR FATHER HAD TAKEN AN INTEREST IN MARS AND IN SPACE DEVELOPMENT.
MY FATHER ...!
CLASS REP-SAN... YOU KNOW ALL THAT?
AFTER WHAT YOU TOLD ME, ALL THE PIECES ARE FITTING TOGETHER.
MORE THAN ANYTHING... THE FACT THAT YOU CAME TO ME ABOUT IT... I...
I NEVER IMAGINED IT WAS ON SUCH A GRAND SCALE.
じわっ
TEARS
ぐすっ
SNIFFLE
I UNDERSTAND, SENSEI! PLEASE! LET ME HELP!
ガッ
EH!? CLASS REP-SAN...
SHE'S SO OVERLY TRUSTING THAT SHE USUALLY SEEMS PRETTY DUMB, BUT THIS LITTLE RICH GIRL'S GOT A GOOD HEAD ON HER SHOULDERS.

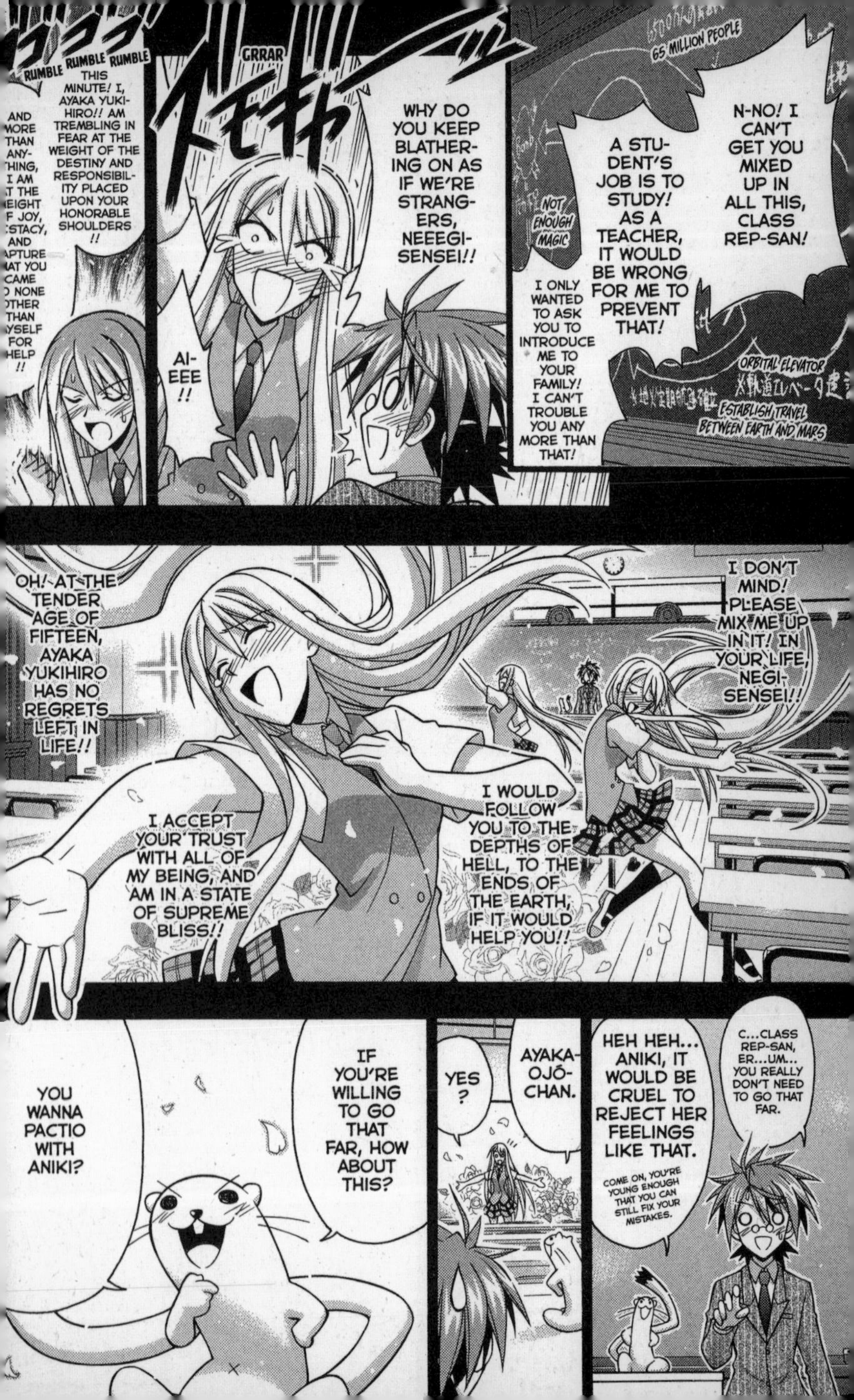
65 MILLION PEOPLE
N-NO! I CAN'T GET YOU MIXED UP IN ALL THIS, CLASS REP-SAN!
A STUDENT'S JOB IS TO STUDY! AS A TEACHER, IT WOULD BE WRONG FOR ME TO PREVENT THAT!
NOT ENOUGH MAGIC
I ONLY WANTED TO ASK YOU TO INTRODUCE ME TO YOUR FAMILY! I CAN'T TROUBLE YOU ANY MORE THAN THAT!
ORBITAL ELEVATOR
ESTABLISH TRAVEL BETWEEN EARTH AND MARS
GRRAR
WHY DO YOU KEEP BLATHERING ON AS IF WE'RE STRANGERS, NEEEGI-SENSEI!!
AI-EEE!!
RUMBLE RUMBLE RUMBLE
THIS MINUTE! I, AYAKA YUKIHIRO!! AM TREMBLING IN FEAR AT THE WEIGHT OF THE DESTINY AND RESPONSIBILITY PLACED UPON YOUR HONORABLE SHOULDERS!!
AND MORE THAN ANYTHING, I AM T THE EIGHT F JOY, CSTACY, AND APTURE AT YOU CAME NONE THER THAN YSELF FOR HELP!!
I DON'T MIND! PLEASE MIX ME UP IN IT! IN YOUR LIFE, NEGI-SENSEI!!
I WOULD FOLLOW YOU TO THE DEPTHS OF HELL, TO THE ENDS OF THE EARTH, IF IT WOULD HELP YOU!!
I ACCEPT YOUR TRUST WITH ALL OF MY BEING, AND AM IN A STATE OF SUPREME BLISS!!
OH! AT THE TENDER AGE OF FIFTEEN, AYAKA YUKIHIRO HAS NO REGRETS LEFT IN LIFE!!
C...CLASS REP-SAN, ER...UM... YOU REALLY DON'T NEED TO GO THAT FAR.
HEH HEH... ANIKI, IT WOULD BE CRUEL TO REJECT HER FEELINGS LIKE THAT.
COME ON, YOU'RE YOUNG ENOUGH THAT YOU CAN STILL FIX YOUR MISTAKES.
AYAKA-OJŌ-CHAN.
YES?
IF YOU'RE WILLING TO GO THAT FAR, HOW ABOUT THIS?
YOU WANNA PACTIO WITH ANIKI?

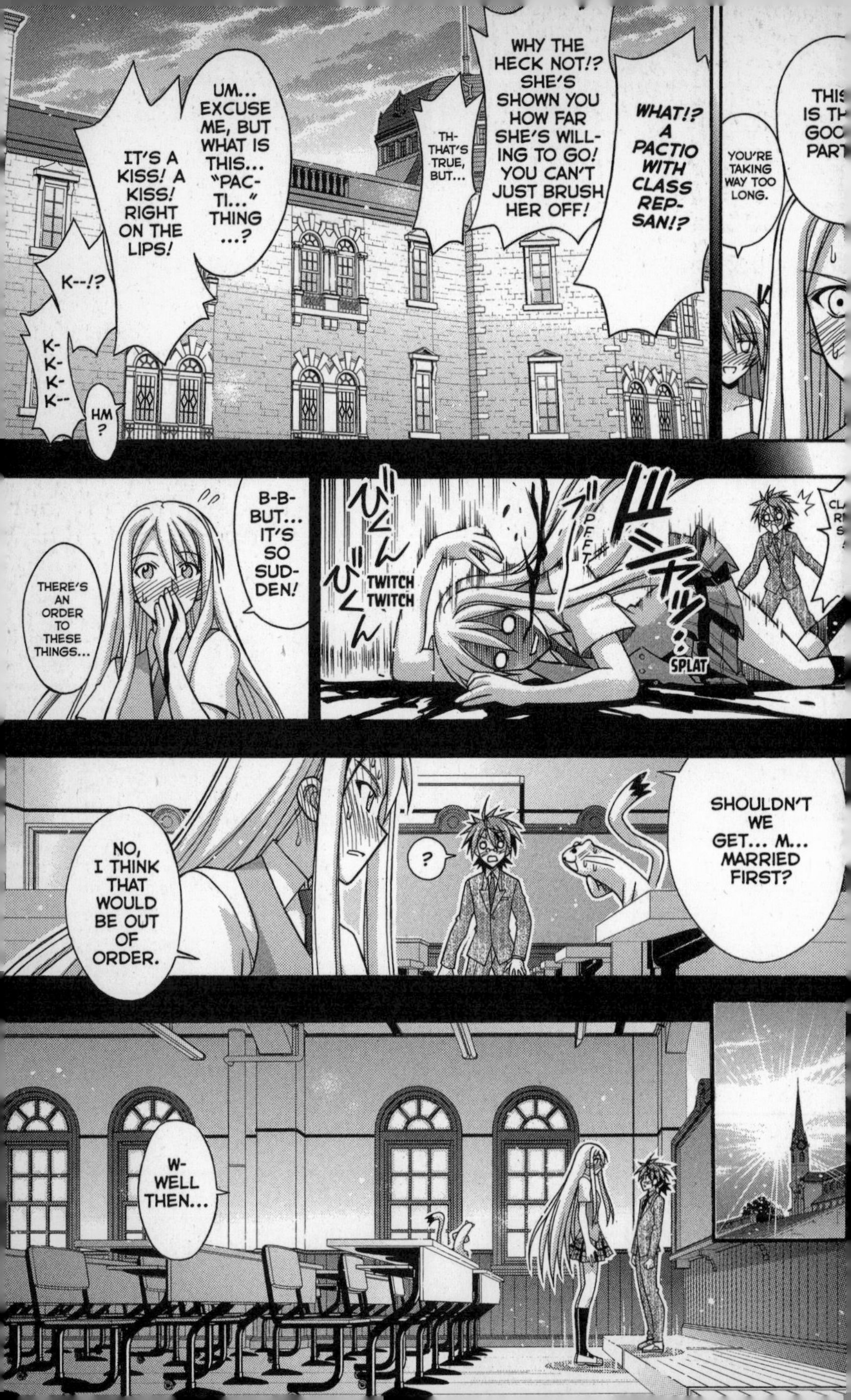
THIS IS TH GOO PART
YOU'RE TAKING WAY TOO LONG.
WHAT!? A PACTIO WITH CLASS REP-SAN!?
WHY THE HECK NOT!? SHE'S SHOWN YOU HOW FAR SHE'S WILL-ING TO GO! YOU CAN'T JUST BRUSH HER OFF!
TH-THAT'S TRUE, BUT...
UM... EXCUSE ME, BUT WHAT IS THIS... "PAC-TI..." THING...?
IT'S A KISS! A KISS! RIGHT ON THE LIPS!
K--!?
K-K-K-K--
HM?
PFFT
SPLAT
びくん びくん
TWITCH TWITCH
B-B-BUT... IT'S SO SUD-DEN!
THERE'S AN ORDER TO THESE THINGS...
SHOULDN'T WE GET... M... MARRIED FIRST?
?
NO, I THINK THAT WOULD BE OUT OF ORDER.
W-WELL THEN...

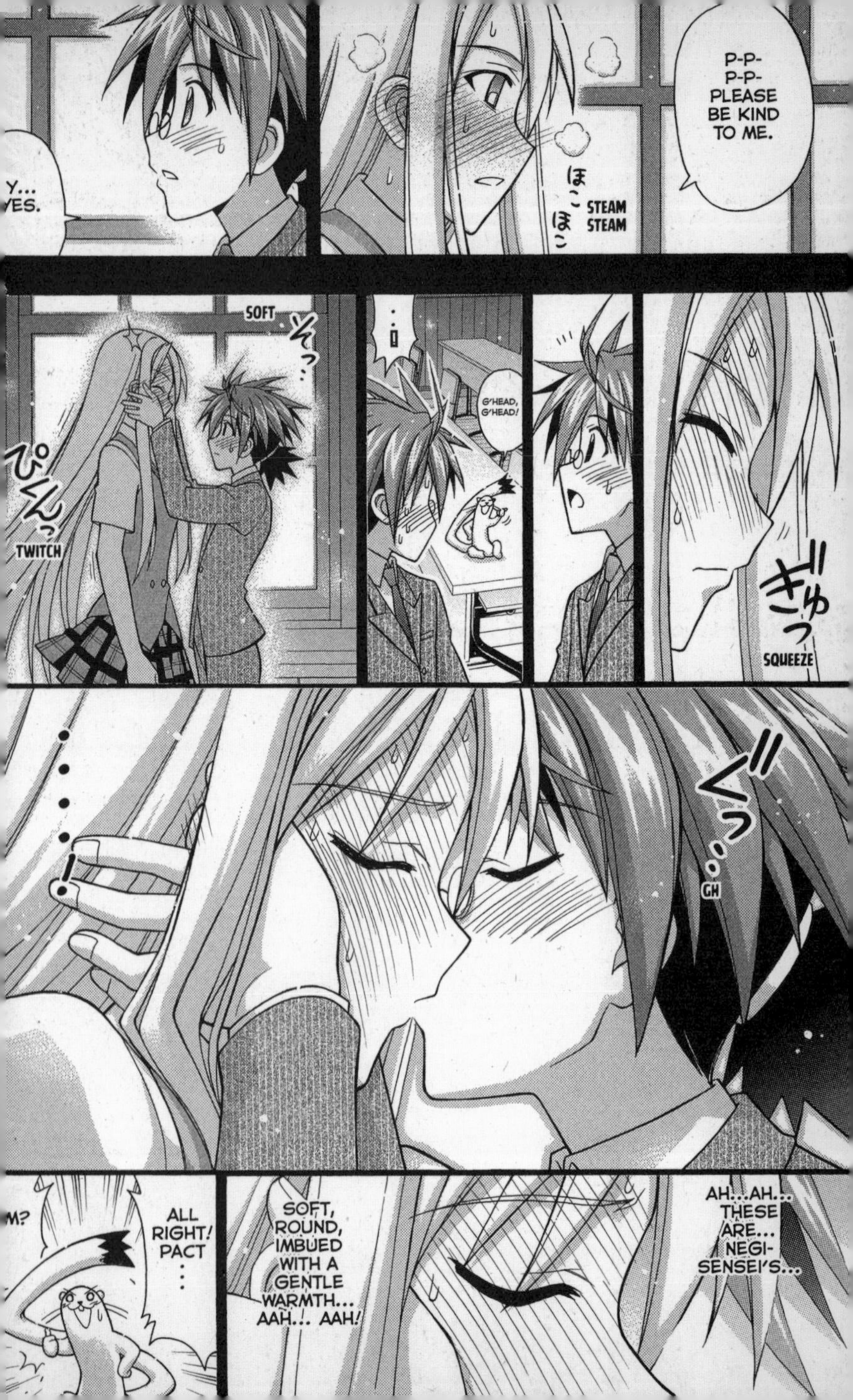
P-P-
P-P-
PLEASE
BE KIND
TO ME.
ほこほこ
STEAM
STEAM
Y...
YES.
ぎゅっ
SQUEEZE
...!
G'HEAD, G'HEAD!
そっ…
SOFT
ぴくんっ
TWITCH
ぐっ…
GH
......!
AH...AH...
THESE
ARE...
NEGI-
SENSEI'S...
SOFT,
ROUND,
IMBUED
WITH A
GENTLE
WARMTH...
AAH...! AAH!
ALL
RIGHT!
PACT
...
M?

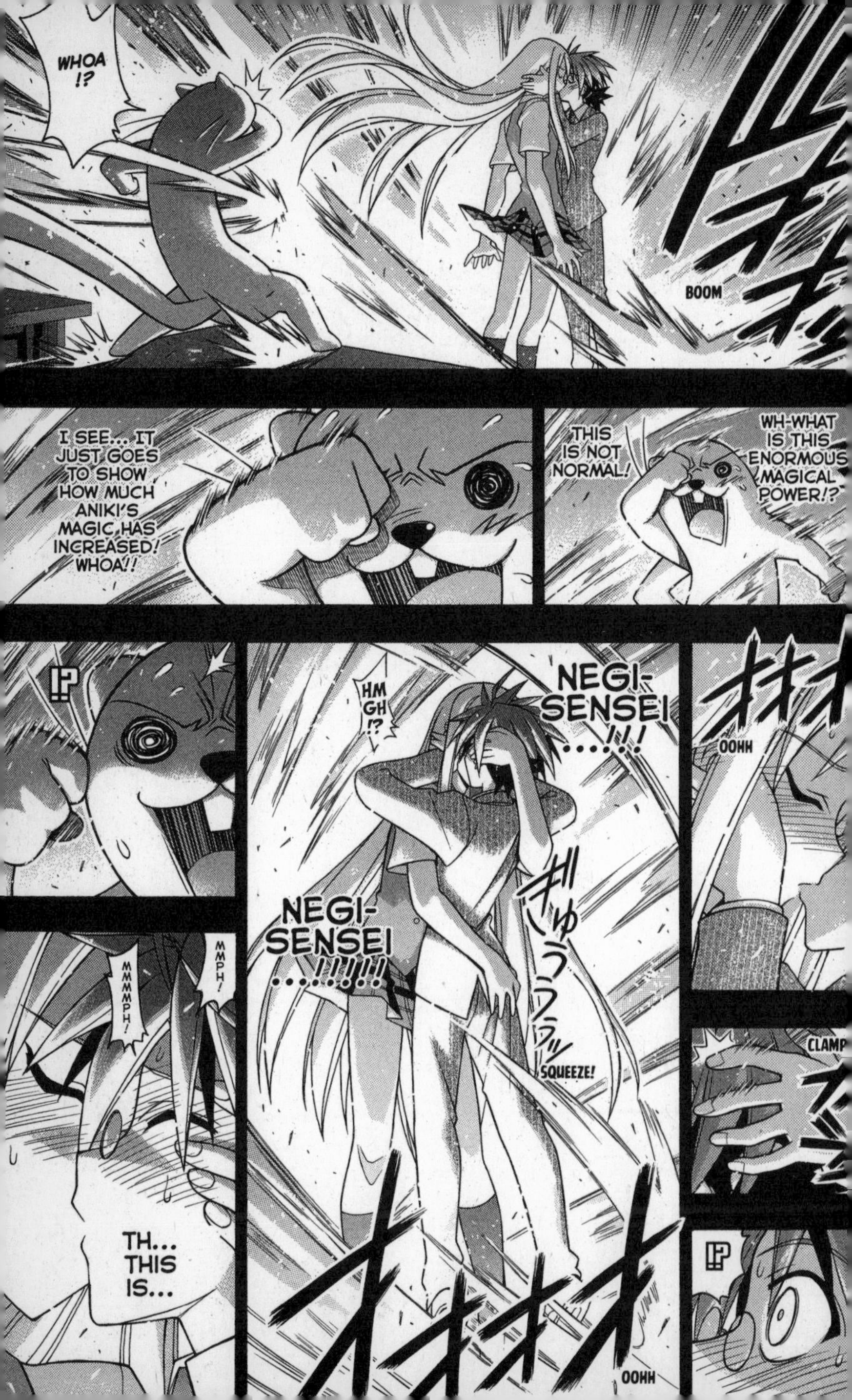
BOOM
WHOA !?
WH-WHAT IS THIS ENORMOUS MAGICAL POWER!?
THIS IS NOT NORMAL!
I SEE... IT JUST GOES TO SHOW HOW MUCH ANIKI'S MAGIC HAS INCREASED! WHOA!!
OOHH
CLAMP
!?
NEGI-SENSEI ...!!!!
HMGH !?
SQUEEZE!
NEGI-SENSEI ...!!!!!!
OOHH
!?
MMPH!
MMMMPH!
TH... THIS IS...

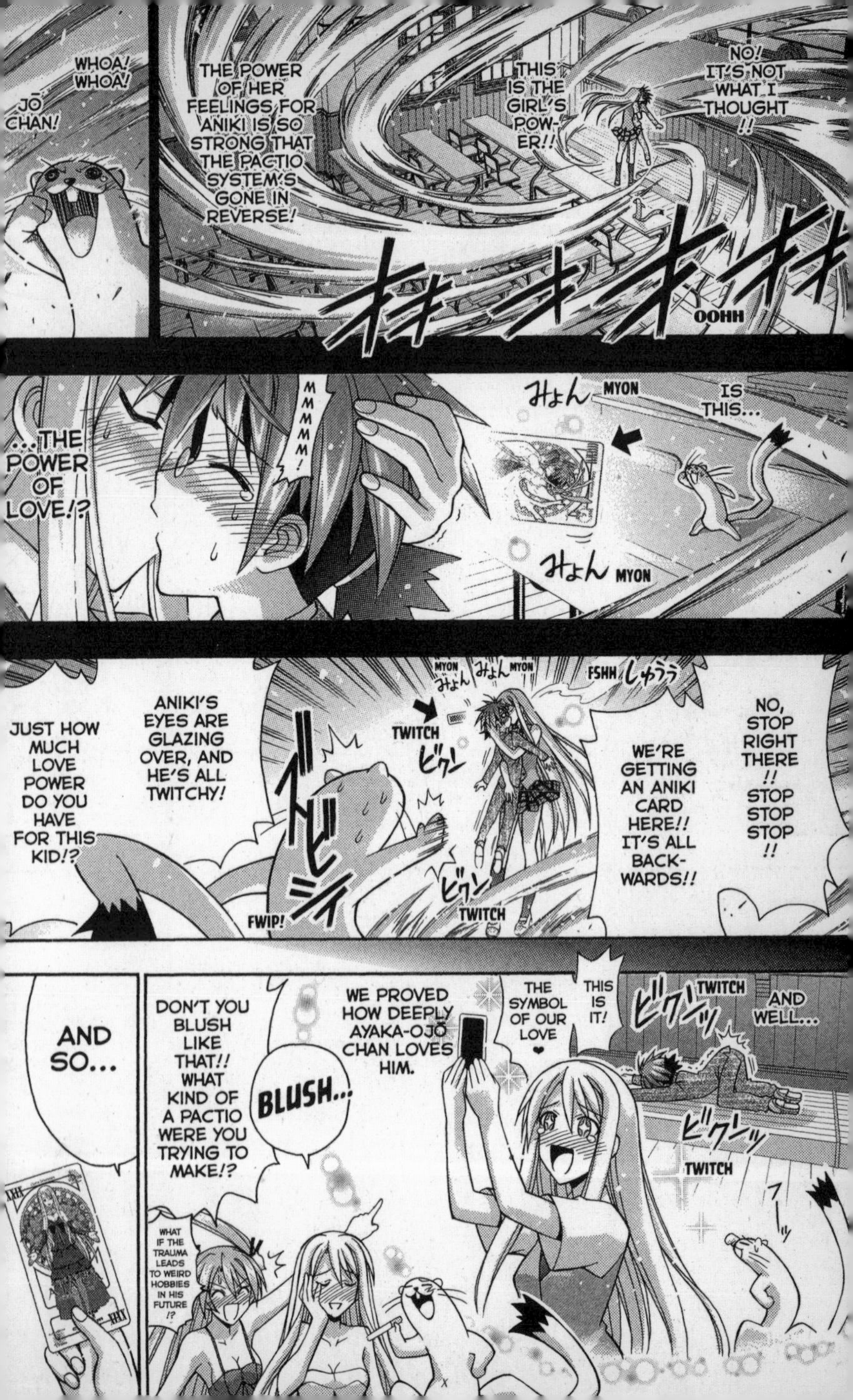
NO! IT'S NOT WHAT I THOUGHT!!
THIS IS THE GIRL'S POW-ER!!
THE POWER OF HER FEELINGS FOR ANIKI IS SO STRONG THAT THE PACTIO SYSTEM'S GONE IN REVERSE!
OOHH
WHOA! WHOA!
JŌ CHAN!
IS THIS...
みょん MYON
みょん MYON
MMMMMM!
...THE POWER OF LOVE!?
NO, STOP RIGHT THERE!! STOP STOP STOP!!
FSHH しゅううう
WE'RE GETTING AN ANIKI CARD HERE!! IT'S ALL BACK-WARDS!!
MYON みょん みょん MYON
TWITCH
TWITCH
FWIP!
ANIKI'S EYES ARE GLAZING OVER, AND HE'S ALL TWITCHY!
JUST HOW MUCH LOVE POWER DO YOU HAVE FOR THIS KID!?
AND WELL...
TWITCH
THIS IS IT!
THE SYMBOL OF OUR LOVE ❤
WE PROVED HOW DEEPLY AYAKA-OJŌ CHAN LOVES HIM.
TWITCH
DON'T YOU BLUSH LIKE THAT!! WHAT KIND OF A PACTIO WERE YOU TRYING TO MAKE!?
BLUSH...
WHAT IF THE TRAUMA LEADS TO WEIRD HOBBIES IN HIS FUTURE!?
AND SO...

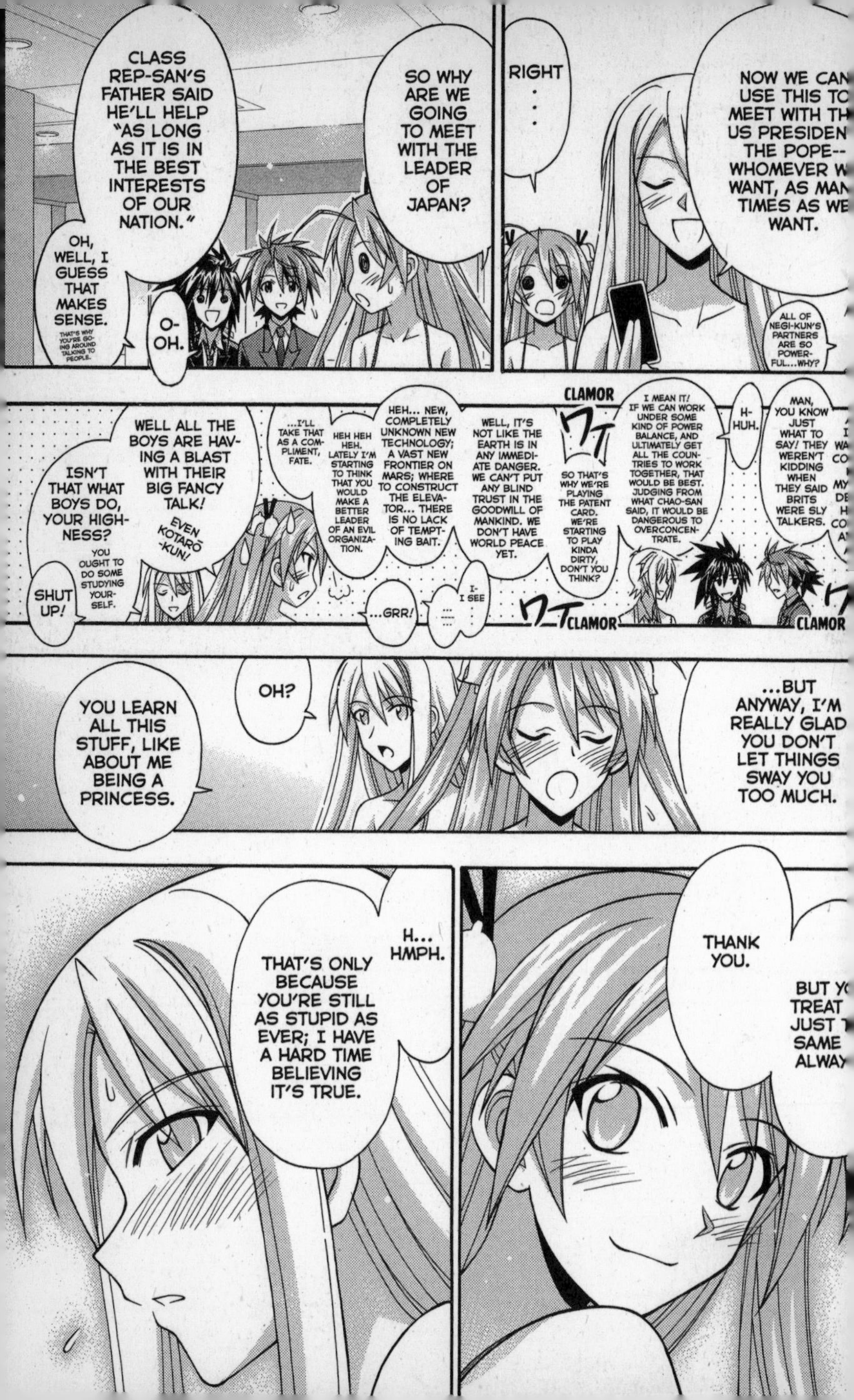
NOW WE CAN USE THIS TO MEET WITH TH US PRESIDEN THE POPE-- WHOMEVER W WANT, AS MAN TIMES AS WE WANT.
RIGHT . . .
ALL OF NEGI-KUN'S PARTNERS ARE SO POWERFUL...WHY?
SO WHY ARE WE GOING TO MEET WITH THE LEADER OF JAPAN?
CLASS REP-SAN'S FATHER SAID HE'LL HELP "AS LONG AS IT IS IN THE BEST INTERESTS OF OUR NATION."
O-OH.
OH, WELL, I GUESS THAT MAKES SENSE.
THAT'S WHY YOU'RE GOING AROUND TALKING TO PEOPLE.
MAN, YOU KNOW JUST WHAT TO SAY! THEY WEREN'T KIDDING WHEN THEY SAID BRITS WERE SLY TALKERS.
CLAMOR
H-HUH.
I MEAN IT! IF WE CAN WORK UNDER SOME KIND OF POWER BALANCE, AND ULTIMATELY GET ALL THE COUNTRIES TO WORK TOGETHER, THAT WOULD BE BEST. JUDGING FROM WHAT CHAO-SAN SAID, IT WOULD BE DANGEROUS TO OVERCONCENTRATE.
CLAMOR
SO THAT'S WHY WE'RE PLAYING THE PATENT CARD. WE'RE STARTING TO PLAY KINDA DIRTY, DON'T YOU THINK?
CLAMOR
WELL, IT'S NOT LIKE THE EARTH IS IN ANY IMMEDIATE DANGER. WE CAN'T PUT ANY BLIND TRUST IN THE GOODWILL OF MANKIND. WE DON'T HAVE WORLD PEACE YET.
HEH... NEW, COMPLETELY UNKNOWN NEW TECHNOLOGY; A VAST NEW FRONTIER ON MARS; WHERE TO CONSTRUCT THE ELEVATOR... THERE IS NO LACK OF TEMPTING BAIT.
HEH HEH HEH. LATELY I'M STARTING TO THINK THAT YOU WOULD MAKE A BETTER LEADER OF AN EVIL ORGANIZATION.
...I'LL TAKE THAT AS A COMPLIMENT, FATE.
I- I SEE
...GRR!
WELL ALL THE BOYS ARE HAVING A BLAST WITH THEIR BIG FANCY TALK!
EVEN KOTARŌ-KUN!
ISN'T THAT WHAT BOYS DO, YOUR HIGHNESS?
YOU OUGHT TO DO SOME STUDYING YOURSELF.
SHUT UP!
...BUT ANYWAY, I'M REALLY GLAD YOU DON'T LET THINGS SWAY YOU TOO MUCH.
OH?
YOU LEARN ALL THIS STUFF, LIKE ABOUT ME BEING A PRINCESS.
THANK YOU.
BUT Y TREAT JUST SAME ALWAY
H... HMPH.
THAT'S ONLY BECAUSE YOU'RE STILL AS STUPID AS EVER; I HAVE A HARD TIME BELIEVING IT'S TRUE.

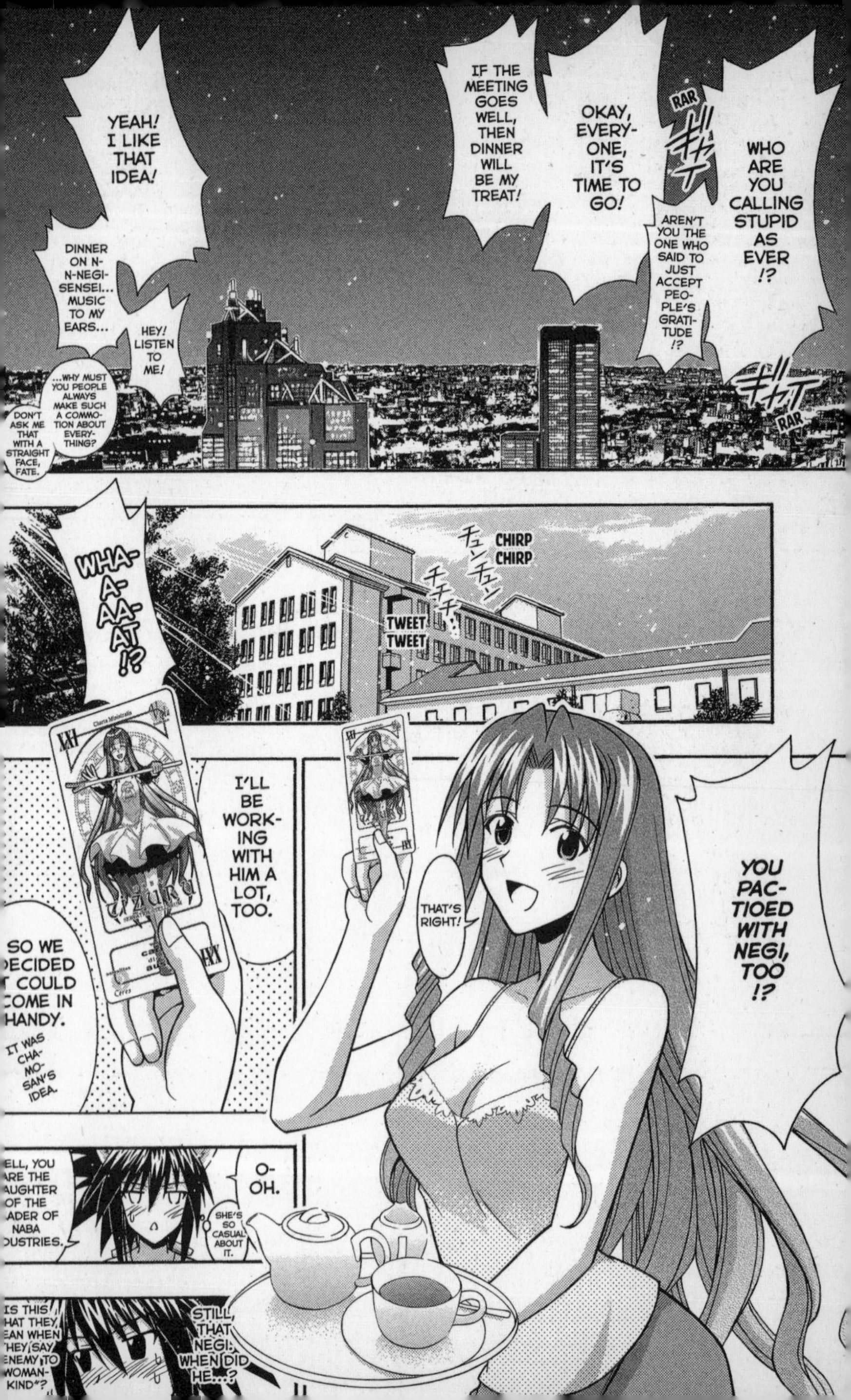
WHO ARE YOU CALLING STUPID AS EVER !?
RAR
AREN'T YOU THE ONE WHO SAID TO JUST ACCEPT PEOPLE'S GRATITUDE !?
RAR
OKAY, EVERYONE, IT'S TIME TO GO!
IF THE MEETING GOES WELL, THEN DINNER WILL BE MY TREAT!
YEAH! I LIKE THAT IDEA!
DINNER ON N-N-NEGI-SENSEI... MUSIC TO MY EARS...
HEY! LISTEN TO ME!
...WHY MUST YOU PEOPLE ALWAYS MAKE SUCH A COMMOTION ABOUT EVERYTHING?
DON'T ASK ME THAT WITH A STRAIGHT FACE, FATE.
CHIRP CHIRP
TWEET TWEET
WHA-A-AA-AT !?
YOU PACTIOED WITH NEGI, TOO !?
THAT'S RIGHT!
I'LL BE WORKING WITH HIM A LOT, TOO.
SO WE DECIDED IT COULD COME IN HANDY.
IT WAS CHAMO-SAN'S IDEA.
O-OH.
SHE'S SO CASUAL ABOUT IT.
WELL, YOU ARE THE DAUGHTER OF THE LEADER OF NABA INDUSTRIES.
STILL, THAT NEGI, WHEN DID HE...?
IS THIS WHAT THEY MEAN WHEN THEY SAY "ENEMY TO WOMANKIND"?

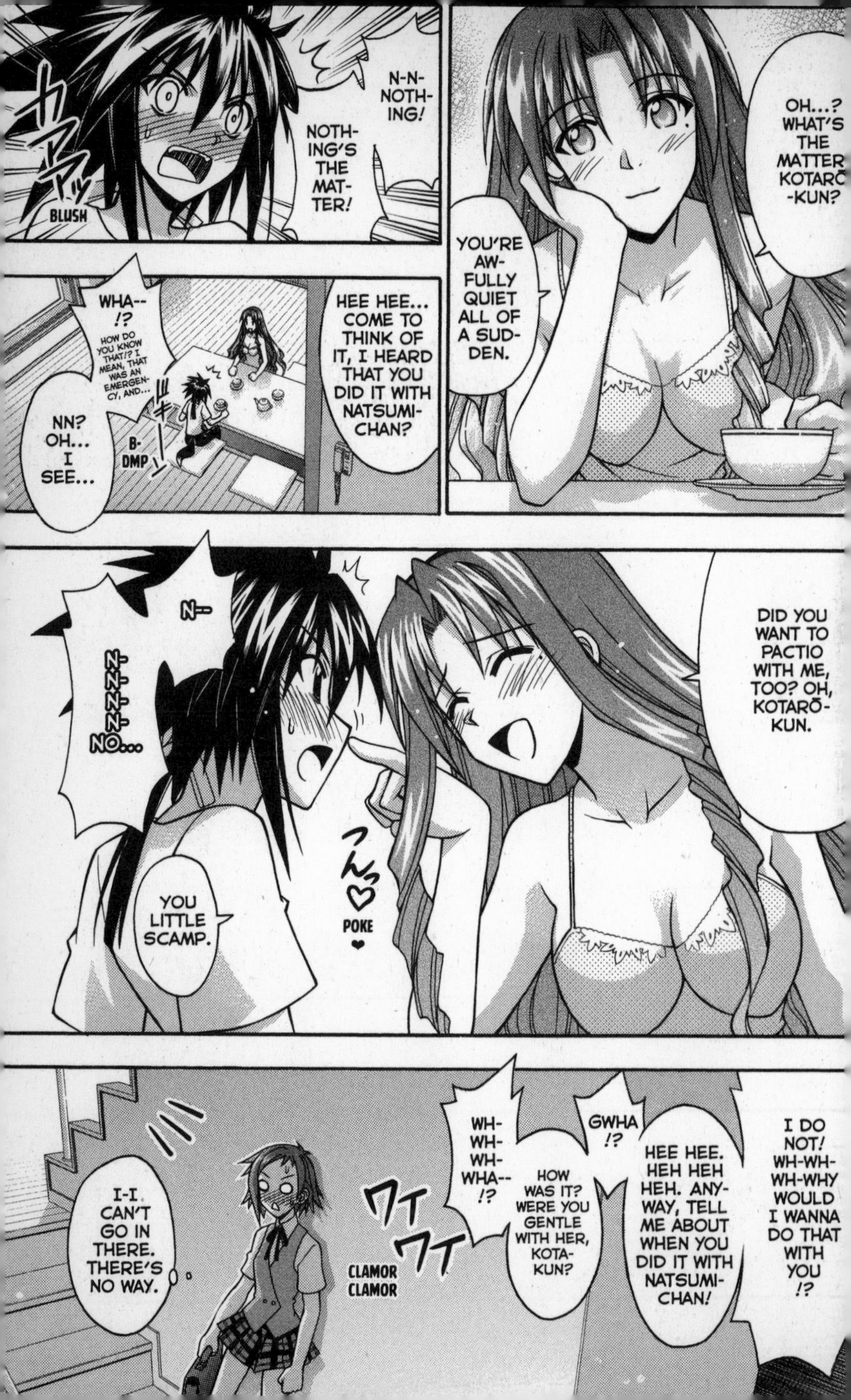
OH...? WHAT'S THE MATTER KOTARŌ-KUN?
YOU'RE AWFULLY QUIET ALL OF A SUDDEN.
N-N-NOTHING!
NOTHING'S THE MATTER!
BLUSH
HEE HEE... COME TO THINK OF IT, I HEARD THAT YOU DID IT WITH NATSUMI-CHAN?
WHA--!?
HOW DO YOU KNOW THAT!? I MEAN, THAT WAS AN EMERGENCY, AND...
B-DMP
NN? OH... I SEE...
DID YOU WANT TO PACTIO WITH ME, TOO? OH, KOTARŌ-KUN.
N--
N-N-N-N-NO...
POKE
YOU LITTLE SCAMP.
I DO NOT! WH-WH-WH-WHY WOULD I WANNA DO THAT WITH YOU!?
HEE HEE. HEH HEH HEH. ANYWAY, TELL ME ABOUT WHEN YOU DID IT WITH NATSUMI-CHAN!
GWHA!?
HOW WAS IT? WERE YOU GENTLE WITH HER, KOTA-KUN?
WH-WH-WH-WHA--!?
CLAMOR CLAMOR
I-I CAN'T GO IN THERE. THERE'S NO WAY.

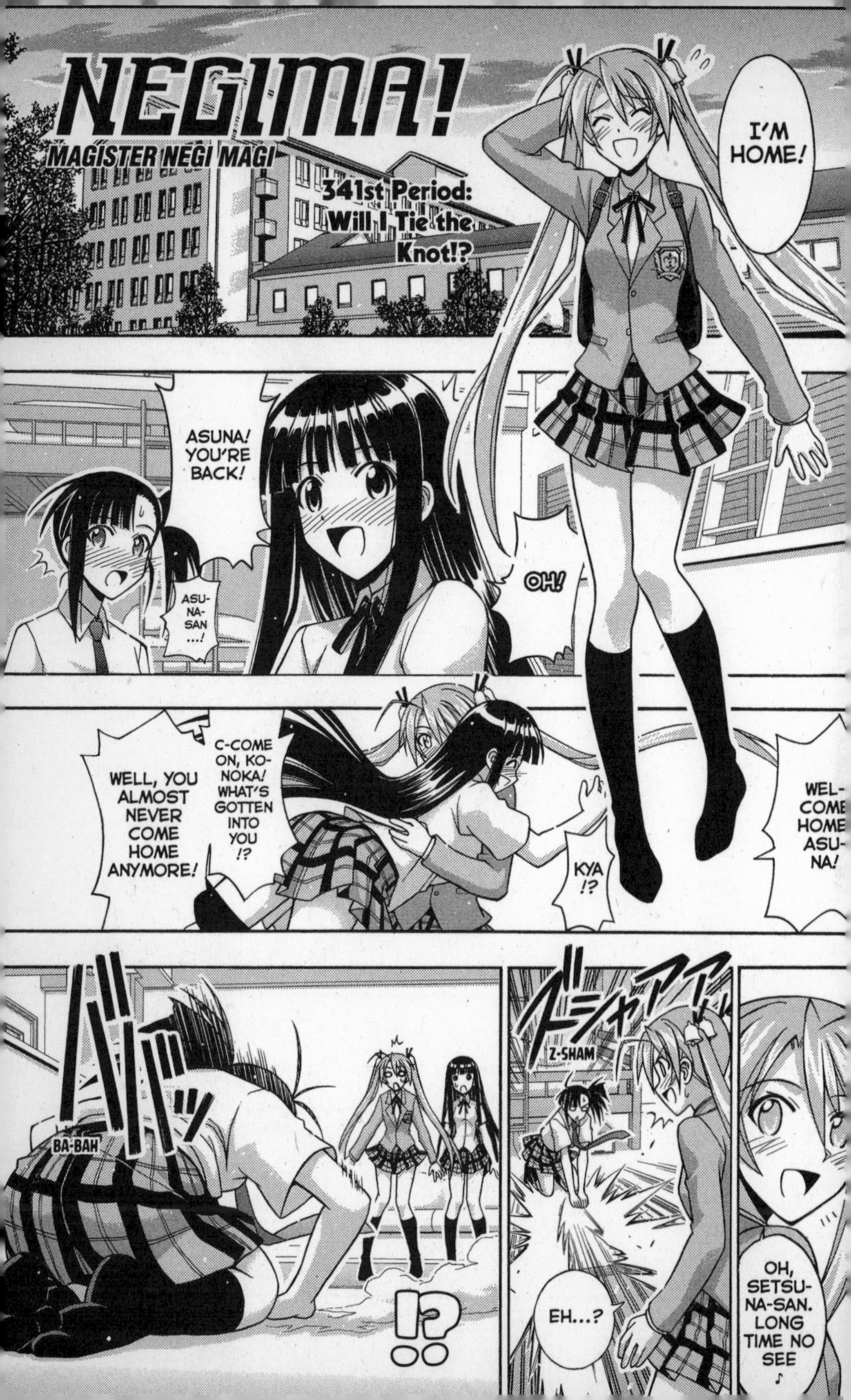
NEGIMA!
MAGISTER NEGI MAGI
341st Period: Will I Tie the Knot!?
I'M HOME!
OH!
ASUNA! YOU'RE BACK!
ASU-NA-SAN...!
WEL-COME HOME ASU-NA!
KYA!?
C-COME ON, KO-NOKA! WHAT'S GOTTEN INTO YOU!?
WELL, YOU ALMOST NEVER COME HOME ANYMORE!
Z-SHAM
OH, SETSU-NA-SAN. LONG TIME NO SEE ♪
EH...?
BA-BAH
!?

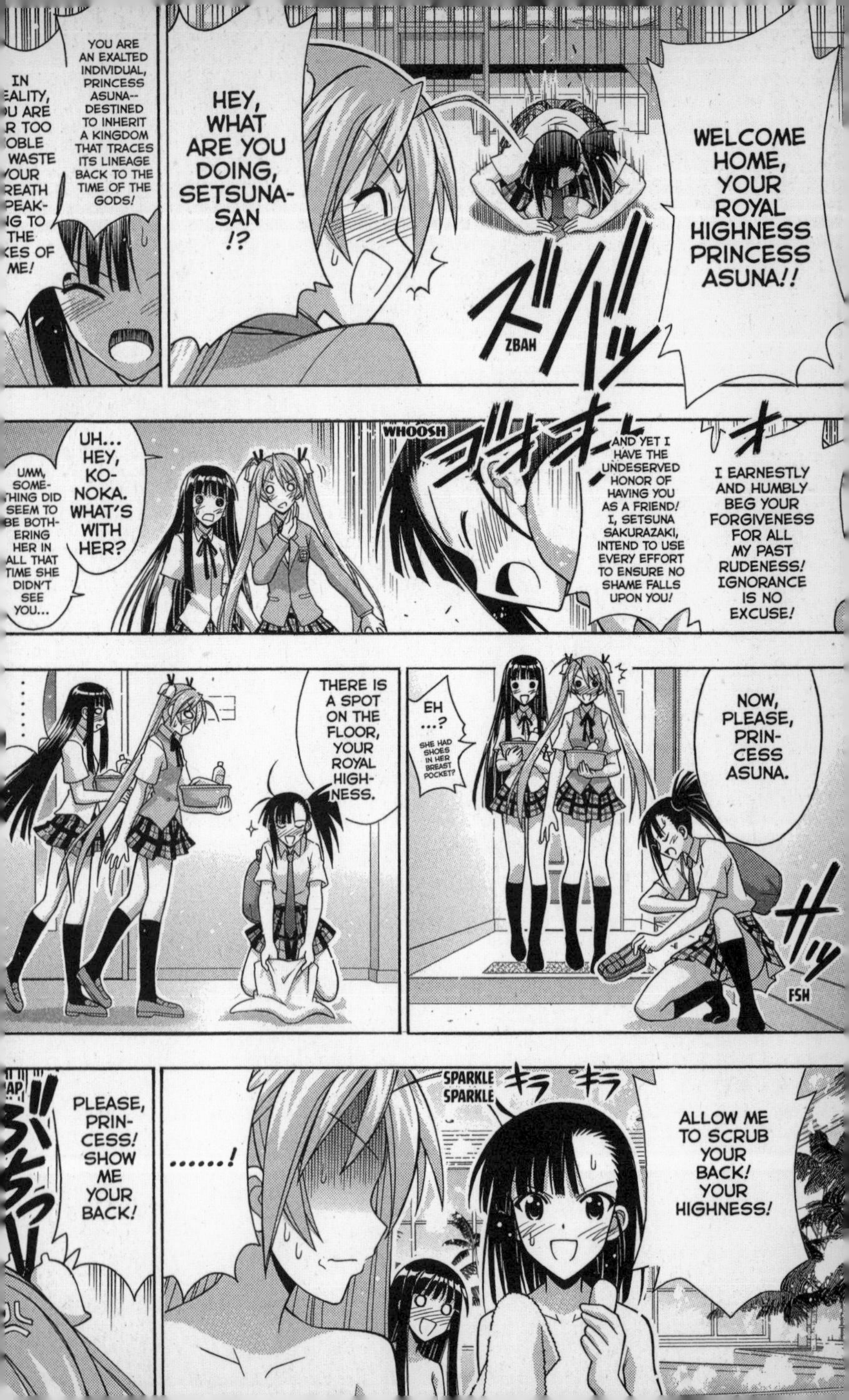

WELCOME HOME, YOUR ROYAL HIGHNESS PRINCESS ASUNA!!
ZBAH
HEY, WHAT ARE YOU DOING, SETSUNA-SAN!?
YOU ARE AN EXALTED INDIVIDUAL, PRINCESS ASUNA-- DESTINED TO INHERIT A KINGDOM THAT TRACES ITS LINEAGE BACK TO THE TIME OF THE GODS!
IN EALITY, OU ARE R TOO OBLE WASTE YOUR REATH PEAK-ING TO THE KES OF ME!
I EARNESTLY AND HUMBLY BEG YOUR FORGIVENESS FOR ALL MY PAST RUDENESS! IGNORANCE IS NO EXCUSE!
AND YET I HAVE THE UNDESERVED HONOR OF HAVING YOU AS A FRIEND! I, SETSUNA SAKURAZAKI, INTEND TO USE EVERY EFFORT TO ENSURE NO SHAME FALLS UPON YOU!
WHOOSH
UH... HEY, KO-NOKA. WHAT'S WITH HER?
UMM, SOME-THING DID SEEM TO BE BOTH-ERING HER IN ALL THAT TIME SHE DIDN'T SEE YOU...
NOW, PLEASE, PRIN-CESS ASUNA.
FSH
EH ...?
SHE HAD SHOES IN HER BREAST POCKET?
THERE IS A SPOT ON THE FLOOR, YOUR ROYAL HIGH-NESS.
......
ALLOW ME TO SCRUB YOUR BACK! YOUR HIGHNESS!
SPARKLE SPARKLE
......!
PLEASE, PRIN-CESS! SHOW ME YOUR BACK!

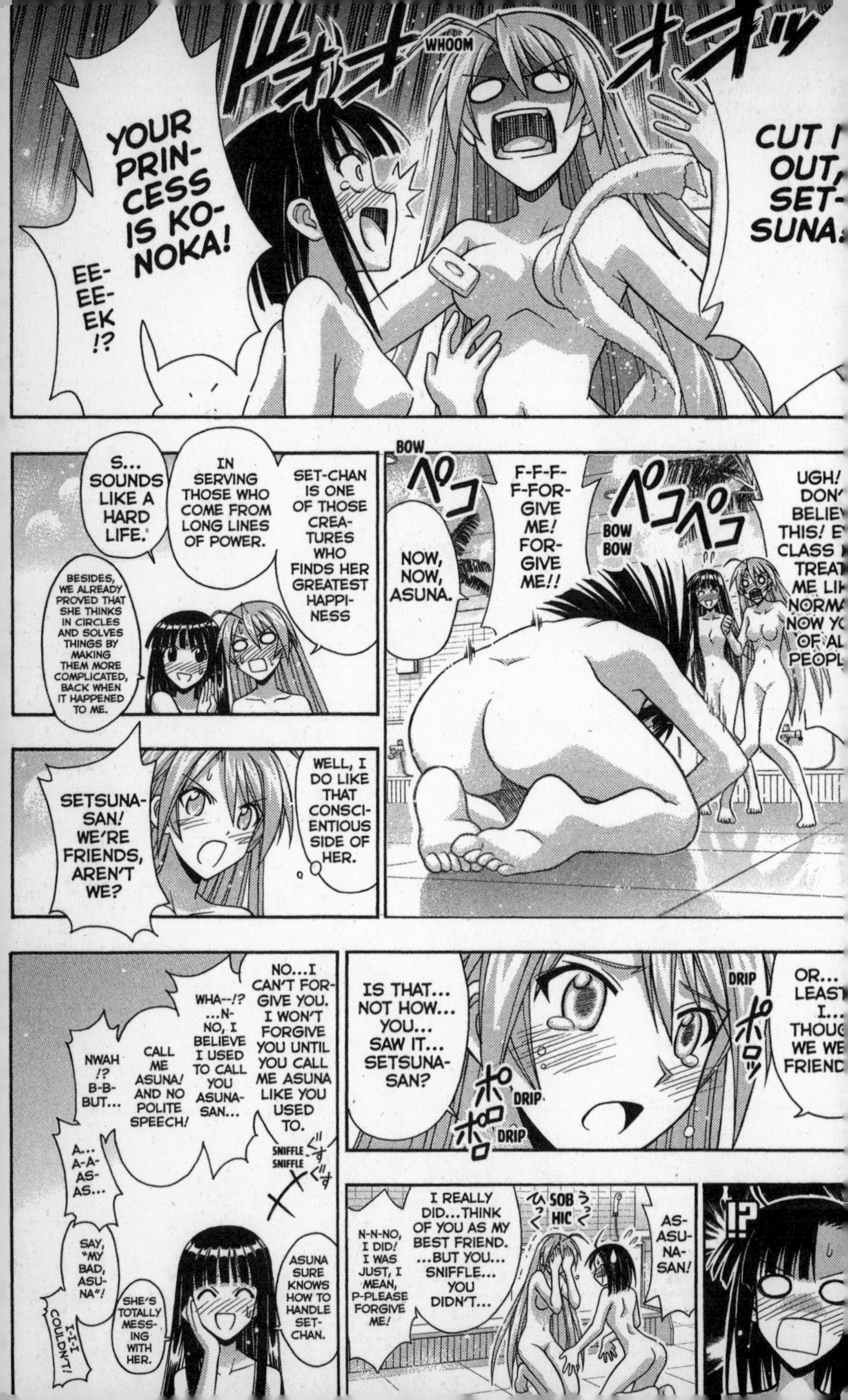
WHOOM
CUT I OUT, SET-SUNA!
YOUR PRIN-CESS IS KO-NOKA!
EE-EE-EK!?
UGH! DON' BELIEV THIS! E CLASS TREAT ME LIK NORMA NOW YO OF AL PEOPL
ペコペコ BOW BOW
F-F-F-F-FOR-GIVE ME! FOR-GIVE ME!!
ペコ BOW
NOW, NOW, ASUNA.
SET-CHAN IS ONE OF THOSE CREA-TURES WHO FINDS HER GREATEST HAPPI-NESS
IN SERVING THOSE WHO COME FROM LONG LINES OF POWER.
S... SOUNDS LIKE A HARD LIFE.
BESIDES, WE ALREADY PROVED THAT SHE THINKS IN CIRCLES AND SOLVES THINGS BY MAKING THEM MORE COMPLICATED, BACK WHEN IT HAPPENED TO ME.
WELL, I DO LIKE THAT CONSCI-ENTIOUS SIDE OF HER.
SETSUNA-SAN! WE'RE FRIENDS, AREN'T WE?
OR... LEAST I... THOUG WE WE FRIEND
ポロッ DRIP
IS THAT... NOT HOW... YOU... SAW IT... SETSUNA-SAN?
ポロポロ DRIP DRIP
!?
AS-ASUNA-SAN!
SOB HIC
I REALLY DID...THINK OF YOU AS MY BEST FRIEND. ...BUT YOU... SNIFFLE... YOU DIDN'T...
N-N-NO, I DID! I WAS JUST, I MEAN, P-PLEASE FORGIVE ME!
NO...I CAN'T FOR-GIVE YOU. I WON'T FORGIVE YOU UNTIL YOU CALL ME ASUNA LIKE YOU USED TO.
WHA--!? ...N-NO, I BELIEVE I USED TO CALL YOU ASUNA-SAN...
CALL ME ASUNA! AND NO POLITE SPEECH!
NWAH!? B-B-BUT...
ぐすぐす SNIFFLE SNIFFLE
A... A-A-AS-AS...
ASUNA SURE KNOWS HOW TO HANDLE SET-CHAN.
SAY, "MY BAD, ASUNA"!
SHE'S TOTALLY MESS-ING WITH HER.
I-I-I COULDN'T!

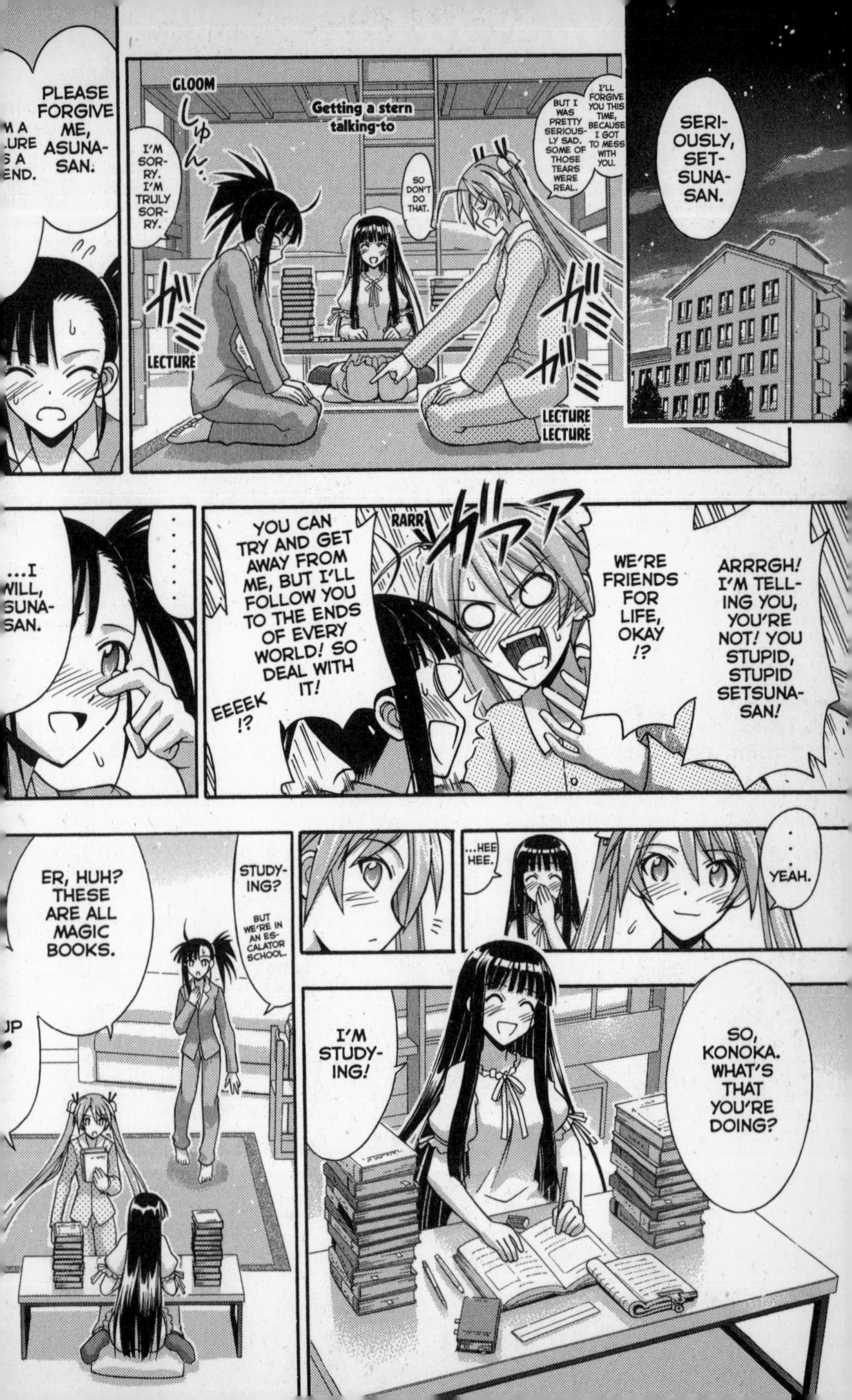
SERIOUSLY, SETSUNA-SAN.
I'LL FORGIVE YOU THIS TIME, BECAUSE I GOT TO MESS WITH YOU.
BUT I WAS PRETTY SERIOUSLY SAD. SOME OF THOSE TEARS WERE REAL.
Getting a stern talking-to
GLOOM
SO DON'T DO THAT.
I'M SORRY. I'M TRULY SORRY.
LECTURE
LECTURE
LECTURE
PLEASE FORGIVE ME, ASUNA-SAN.
ARRRGH! I'M TELLING YOU, YOU'RE NOT! YOU STUPID, STUPID SETSUNA-SAN!
WE'RE FRIENDS FOR LIFE, OKAY!?
RARR
YOU CAN TRY AND GET AWAY FROM ME, BUT I'LL FOLLOW YOU TO THE ENDS OF EVERY WORLD! SO DEAL WITH IT!
EEEEK!?
......
...YEAH.
...HEE HEE.
SO, KONOKA. WHAT'S THAT YOU'RE DOING?
I'M STUDYING!
STUDYING?
BUT WE'RE IN AN ESCALATOR SCHOOL.
ER, HUH? THESE ARE ALL MAGIC BOOKS.

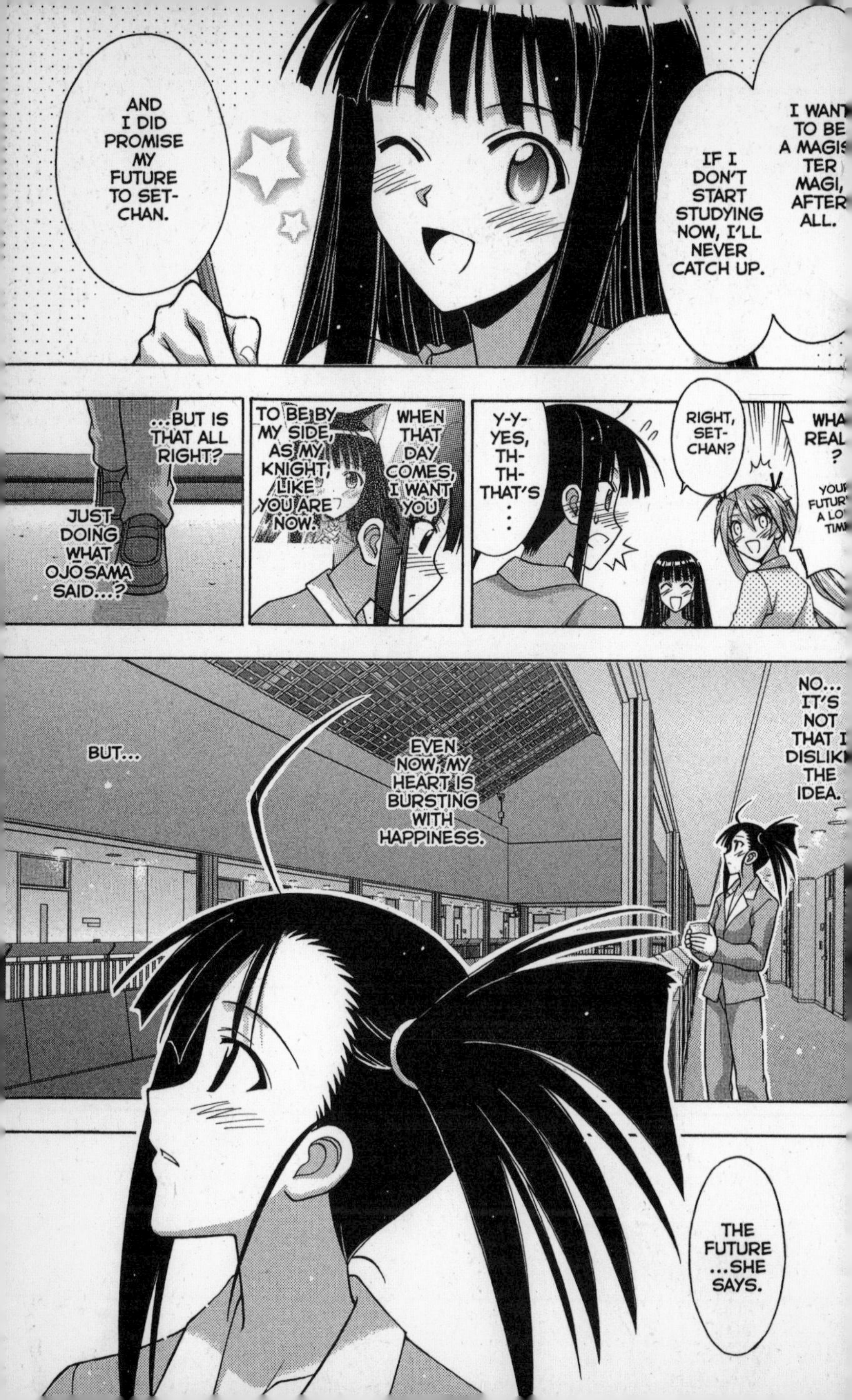
I WANT TO BE A MAGISTER MAGI, AFTER ALL.
IF I DON'T START STUDYING NOW, I'LL NEVER CATCH UP.
AND I DID PROMISE MY FUTURE TO SET-CHAN.
WHA REAL?
RIGHT, SET-CHAN?
Y-Y-YES, TH-TH-THAT'S...
WHEN THAT DAY COMES, I WANT YOU
TO BE BY MY SIDE, AS MY KNIGHT, LIKE YOU ARE NOW.
...BUT IS THAT ALL RIGHT?
JUST DOING WHAT OJŌSAMA SAID...?
NO... IT'S NOT THAT I DISLIKE THE IDEA.
EVEN NOW, MY HEART IS BURSTING WITH HAPPINESS.
BUT...
THE FUTURE ...SHE SAYS.

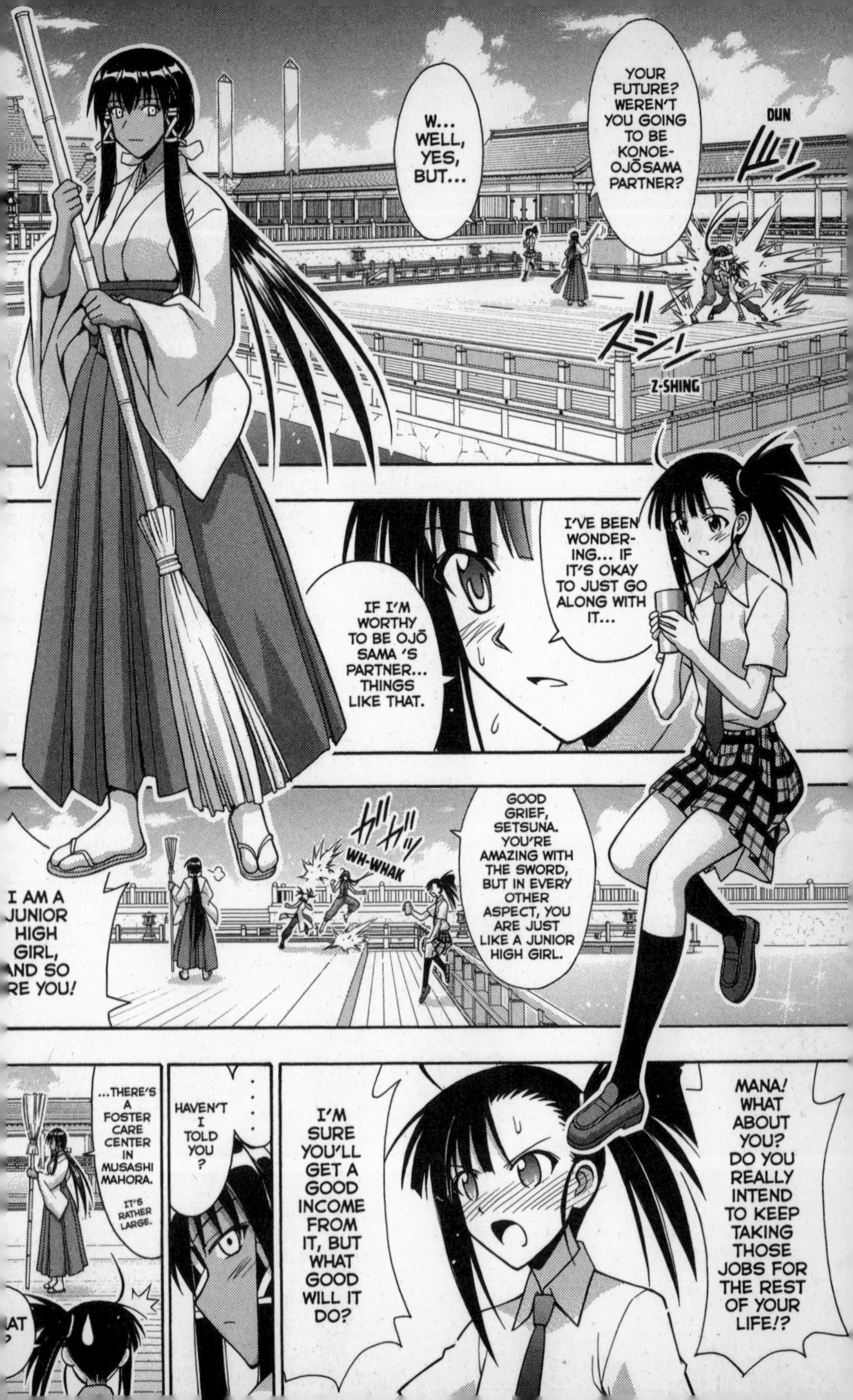

YOUR FUTURE? WEREN'T YOU GOING TO BE KONOE-OJŌSAMA PARTNER?
DUN
W... WELL, YES, BUT...
Z-SHING
I'VE BEEN WONDERING... IF IT'S OKAY TO JUST GO ALONG WITH IT...
IF I'M WORTHY TO BE OJŌ SAMA 'S PARTNER... THINGS LIKE THAT.
GOOD GRIEF, SETSUNA. YOU'RE AMAZING WITH THE SWORD, BUT IN EVERY OTHER ASPECT, YOU ARE JUST LIKE A JUNIOR HIGH GIRL.
WH-WHAK
I AM A JUNIOR HIGH GIRL, AND SO RE YOU!
MANA! WHAT ABOUT YOU? DO YOU REALLY INTEND TO KEEP TAKING THOSE JOBS FOR THE REST OF YOUR LIFE!?
I'M SURE YOU'LL GET A GOOD INCOME FROM IT, BUT WHAT GOOD WILL IT DO?
...
HAVEN'T I TOLD YOU?
...THERE'S A FOSTER CARE CENTER IN MUSASHI MAHORA.
IT'S RATHER LARGE.

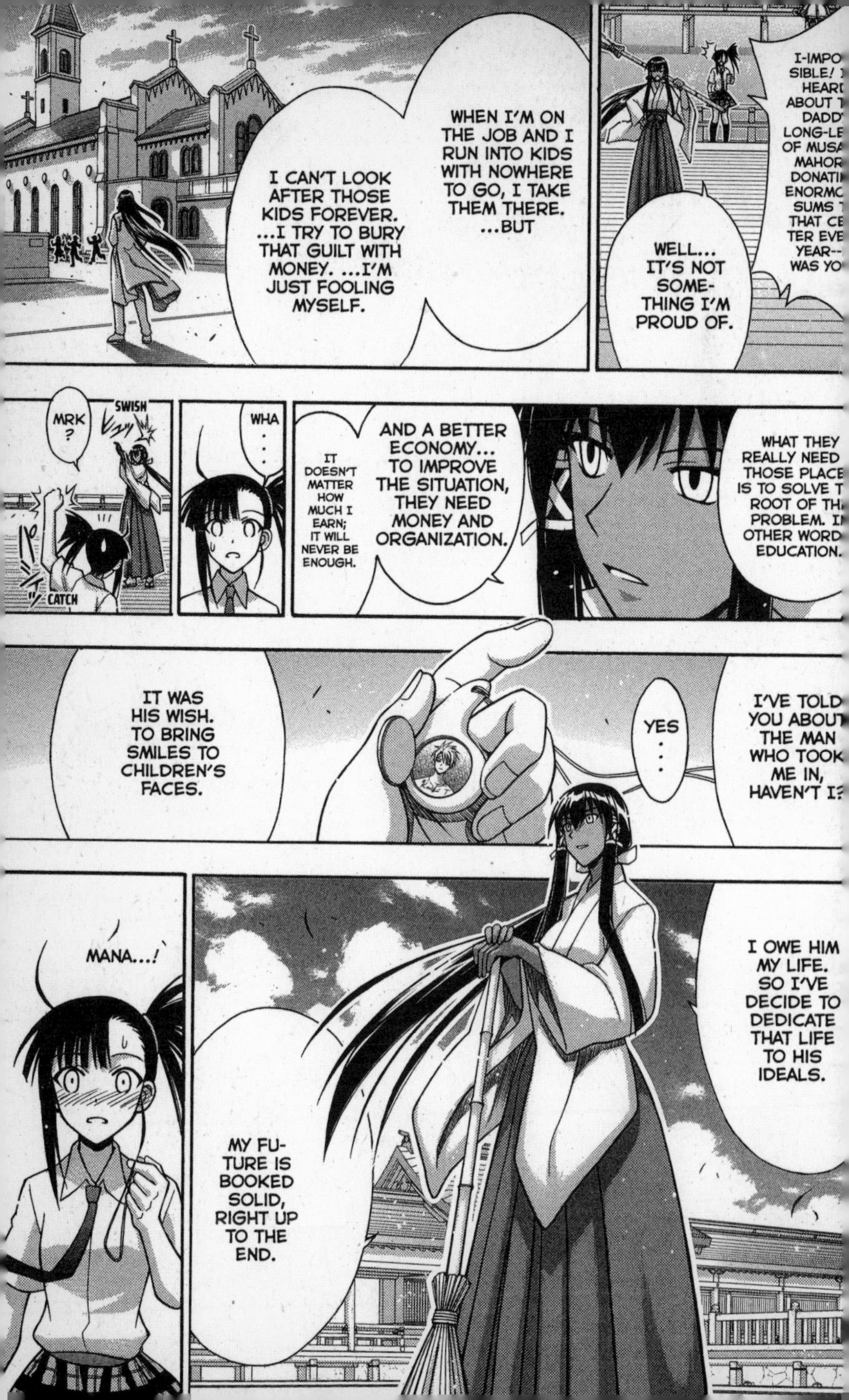
I-IMPO SIBLE! I HEARD ABOUT T DADDY LONG-LE OF MUSA MAHOR DONATI ENORMO SUMS T THAT CE TER EVE YEAR-- WAS YO
WELL... IT'S NOT SOME-THING I'M PROUD OF.
WHEN I'M ON THE JOB AND I RUN INTO KIDS WITH NOWHERE TO GO, I TAKE THEM THERE. ...BUT
I CAN'T LOOK AFTER THOSE KIDS FOREVER. ...I TRY TO BURY THAT GUILT WITH MONEY. ...I'M JUST FOOLING MYSELF.
WHAT THEY REALLY NEED THOSE PLACE IS TO SOLVE T ROOT OF TH PROBLEM. I OTHER WORD EDUCATION.
AND A BETTER ECONOMY... TO IMPROVE THE SITUATION, THEY NEED MONEY AND ORGANIZATION.
IT DOESN'T MATTER HOW MUCH I EARN; IT WILL NEVER BE ENOUGH.
WHA...
SWISH
MRK?
CATCH
I'VE TOLD YOU ABOUT THE MAN WHO TOOK ME IN, HAVEN'T I?
YES...
IT WAS HIS WISH. TO BRING SMILES TO CHILDREN'S FACES.
I OWE HIM MY LIFE. SO I'VE DECIDE TO DEDICATE THAT LIFE TO HIS IDEALS.
MY FU-TURE IS BOOKED SOLID, RIGHT UP TO THE END.
MANA...!

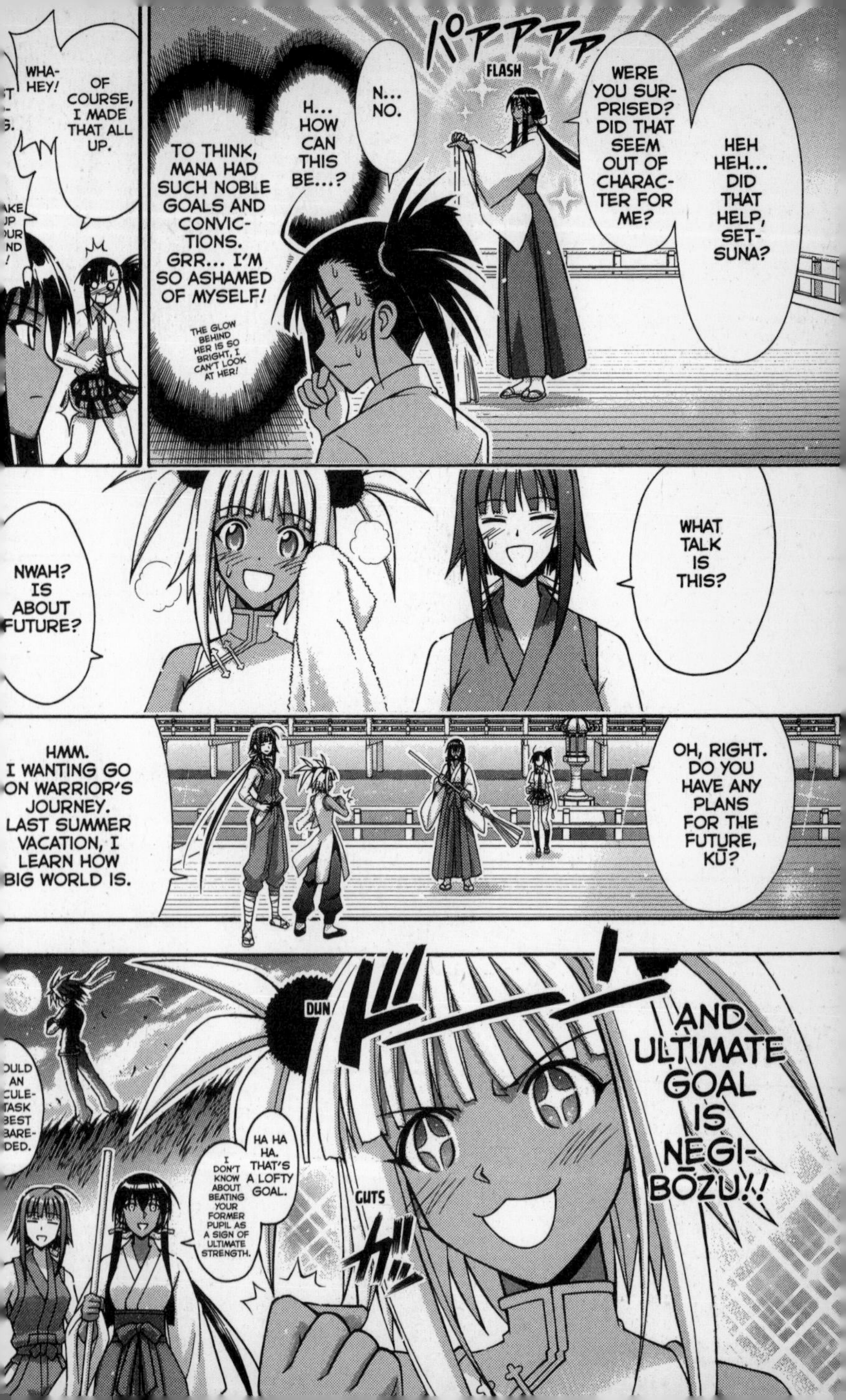
パアアアア
FLASH
HEH HEH... DID THAT HELP, SET-SUNA?
WERE YOU SURPRISED? DID THAT SEEM OUT OF CHARACTER FOR ME?
N... NO.
H... HOW CAN THIS BE...?
TO THINK, MANA HAD SUCH NOBLE GOALS AND CONVICTIONS. GRR... I'M SO ASHAMED OF MYSELF!
THE GLOW BEHIND HER IS SO BRIGHT, I CAN'T LOOK AT HER!
OF COURSE, I MADE THAT ALL UP.
WHA- HEY!
WHAT TALK IS THIS?
NWAH? IS ABOUT FUTURE?
OH, RIGHT. DO YOU HAVE ANY PLANS FOR THE FUTURE, KŪ?
HMM. I WANTING GO ON WARRIOR'S JOURNEY. LAST SUMMER VACATION, I LEARN HOW BIG WORLD IS.
AND ULTIMATE GOAL IS NEGI-BŌZU!!
DUN
GUTS
HA HA HA. THAT'S A LOFTY GOAL.
I DON'T KNOW ABOUT BEATING YOUR FORMER PUPIL AS A SIGN OF ULTIMATE STRENGTH.

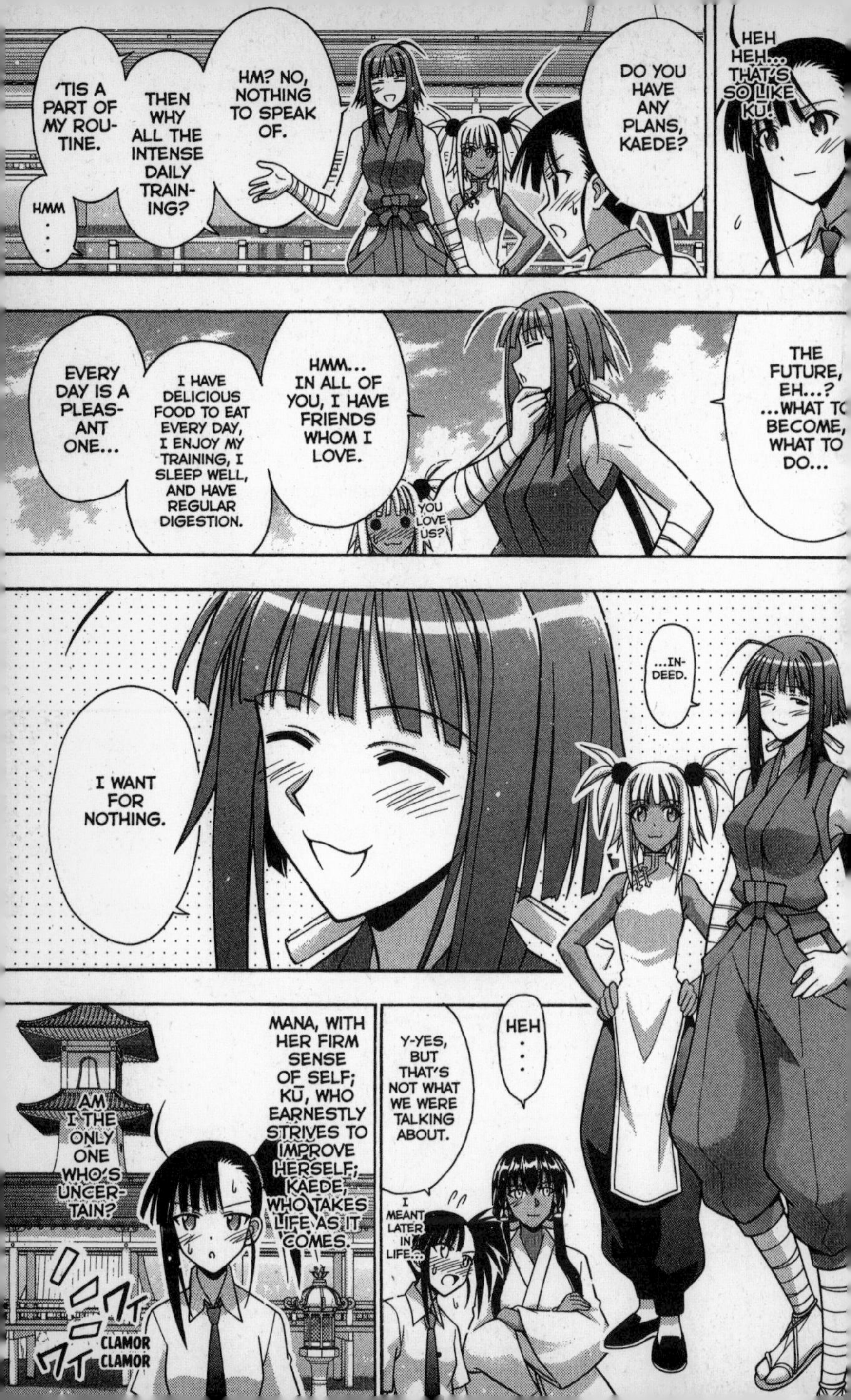
HEH HEH... THAT'S SO LIKE KU!
DO YOU HAVE ANY PLANS, KAEDE?
HM? NO, NOTHING TO SPEAK OF.
THEN WHY ALL THE INTENSE DAILY TRAINING?
'TIS A PART OF MY ROUTINE.
HMM...
THE FUTURE, EH...? ...WHAT TO BECOME, WHAT TO DO...
HMM... IN ALL OF YOU, I HAVE FRIENDS WHOM I LOVE.
YOU LOVE US?
I HAVE DELICIOUS FOOD TO EAT EVERY DAY, I ENJOY MY TRAINING, I SLEEP WELL, AND HAVE REGULAR DIGESTION.
EVERY DAY IS A PLEASANT ONE...
...INDEED.
I WANT FOR NOTHING.
HEH...
Y-YES, BUT THAT'S NOT WHAT WE WERE TALKING ABOUT.
I MEANT LATER IN LIFE...
MANA, WITH HER FIRM SENSE OF SELF; KŪ, WHO EARNESTLY STRIVES TO IMPROVE HERSELF; KAEDE, WHO TAKES LIFE AS IT COMES.
AM I THE ONLY ONE WHO'S UNCERTAIN?
CLAMOR CLAMOR

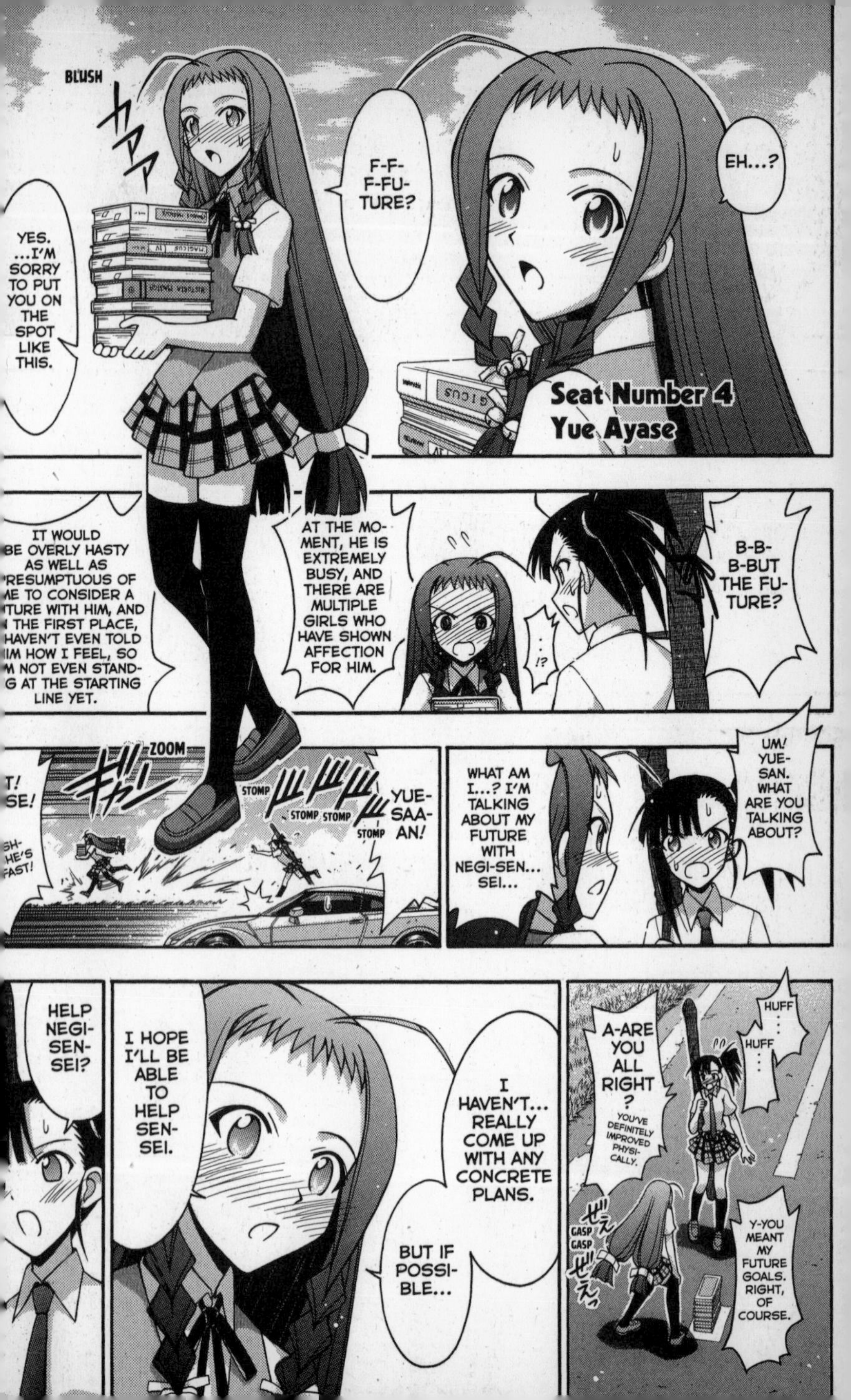
EH...?
F-F-F-FU-TURE?
Seat Number 4 Yue Ayase
BLUSH
YES. ...I'M SORRY TO PUT YOU ON THE SPOT LIKE THIS.
B-B-B-BUT THE FU-TURE?
...!?
AT THE MO-MENT, HE IS EXTREMELY BUSY, AND THERE ARE MULTIPLE GIRLS WHO HAVE SHOWN AFFECTION FOR HIM.
IT WOULD BE OVERLY HASTY AS WELL AS 'RESUMPTUOUS OF ME TO CONSIDER A TURE WITH HIM, AND THE FIRST PLACE, HAVEN'T EVEN TOLD IM HOW I FEEL, SO M NOT EVEN STAND-G AT THE STARTING LINE YET.
UM! YUE-SAN. WHAT ARE YOU TALKING ABOUT?
WHAT AM I...? I'M TALKING ABOUT MY FUTURE WITH NEGI-SEN... SEI...
YUE-SAA-AN!
STOMP STOMP STOMP STOMP
ZOOM
T! SE!
SH-HE'S FAST!
HUFF... HUFF...
A-ARE YOU ALL RIGHT?
YOU'VE DEFINITELY IMPROVED PHYSI-CALLY.
GASP GASP
Y-YOU MEANT MY FUTURE GOALS. RIGHT, OF COURSE.
I HAVEN'T... REALLY COME UP WITH ANY CONCRETE PLANS.
BUT IF POSSI-BLE...
I HOPE I'LL BE ABLE TO HELP SEN-SEI.
HELP NEGI-SEN-SEI?

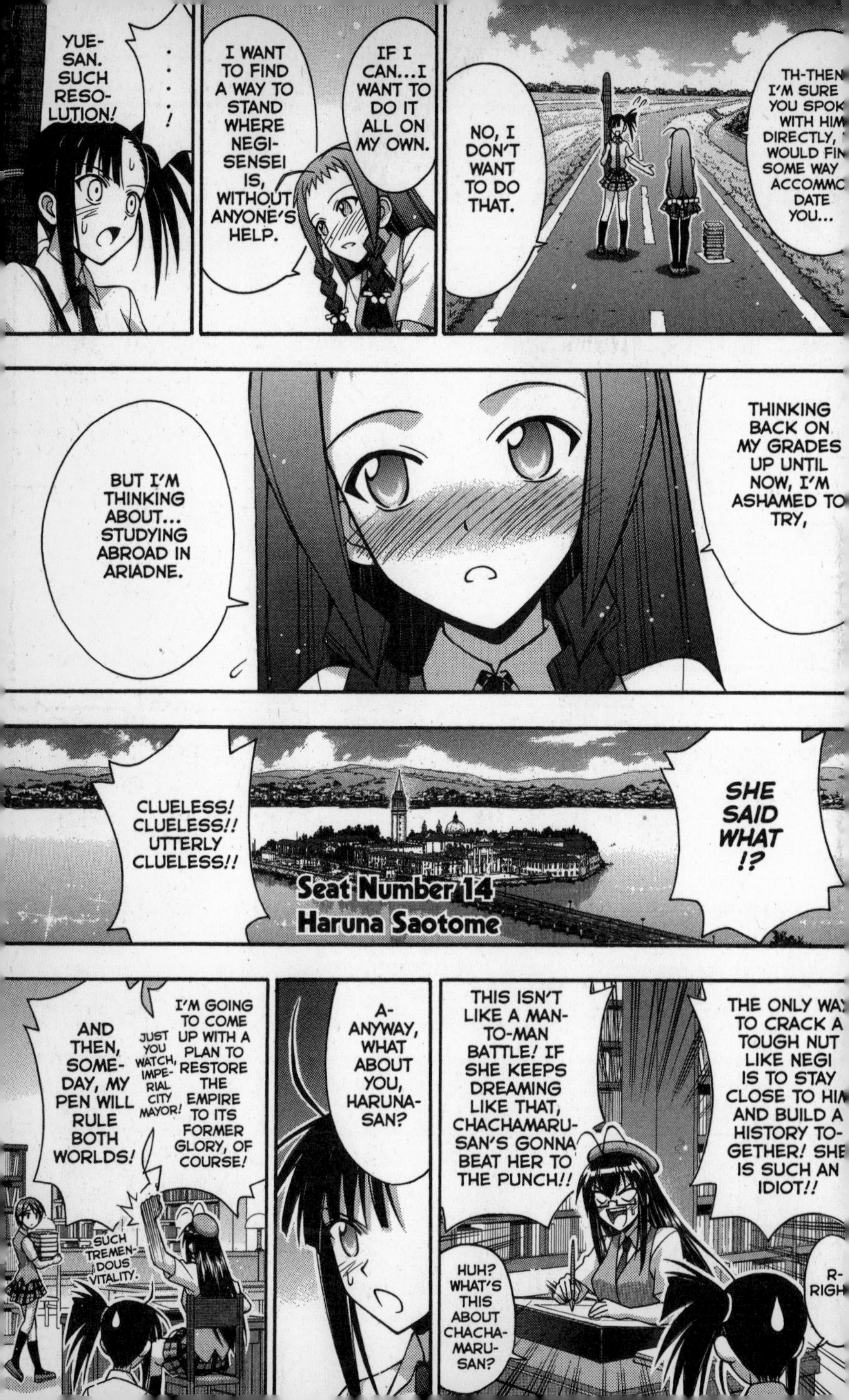
TH-THEN I'M SURE YOU SPOK WITH HIM DIRECTLY, WOULD FIN SOME WAY ACCOMMO DATE YOU...
NO, I DON'T WANT TO DO THAT.
IF I CAN...I WANT TO DO IT ALL ON MY OWN.
I WANT TO FIND A WAY TO STAND WHERE NEGI-SENSEI IS, WITHOUT ANYONE'S HELP.
....!
YUE-SAN. SUCH RESO-LUTION!
THINKING BACK ON MY GRADES UP UNTIL NOW, I'M ASHAMED TO TRY,
BUT I'M THINKING ABOUT... STUDYING ABROAD IN ARIADNE.
SHE SAID WHAT !?
CLUELESS! CLUELESS!! UTTERLY CLUELESS!!
Seat Number 14
Haruna Saotome
THE ONLY WAY TO CRACK A TOUGH NUT LIKE NEGI IS TO STAY CLOSE TO HI AND BUILD A HISTORY TO-GETHER! SHE IS SUCH AN IDIOT!!
R- RIGH
THIS ISN'T LIKE A MAN-TO-MAN BATTLE! IF SHE KEEPS DREAMING LIKE THAT, CHACHAMARU-SAN'S GONNA BEAT HER TO THE PUNCH!!
HUH? WHAT'S THIS ABOUT CHACHA-MARU-SAN?
A- ANYWAY, WHAT ABOUT YOU, HARUNA-SAN?
I'M GOING TO COME UP WITH A PLAN TO RESTORE THE EMPIRE TO ITS FORMER GLORY, OF COURSE!
JUST YOU WATCH, IMPE-RIAL CITY MAYOR!
AND THEN, SOME-DAY, MY PEN WILL RULE BOTH WORLDS!
SUCH TREMEN-DOUS VITALITY.

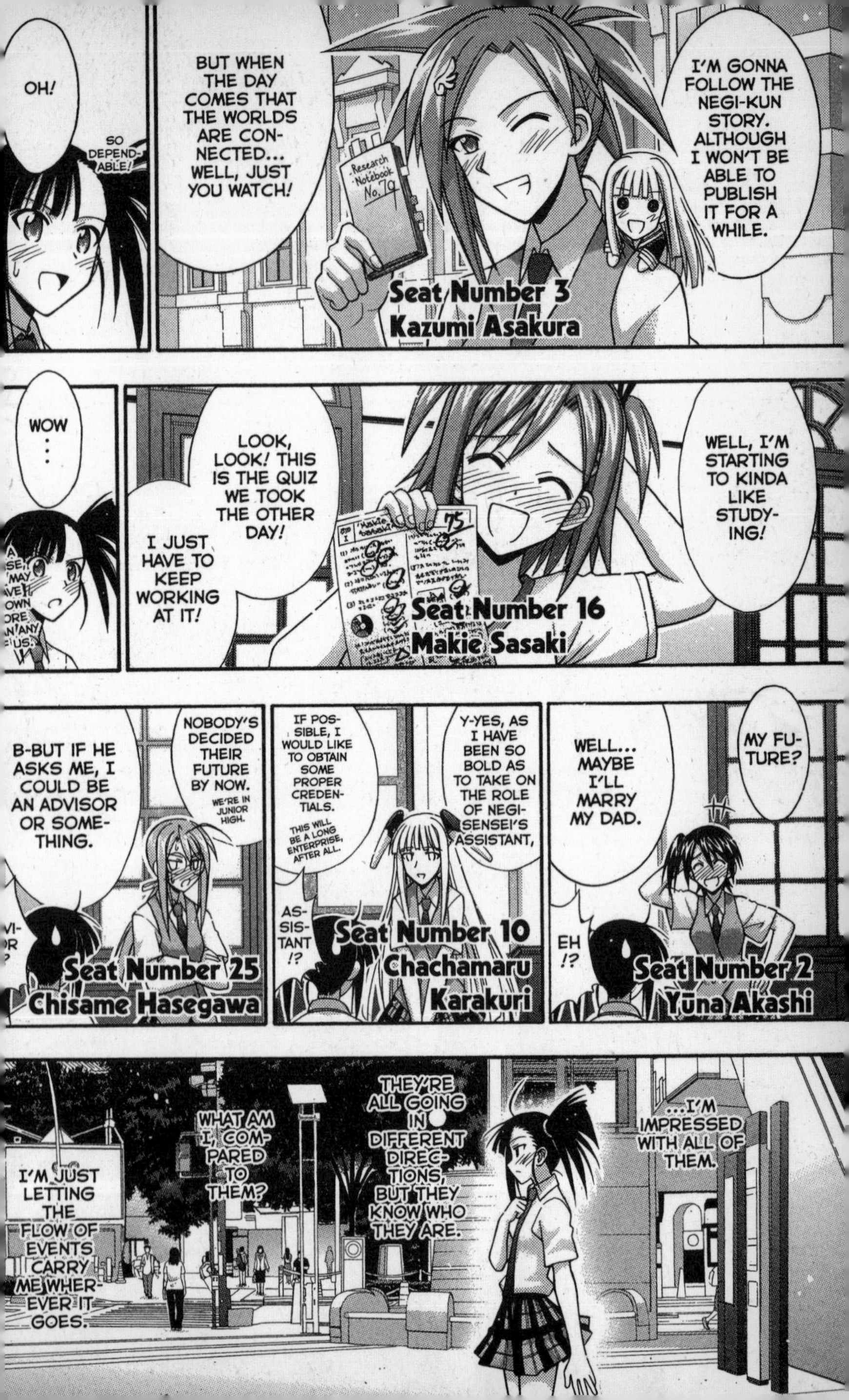
I'M GONNA FOLLOW THE NEGI-KUN STORY. ALTHOUGH I WON'T BE ABLE TO PUBLISH IT FOR A WHILE.
BUT WHEN THE DAY COMES THAT THE WORLDS ARE CONNECTED... WELL, JUST YOU WATCH!
Research Notebook No.79
Seat Number 3 Kazumi Asakura
OH!
SO DEPENDABLE!
WELL, I'M STARTING TO KINDA LIKE STUDYING!
LOOK, LOOK! THIS IS THE QUIZ WE TOOK THE OTHER DAY!
I JUST HAVE TO KEEP WORKING AT IT!
75
Seat Number 16 Makie Sasaki
WOW...
MY FUTURE?
WELL... MAYBE I'LL MARRY MY DAD.
EH!?
Seat Number 2 Yūna Akashi
Y-YES, AS I HAVE BEEN SO BOLD AS TO TAKE ON THE ROLE OF NEGI-SENSEI'S ASSISTANT,
IF POSSIBLE, I WOULD LIKE TO OBTAIN SOME PROPER CREDENTIALS.
THIS WILL BE A LONG ENTERPRISE, AFTER ALL.
ASSISTANT!?
Seat Number 10 Chachamaru Karakuri
NOBODY'S DECIDED THEIR FUTURE BY NOW.
WE'RE IN JUNIOR HIGH.
B-BUT IF HE ASKS ME, I COULD BE AN ADVISOR OR SOMETHING.
Seat Number 25 Chisame Hasegawa
...I'M IMPRESSED WITH ALL OF THEM.
THEY'RE ALL GOING IN DIFFERENT DIRECTIONS, BUT THEY KNOW WHO THEY ARE.
WHAT AM I, COMPARED TO THEM?
I'M JUST LETTING THE FLOW OF EVENTS CARRY ME WHEREVER IT GOES.

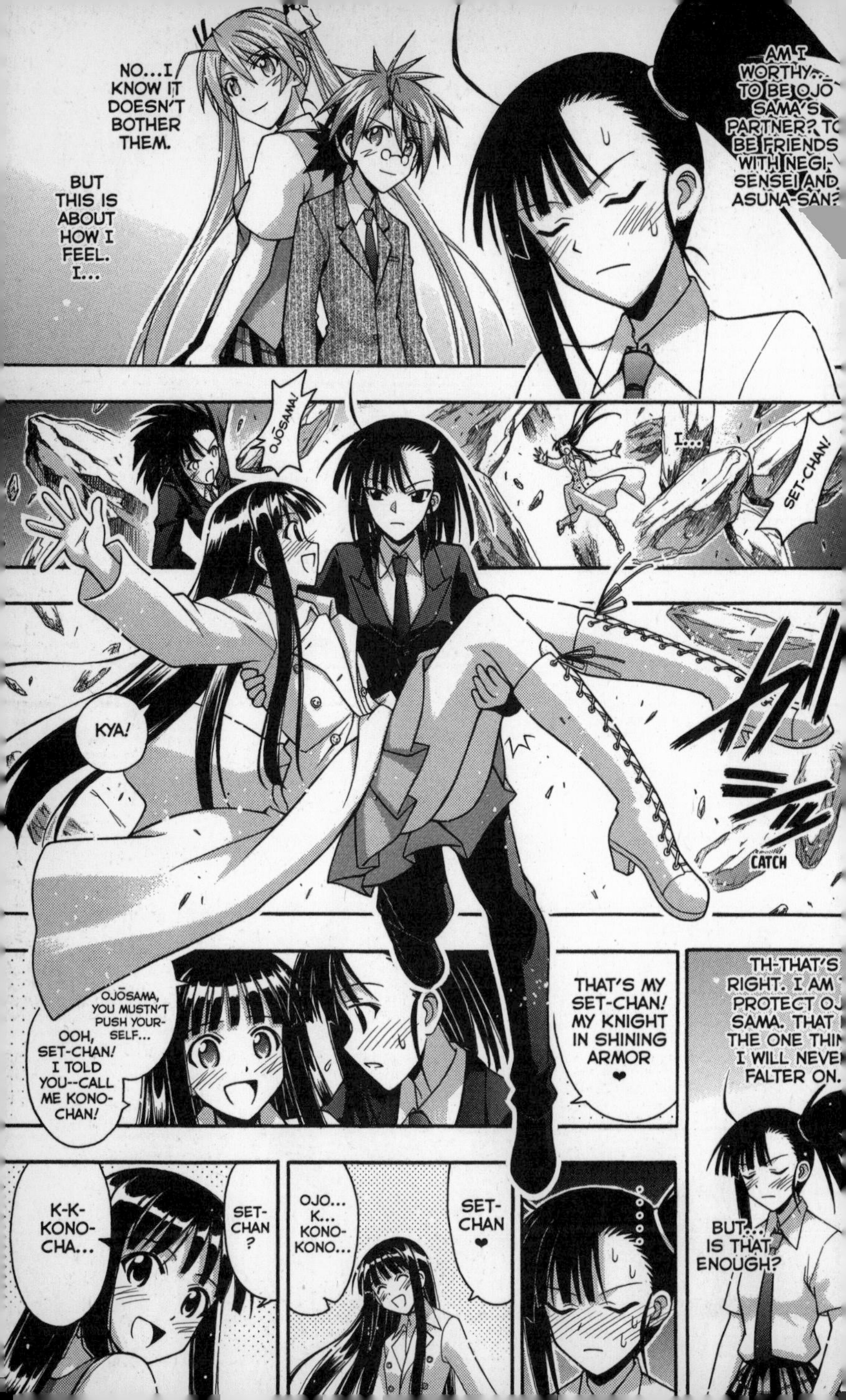
AM I WORTHY... TO BE OJO SAMA'S PARTNER? TO BE FRIENDS WITH NEGI-SENSEI AND ASUNA-SAN?
NO...I KNOW IT DOESN'T BOTHER THEM.
BUT THIS IS ABOUT HOW I FEEL. I...
SET-CHAN!
I...
OJŌSAMA!
KYA!
CATCH
TH-THAT'S RIGHT. I AM PROTECT OJ SAMA. THAT THE ONE THIN I WILL NEVE FALTER ON.
THAT'S MY SET-CHAN! MY KNIGHT IN SHINING ARMOR ❤
OJŌSAMA, YOU MUSTN'T PUSH YOUR-SELF...
OOH, SET-CHAN! I TOLD YOU--CALL ME KONO-CHAN!
BUT... IS THAT ENOUGH?
SET-CHAN ❤
OJO... K... KONO-KONO...
SET-CHAN ?
K-K-KONO-CHA...

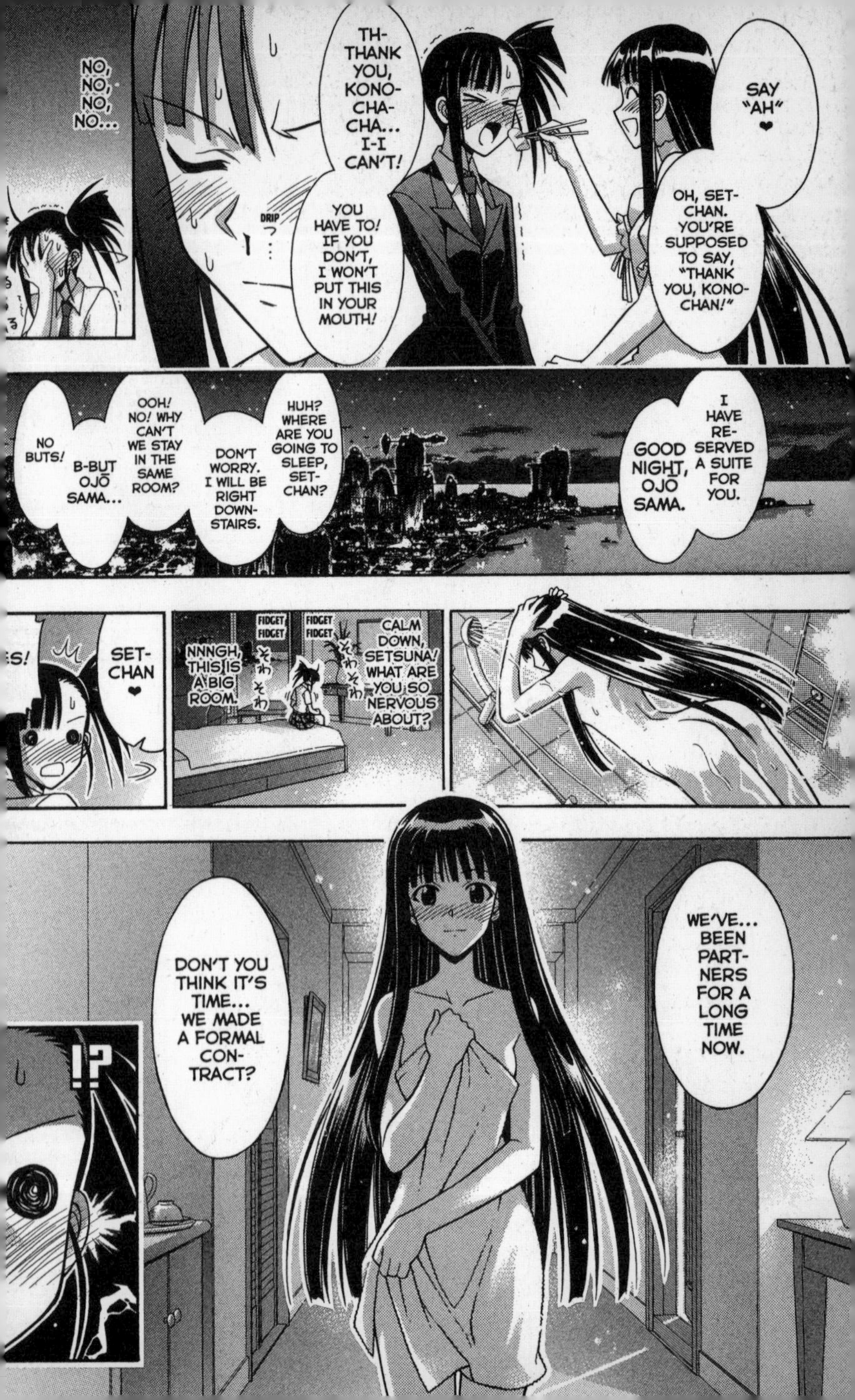
SAY "AH" ❤
OH, SET-CHAN. YOU'RE SUPPOSED TO SAY, "THANK YOU, KONO-CHAN!"
TH-THANK YOU, KONO-CHACHA... I-I CAN'T!
YOU HAVE TO! IF YOU DON'T, I WON'T PUT THIS IN YOUR MOUTH!
DRIP
NO, NO, NO, NO...
I HAVE RE-SERVED A SUITE FOR YOU.
GOOD NIGHT, OJŌ SAMA.
HUH? WHERE ARE YOU GOING TO SLEEP, SET-CHAN?
DON'T WORRY. I WILL BE RIGHT DOWN-STAIRS.
OOH! NO! WHY CAN'T WE STAY IN THE SAME ROOM?
B-BUT OJŌ SAMA...
NO BUTS!
CALM DOWN, SETSUNA! WHAT ARE YOU SO NERVOUS ABOUT?
FIDGET FIDGET
そわそわ
FIDGET FIDGET
そわそわ
NNNGH, THIS IS A BIG ROOM.
SET-CHAN ❤
WE'VE... BEEN PART-NERS FOR A LONG TIME NOW.
DON'T YOU THINK IT'S TIME... WE MADE A FORMAL CON-TRACT?
!?

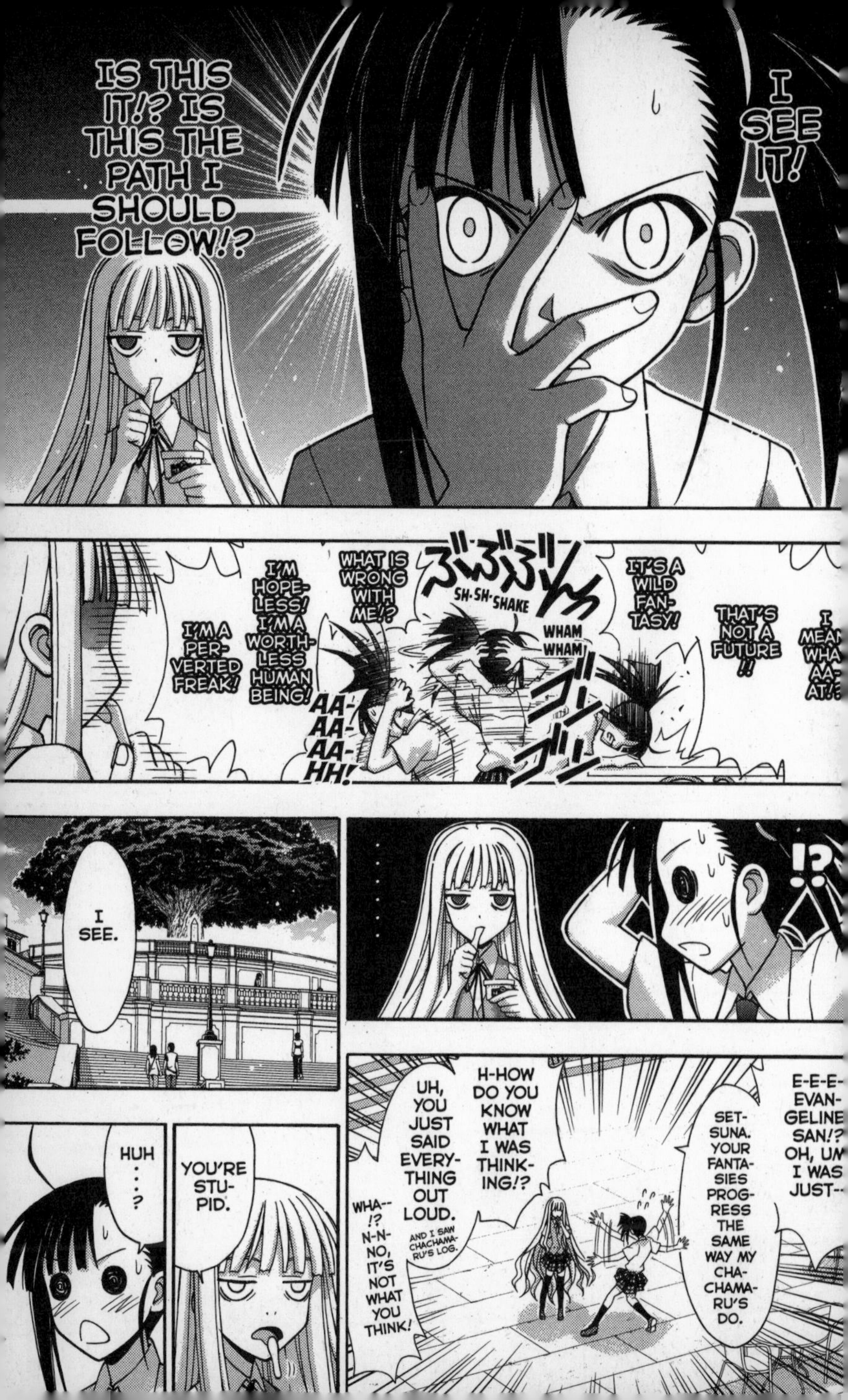
I SEE IT!
IS THIS IT!? IS THIS THE PATH I SHOULD FOLLOW!?
I MEAN WHA AA- AT!?
THAT'S NOT A FUTURE!!
IT'S A WILD FAN- TASY!
WHAM WHAM
ぶぶぶん
SH-SH-SHAKE
WHAT IS WRONG WITH ME!?
I'M HOPE- LESS! I'M A WORTH- LESS HUMAN BEING!
I'M A PER- VERTED FREAK!
AA- AA- AA- HH!
!?
I SEE.
E-E-E- EVAN- GELINE SAN!? OH, UM I WAS JUST--
SET- SUNA. YOUR FANTA- SIES PROG- RESS THE SAME WAY MY CHA- CHAMA- RU'S DO.
H-HOW DO YOU KNOW WHAT I WAS THINK- ING!?
UH, YOU JUST SAID EVERY- THING OUT LOUD.
AND I SAW CHACHAMA- RU'S LOG.
WHA-- !? N-N- NO, IT'S NOT WHAT YOU THINK!
YOU'RE STU- PID.
HUH ...?

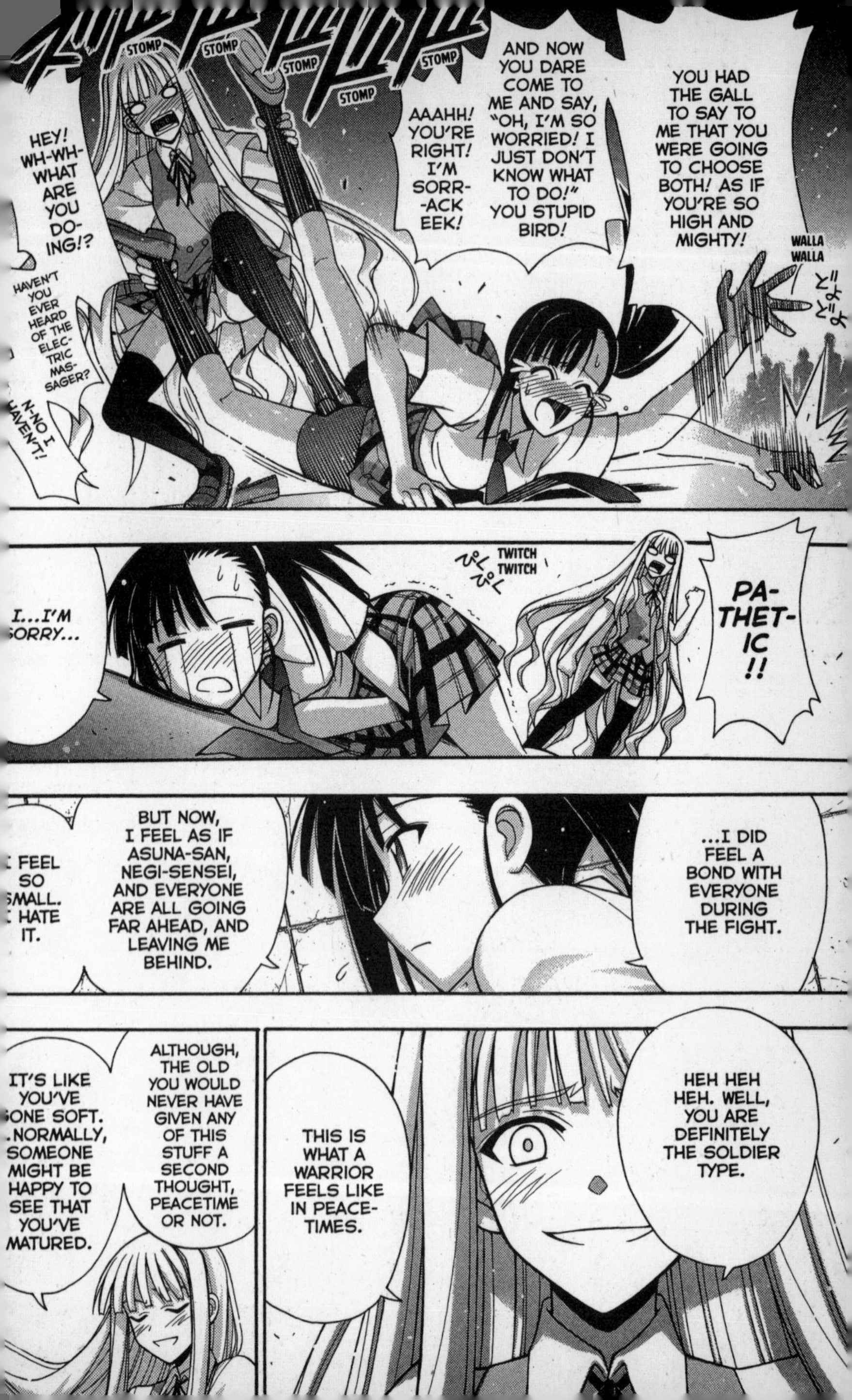
STOMP STOMP STOMP STOMP STOMP
YOU HAD THE GALL TO SAY TO ME THAT YOU WERE GOING TO CHOOSE BOTH! AS IF YOU'RE SO HIGH AND MIGHTY!
AND NOW YOU DARE COME TO ME AND SAY, "OH, I'M SO WORRIED! I JUST DON'T KNOW WHAT TO DO!" YOU STUPID BIRD!
AAAHH! YOU'RE RIGHT! I'M SORR--ACK EEK!
WALLA WALLA
HEY! WH-WH-WHAT ARE YOU DO-ING!?
HAVEN'T YOU EVER HEARD OF THE ELEC-TRIC MAS-SAGER?
N-NO I HAVEN'T!
PA-THET-IC!!
TWITCH TWITCH
I...I'M SORRY...
...I DID FEEL A BOND WITH EVERYONE DURING THE FIGHT.
BUT NOW, I FEEL AS IF ASUNA-SAN, NEGI-SENSEI, AND EVERYONE ARE ALL GOING FAR AHEAD, AND LEAVING ME BEHIND.
FEEL SO SMALL. HATE IT.
HEH HEH HEH. WELL, YOU ARE DEFINITELY THE SOLDIER TYPE.
THIS IS WHAT A WARRIOR FEELS LIKE IN PEACE-TIMES.
ALTHOUGH, THE OLD YOU WOULD NEVER HAVE GIVEN ANY OF THIS STUFF A SECOND THOUGHT, PEACETIME OR NOT.
IT'S LIKE YOU'VE ONE SOFT. NORMALLY, SOMEONE MIGHT BE HAPPY TO SEE THAT YOU'VE MATURED.

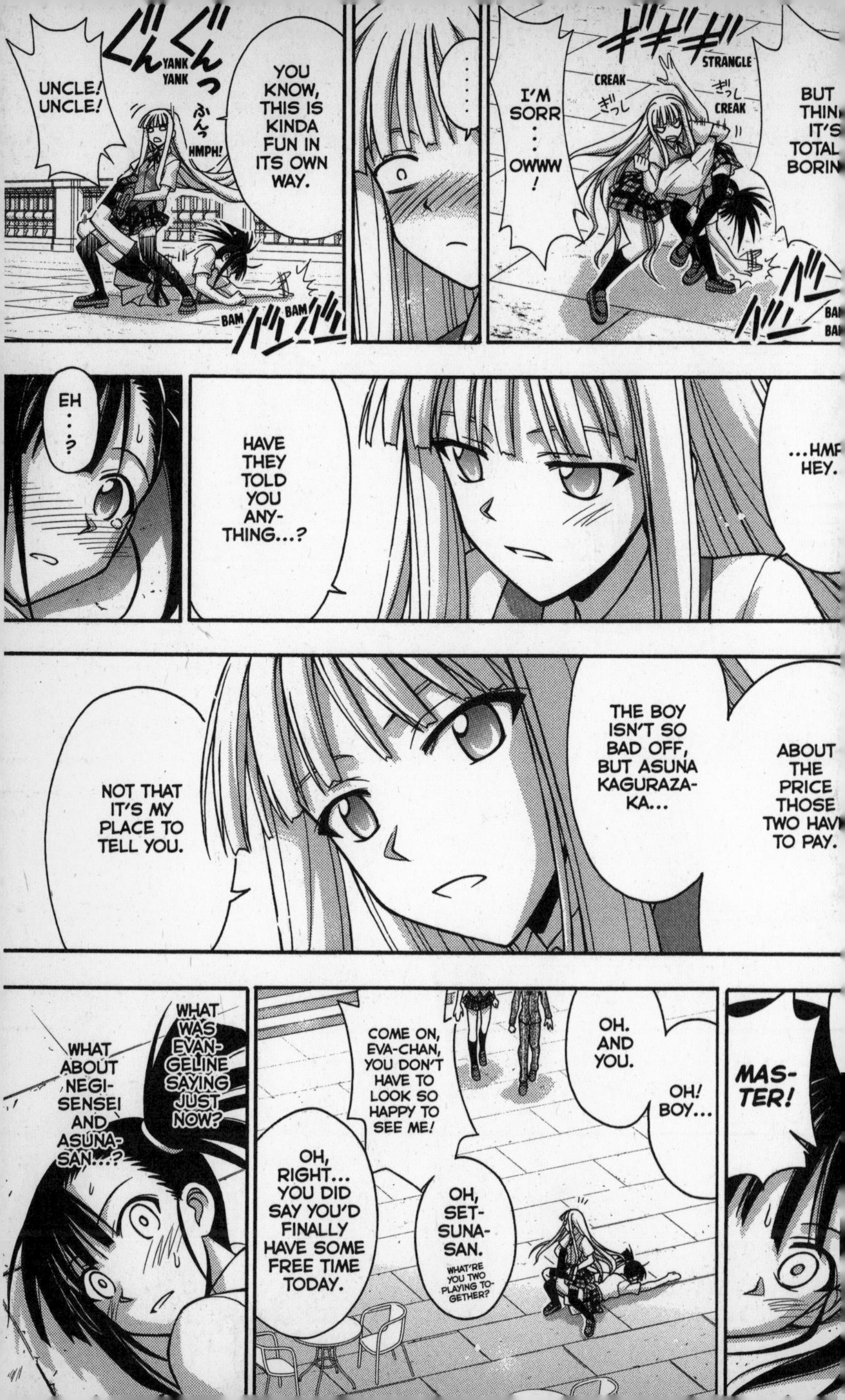
BUT THIN
IT'S
TOTAL
BORIN
STRANGLE
CREAK
ぎっし ぎっし CREAK
I'M SORR... OWWW!
......
YOU KNOW, THIS IS KINDA FUN IN ITS OWN WAY.
ぐんぐんっ YANK YANK
UNCLE! UNCLE!
ふんっ HMPH!
BAM BAM
...HMP HEY.
HAVE THEY TOLD YOU ANY-THING...?
EH...?
ABOUT THE PRICE THOSE TWO HAV TO PAY.
THE BOY ISN'T SO BAD OFF, BUT ASUNA KAGURAZA-KA...
NOT THAT IT'S MY PLACE TO TELL YOU.
MAS-TER!
OH. AND YOU.
OH! BOY...
COME ON, EVA-CHAN, YOU DON'T HAVE TO LOOK SO HAPPY TO SEE ME!
OH, SET-SUNA-SAN.
WHAT'RE YOU TWO PLAYING TO-GETHER?
OH, RIGHT... YOU DID SAY YOU'D FINALLY HAVE SOME FREE TIME TODAY.
WHAT WAS EVAN-GELINE SAYING JUST NOW?
WHAT ABOUT NEGI-SENSEI AND ASUNA-SAN...?

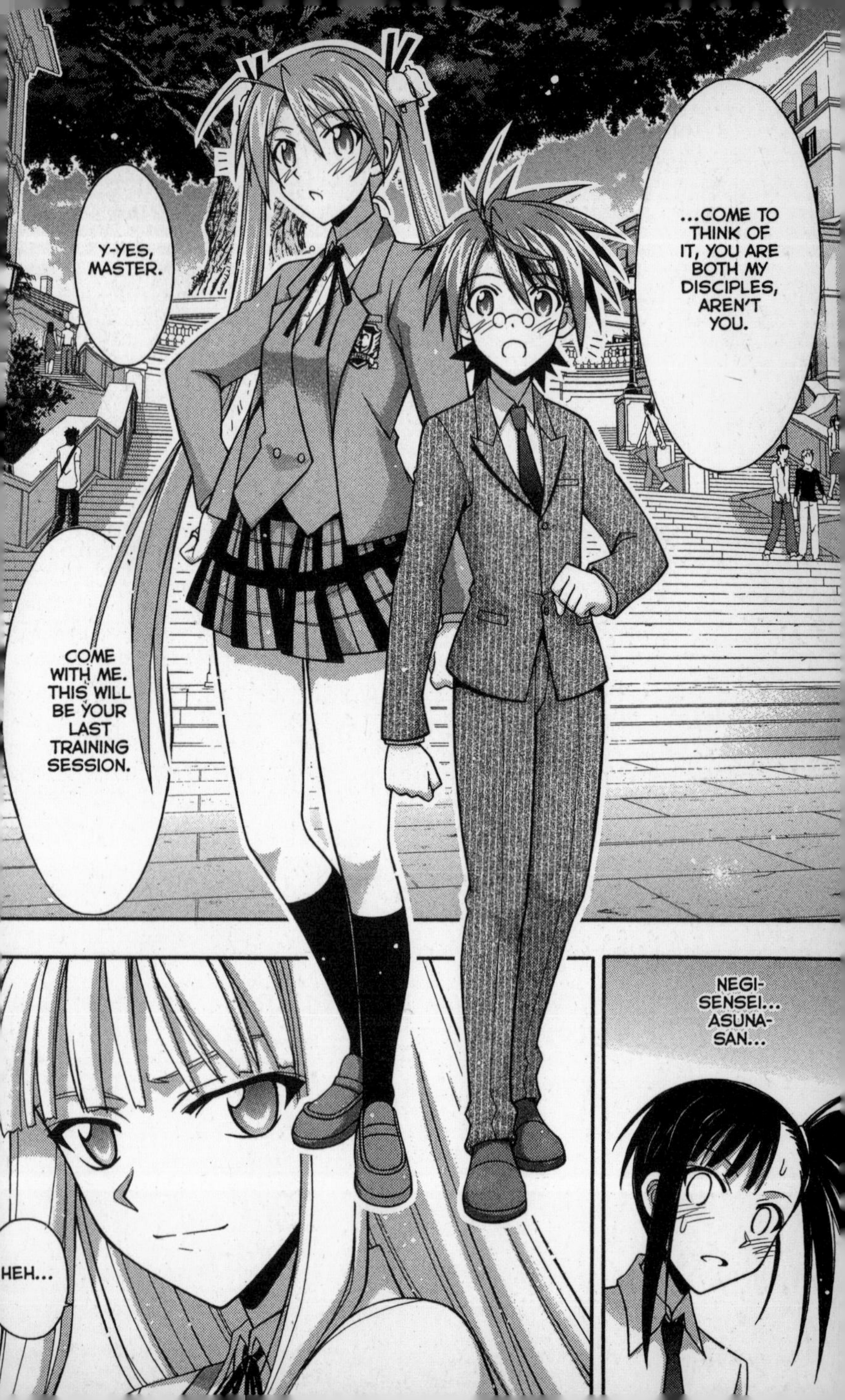
...COME TO THINK OF IT, YOU ARE BOTH MY DISCIPLES, AREN'T YOU.
Y-YES, MASTER.
COME WITH ME. THIS WILL BE YOUR LAST TRAINING SESSION.
NEGI-SENSEI... ASUNA-SAN...
HEH...

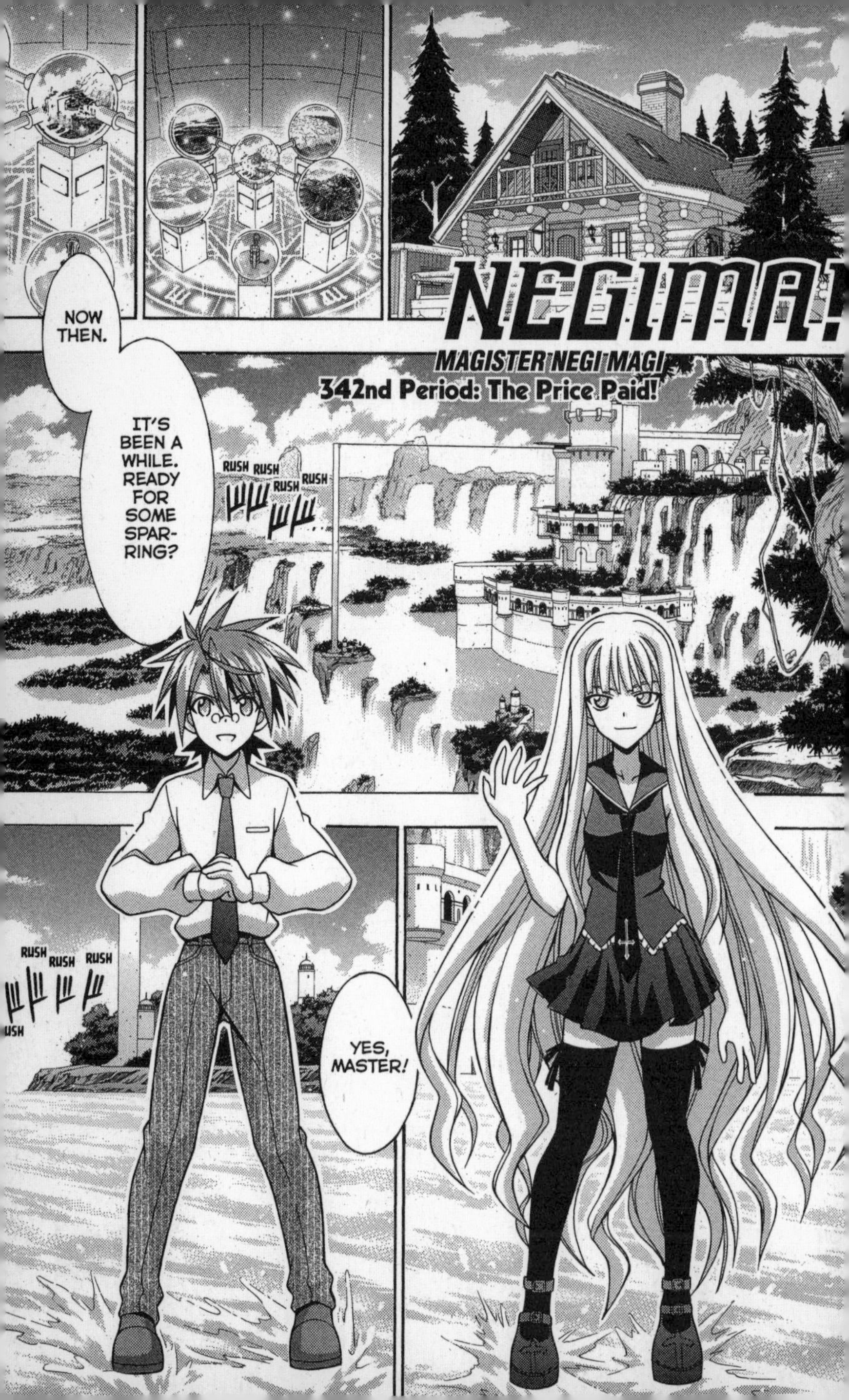
NEGIMA!
MAGISTER NEGI MAGI
342nd Period: The Price Paid!
NOW THEN.
IT'S BEEN A WHILE. READY FOR SOME SPAR-RING?
RUSH RUSH RUSH RUSH
YES, MASTER!
RUSH RUSH RUSH
USH

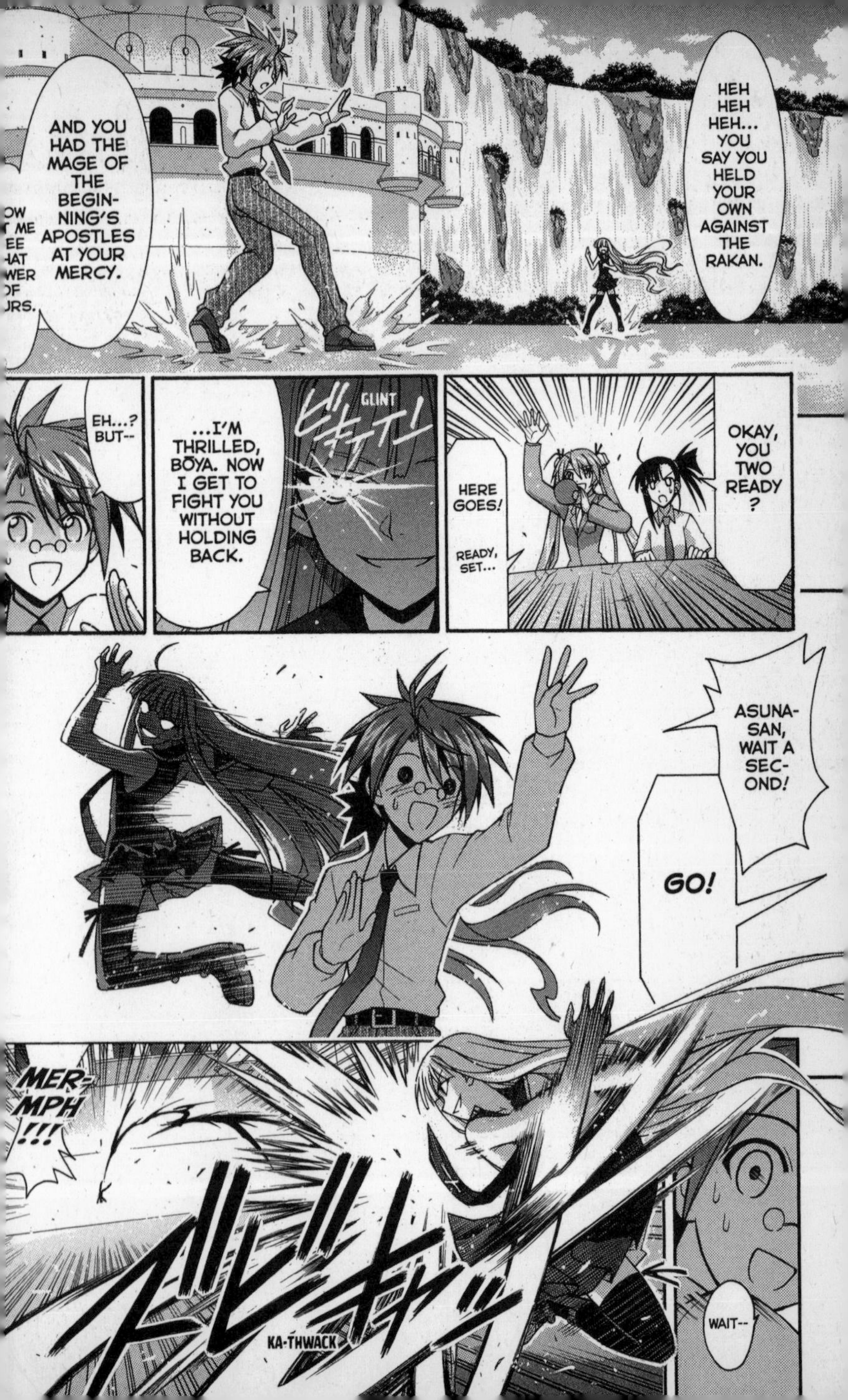
HEH HEH HEH... YOU SAY YOU HELD YOUR OWN AGAINST THE RAKAN.
AND YOU HAD THE MAGE OF THE BEGINNING'S APOSTLES AT YOUR MERCY.
OKAY, YOU TWO READY?
HERE GOES!
READY, SET...
GLINT
...I'M THRILLED, BŌYA. NOW I GET TO FIGHT YOU WITHOUT HOLDING BACK.
EH...? BUT--
ASUNA-SAN, WAIT A SECOND!
GO!
WAIT--
KA-THWACK
MERMPH!!!...

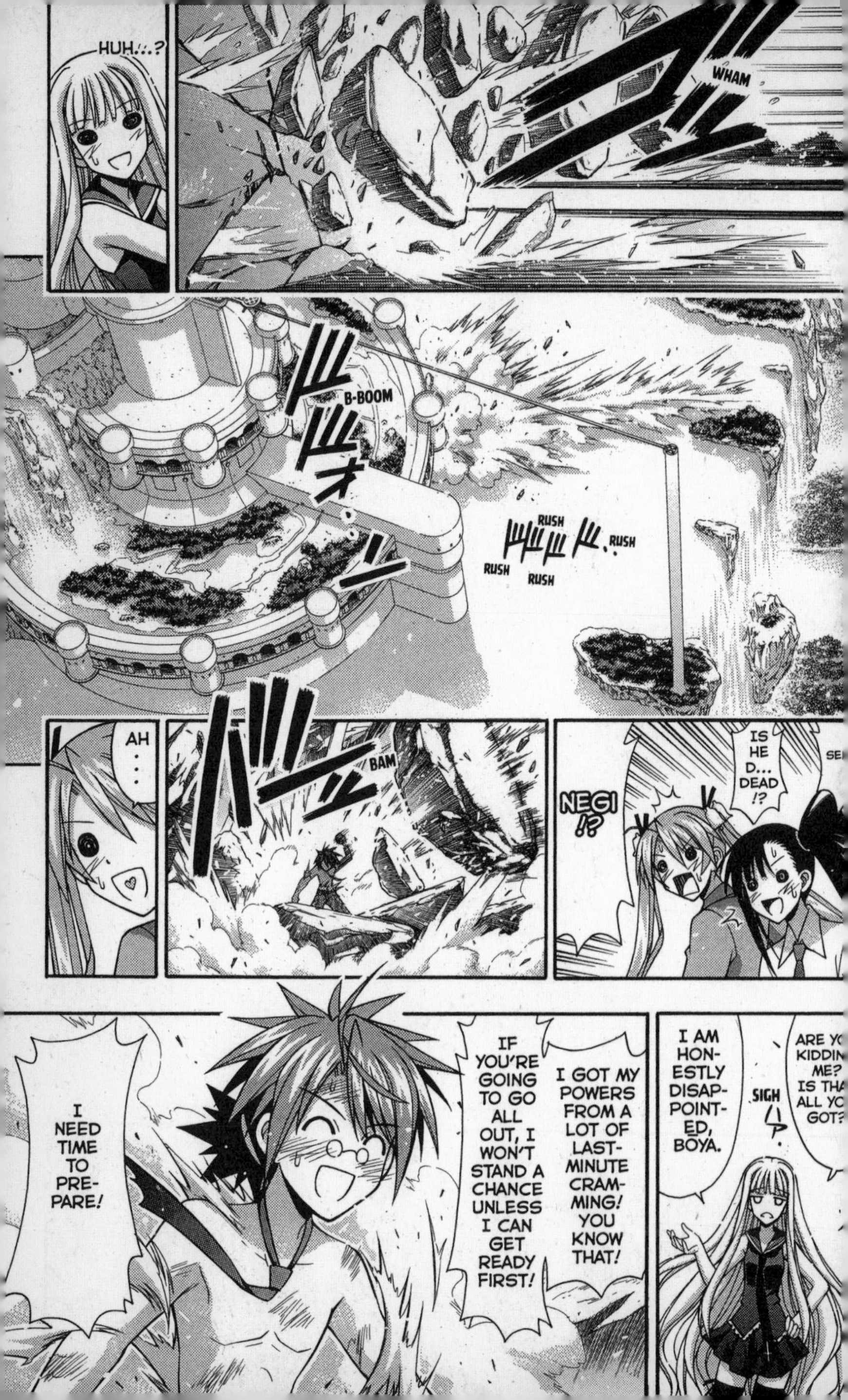
WHAM
HUH!?..?
B-BOOM
RUSH RUSH RUSH RUSH
IS HE D... DEAD!?
NEGI!?
BAM
AH...
ARE YOU KIDDING ME? IS THAT ALL YOU GOT?
SIGH
I AM HON-ESTLY DISAP-POINT-ED, BOYA.
I GOT MY POWERS FROM A LOT OF LAST-MINUTE CRAM-MING! YOU KNOW THAT!
IF YOU'RE GOING TO GO ALL OUT, I WON'T STAND A CHANCE UNLESS I CAN GET READY FIRST!
I NEED TIME TO PRE-PARE!

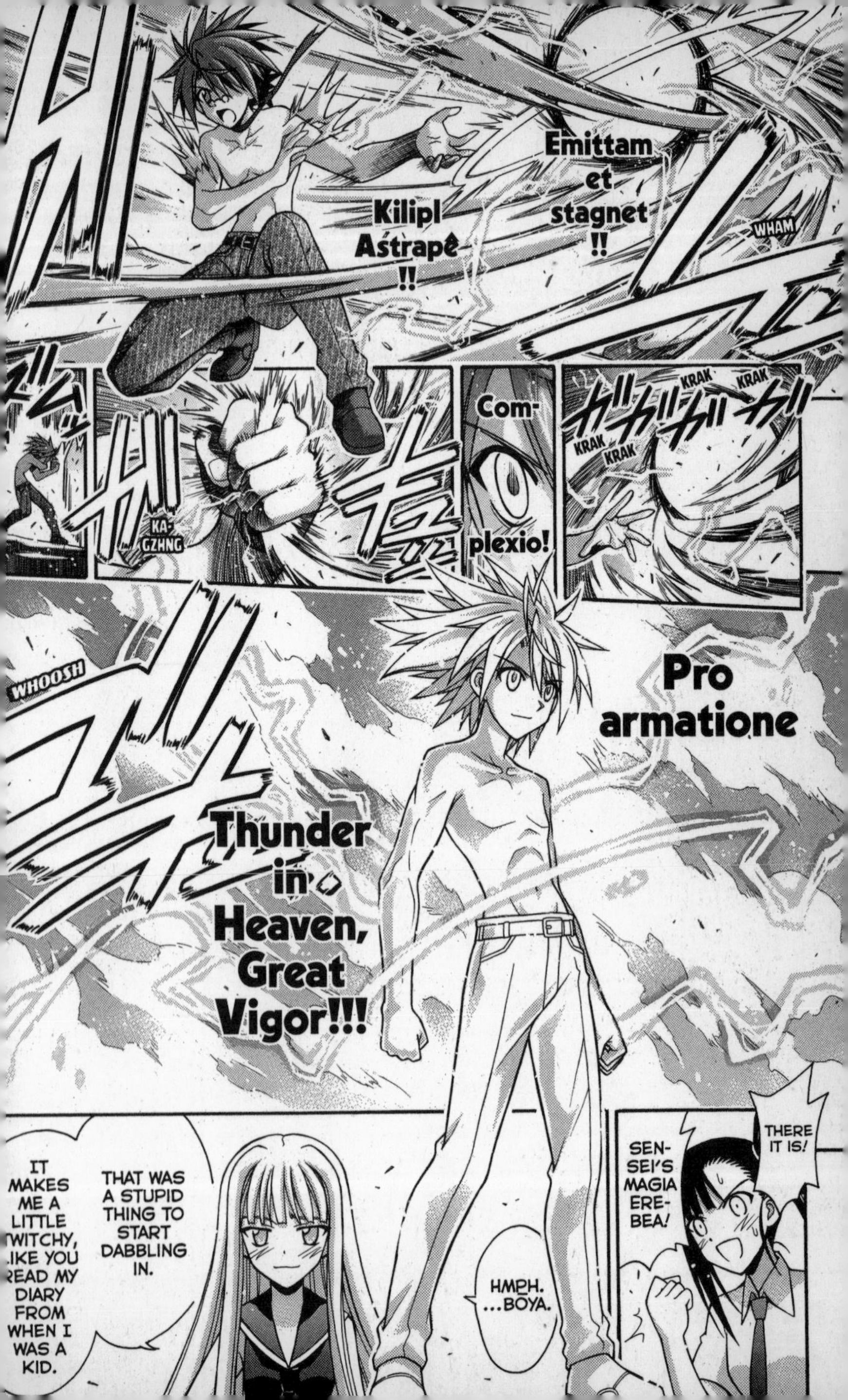
Emittam et stagnet!!
WHAM
Kilipl Astrapê!!
KRAK
KRAK
KRAK
KRAK
Com-plexio!
KA-GZHNG
Pro armatione
Thunder in Heaven, Great Vigor!!!
WHOOSH
THERE IT IS!
SEN-SEI'S MAGIA ERE-BEA!
HMPH. ...BOYA.
THAT WAS A STUPID THING TO START DABBLING IN.
IT MAKES ME A LITTLE TWITCHY, LIKE YOU READ MY DIARY FROM WHEN I WAS A KID.

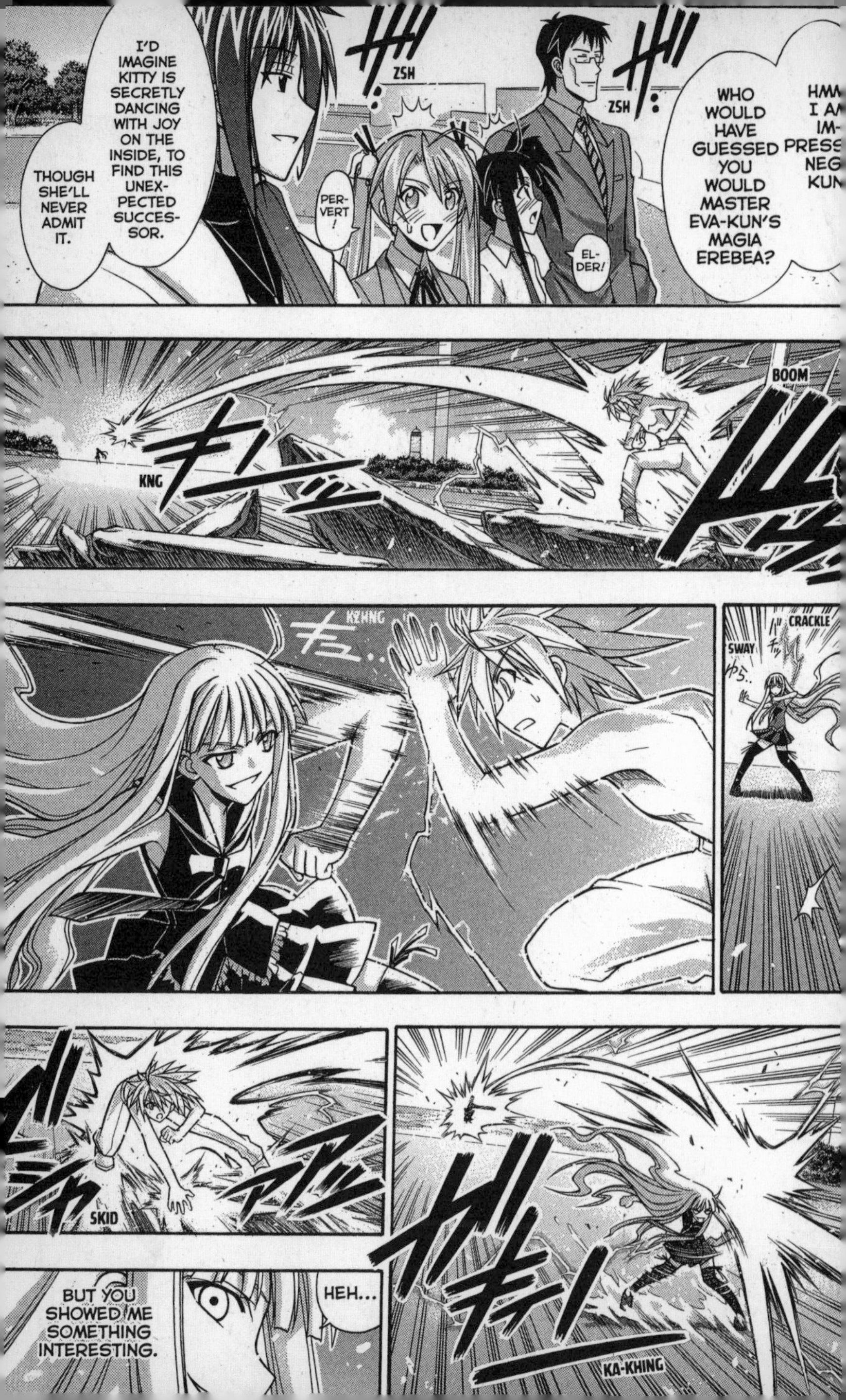
HMM I AM IM- PRESS NEG KUN
WHO WOULD HAVE GUESSED YOU WOULD MASTER EVA-KUN'S MAGIA EREBEA?
ZSH
EL- DER!
PER- VERT!
ZSH
I'D IMAGINE KITTY IS SECRETLY DANCING WITH JOY ON THE INSIDE, TO FIND THIS UNEX- PECTED SUCCES- SOR.
THOUGH SHE'LL NEVER ADMIT IT.
BOOM
KNG
CRACKLE
SWAY
KYHNG
KA-KHING
SKID
HEH...
BUT YOU SHOWED ME SOMETHING INTERESTING.

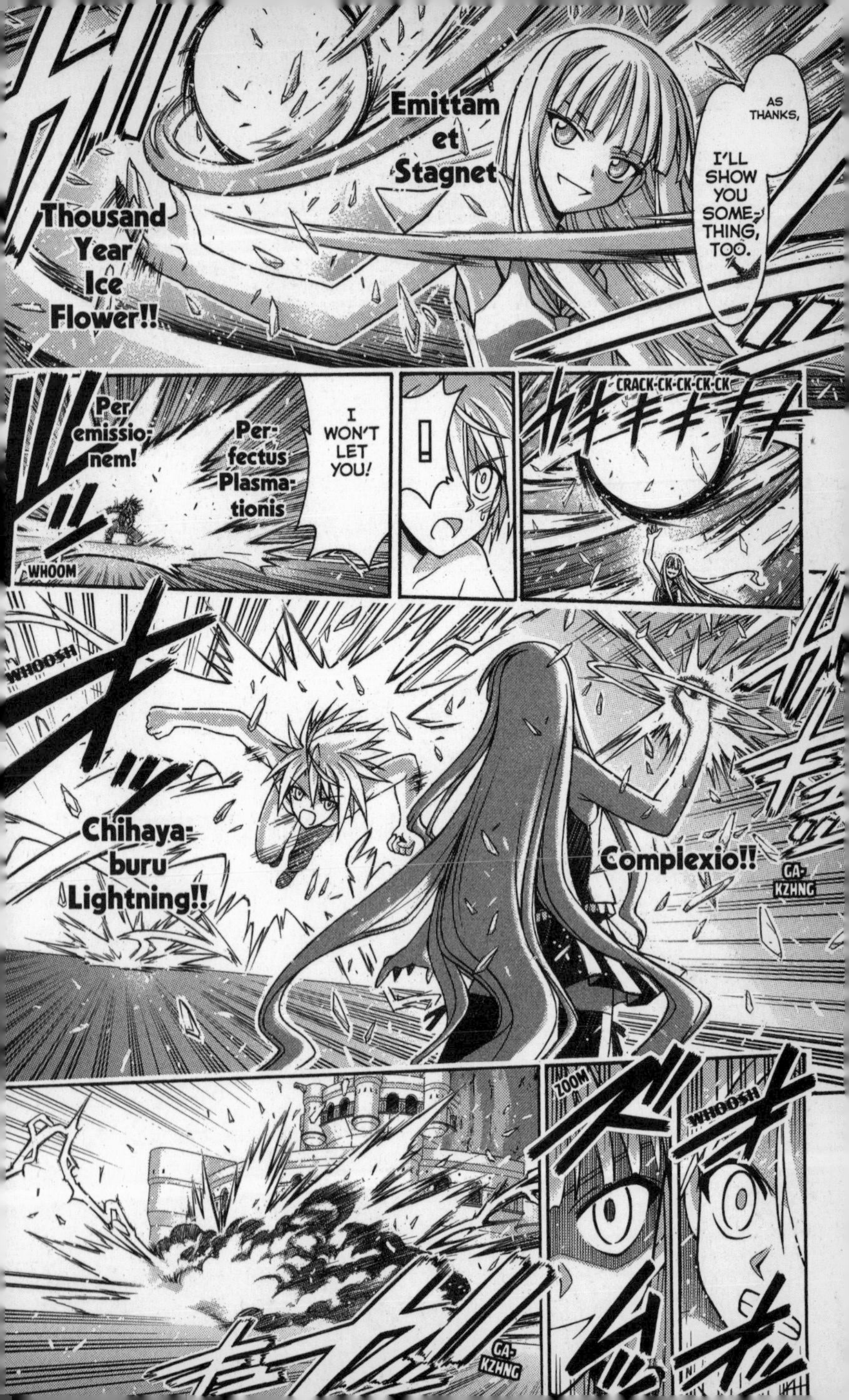

AS THANKS, I'LL SHOW YOU SOMETHING, TOO.
Emittam et Stagnet
Thousand Year Ice Flower!!
CRACK-CK-CK-CK-CK
!
I WON'T LET YOU!
Perfectus Plasmationis
Per emissionem!
WHOOM
GA-KZHNG
Complexio!!
Chihayaburu Lightning!!
WHOOSH
WHOOSH
ZOOM
GA-KZHNG

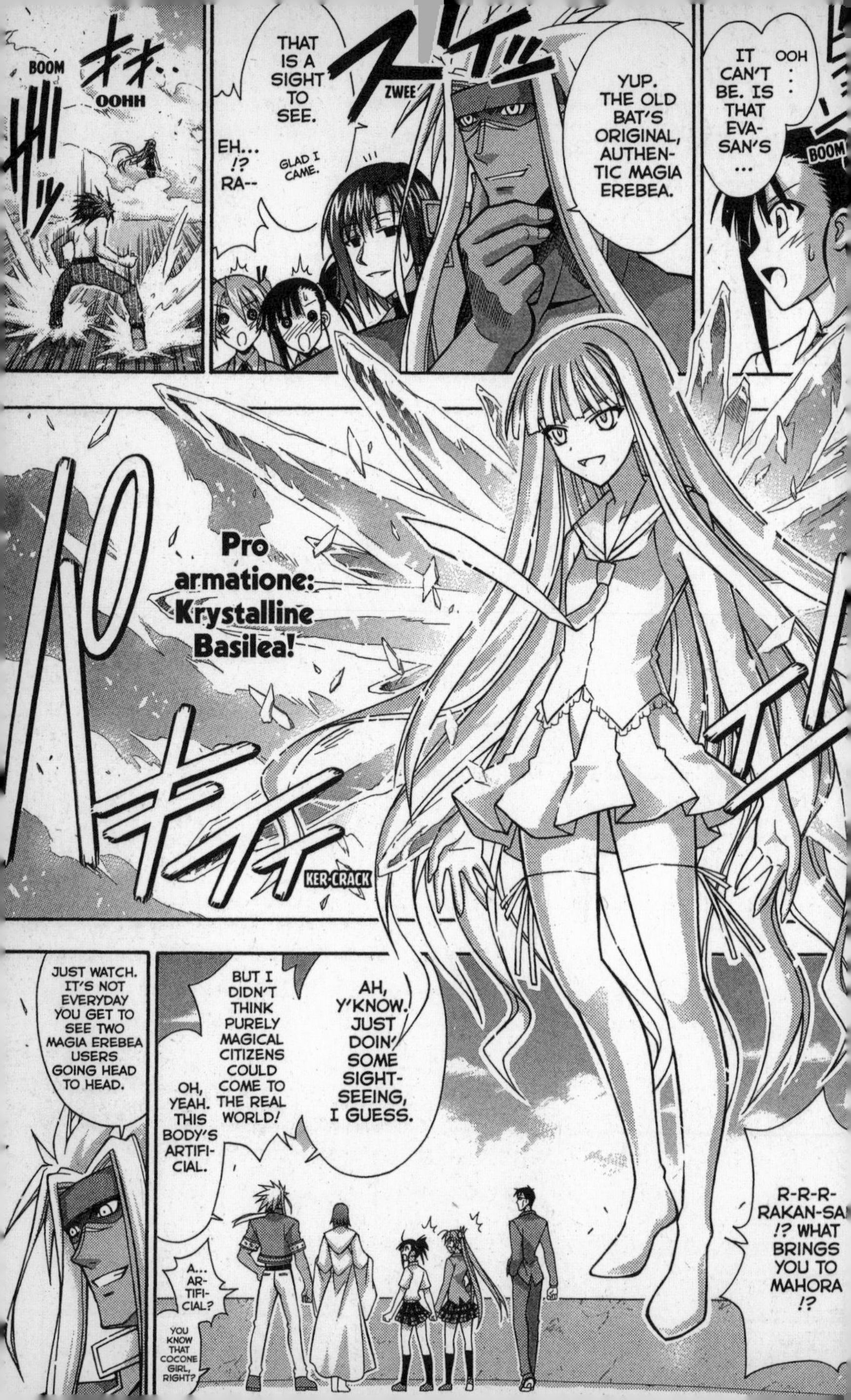

OOH...
IT CAN'T BE. IS THAT EVA-SAN'S ...
BOOM
ZWEE
YUP. THE OLD BAT'S ORIGINAL, AUTHENTIC MAGIA EREBEA.
THAT IS A SIGHT TO SEE.
GLAD I CAME.
EH... !? RA--
BOOM
OOHH
Pro armatione: Krystalline Basilea!
KER-CRACK
R-R-R-RAKAN-SA !? WHAT BRINGS YOU TO MAHORA !?
AH, Y'KNOW. JUST DOIN' SOME SIGHT-SEEING, I GUESS.
BUT I DIDN'T THINK PURELY MAGICAL CITIZENS COULD COME TO THE REAL WORLD!
OH, YEAH. THIS BODY'S ARTIFICIAL.
A... ARTIFICIAL?
YOU KNOW THAT COCONE GIRL, RIGHT?
JUST WATCH. IT'S NOT EVERYDAY YOU GET TO SEE TWO MAGIA EREBEA USERS GOING HEAD TO HEAD.

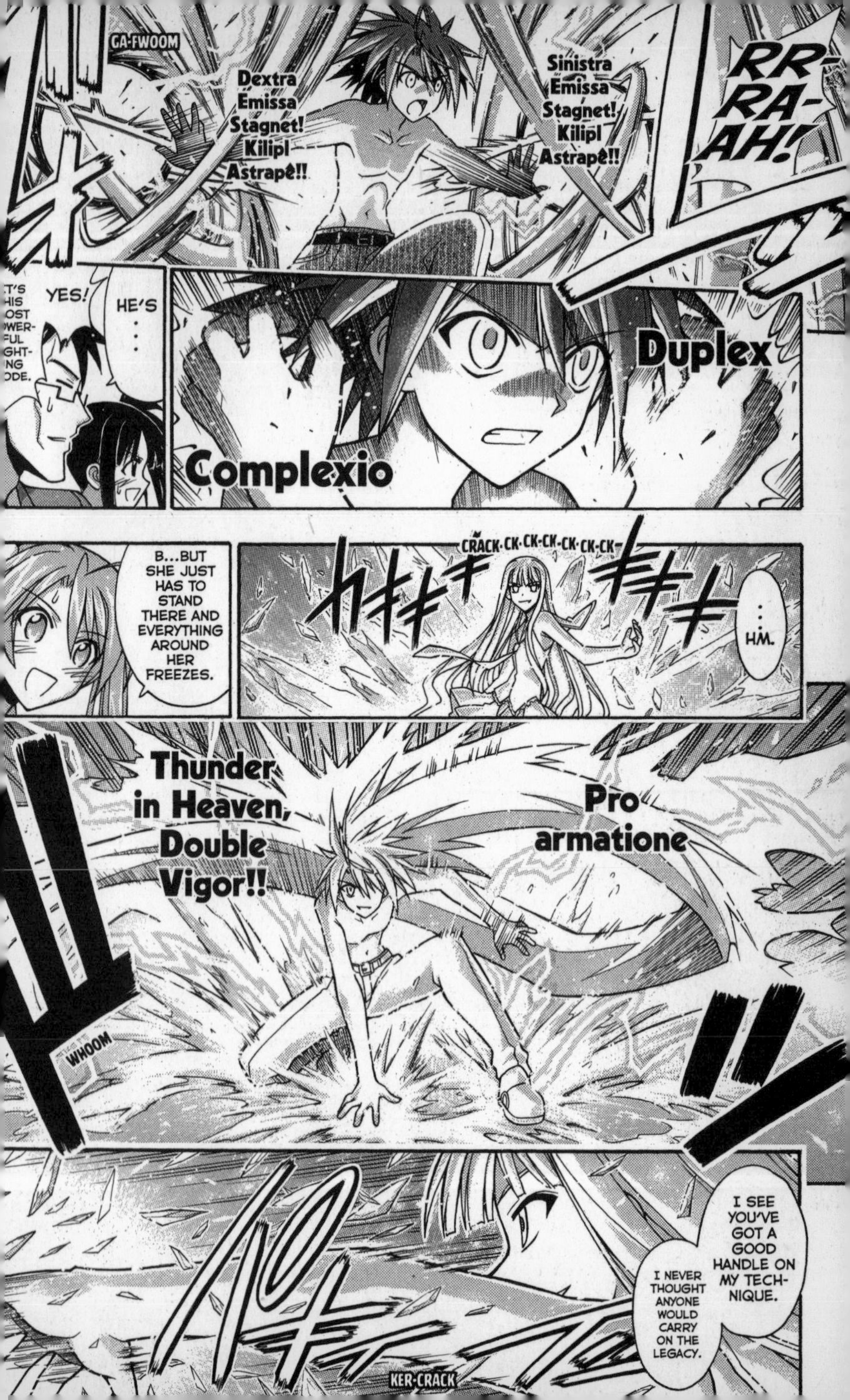
RR-RA-AH!
Sinistra Emissa Stagnet! Kilipl Astrapê!!
Dextra Emissa Stagnet! Kilipl Astrapê!!
GA-FWOOM
Duplex
Complexio
HE'S . . .
YES!
T'S HIS OST OWER-FUL GHT-NG ODE.
CRACK-CK-CK-CK-CK-CK-CK
. . . HM.
B...BUT SHE JUST HAS TO STAND THERE AND EVERYTHING AROUND HER FREEZES.
Pro armatione
Thunder in Heaven, Double Vigor!!
WHOOM
I SEE YOU'VE GOT A GOOD HANDLE ON MY TECH-NIQUE.
I NEVER THOUGHT ANYONE WOULD CARRY ON THE LEGACY.
KER-CRACK

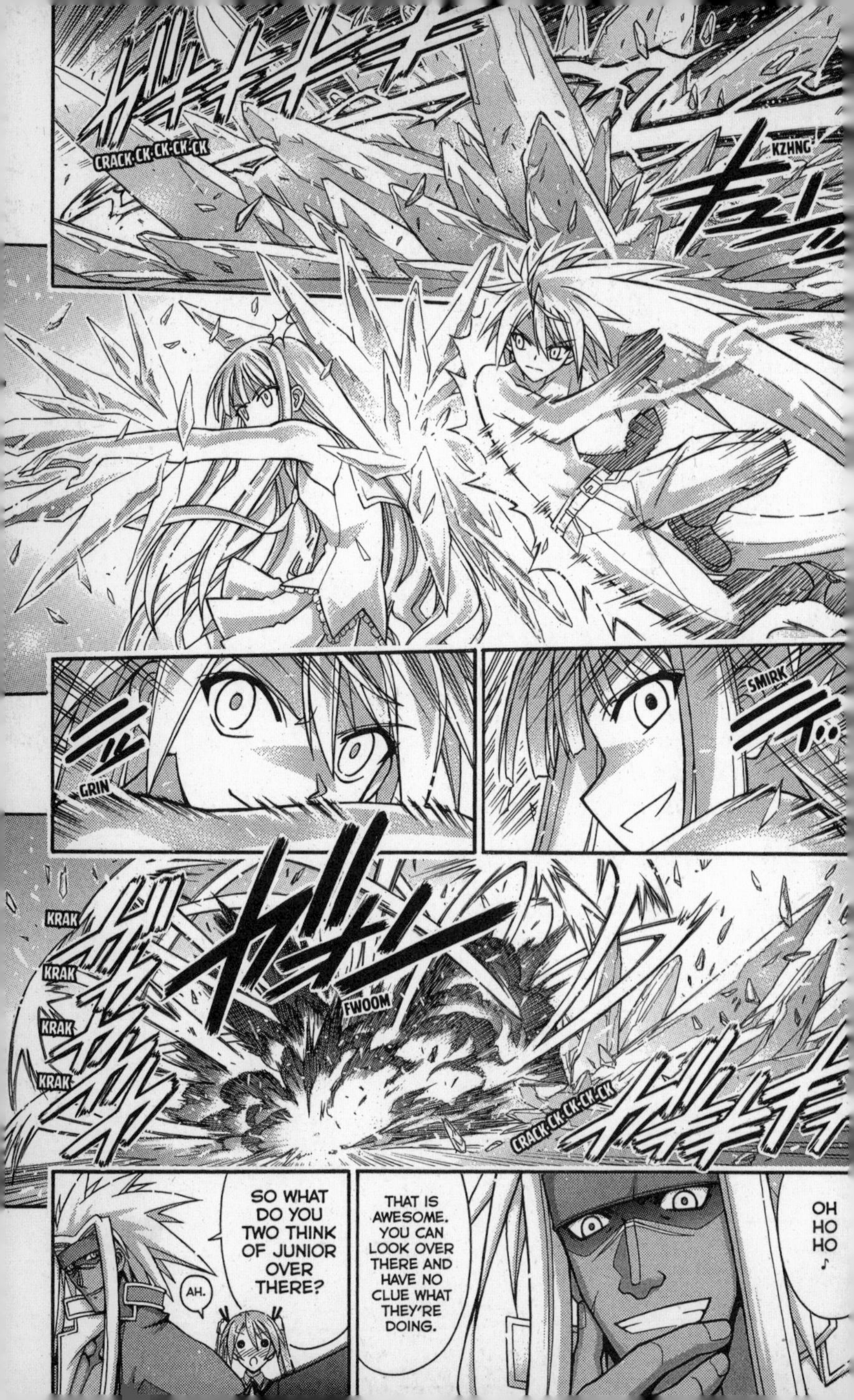
KZHNG
CRACK-CK-CK-CK-CK
SMIRK
GRIN
KRAK
KRAK
KRAK
KRAK
FWOOM
CRACK-CK-CK-CK-CK
OH HO HO ♪
THAT IS AWESOME. YOU CAN LOOK OVER THERE AND HAVE NO CLUE WHAT THEY'RE DOING.
SO WHAT DO YOU TWO THINK OF JUNIOR OVER THERE?
AH.

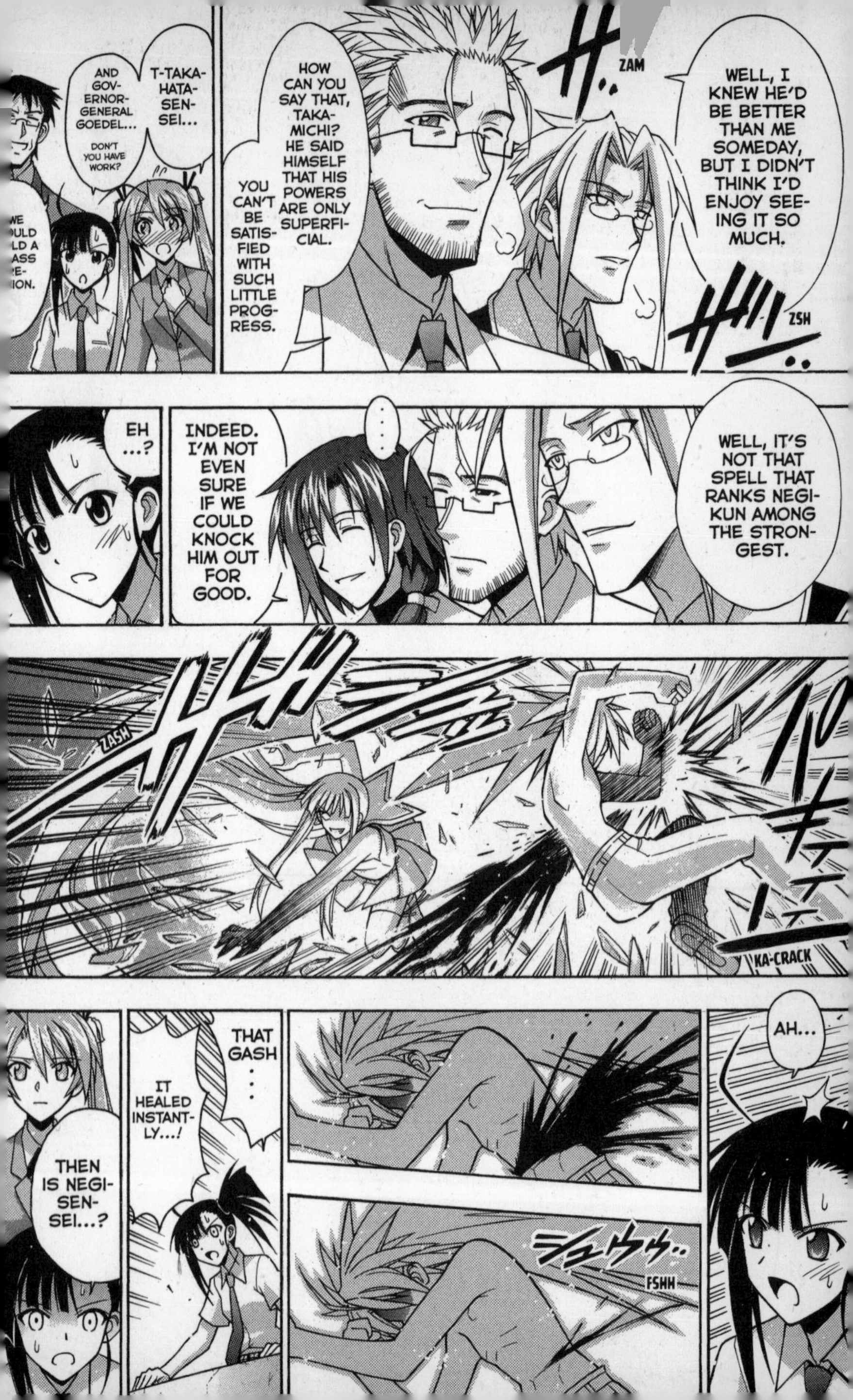
ZAM
WELL, I KNEW HE'D BE BETTER THAN ME SOMEDAY, BUT I DIDN'T THINK I'D ENJOY SEEING IT SO MUCH.
ZSH
HOW CAN YOU SAY THAT, TAKAMICHI? HE SAID HIMSELF THAT HIS POWERS ARE ONLY SUPERFICIAL.
YOU CAN'T BE SATISFIED WITH SUCH LITTLE PROGRESS.
T-TAKAHATA-SENSEI...
AND GOVERNOR-GENERAL GOEDEL...
DON'T YOU HAVE WORK?
WELL, IT'S NOT THAT SPELL THAT RANKS NEGI-KUN AMONG THE STRONGEST.
...
INDEED. I'M NOT EVEN SURE IF WE COULD KNOCK HIM OUT FOR GOOD.
EH ...?
KA-CRACK
ZASH
AH...
FSHH
THAT GASH ...
IT HEALED INSTANTLY...!
THEN IS NEGI-SENSEI...?

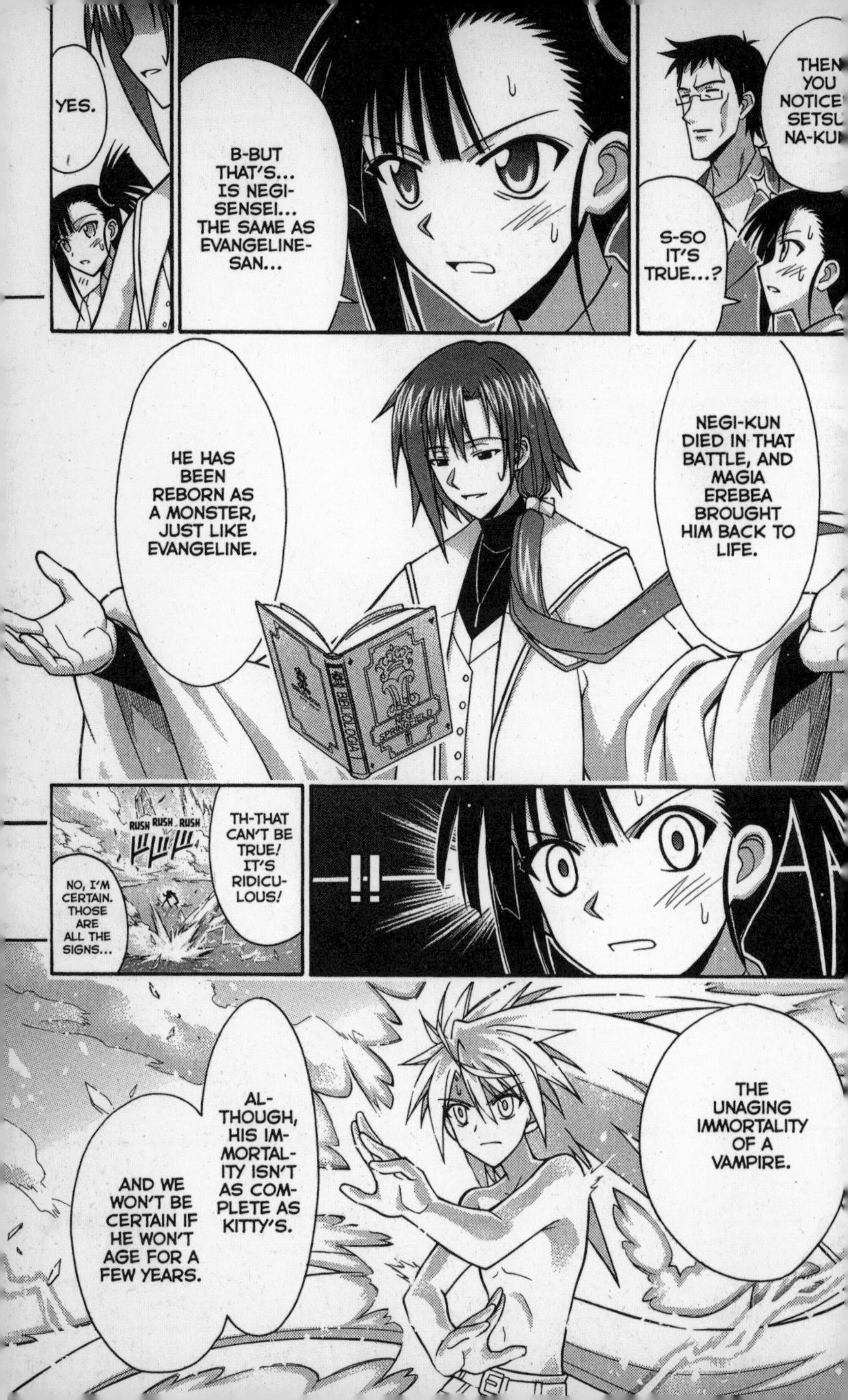
THEN YOU NOTICE SETSUNA-KU
S-SO IT'S TRUE...?
B-BUT THAT'S... IS NEGI-SENSEI... THE SAME AS EVANGELINE-SAN...
YES.
NEGI-KUN DIED IN THAT BATTLE, AND MAGIA EREBEA BROUGHT HIM BACK TO LIFE.
HE HAS BEEN REBORN AS A MONSTER, JUST LIKE EVANGELINE.
!!
TH-THAT CAN'T BE TRUE! IT'S RIDICULOUS!
RUSH RUSH RUSH
NO, I'M CERTAIN. THOSE ARE ALL THE SIGNS...
THE UNAGING IMMORTALITY OF A VAMPIRE.
ALTHOUGH, HIS IMMORTALITY ISN'T AS COMPLETE AS KITTY'S.
AND WE WON'T BE CERTAIN IF HE WON'T AGE FOR A FEW YEARS.

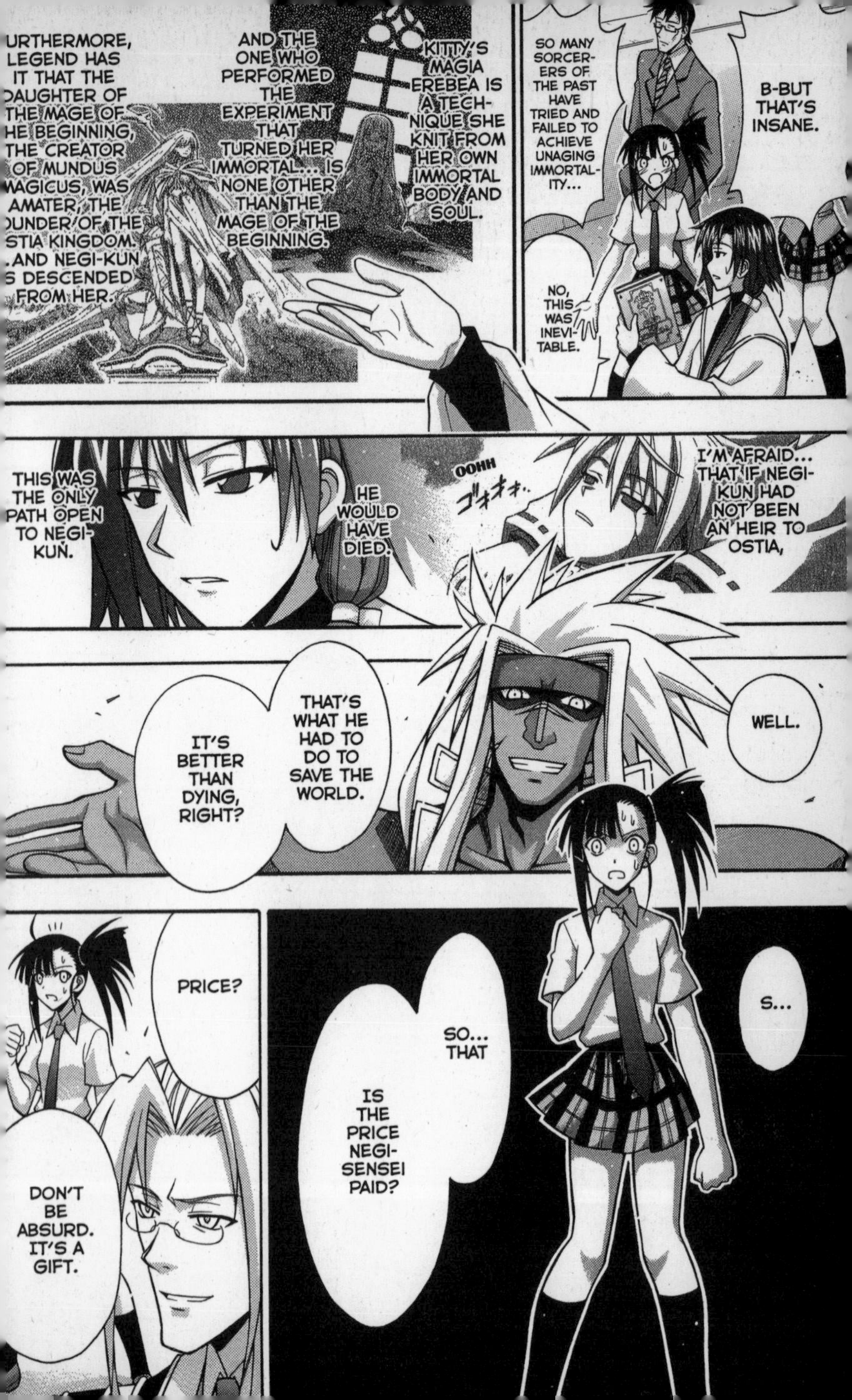
B-BUT THAT'S INSANE.
SO MANY SORCERERS OF THE PAST HAVE TRIED AND FAILED TO ACHIEVE UNAGING IMMORTALITY...
NO, THIS WAS INEVITABLE.
KITTY'S MAGIA EREBEA IS A TECHNIQUE SHE KNIT FROM HER OWN IMMORTAL BODY AND SOUL.
AND THE ONE WHO PERFORMED THE EXPERIMENT THAT TURNED HER IMMORTAL... IS NONE OTHER THAN THE MAGE OF THE BEGINNING.
FURTHERMORE, LEGEND HAS IT THAT THE DAUGHTER OF THE MAGE OF THE BEGINNING, THE CREATOR OF MUNDUS MAGICUS, WAS AMATER, THE FOUNDER OF THE OSTIA KINGDOM. ...AND NEGI-KUN IS DESCENDED FROM HER.
I'M AFRAID... THAT IF NEGI-KUN HAD NOT BEEN AN HEIR TO OSTIA,
OOHH
ゴオオオ..
HE WOULD HAVE DIED.
THIS WAS THE ONLY PATH OPEN TO NEGI-KUN.
WELL.
THAT'S WHAT HE HAD TO DO TO SAVE THE WORLD.
IT'S BETTER THAN DYING, RIGHT?
S...
SO... THAT IS THE PRICE NEGI-SENSEI PAID?
PRICE?
DON'T BE ABSURD. IT'S A GIFT.

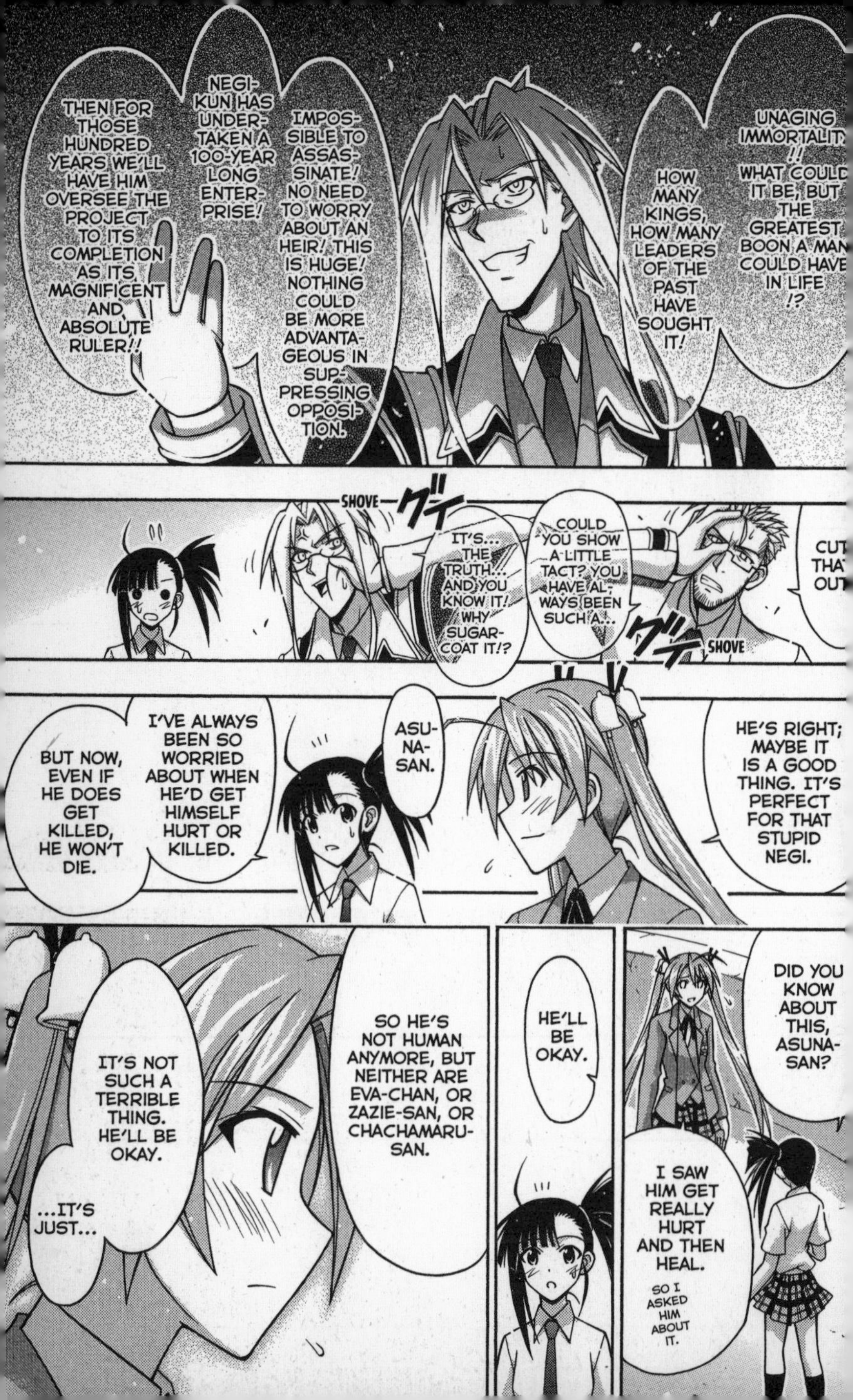
UNAGING IMMORTALIT !! WHAT COULD IT BE, BUT THE GREATEST BOON A MAN COULD HAVE IN LIFE !?
HOW MANY KINGS, HOW MANY LEADERS OF THE PAST HAVE SOUGHT IT!
IMPOSSIBLE TO ASSASSINATE! NO NEED TO WORRY ABOUT AN HEIR! THIS IS HUGE! NOTHING COULD BE MORE ADVANTAGEOUS IN SUPPRESSING OPPOSITION.
NEGI-KUN HAS UNDERTAKEN A 100-YEAR LONG ENTERPRISE!
THEN FOR THOSE HUNDRED YEARS WE'LL HAVE HIM OVERSEE THE PROJECT TO ITS COMPLETION AS ITS MAGNIFICENT AND ABSOLUTE RULER!!
CUT THAT OUT
SHOVE
COULD YOU SHOW A LITTLE TACT? YOU HAVE ALWAYS BEEN SUCH A...
SHOVE
IT'S... THE TRUTH... AND YOU KNOW IT! WHY SUGARCOAT IT!?
HE'S RIGHT; MAYBE IT IS A GOOD THING. IT'S PERFECT FOR THAT STUPID NEGI.
ASUNA-SAN.
I'VE ALWAYS BEEN SO WORRIED ABOUT WHEN HE'D GET HIMSELF HURT OR KILLED.
BUT NOW, EVEN IF HE DOES GET KILLED, HE WON'T DIE.
DID YOU KNOW ABOUT THIS, ASUNA-SAN?
I SAW HIM GET REALLY HURT AND THEN HEAL.
SO I ASKED HIM ABOUT IT.
HE'LL BE OKAY.
SO HE'S NOT HUMAN ANYMORE, BUT NEITHER ARE EVA-CHAN, OR ZAZIE-SAN, OR CHACHAMARU-SAN.
IT'S NOT SUCH A TERRIBLE THING. HE'LL BE OKAY.
...IT'S JUST...

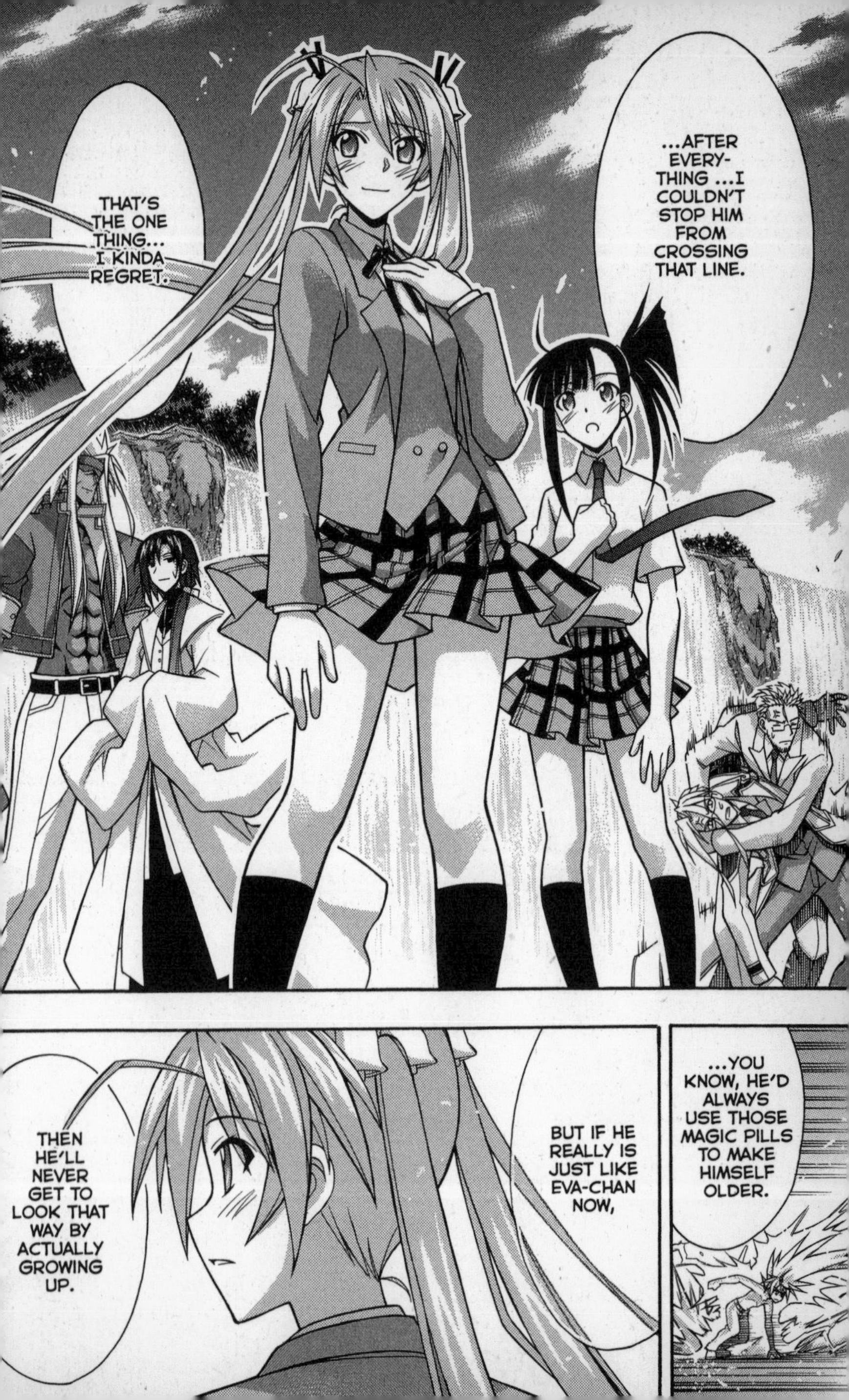
...AFTER EVERY-THING ...I COULDN'T STOP HIM FROM CROSSING THAT LINE.
THAT'S THE ONE THING... I KINDA REGRET.
...YOU KNOW, HE'D ALWAYS USE THOSE MAGIC PILLS TO MAKE HIMSELF OLDER.
BUT IF HE REALLY IS JUST LIKE EVA-CHAN NOW,
THEN HE'LL NEVER GET TO LOOK THAT WAY BY ACTUALLY GROWING UP.

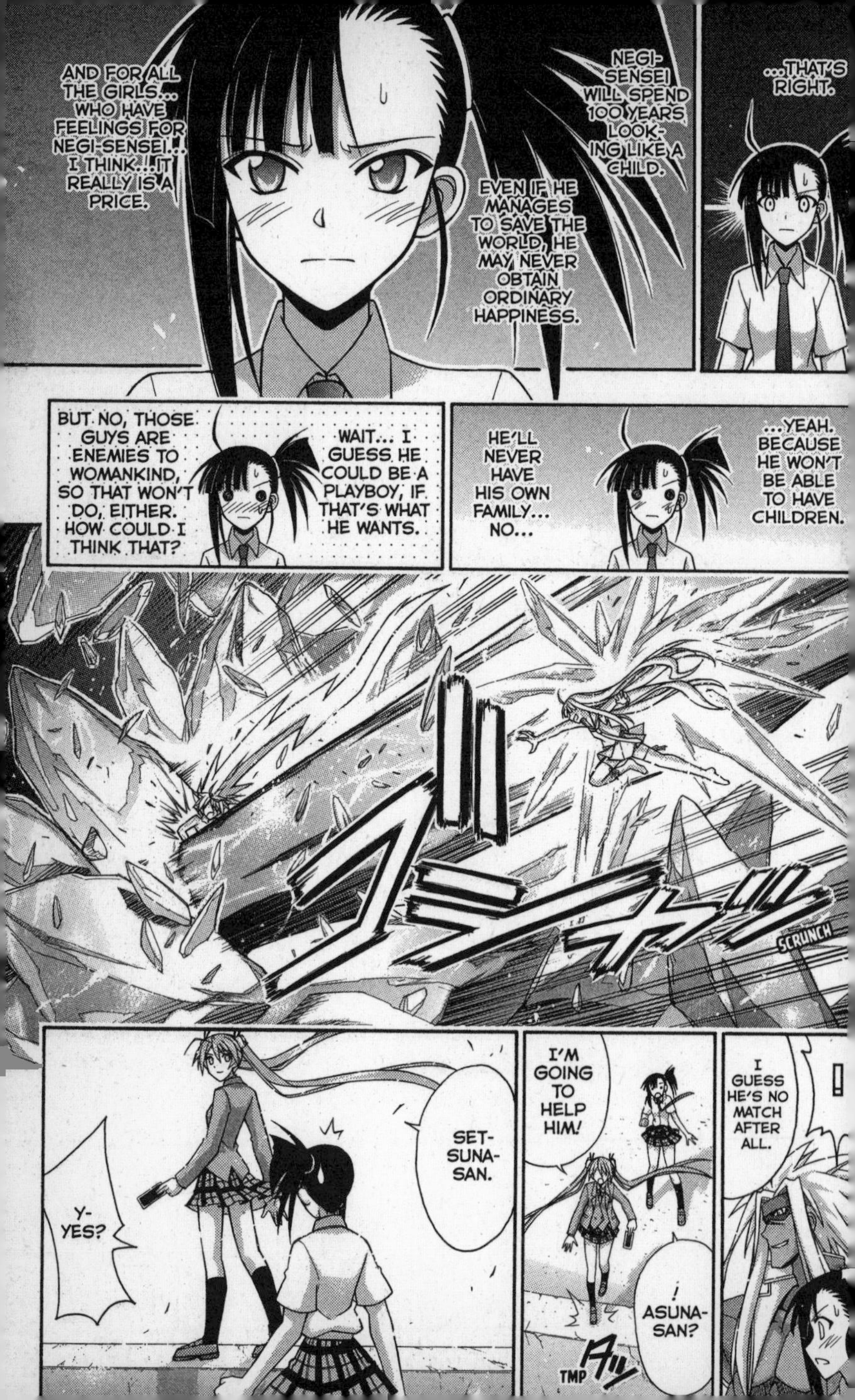
...THAT'S RIGHT.
NEGI-SENSEI WILL SPEND 100 YEARS LOOKING LIKE A CHILD.
EVEN IF HE MANAGES TO SAVE THE WORLD, HE MAY NEVER OBTAIN ORDINARY HAPPINESS.
AND FOR ALL THE GIRLS... WHO HAVE FEELINGS FOR NEGI-SENSEI... I THINK... IT REALLY IS A PRICE.
...YEAH. BECAUSE HE WON'T BE ABLE TO HAVE CHILDREN.
HE'LL NEVER HAVE HIS OWN FAMILY... NO...
WAIT... I GUESS HE COULD BE A PLAYBOY, IF THAT'S WHAT HE WANTS.
BUT NO, THOSE GUYS ARE ENEMIES TO WOMANKIND, SO THAT WON'T DO, EITHER. HOW COULD I THINK THAT?
SCRUNCH
!
I GUESS HE'S NO MATCH AFTER ALL.
I'M GOING TO HELP HIM!
! ASUNA-SAN?
TMP
SET-SUNA-SAN.
Y-YES?

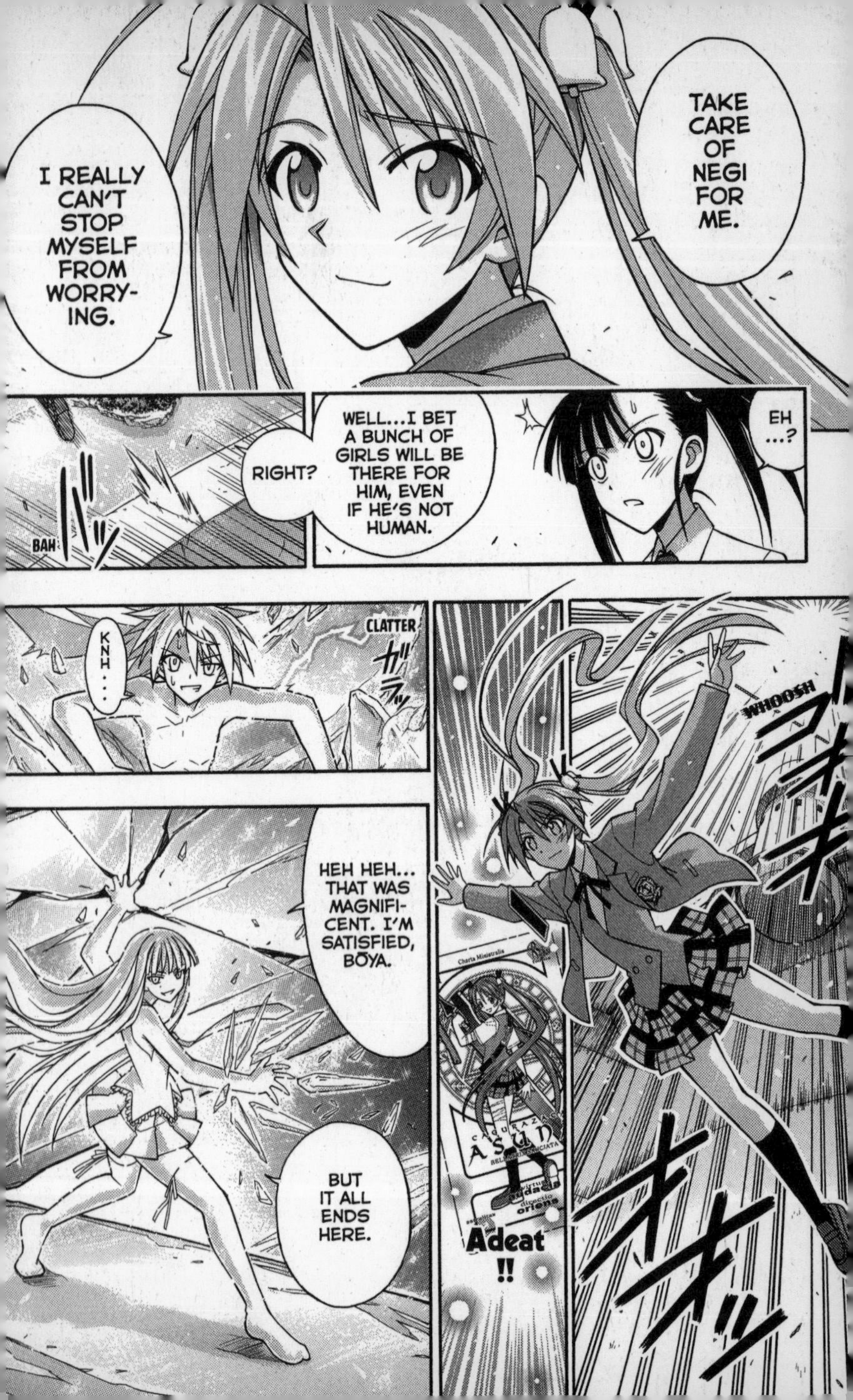
TAKE CARE OF NEGI FOR ME.
I REALLY CAN'T STOP MYSELF FROM WORRYING.
EH ...?
WELL...I BET A BUNCH OF GIRLS WILL BE THERE FOR HIM, EVEN IF HE'S NOT HUMAN.
RIGHT?
BAH
WHOOSH
Adeat !!
KNH...
CLATTER
HEH HEH... THAT WAS MAGNIFICENT. I'M SATISFIED, BŌYA.
BUT IT ALL ENDS HERE.

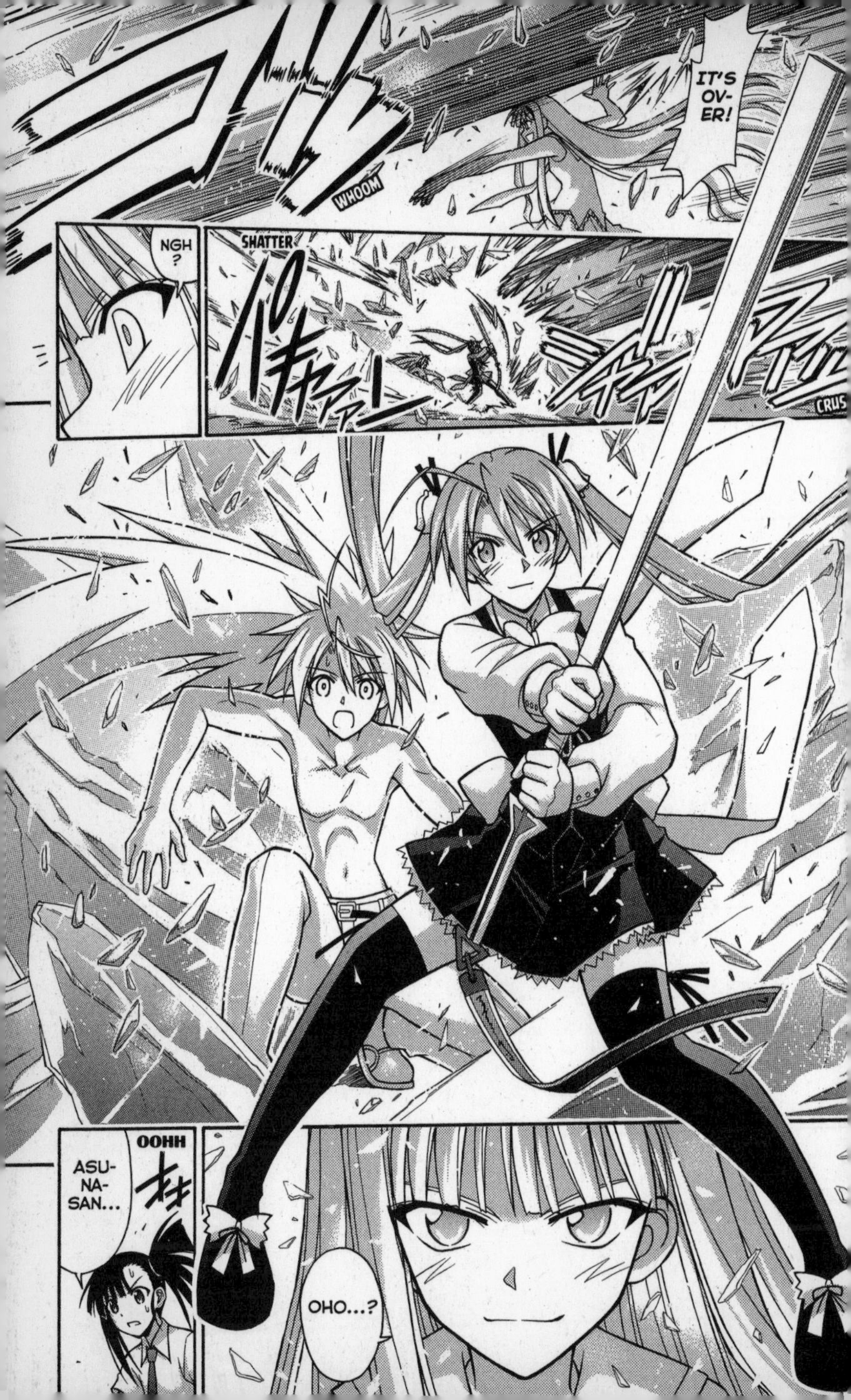
IT'S OV-ER!
WHOOM
CRUS
SHATTER
NGH?
OHO...?
OOHH
ASU-NA-SAN...

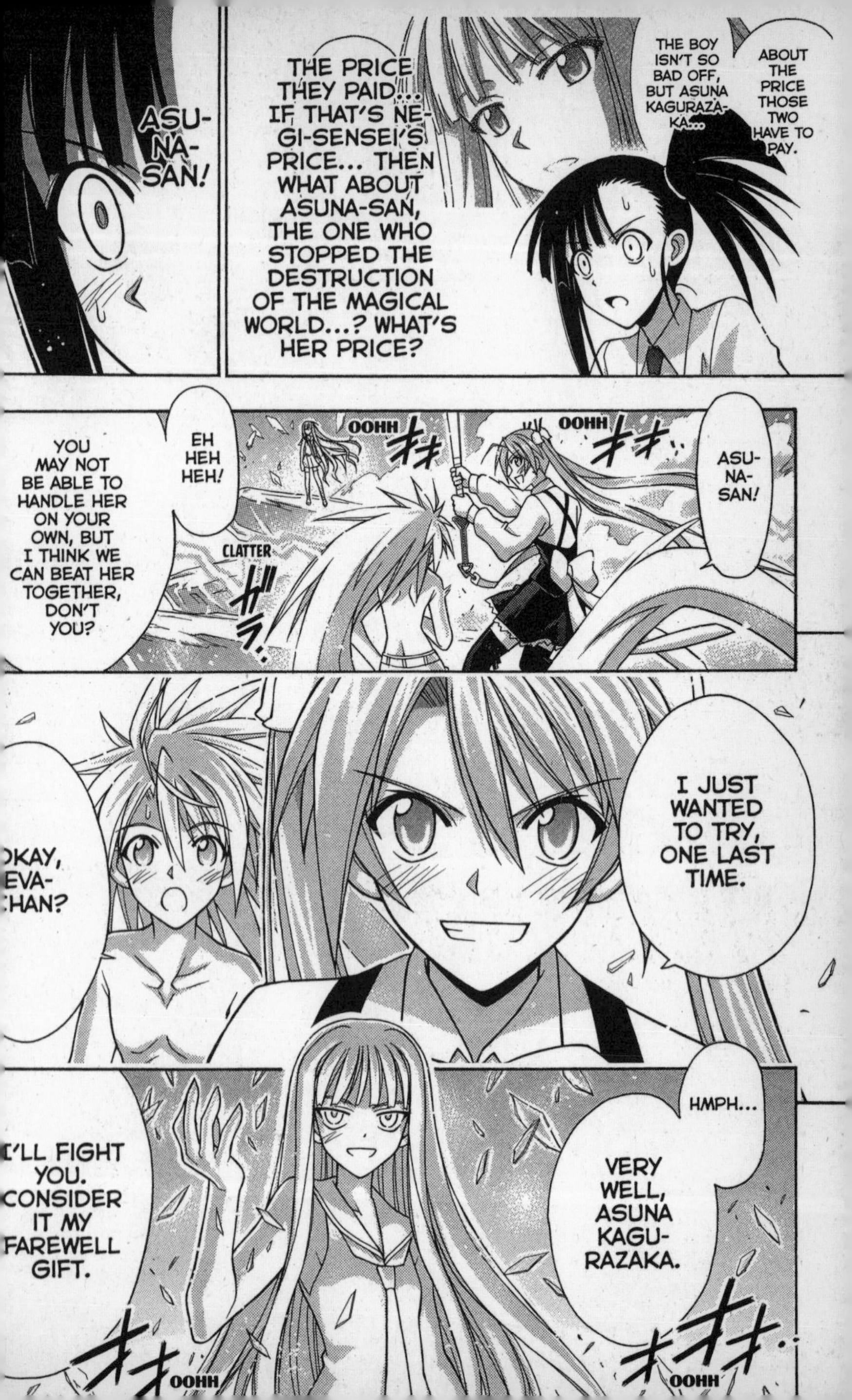
ABOUT THE PRICE THOSE TWO HAVE TO PAY.
THE BOY ISN'T SO BAD OFF, BUT ASUNA KAGURAZAKA...
THE PRICE THEY PAID... IF THAT'S NEGI-SENSEI'S PRICE... THEN WHAT ABOUT ASUNA-SAN, THE ONE WHO STOPPED THE DESTRUCTION OF THE MAGICAL WORLD...? WHAT'S HER PRICE?
ASUNA-SAN!
ASUNA-SAN!
OOHH
OOHH
EH HEH HEH!
YOU MAY NOT BE ABLE TO HANDLE HER ON YOUR OWN, BUT I THINK WE CAN BEAT HER TOGETHER, DON'T YOU?
CLATTER
I JUST WANTED TO TRY, ONE LAST TIME.
OKAY, EVA-CHAN?
HMPH...
VERY WELL, ASUNA KAGURAZAKA.
I'LL FIGHT YOU. CONSIDER IT MY FAREWELL GIFT.
OOHH
OOHH

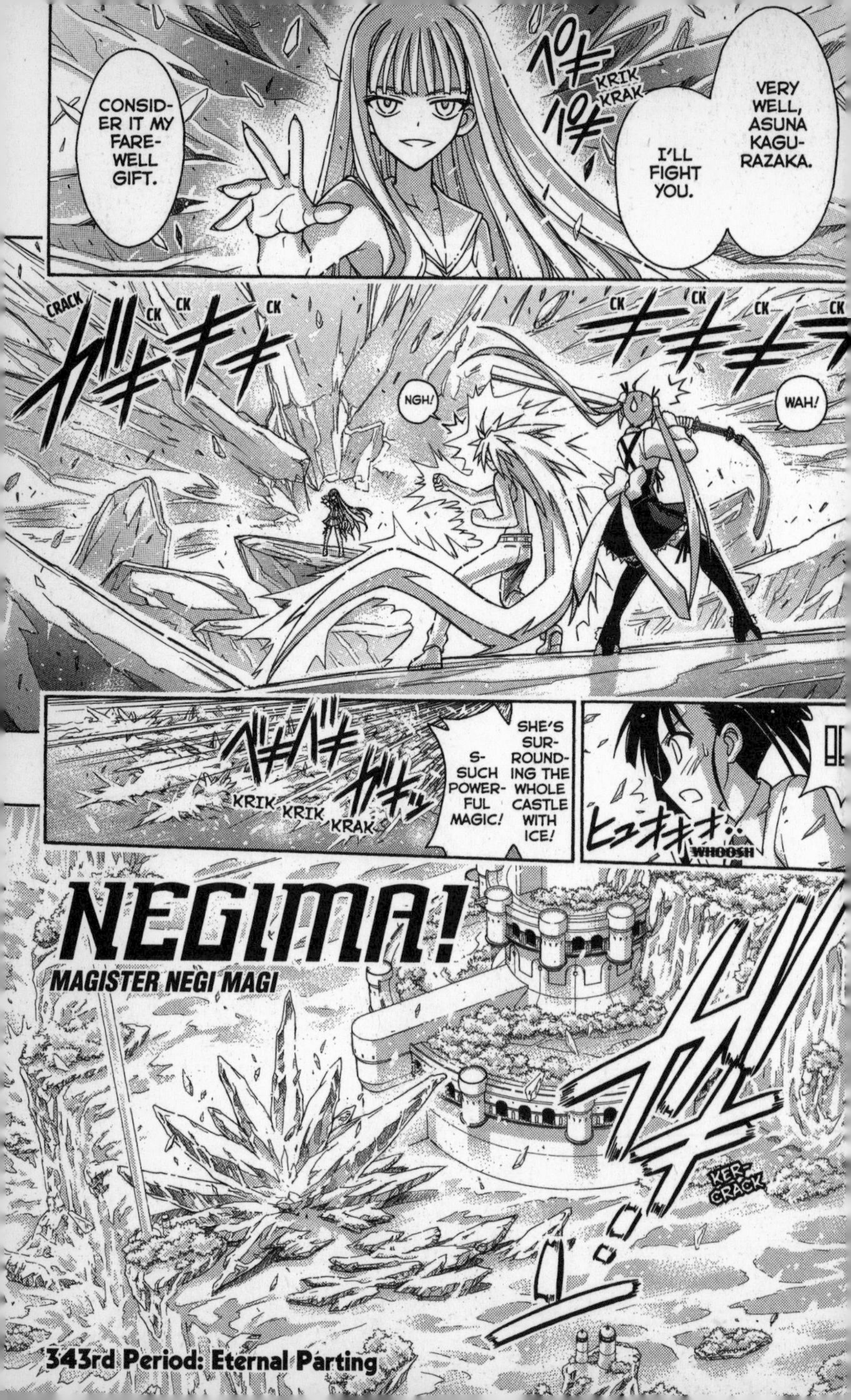
VERY WELL, ASUNA KAGURAZAKA.
I'LL FIGHT YOU.
KRIK KRAK
CONSIDER IT MY FAREWELL GIFT.
CK CK CK CK
WAH!
NGH!
CRACK CK CK CK
WHOOSH
SHE'S SURROUNDING THE WHOLE CASTLE WITH ICE!
S-SUCH POWERFUL MAGIC!
KRIK KRIK KRAK
KER-CRACK
NEGIMA!
MAGISTER NEGI MAGI
343rd Period: Eternal Parting

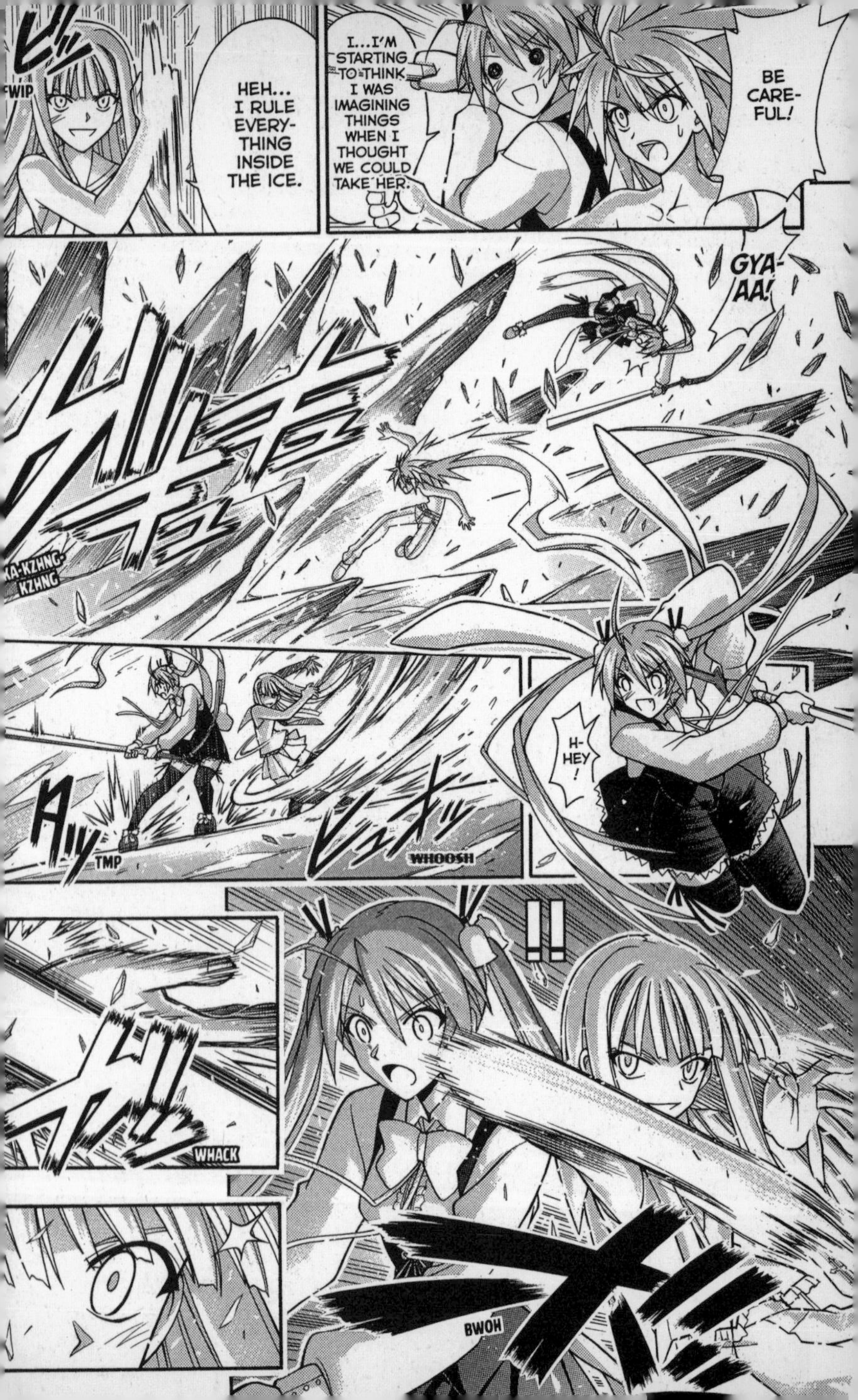
BE CARE-FUL!
I...I'M STARTING TO THINK I WAS IMAGINING THINGS WHEN I THOUGHT WE COULD TAKE HER.
FWIP
HEH... I RULE EVERY-THING INSIDE THE ICE.
GYA-AA!
KA-KZHNG-KZHNG
H-HEY!
WHOOSH
TMP
!!
BWOH
WHACK

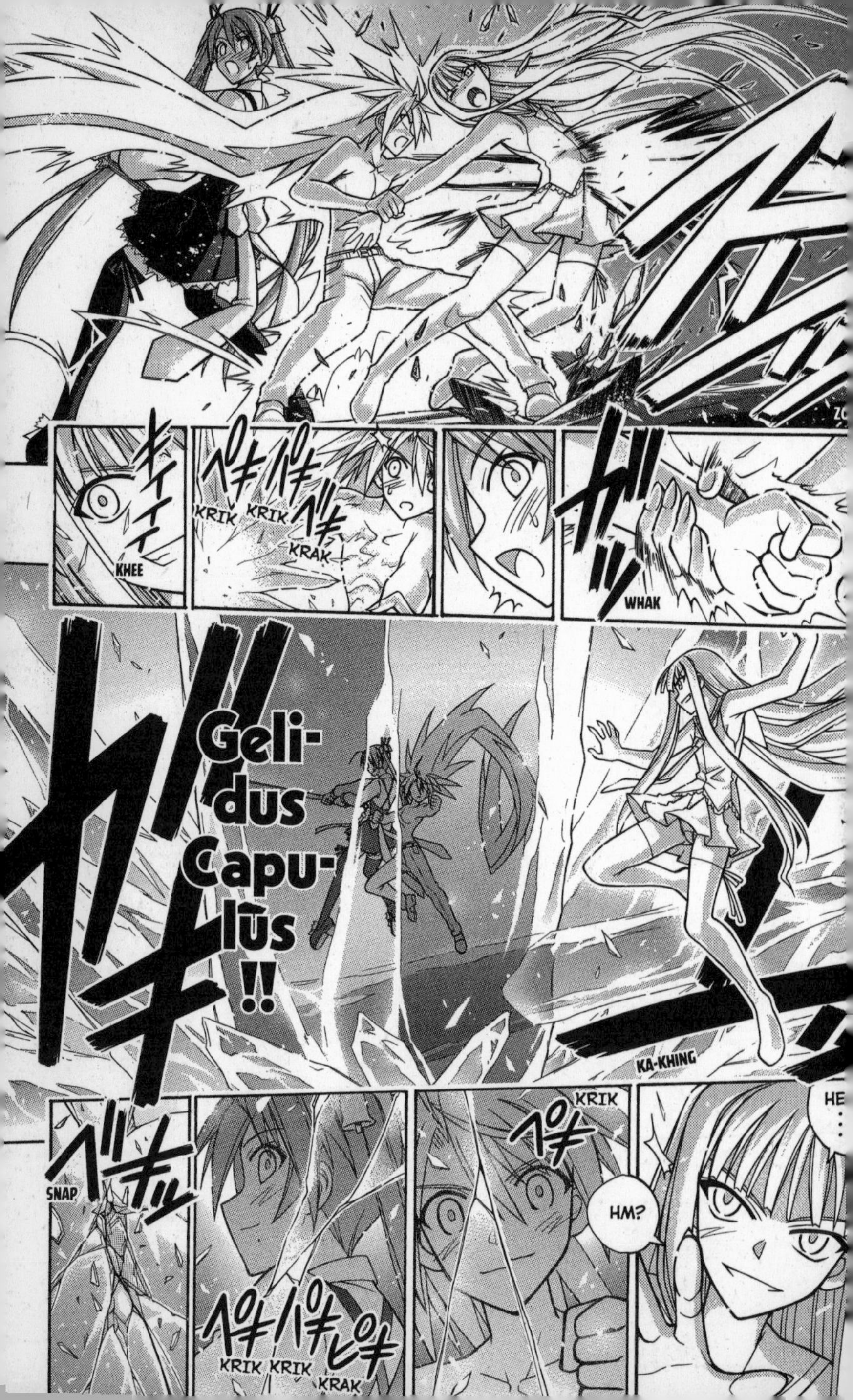
WHAK
KRIK
KRIK
KRAK
KHEE
Geli-
dus
Capu-
lūs
!!
KA-KHING
HE...
HM?
KRIK
KRIK
KRIK
KRAK
SNAP

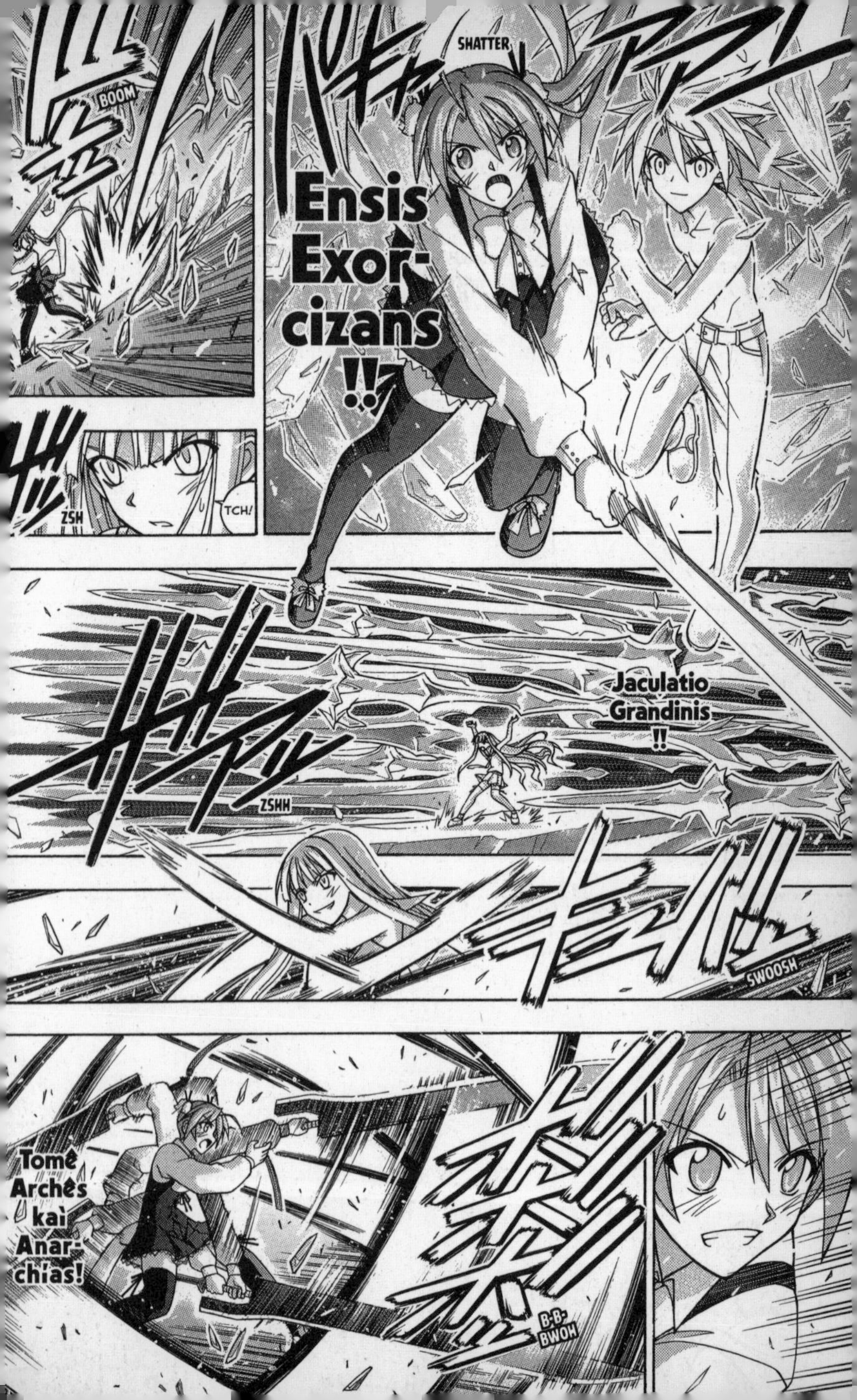
SHATTER
Ensis Exor-cizans!!
BOOM
ZSH
TCH!
Jaculatio Grandinis!!
ZSHH
SWOOSH
Tomê Archês kaì Anar-chías!
B-B-BWOH

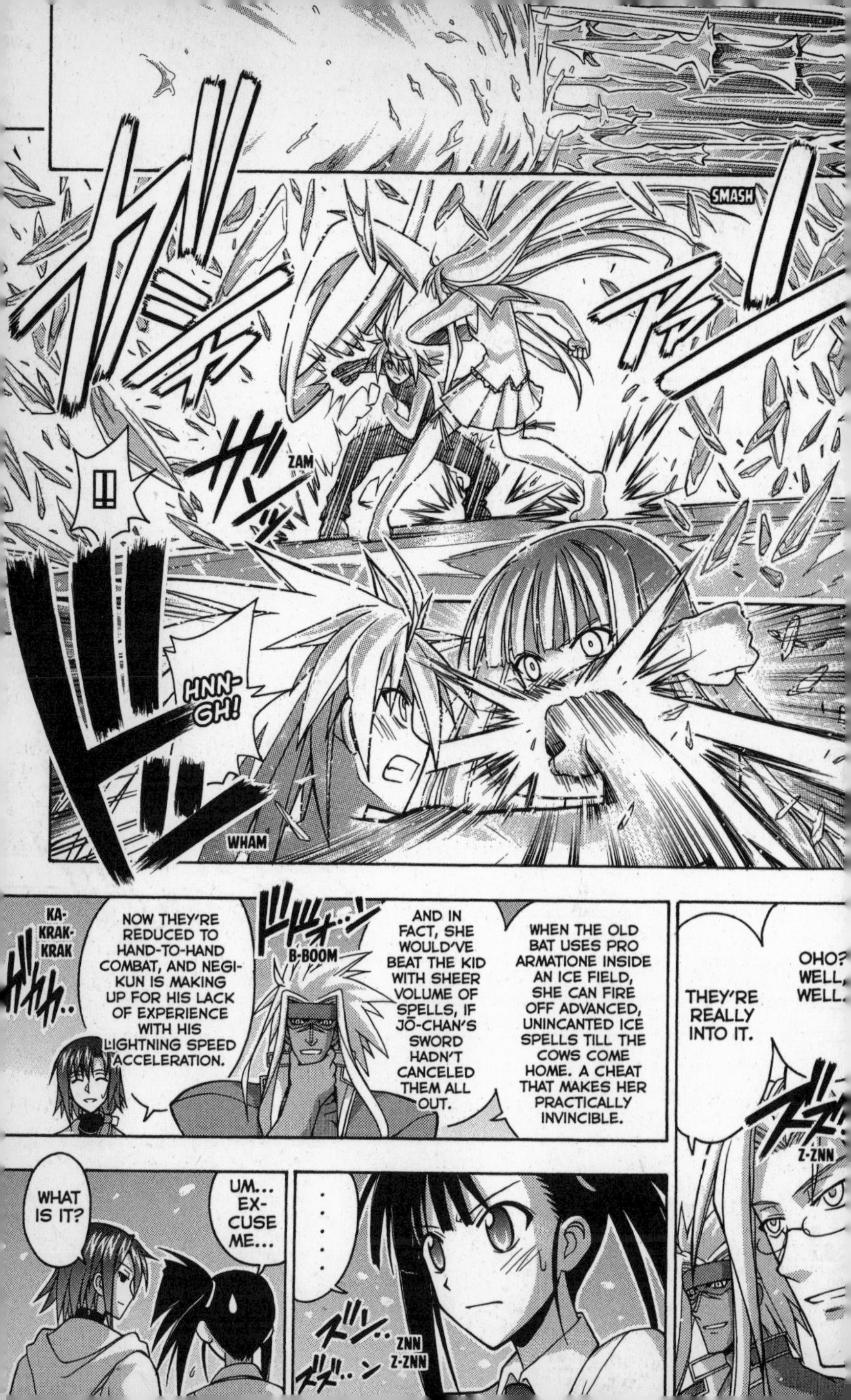
SMASH
ZAM
!!
HNN-GH!
WHAM
OHO? WELL, WELL.
THEY'RE REALLY INTO IT.
Z-ZNN
WHEN THE OLD BAT USES PRO ARMATIONE INSIDE AN ICE FIELD, SHE CAN FIRE OFF ADVANCED, UNINCANTED ICE SPELLS TILL THE COWS COME HOME. A CHEAT THAT MAKES HER PRACTICALLY INVINCIBLE.
AND IN FACT, SHE WOULD'VE BEAT THE KID WITH SHEER VOLUME OF SPELLS, IF JŌ-CHAN'S SWORD HADN'T CANCELED THEM ALL OUT.
B-BOOM
NOW THEY'RE REDUCED TO HAND-TO-HAND COMBAT, AND NEGI-KUN IS MAKING UP FOR HIS LACK OF EXPERIENCE WITH HIS LIGHTNING SPEED ACCELERATION.
KA-KRAK-KRAK
......
ZNN Z-ZNN
UM... EXCUSE ME...
WHAT IS IT?

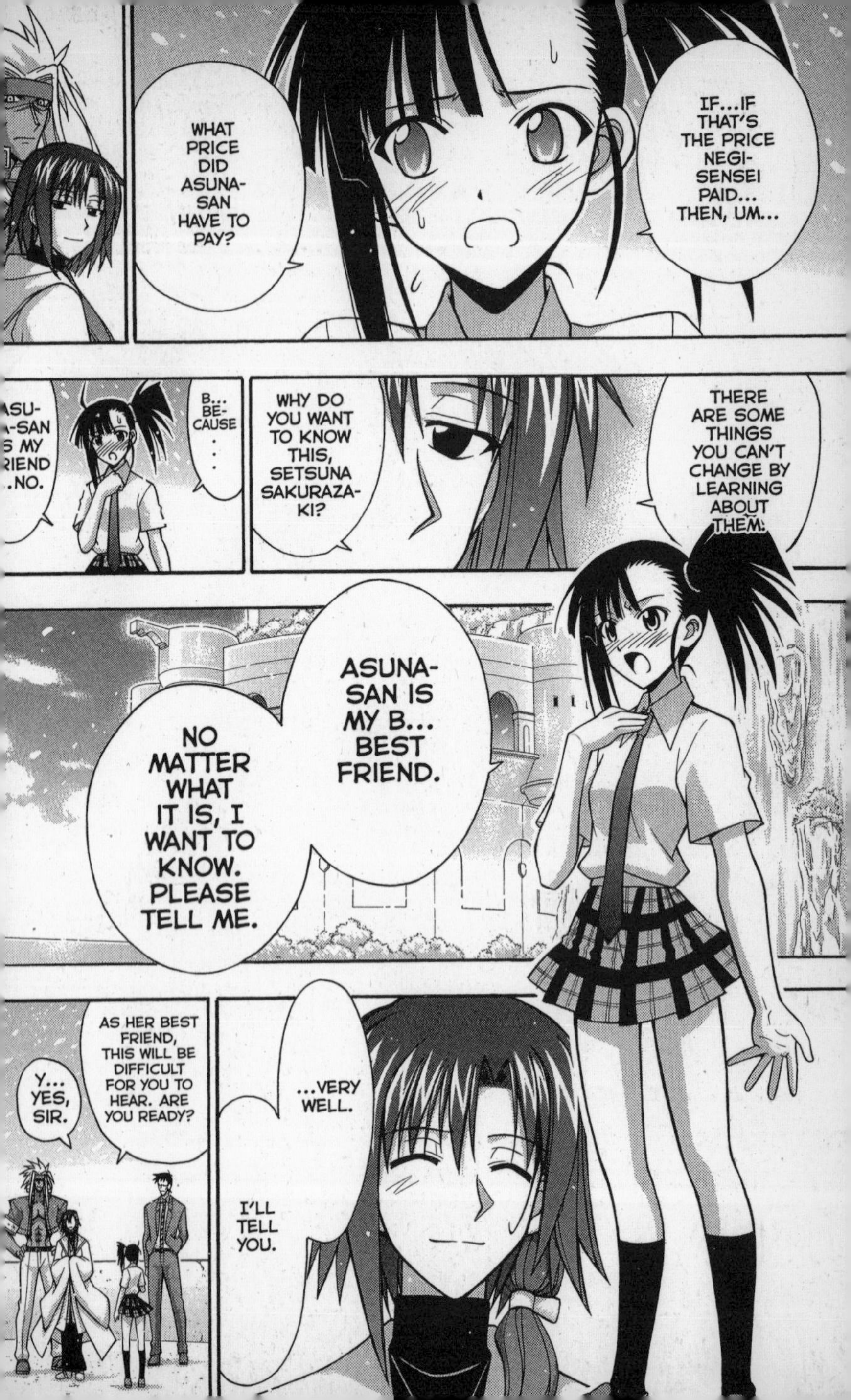
IF...IF THAT'S THE PRICE NEGI-SENSEI PAID... THEN, UM...
WHAT PRICE DID ASUNA-SAN HAVE TO PAY?
THERE ARE SOME THINGS YOU CAN'T CHANGE BY LEARNING ABOUT THEM.
WHY DO YOU WANT TO KNOW THIS, SETSUNA SAKURAZAKI?
B... BE-CAUSE . . .
ASU- -SAN S MY RIEND .NO.
ASUNA-SAN IS MY B... BEST FRIEND.
NO MATTER WHAT IT IS, I WANT TO KNOW. PLEASE TELL ME.
...VERY WELL.
I'LL TELL YOU.
AS HER BEST FRIEND, THIS WILL BE DIFFICULT FOR YOU TO HEAR. ARE YOU READY?
Y... YES, SIR.

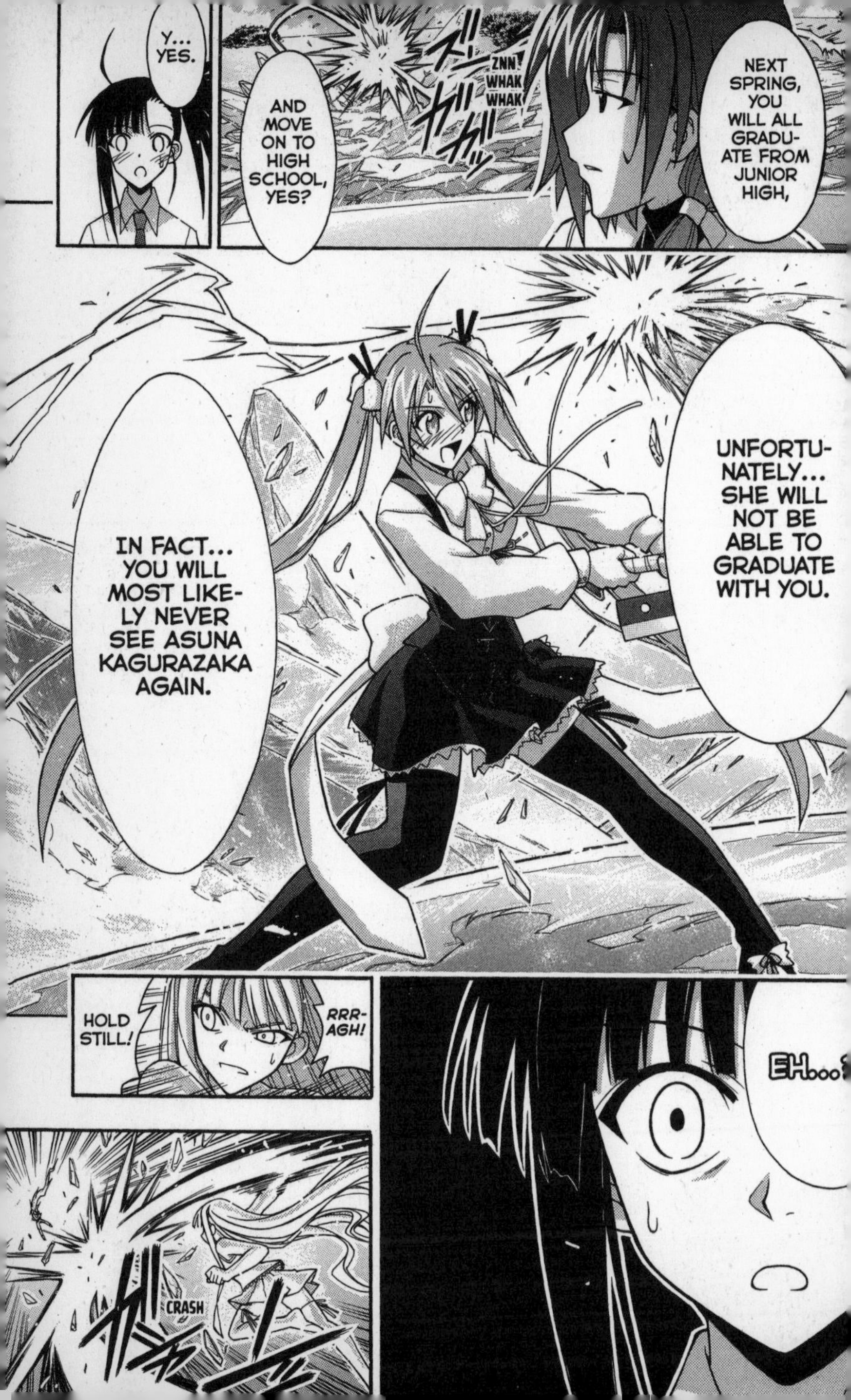
NEXT SPRING, YOU WILL ALL GRADUATE FROM JUNIOR HIGH,
ZNN WHAK WHAK
AND MOVE ON TO HIGH SCHOOL, YES?
Y... YES.
UNFORTUNATELY... SHE WILL NOT BE ABLE TO GRADUATE WITH YOU.
IN FACT... YOU WILL MOST LIKELY NEVER SEE ASUNA KAGURAZAKA AGAIN.
EH...?
RRR-AGH!
HOLD STILL!
CRASH

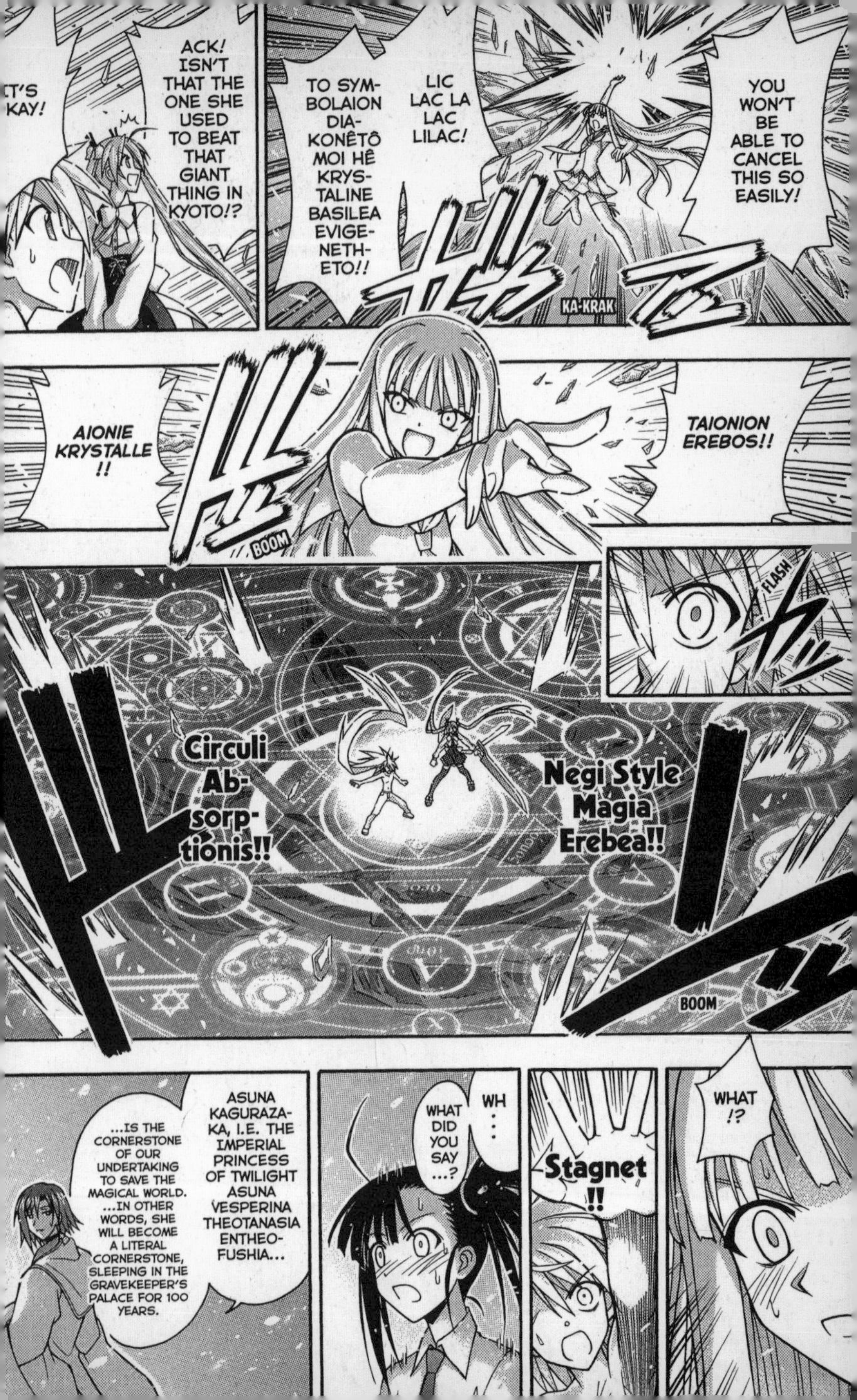
YOU WON'T BE ABLE TO CANCEL THIS SO EASILY!
LIC LAC LA LAC LILAC!
TO SYMBOLAION DIAKONÊTÔ MOI HÊ KRYSTALINE BASILEA EVIGENETHETO!!
KA-KRAK
ACK! ISN'T THAT THE ONE SHE USED TO BEAT THAT GIANT THING IN KYOTO!?
T'S KAY!
TAIONION EREBOS!!
AIONIE KRYSTALLE !!
BOOM
FLASH
Negi Style Magia Erebea!!
Circuli Absorptionis!!
BOOM
WHAT !?
Stagnet !!
WH . . .
WHAT DID YOU SAY ...?
ASUNA KAGURAZAKA, I.E. THE IMPERIAL PRINCESS OF TWILIGHT ASUNA VESPERINA THEOTANASIA ENTHEOFUSHIA...
...IS THE CORNERSTONE OF OUR UNDERTAKING TO SAVE THE MAGICAL WORLD. ...IN OTHER WORDS, SHE WILL BECOME A LITERAL CORNERSTONE, SLEEPING IN THE GRAVEKEEPER'S PALACE FOR 100 YEARS.

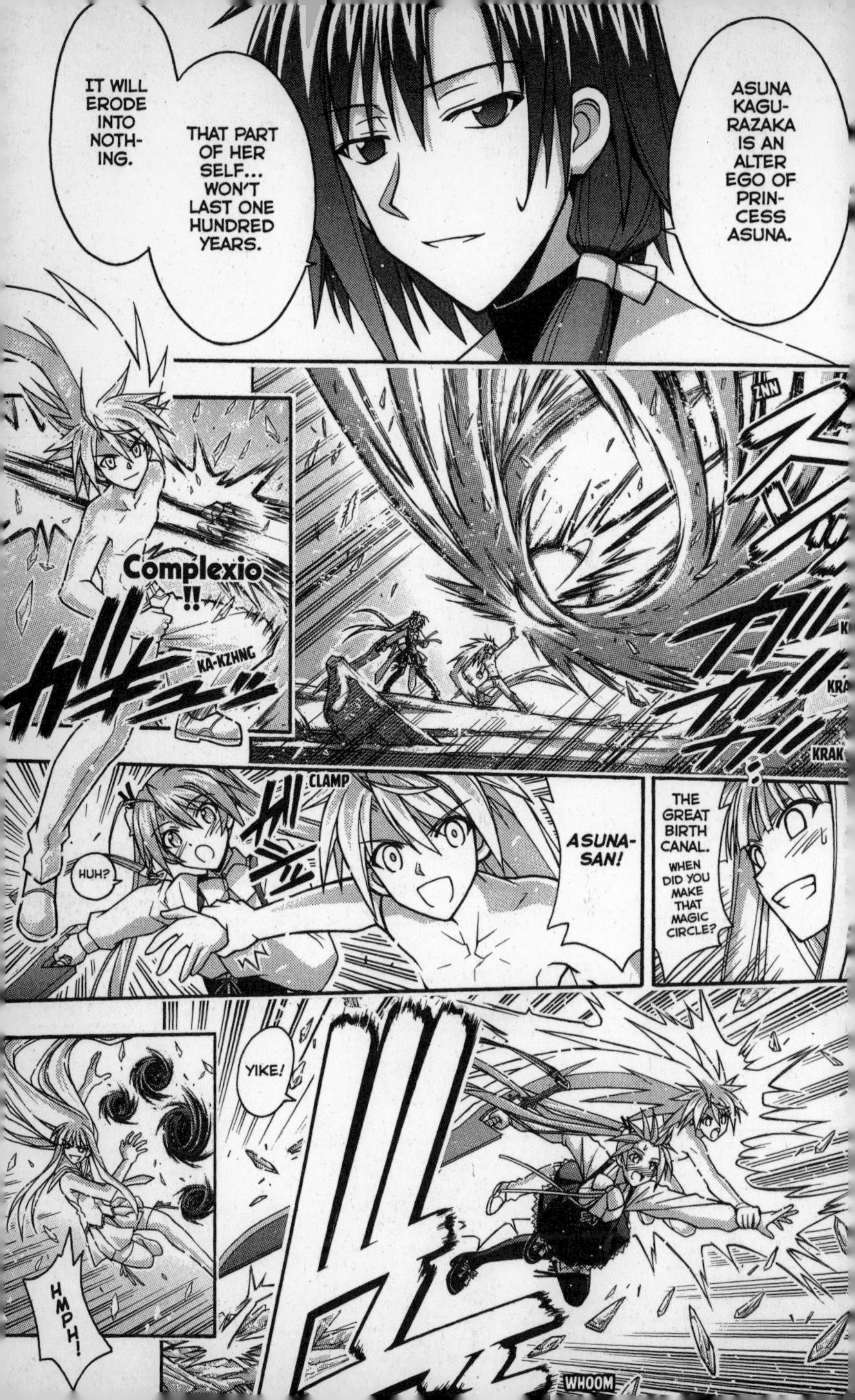
ASUNA KAGURAZAKA IS AN ALTER EGO OF PRINCESS ASUNA.
THAT PART OF HER SELF... WON'T LAST ONE HUNDRED YEARS.
IT WILL ERODE INTO NOTHING.
ZNN
KRA
KRAK
Complexio!!
KA-KZHNG
THE GREAT BIRTH CANAL.
WHEN DID YOU MAKE THAT MAGIC CIRCLE?
ASUNA-SAN!
CLAMP
HUH?
YIKE!
WHOOM
HMPH!

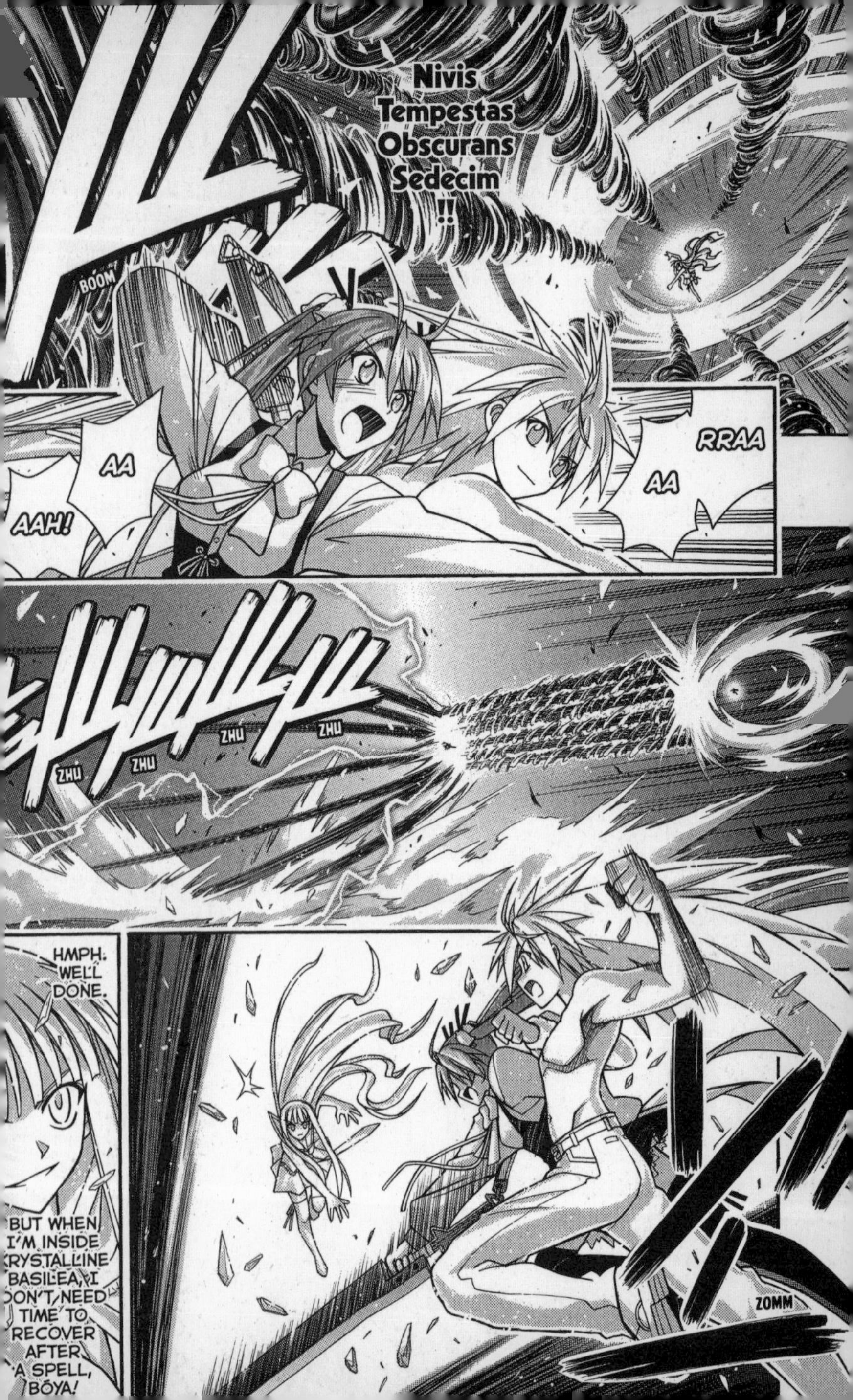
Nivis Tempestas Obscurans Sedecim !!
BOOM
RRAA AA
AA AAH!
ZHU ZHU ZHU ZHU
HMPH. WELL DONE.
ZOMM
BUT WHEN I'M INSIDE KRYSTALLINE BASILEA, I DON'T NEED TIME TO RECOVER AFTER A SPELL, BÔYA!

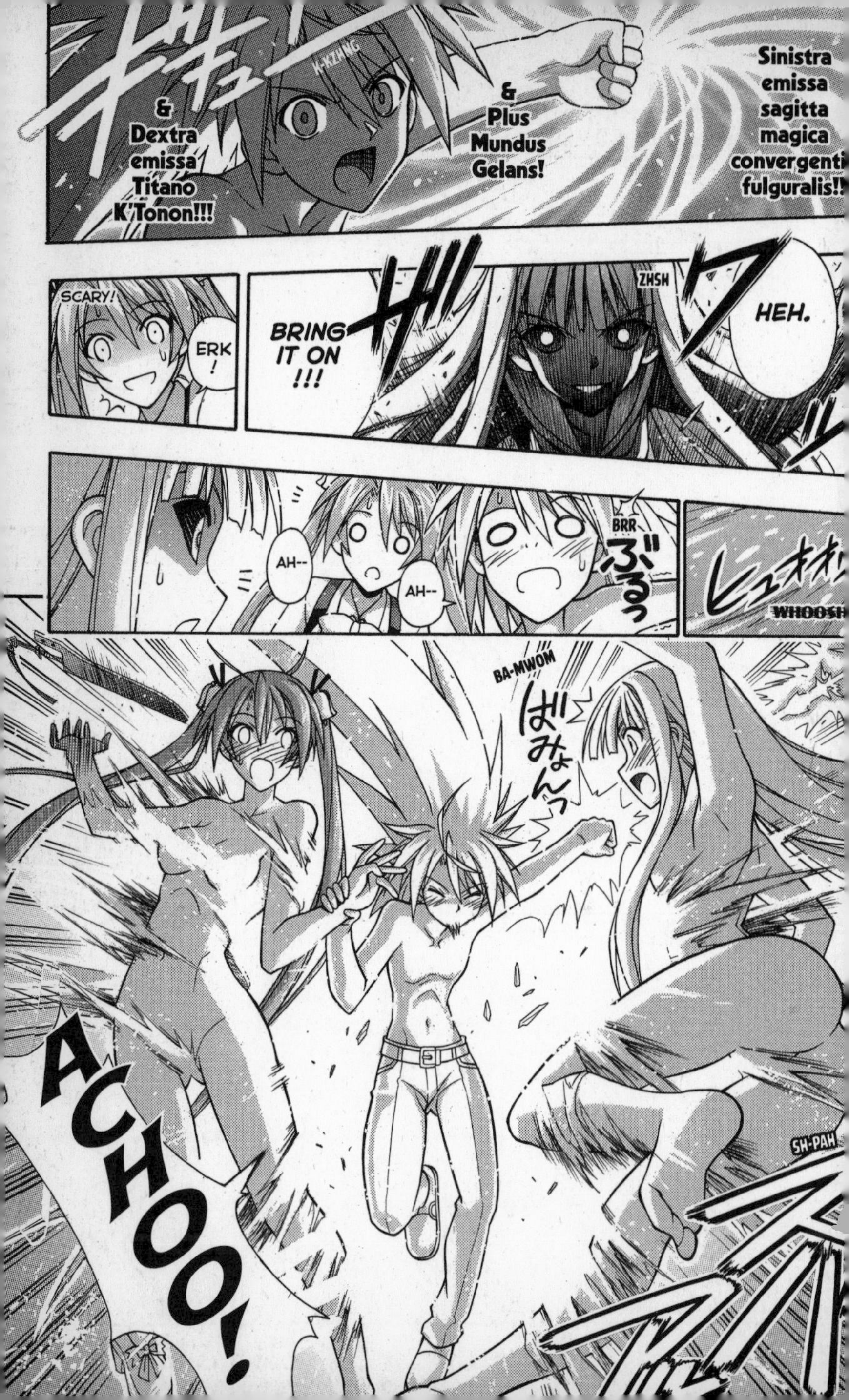
Sinistra emissa sagitta magica convergenti fulguralis!!
& Plus Mundus Gelans!
K-HZHNG
& Dextra emissa Titano K'Tonon!!!
HEH.
ZHSH
BRING IT ON !!!
SCARY!
ERK !
WHOOSH
BRR
ぶるっ
AH--
AH--
BA-MWOM
ばみょんっ
SH-PAH
ACHOO!

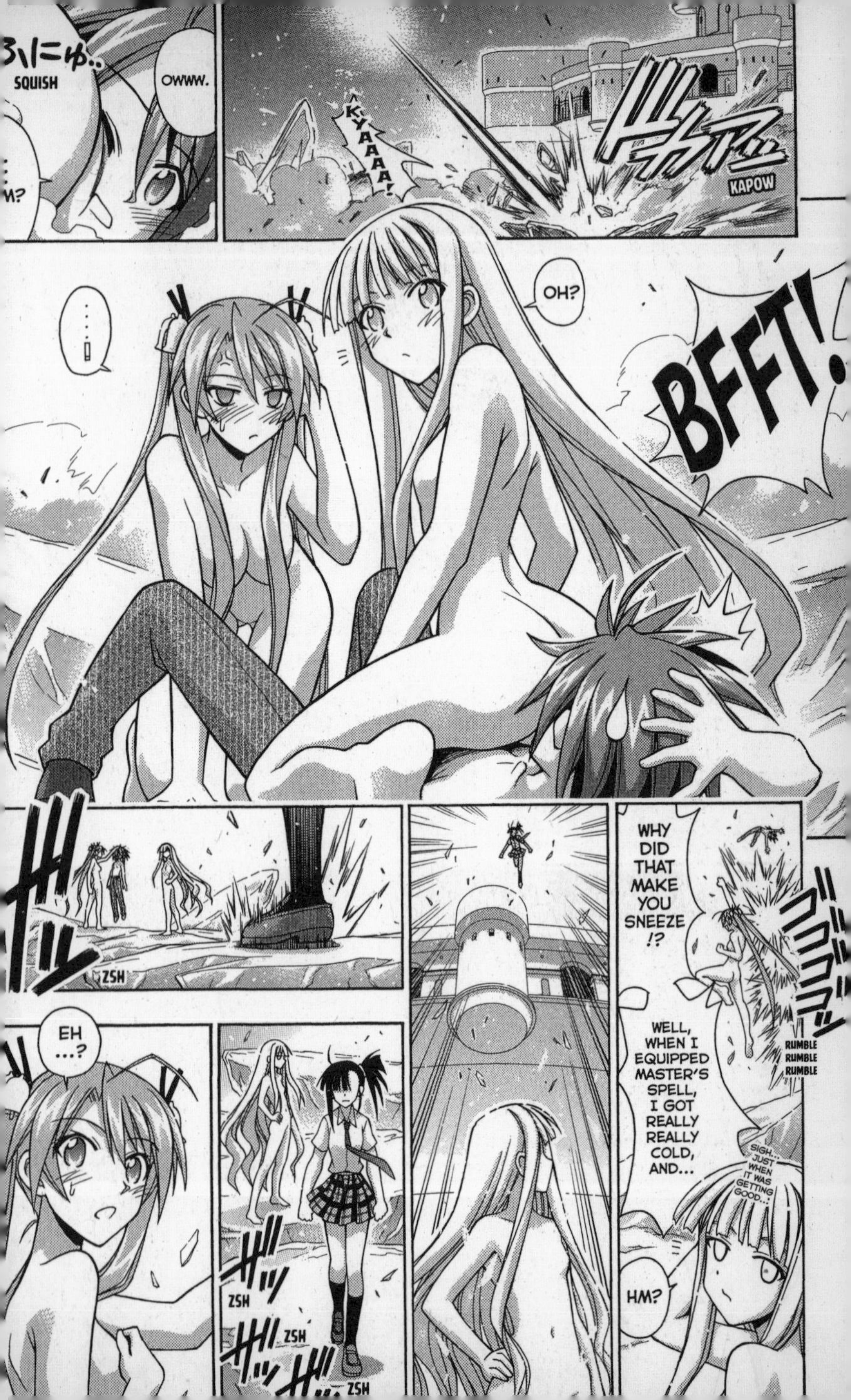
KYAAAA!
KAPOW
OWWW.
SQUISH
...M?
OH?
BFFT!
...!
WHY DID THAT MAKE YOU SNEEZE!?
RUMBLE RUMBLE RUMBLE
ZSH
WELL, WHEN I EQUIPPED MASTER'S SPELL, I GOT REALLY REALLY COLD, AND...
SIGH... JUST WHEN IT WAS GETTING GOOD...
HM?
ZSH
ZSH
ZSH
EH ...?

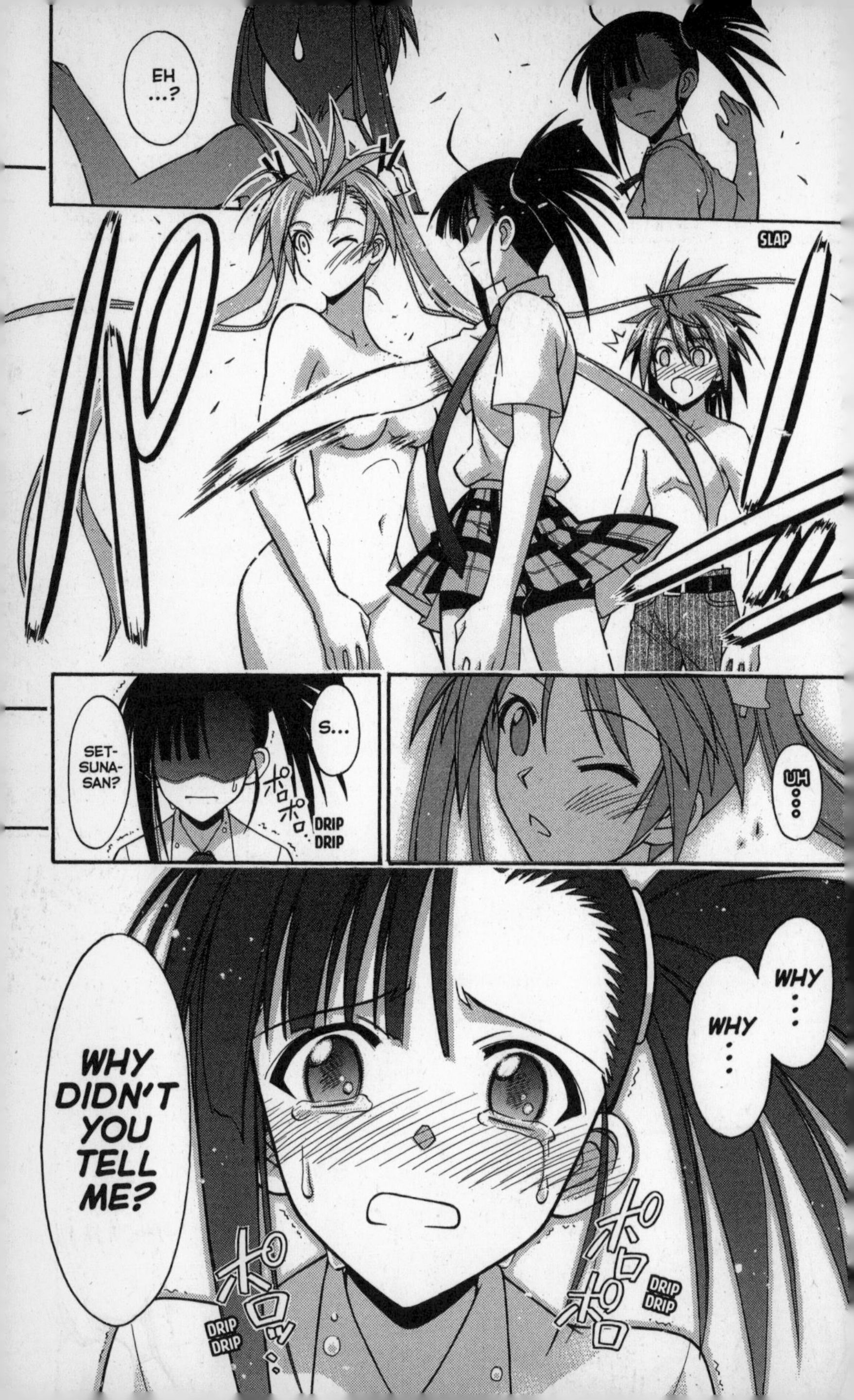
EH ...?
SLAP
UH...
S...
SET-SUNA-SAN?
ポロポロ
DRIP DRIP
WHY...
WHY...
WHY DIDN'T YOU TELL ME?
ポロポロ
DRIP DRIP
ポロッ
DRIP DRIP

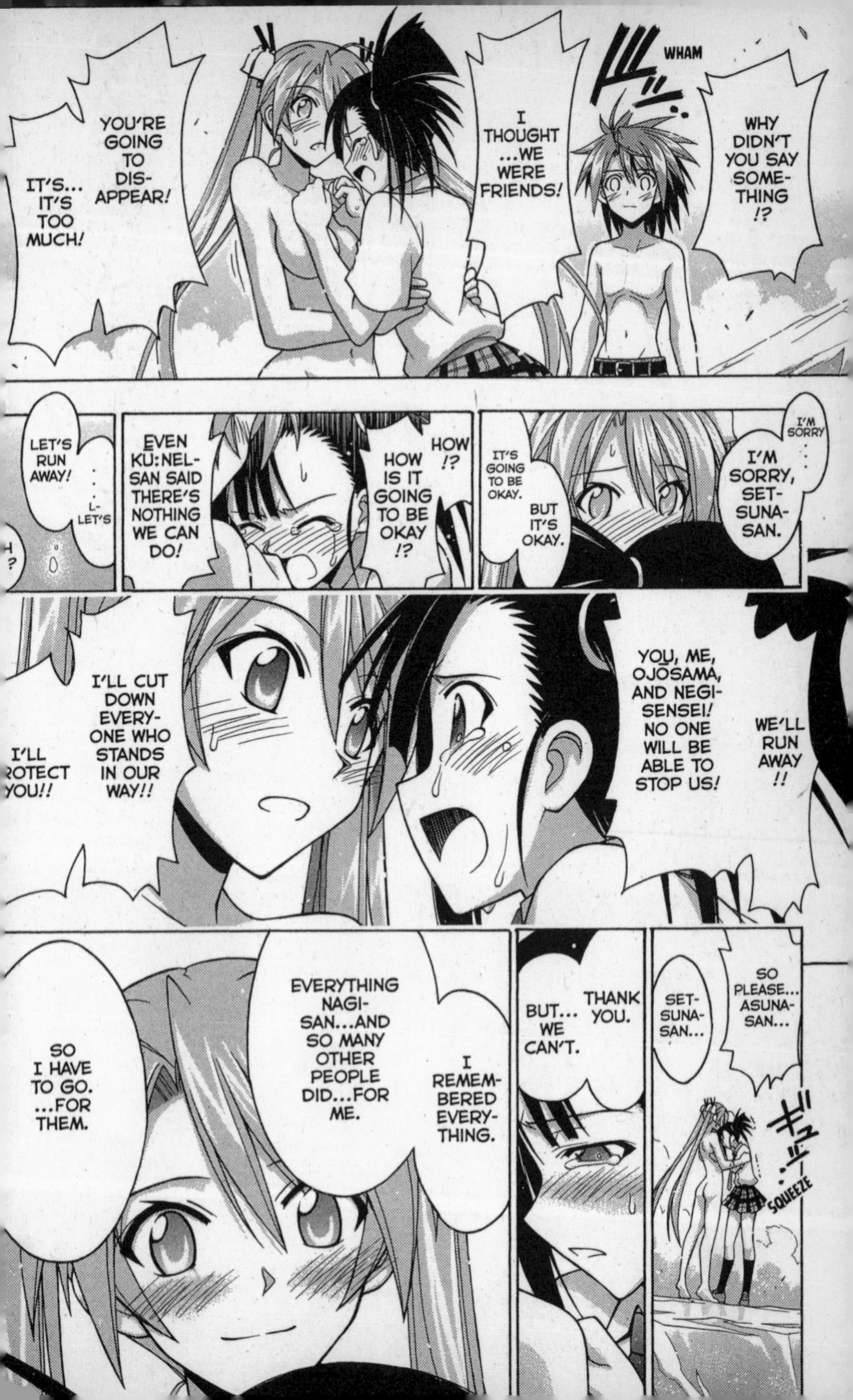
WHAM
WHY DIDN'T YOU SAY SOMETHING!?
I THOUGHT ...WE WERE FRIENDS!
YOU'RE GOING TO DISAPPEAR!
IT'S... IT'S TOO MUCH!
I'M SORRY
I'M SORRY, SETSUNA-SAN.
BUT IT'S OKAY.
IT'S GOING TO BE OKAY.
HOW!?
HOW IS IT GOING TO BE OKAY!?
EVEN KU:NEL-SAN SAID THERE'S NOTHING WE CAN DO!
L-LET'S...
LET'S RUN AWAY!
WE'LL RUN AWAY!!
YOU, ME, OJŌSAMA, AND NEGI-SENSEI! NO ONE WILL BE ABLE TO STOP US!
I'LL CUT DOWN EVERYONE WHO STANDS IN OUR WAY!!
I'LL ROTECT YOU!!
SO PLEASE... ASUNA-SAN...
SETSUNA-SAN...
SQUEEZE
THANK YOU.
BUT... WE CAN'T.
I REMEMBERED EVERYTHING.
EVERYTHING NAGI-SAN...AND SO MANY OTHER PEOPLE DID...FOR ME.
SO I HAVE TO GO. ...FOR THEM.

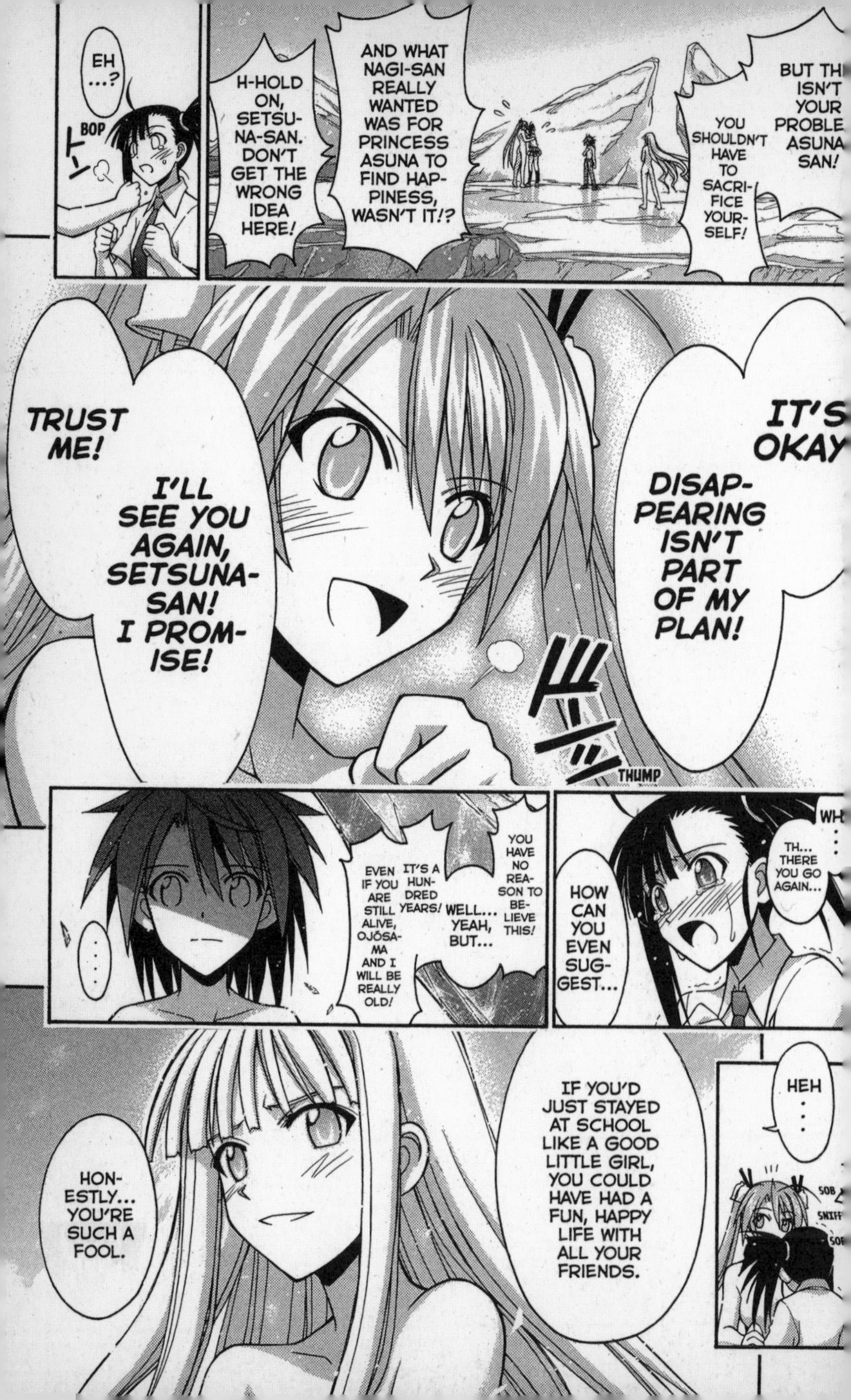
BUT THI ISN'T YOUR PROBLE ASUNA-SAN!
YOU SHOULDN'T HAVE TO SACRIFICE YOURSELF!
AND WHAT NAGI-SAN REALLY WANTED WAS FOR PRINCESS ASUNA TO FIND HAPPINESS, WASN'T IT!?
H-HOLD ON, SETSUNA-SAN. DON'T GET THE WRONG IDEA HERE!
EH ...?
BOP
IT'S OKAY
DISAPPEARING ISN'T PART OF MY PLAN!
THUMP
TRUST ME!
I'LL SEE YOU AGAIN, SETSUNA-SAN! I PROMISE!
WH ...
TH... THERE YOU GO AGAIN...
HOW CAN YOU EVEN SUGGEST...
YOU HAVE NO REASON TO BELIEVE THIS!
IT'S A HUNDRED YEARS!
WELL... YEAH, BUT...
EVEN IF YOU ARE STILL ALIVE, OJŌSAMA AND I WILL BE REALLY OLD!
......
HEH ...
SOB
SNIFF
SOB
IF YOU'D JUST STAYED AT SCHOOL LIKE A GOOD LITTLE GIRL, YOU COULD HAVE HAD A FUN, HAPPY LIFE WITH ALL YOUR FRIENDS.
HONESTLY... YOU'RE SUCH A FOOL.

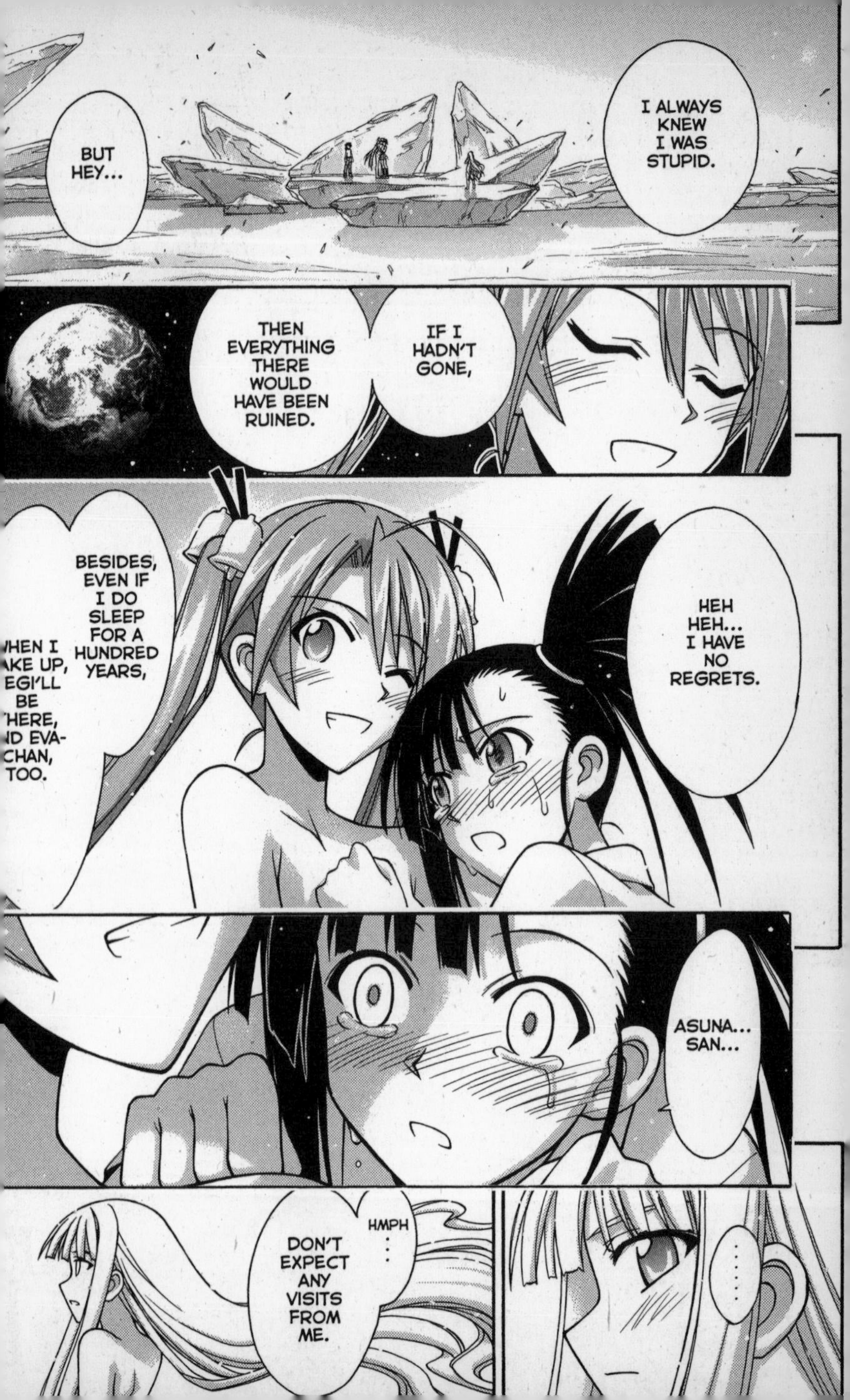
I ALWAYS KNEW I WAS STUPID.
BUT HEY...
IF I HADN'T GONE,
THEN EVERYTHING THERE WOULD HAVE BEEN RUINED.
HEH HEH... I HAVE NO REGRETS.
BESIDES, EVEN IF I DO SLEEP FOR A HUNDRED YEARS,
HEN I AKE UP, EGI'LL BE HERE, ND EVA-CHAN, TOO.
ASUNA... SAN...
......
HMPH...
DON'T EXPECT ANY VISITS FROM ME.

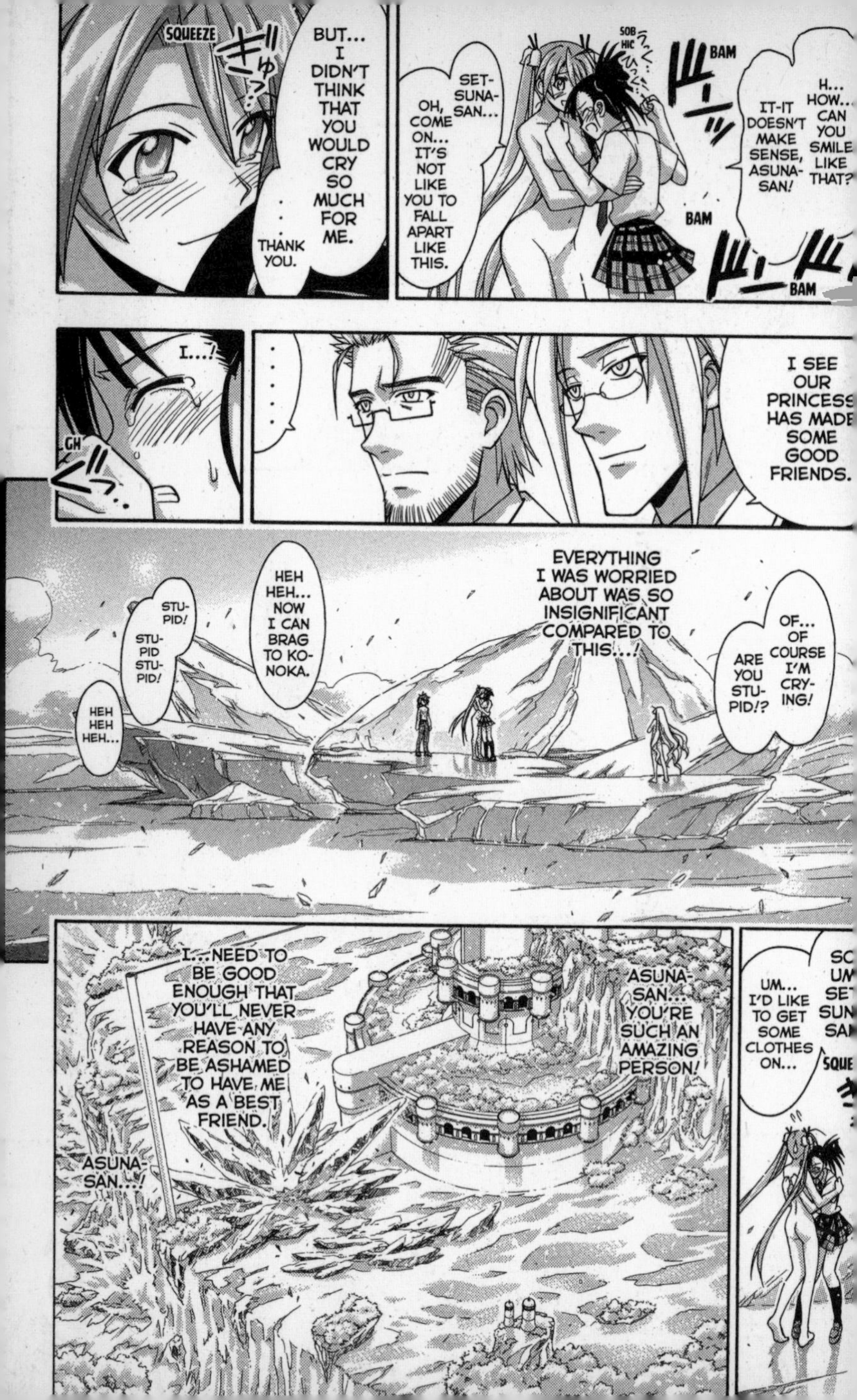
BAM
H... HOW... CAN YOU SMILE LIKE THAT?
IT-IT DOESN'T MAKE SENSE, ASUNA-SAN!
BAM
BAM
SOB HIC
SET-SUNA-SAN...
OH, COME ON... IT'S NOT LIKE YOU TO FALL APART LIKE THIS.
SQUEEZE
BUT... I DIDN'T THINK THAT YOU WOULD CRY SO MUCH FOR ME.
... THANK YOU.
I SEE OUR PRINCESS HAS MADE SOME GOOD FRIENDS.
......
I...!
GH
OF... OF COURSE I'M CRY-ING!
ARE YOU STU-PID!?
EVERYTHING I WAS WORRIED ABOUT WAS SO INSIGNIFICANT COMPARED TO THIS...!
HEH HEH... NOW I CAN BRAG TO KO-NOKA.
STU-PID! STU-PID STU-PID!
HEH HEH HEH...
UM... I'D LIKE TO GET SOME CLOTHES ON...
ASUNA-SAN... YOU'RE SUCH AN AMAZING PERSON!
I...NEED TO BE GOOD ENOUGH THAT YOU'LL NEVER HAVE ANY REASON TO BE ASHAMED TO HAVE ME AS A BEST FRIEND.
ASUNA-SAN...!

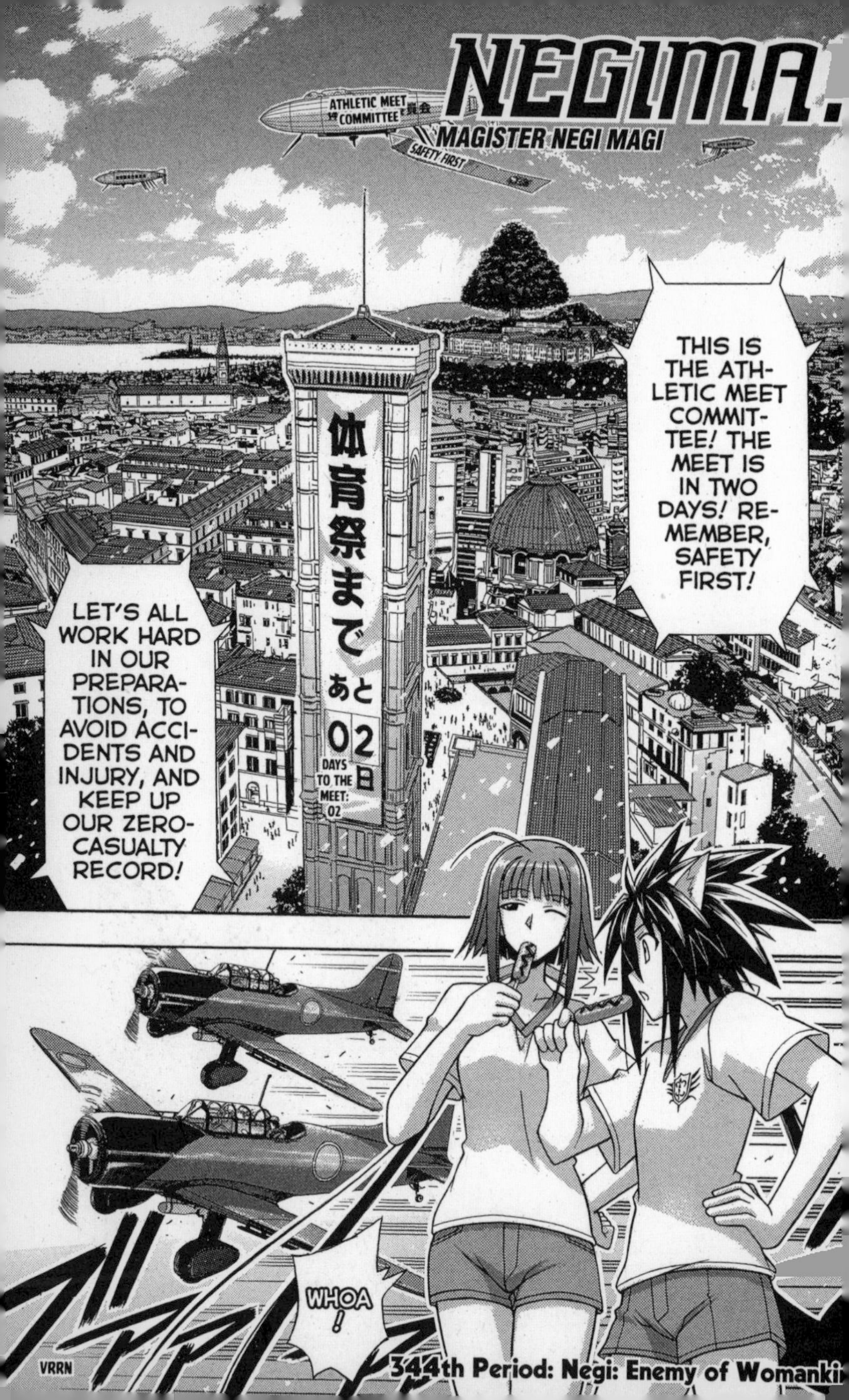
NEGIMA
MAGISTER NEGI MAGI
ATHLETIC MEET COMMITTEE
SAFETY FIRST
THIS IS THE ATHLETIC MEET COMMITTEE! THE MEET IS IN TWO DAYS! REMEMBER, SAFETY FIRST!
体育祭まで あと 02日
DAYS TO THE MEET: 02
LET'S ALL WORK HARD IN OUR PREPARATIONS, TO AVOID ACCIDENTS AND INJURY, AND KEEP UP OUR ZERO-CASUALTY RECORD!
WHOA!
VRRN
344th Period: Negi: Enemy of Womanki

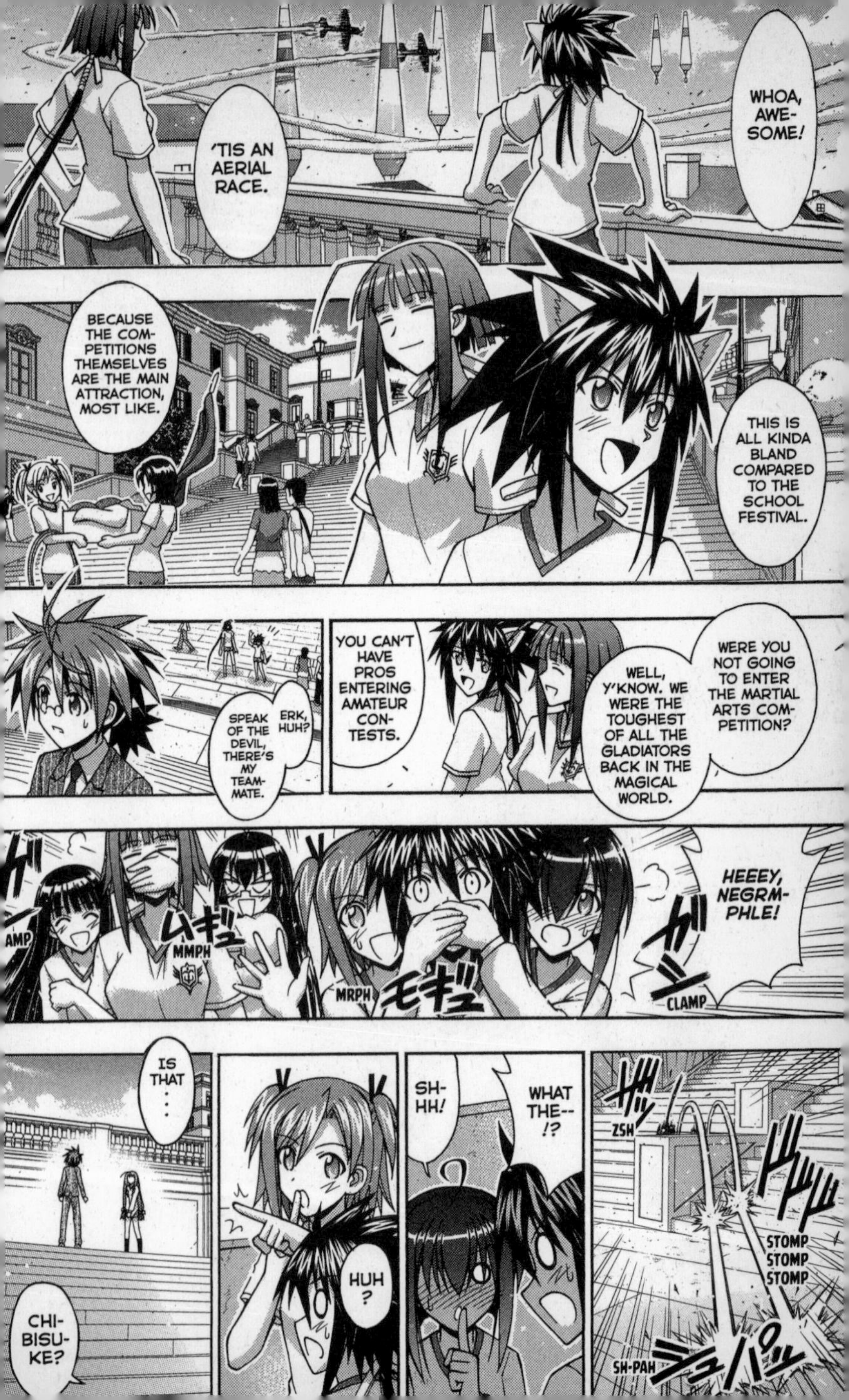
WHOA, AWESOME!
'TIS AN AERIAL RACE.
THIS IS ALL KINDA BLAND COMPARED TO THE SCHOOL FESTIVAL.
BECAUSE THE COMPETITIONS THEMSELVES ARE THE MAIN ATTRACTION, MOST LIKE.
WERE YOU NOT GOING TO ENTER THE MARTIAL ARTS COMPETITION?
WELL, Y'KNOW. WE WERE THE TOUGHEST OF ALL THE GLADIATORS BACK IN THE MAGICAL WORLD.
YOU CAN'T HAVE PROS ENTERING AMATEUR CONTESTS.
ERK, HUH?
SPEAK OF THE DEVIL, THERE'S MY TEAMMATE.
HEEEY, NEGRMPHLE!
CLAMP
MRPH
MMPH
AMP
ZSH
STOMP STOMP STOMP
SH-PAH
WHAT THE--!?
SH-HH!
HUH?
IS THAT . . .
CHIBISUKE?

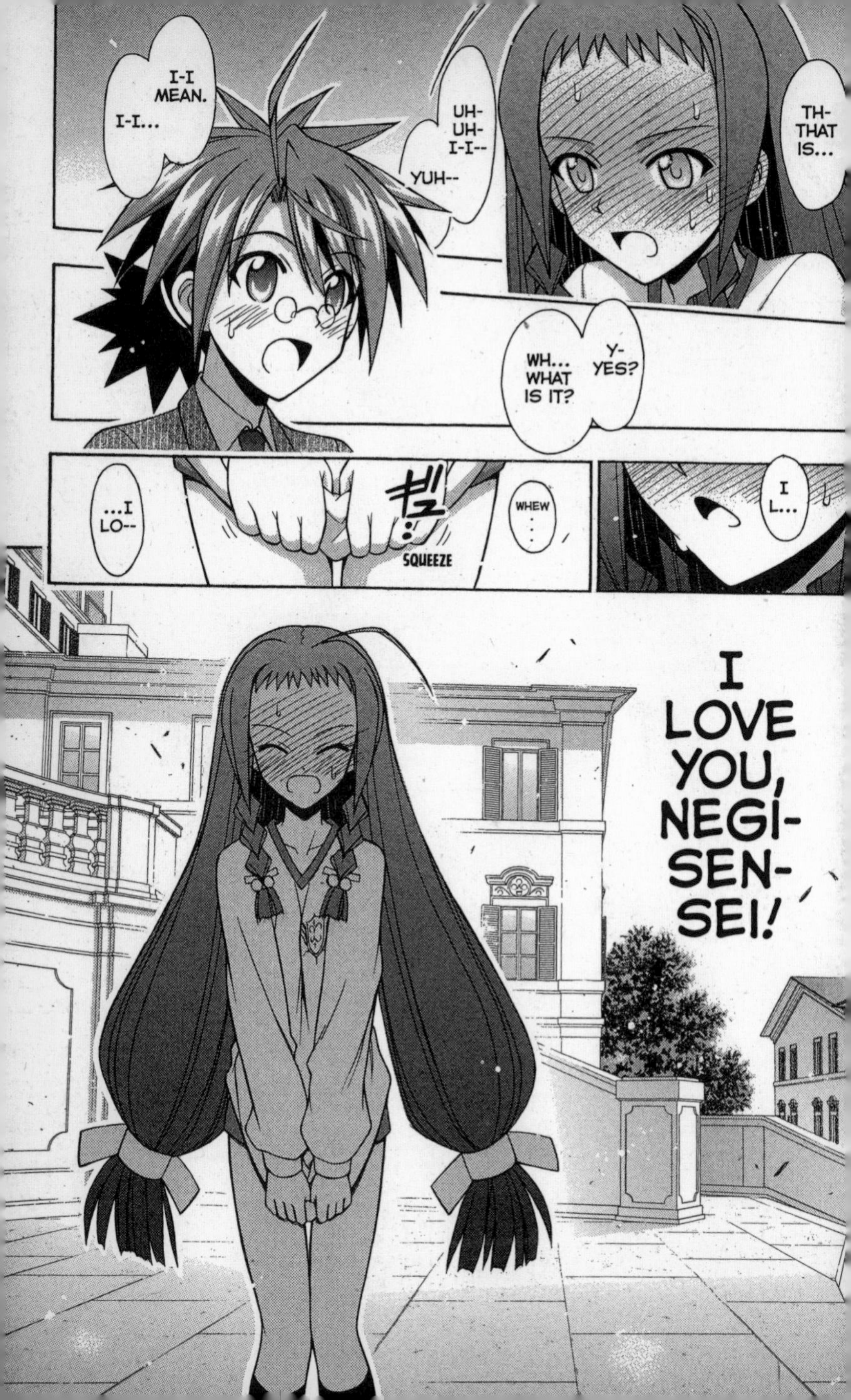

TH- THAT IS...
UH- UH- I-I--
YUH--
I-I MEAN. I-I...
Y- YES?
WH... WHAT IS IT?
I L...
WHEW...
SQUEEZE
...I LO--
I LOVE YOU, NEGI-SENSEI!

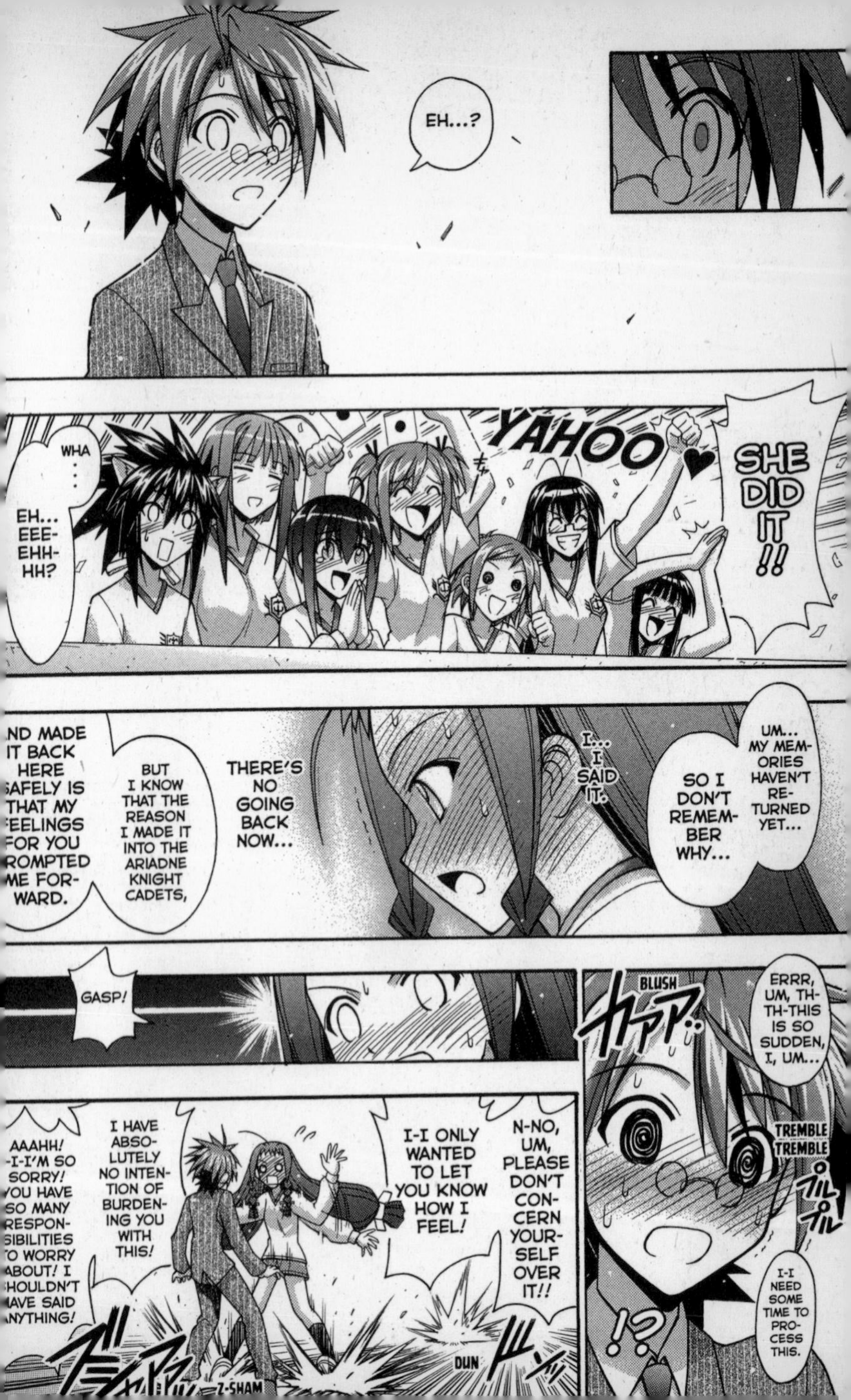
EH...?
SHE DID IT!!
YAHOO ♥
WHA... EH... EEE-EHH-HH?
UM... MY MEMORIES HAVEN'T RETURNED YET...
SO I DON'T REMEMBER WHY...
I... I SAID IT.
THERE'S NO GOING BACK NOW...
BUT I KNOW THAT THE REASON I MADE IT INTO THE ARIADNE KNIGHT CADETS,
ND MADE IT BACK HERE SAFELY IS THAT MY FEELINGS FOR YOU ROMPTED ME FORWARD.
BLUSH
ERRR, UM, TH-TH-THIS IS SO SUDDEN, I, UM...
TREMBLE TREMBLE
I-I NEED SOME TIME TO PROCESS THIS.
GASP!
N-NO, UM, PLEASE DON'T CONCERN YOURSELF OVER IT!!
I-I ONLY WANTED TO LET YOU KNOW HOW I FEEL!
I HAVE ABSOLUTELY NO INTENTION OF BURDENING YOU WITH THIS!
AAAHH! I-I'M SO SORRY! YOU HAVE SO MANY RESPONSIBILITIES TO WORRY ABOUT! I SHOULDN'T HAVE SAID ANYTHING!
DUN
Z-SHAM

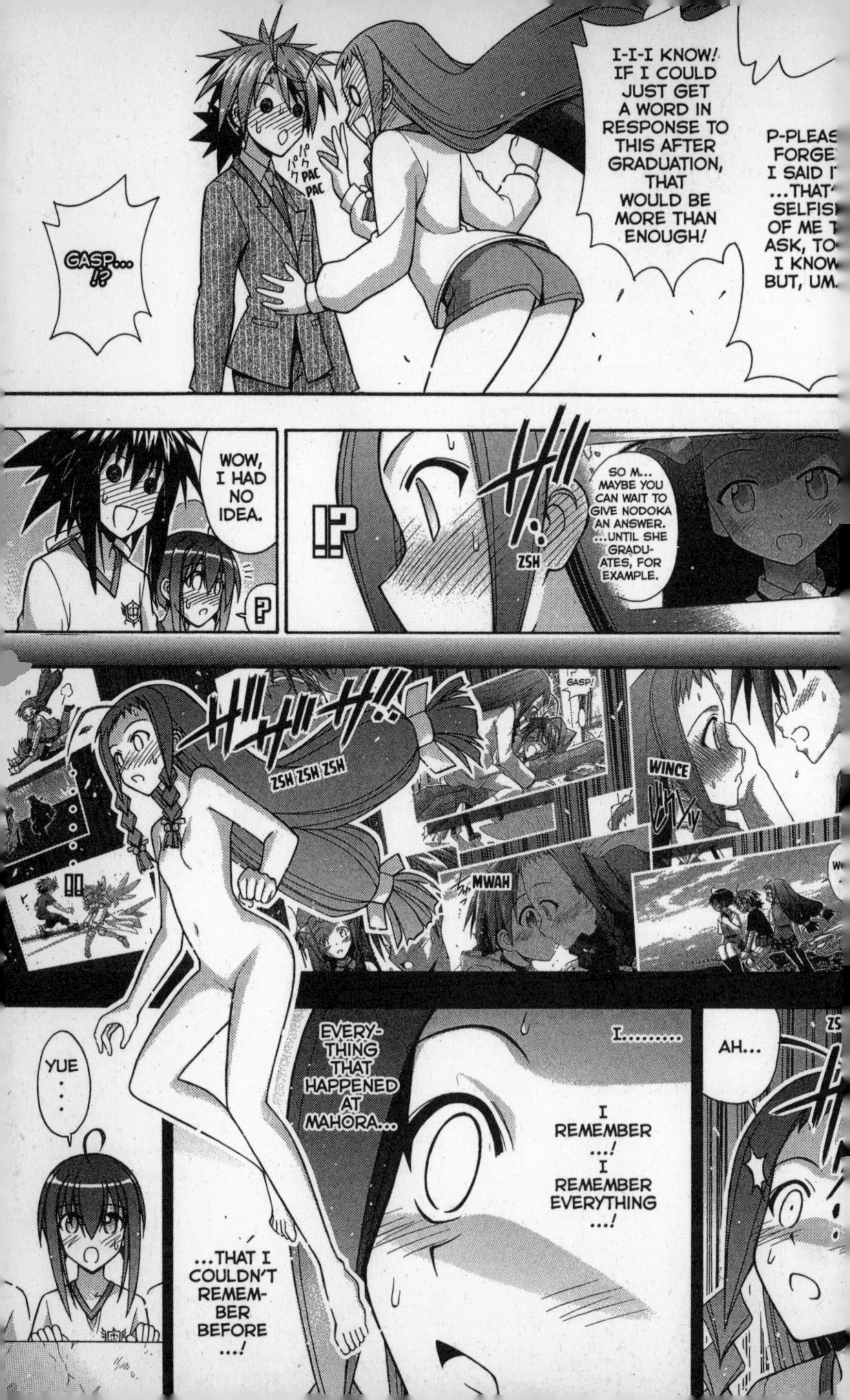

P-PLEAS FORGE I SAID I ...THAT' SELFIS OF ME T ASK, TO I KNOW BUT, UM.
I-I-I KNOW! IF I COULD JUST GET A WORD IN RESPONSE TO THIS AFTER GRADUATION, THAT WOULD BE MORE THAN ENOUGH!
PAC PAC
GASP... !?
SO M... MAYBE YOU CAN WAIT TO GIVE NODOKA AN ANSWER. ...UNTIL SHE GRADUATES, FOR EXAMPLE.
ZSH
!?
WOW, I HAD NO IDEA.
!?
GASP!
WINCE
MWAH
ZSH ZSH ZSH
!!
AH...
I.........
I REMEMBER ...! I REMEMBER EVERYTHING ...!
EVERYTHING THAT HAPPENED AT MAHORA...
...THAT I COULDN'T REMEMBER BEFORE ...!
YUE ...

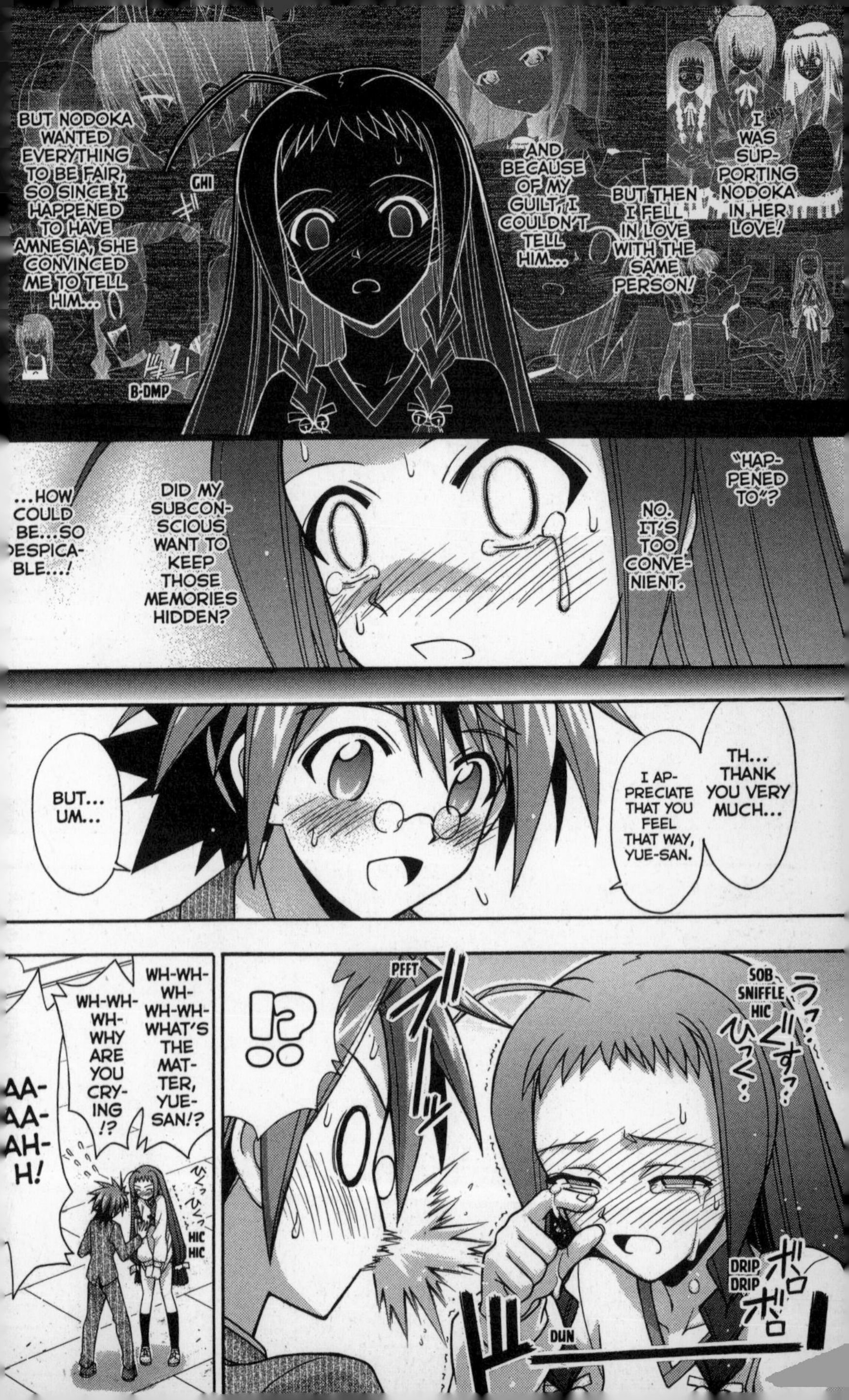
I WAS SUPPORTING NODOKA IN HER LOVE!
BUT THEN I FELL IN LOVE WITH THE SAME PERSON!
AND BECAUSE OF MY GUILT, I COULDN'T TELL HIM...
GHI
BUT NODOKA WANTED EVERYTHING TO BE FAIR, SO SINCE I HAPPENED TO HAVE AMNESIA, SHE CONVINCED ME TO TELL HIM...
B-DMP
"HAPPENED TO"?
NO. IT'S TOO CONVENIENT.
DID MY SUBCONSCIOUS WANT TO KEEP THOSE MEMORIES HIDDEN?
...HOW COULD BE...SO DESPICABLE...!
TH... THANK YOU VERY MUCH...
I APPRECIATE THAT YOU FEEL THAT WAY, YUE-SAN.
BUT... UM...
SOB SNIFFLE HIC
PFFT
!?
DRIP DRIP
DUN
WH-WH-WH-WH-WH-WHAT'S THE MATTER, YUE-SAN!?
WH-WH-WH-WHY ARE YOU CRYING!?
AAAAAH!
HIC HIC

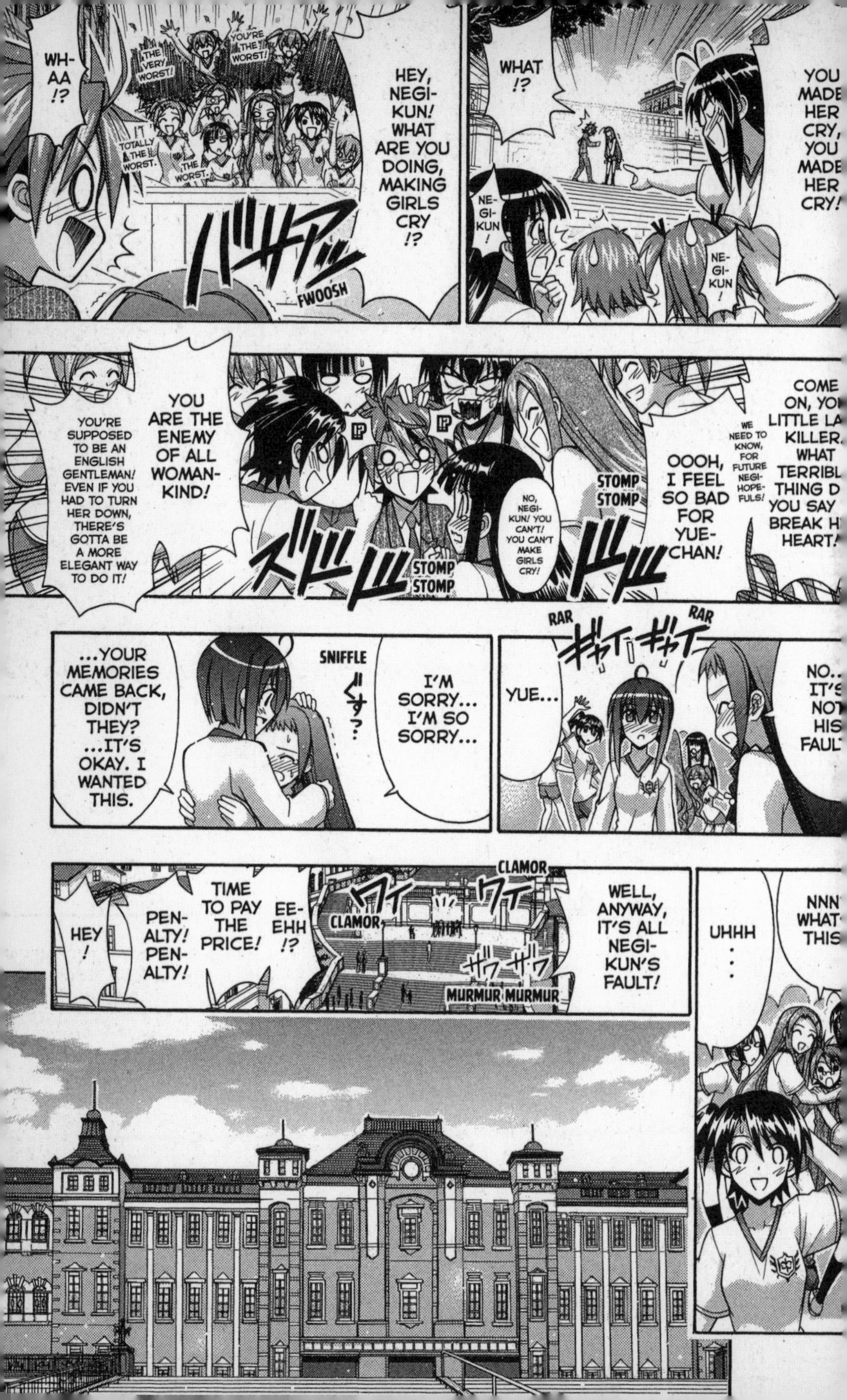

YOU MADE HER CRY, YOU MADE HER CRY!
WHAT!?
NEGI-KUN!
NEGI-KUN!
HEY, NEGI-KUN! WHAT ARE YOU DOING, MAKING GIRLS CRY!?
YOU'RE THE WORST!
THE VERY WORST!
IT TOTALLY THE WORST.
THE WORST.
WH-AA!?
FWOOSH
COME ON, YO LITTLE LA KILLER. WHAT TERRIBL THING D YOU SAY BREAK H HEART!
WE NEED TO KNOW, FOR FUTURE NEGI-HOPE-FULS!
OOOH, I FEEL SO BAD FOR YUE-CHAN!
STOMP STOMP
NO, NEGI-KUN! YOU CAN'T! YOU CAN'T MAKE GIRLS CRY!
YOU ARE THE ENEMY OF ALL WOMAN-KIND!
YOU'RE SUPPOSED TO BE AN ENGLISH GENTLEMAN! EVEN IF YOU HAD TO TURN HER DOWN, THERE'S GOTTA BE A MORE ELEGANT WAY TO DO IT!
STOMP STOMP
NO... IT'S NOT HIS FAUL
RAR RAR
YUE...
I'M SORRY... I'M SO SORRY...
SNIFFLE
...YOUR MEMORIES CAME BACK, DIDN'T THEY? ...IT'S OKAY. I WANTED THIS.
NNN WHAT' THIS
UHHH...
WELL, ANYWAY, IT'S ALL NEGI-KUN'S FAULT!
CLAMOR
EE-EHH!?
TIME TO PAY THE PRICE!
PEN-ALTY! PEN-ALTY!
HEY!
CLAMOR
MURMUR MURMUR

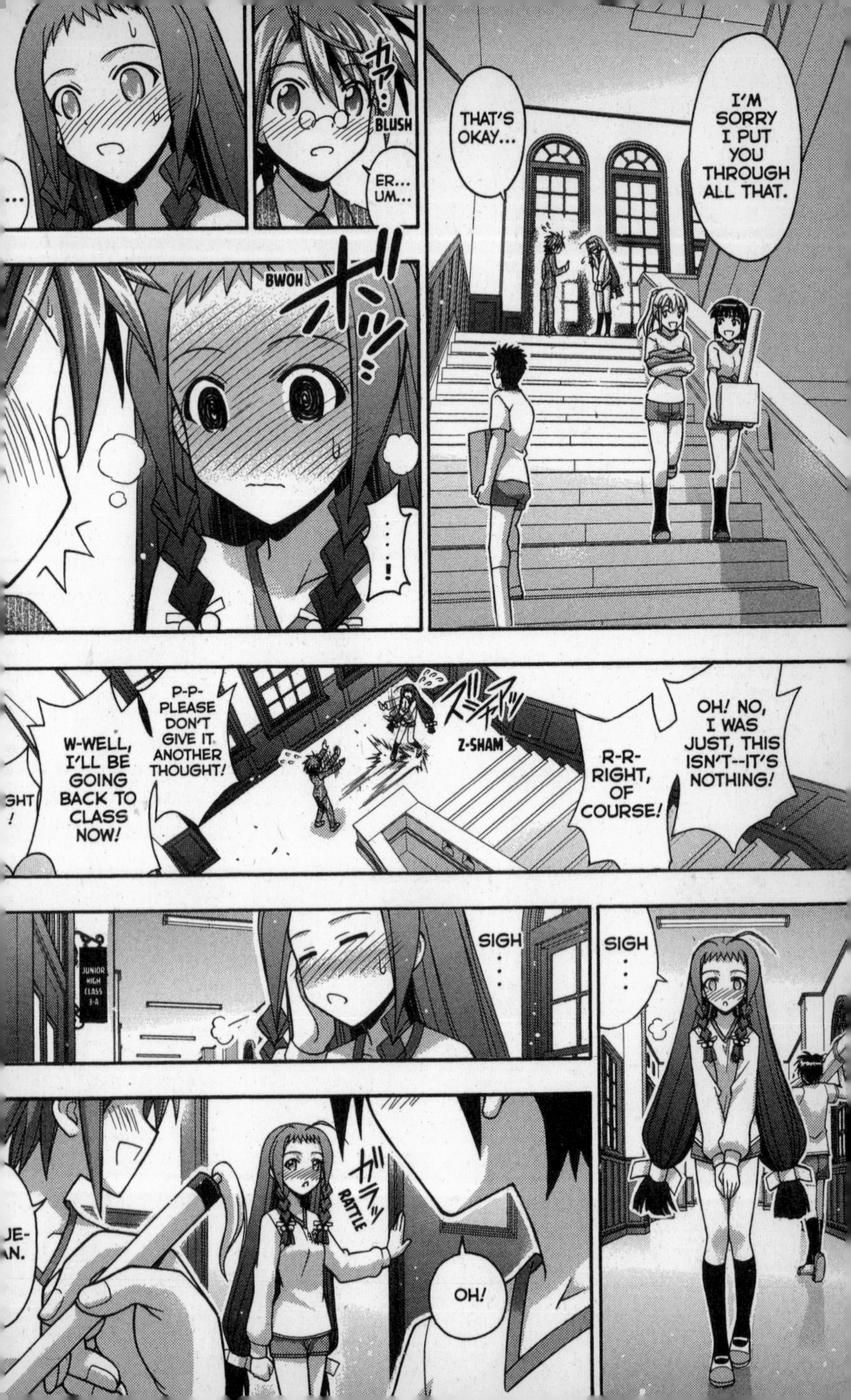
I'M SORRY I PUT YOU THROUGH ALL THAT.
THAT'S OKAY...
BLUSH
ER... UM...
...
BWOH
...!
OH! NO, I WAS JUST, THIS ISN'T--IT'S NOTHING!
R-R-RIGHT, OF COURSE!
Z-SHAM
P-P-PLEASE DON'T GIVE IT ANOTHER THOUGHT!
W-WELL, I'LL BE GOING BACK TO CLASS NOW!
SIGH...
SIGH...
JUNIOR HIGH CLASS 3-A
RATTLE
OH!

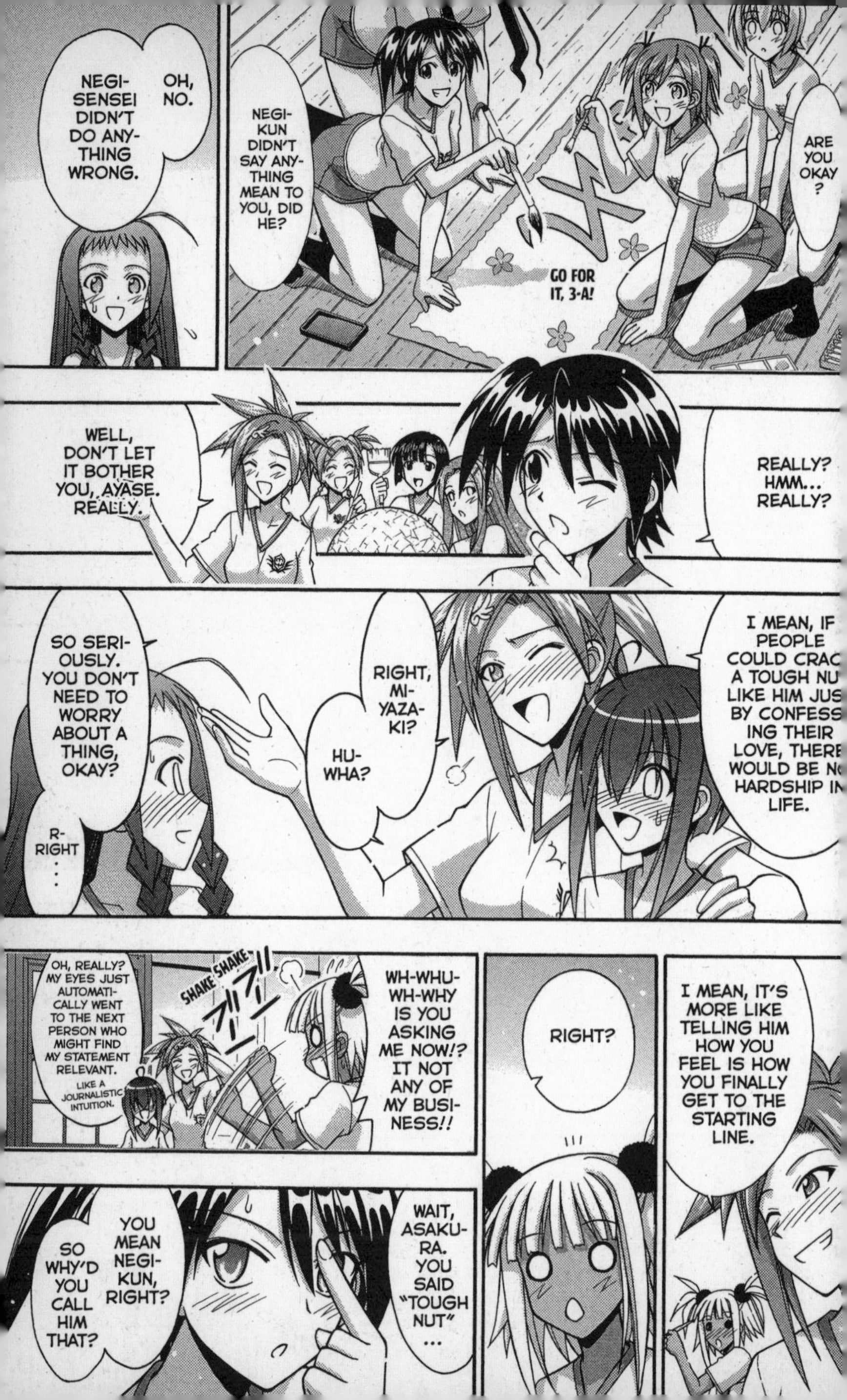
ARE YOU OKAY?
GO FOR IT, 3-A!
NEGI-KUN DIDN'T SAY ANYTHING MEAN TO YOU, DID HE?
OH, NO.
NEGI-SENSEI DIDN'T DO ANYTHING WRONG.
REALLY? HMM... REALLY?
WELL, DON'T LET IT BOTHER YOU, AYASE. REALLY.
I MEAN, IF PEOPLE COULD CRAC A TOUGH NU LIKE HIM JUS BY CONFESS ING THEIR LOVE, THERE WOULD BE N HARDSHIP IN LIFE.
RIGHT, MIYAZAKI?
HU-WHA?
SO SERIOUSLY. YOU DON'T NEED TO WORRY ABOUT A THING, OKAY?
R-RIGHT...
I MEAN, IT'S MORE LIKE TELLING HIM HOW YOU FEEL IS HOW YOU FINALLY GET TO THE STARTING LINE.
RIGHT?
WH-WHU-WH-WHY IS YOU ASKING ME NOW!? IT NOT ANY OF MY BUSINESS!!
SHAKE SHAKE
OH, REALLY? MY EYES JUST AUTOMATICALLY WENT TO THE NEXT PERSON WHO MIGHT FIND MY STATEMENT RELEVANT.
LIKE A JOURNALISTIC INTUITION.
WAIT, ASAKURA. YOU SAID "TOUGH NUT"...
YOU MEAN NEGI-KUN, RIGHT?
SO WHY'D YOU CALL HIM THAT?

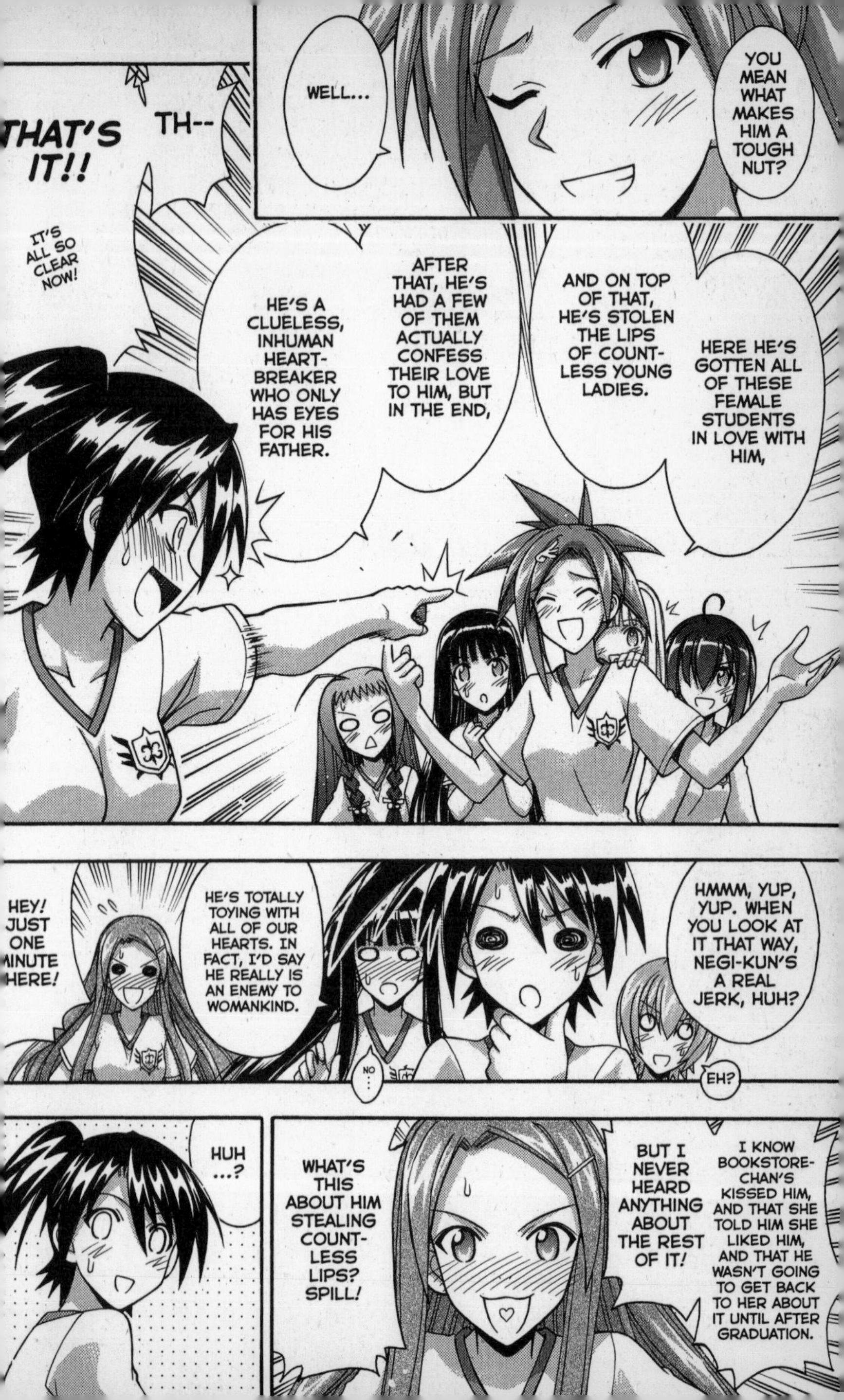
YOU MEAN WHAT MAKES HIM A TOUGH NUT?
WELL...
TH--
THAT'S IT!!
IT'S ALL SO CLEAR NOW!
HERE HE'S GOTTEN ALL OF THESE FEMALE STUDENTS IN LOVE WITH HIM,
AND ON TOP OF THAT, HE'S STOLEN THE LIPS OF COUNT-LESS YOUNG LADIES.
AFTER THAT, HE'S HAD A FEW OF THEM ACTUALLY CONFESS THEIR LOVE TO HIM, BUT IN THE END,
HE'S A CLUELESS, INHUMAN HEART-BREAKER WHO ONLY HAS EYES FOR HIS FATHER.
HMMM, YUP, YUP. WHEN YOU LOOK AT IT THAT WAY, NEGI-KUN'S A REAL JERK, HUH?
EH?
NO...
HE'S TOTALLY TOYING WITH ALL OF OUR HEARTS. IN FACT, I'D SAY HE REALLY IS AN ENEMY TO WOMANKIND.
HEY! JUST ONE MINUTE HERE!
I KNOW BOOKSTORE-CHAN'S KISSED HIM, AND THAT SHE TOLD HIM SHE LIKED HIM, AND THAT HE WASN'T GOING TO GET BACK TO HER ABOUT IT UNTIL AFTER GRADUATION.
BUT I NEVER HEARD ANYTHING ABOUT THE REST OF IT!
WHAT'S THIS ABOUT HIM STEALING COUNT-LESS LIPS? SPILL!
HUH ...?

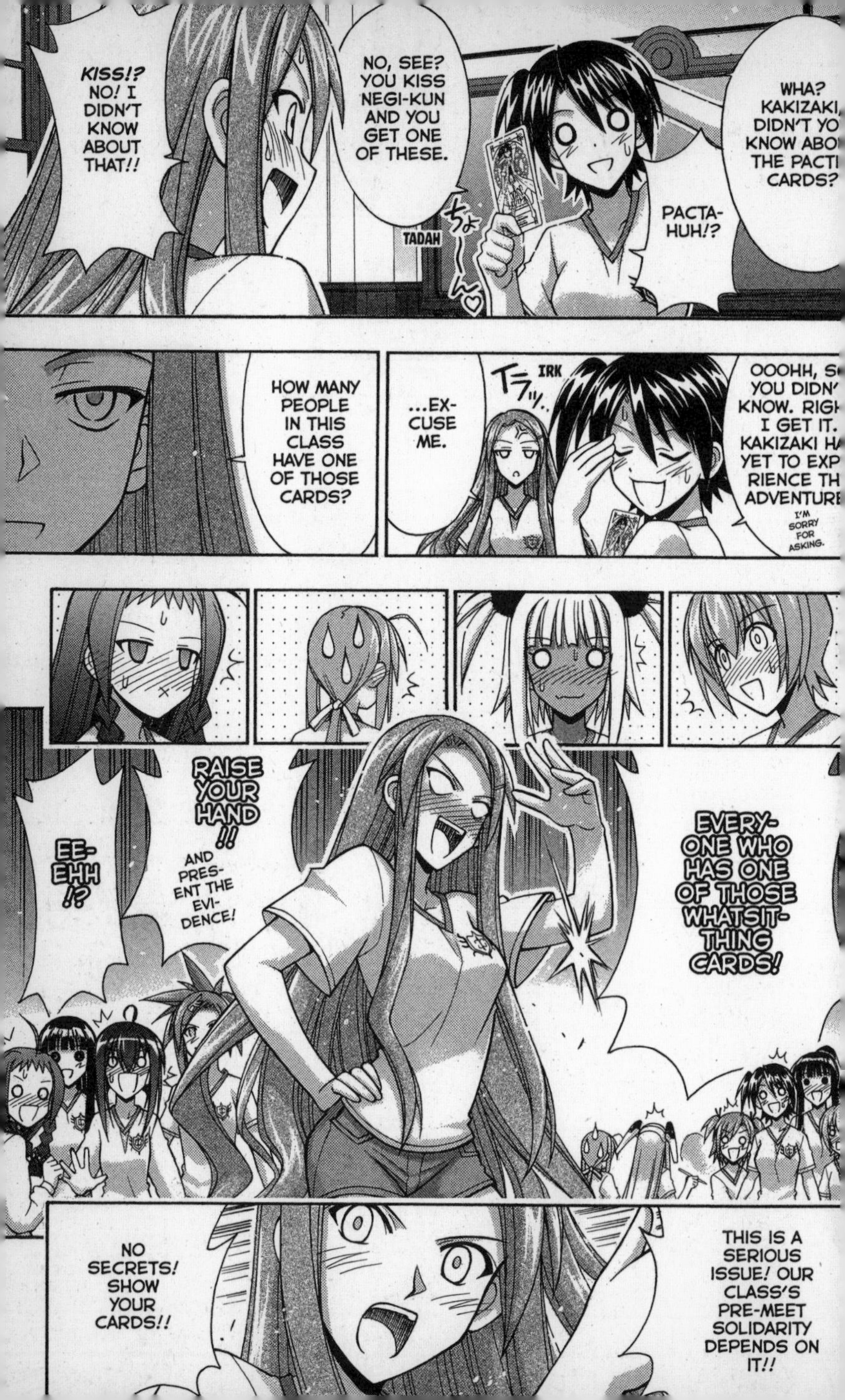
WHA? KAKIZAKI, DIDN'T YO KNOW ABO THE PACTI CARDS?
PACTA-HUH!?
NO, SEE? YOU KISS NEGI-KUN AND YOU GET ONE OF THESE.
TADAH
KISS!? NO! I DIDN'T KNOW ABOUT THAT!!
OOOHH, S YOU DIDN' KNOW. RIGH I GET IT. KAKIZAKI H YET TO EXP RIENCE TH ADVENTURE
I'M SORRY FOR ASKING.
IRK
...EX-CUSE ME.
HOW MANY PEOPLE IN THIS CLASS HAVE ONE OF THOSE CARDS?
EVERY-ONE WHO HAS ONE OF THOSE WHATSIT-THING CARDS!
RAISE YOUR HAND!!
AND PRES-ENT THE EVI-DENCE!
EE-EHH!?
THIS IS A SERIOUS ISSUE! OUR CLASS'S PRE-MEET SOLIDARITY DEPENDS ON IT!!
NO SECRETS! SHOW YOUR CARDS!!

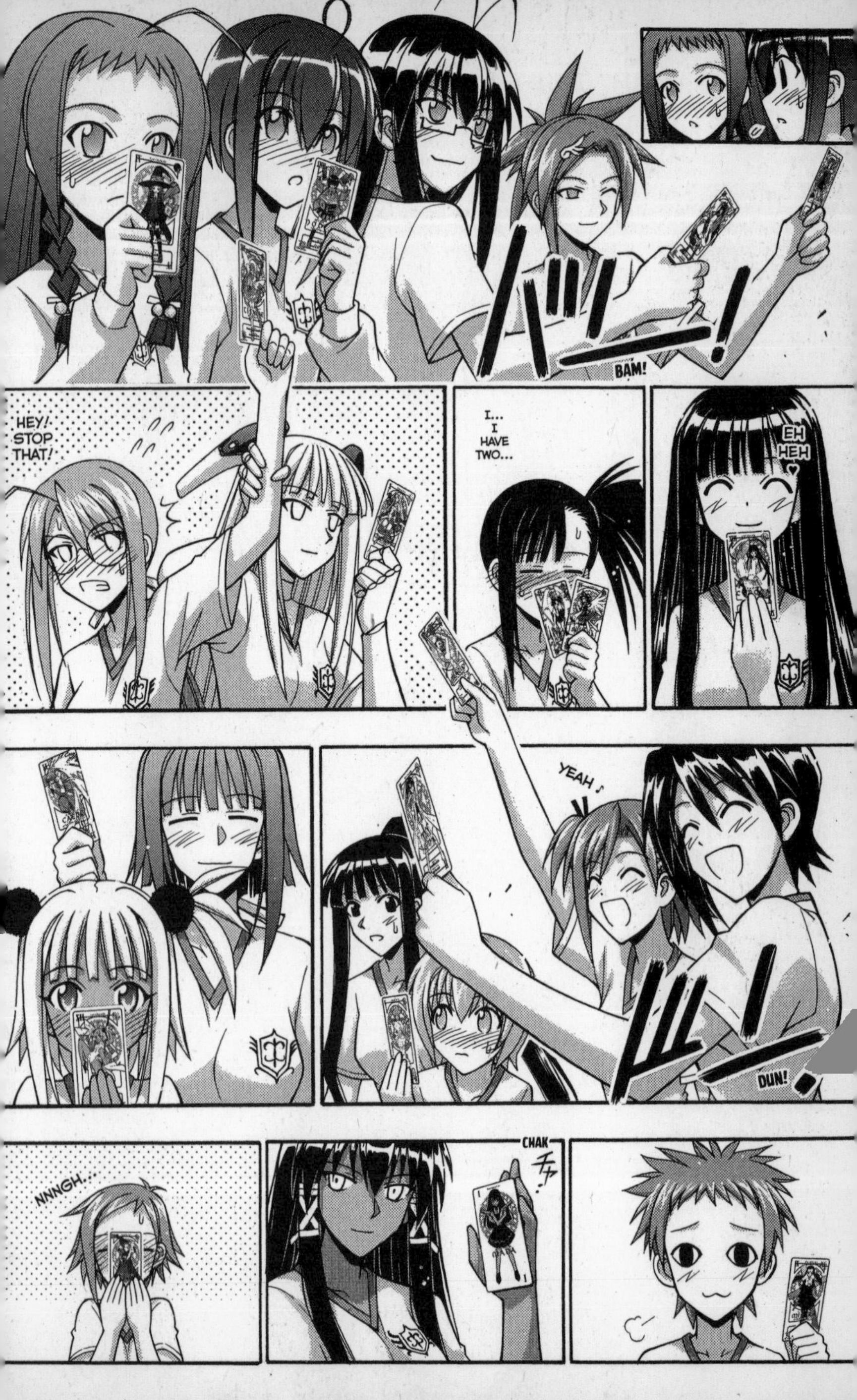
BAM!
EH HEH ♥
I... I HAVE TWO...
HEY! STOP THAT!
YEAH ♪
DUN!
CHAK
NNNGH...

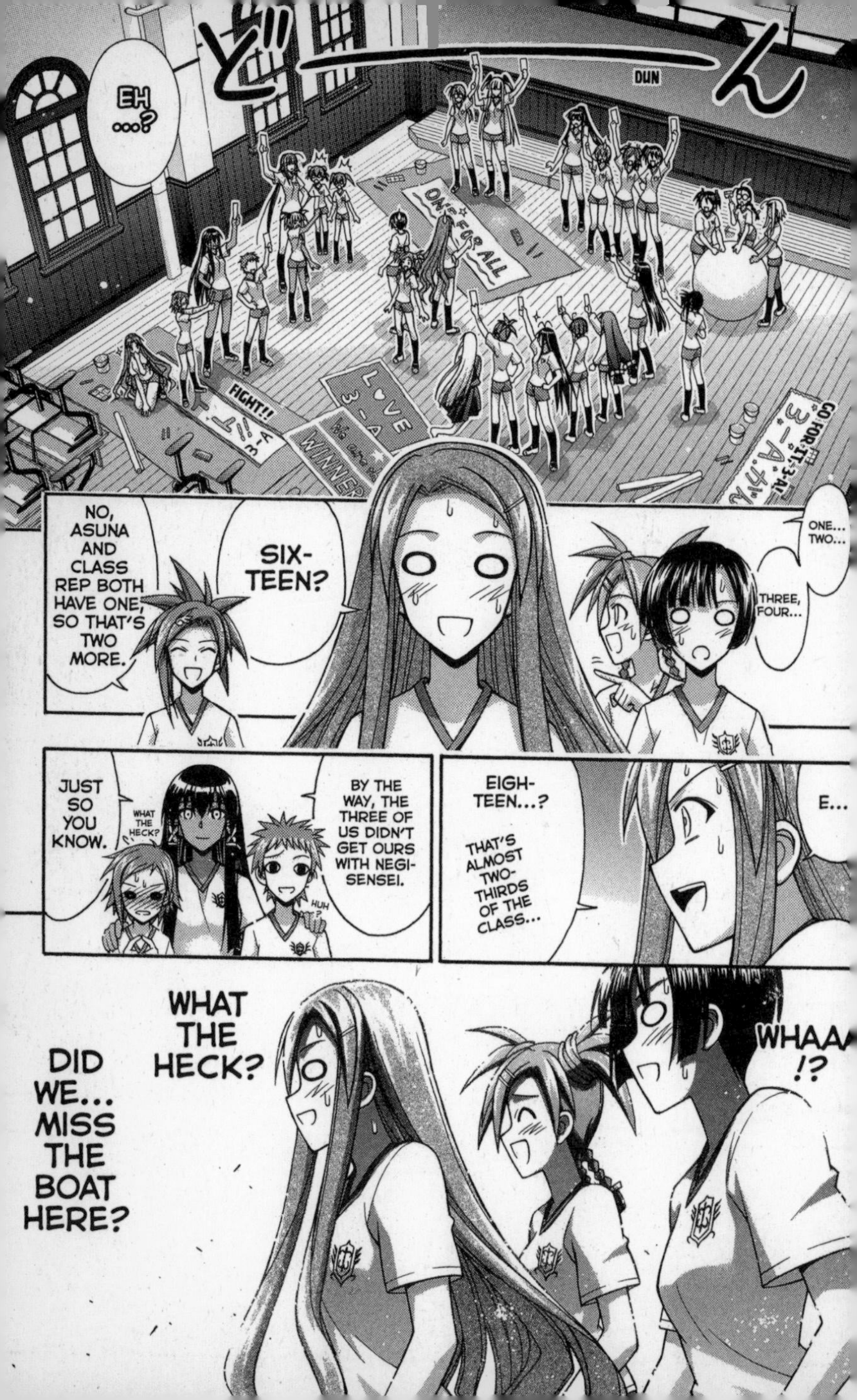

どーーーん
DUN
EH...?
ONE FOR ALL
GO FOR IT, 3-A!
LOVE 3-A
WINNER
FIGHT!!
ONE... TWO...
THREE, FOUR...
SIX-TEEN?
NO, ASUNA AND CLASS REP BOTH HAVE ONE, SO THAT'S TWO MORE.
E...
EIGH-TEEN...?
THAT'S ALMOST TWO-THIRDS OF THE CLASS...
BY THE WAY, THE THREE OF US DIDN'T GET OURS WITH NEGI-SENSEI.
HUH?
WHAT THE HECK?
JUST SO YOU KNOW.
WHAAA!?
WHAT THE HECK?
DID WE... MISS THE BOAT HERE?

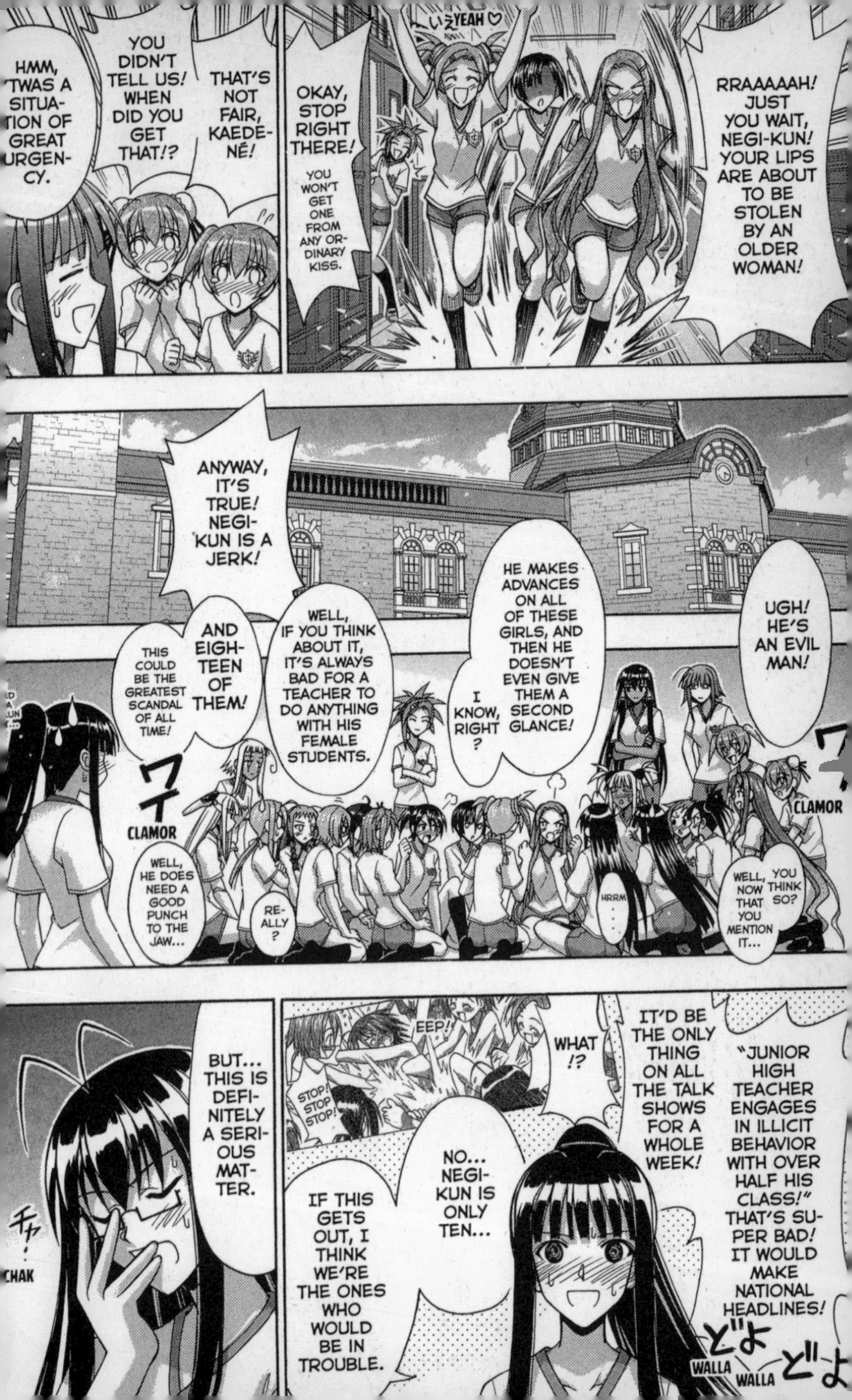
いえYEAH ♡
RRAAAAAH! JUST YOU WAIT, NEGI-KUN! YOUR LIPS ARE ABOUT TO BE STOLEN BY AN OLDER WOMAN!
OKAY, STOP RIGHT THERE!
YOU WON'T GET ONE FROM ANY ORDINARY KISS.
THAT'S NOT FAIR, KAEDE-NÉ!
YOU DIDN'T TELL US! WHEN DID YOU GET THAT!?
HMM, 'TWAS A SITUATION OF GREAT URGENCY.
UGH! HE'S AN EVIL MAN!
HE MAKES ADVANCES ON ALL OF THESE GIRLS, AND THEN HE DOESN'T EVEN GIVE THEM A SECOND GLANCE!
I KNOW, RIGHT?
WELL, IF YOU THINK ABOUT IT, IT'S ALWAYS BAD FOR A TEACHER TO DO ANYTHING WITH HIS FEMALE STUDENTS.
ANYWAY, IT'S TRUE! NEGI-KUN IS A JERK!
AND EIGHTEEN OF THEM!
THIS COULD BE THE GREATEST SCANDAL OF ALL TIME!
CLAMOR
YOU THINK SO?
WELL, NOW THAT YOU MENTION IT...
HRRM...
REALLY?
WELL, HE DOES NEED A GOOD PUNCH TO THE JAW...
CLAMOR
"JUNIOR HIGH TEACHER ENGAGES IN ILLICIT BEHAVIOR WITH OVER HALF HIS CLASS!" THAT'S SUPER BAD! IT WOULD MAKE NATIONAL HEADLINES!
IT'D BE THE ONLY THING ON ALL THE TALK SHOWS FOR A WHOLE WEEK!
WHAT!?
EEP!!
STOP! STOP STOP!
NO... NEGI-KUN IS ONLY TEN...
IF THIS GETS OUT, I THINK WE'RE THE ONES WHO WOULD BE IN TROUBLE.
WALLA WALLA
BUT... THIS IS DEFINITELY A SERIOUS MATTER.
CHAK

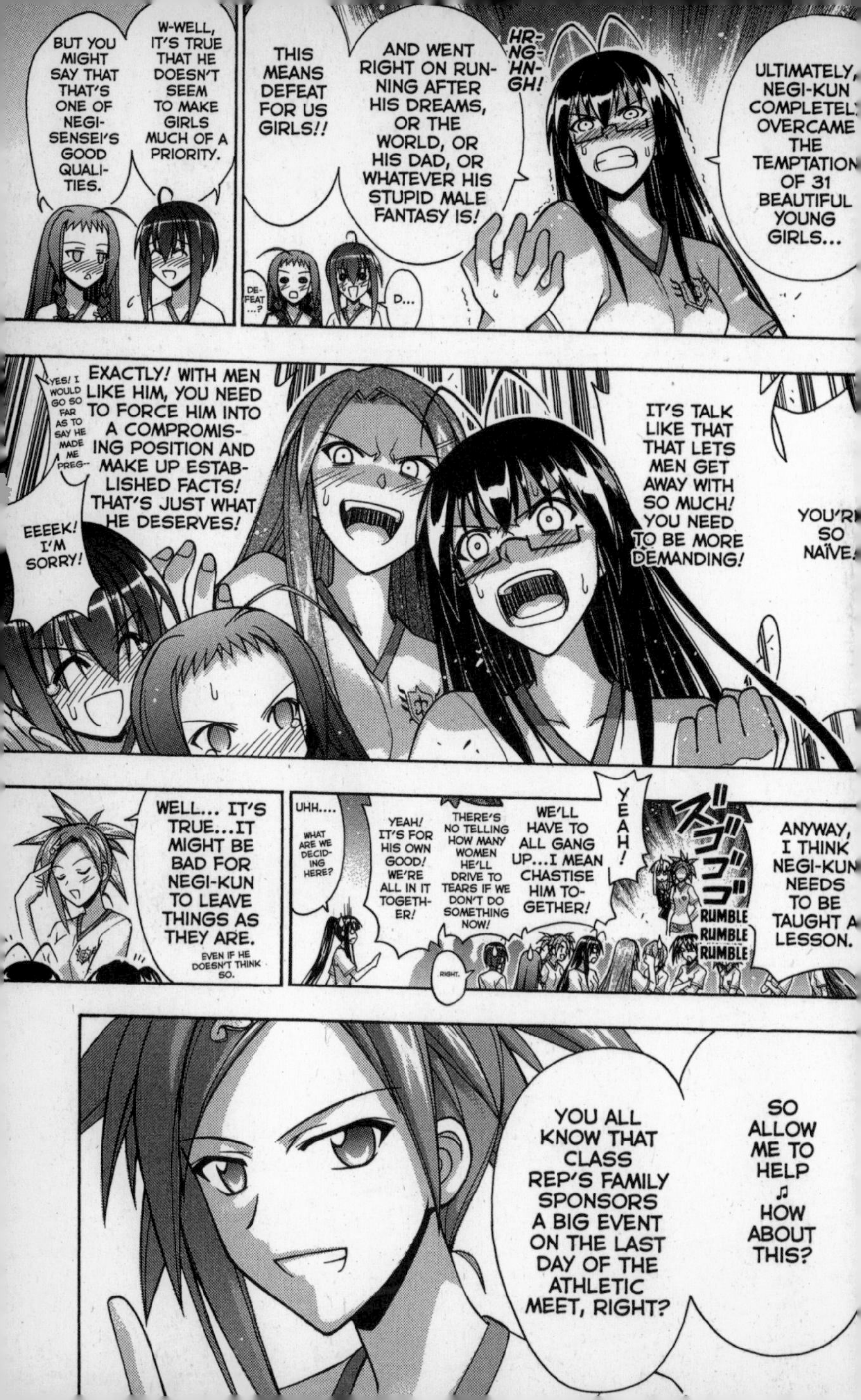
ULTIMATELY, NEGI-KUN COMPLETEL OVERCAME THE TEMPTATION OF 31 BEAUTIFUL YOUNG GIRLS...
HRNGHNGH!
AND WENT RIGHT ON RUNNING AFTER HIS DREAMS, OR THE WORLD, OR HIS DAD, OR WHATEVER HIS STUPID MALE FANTASY IS!
THIS MEANS DEFEAT FOR US GIRLS!!
D...
DEFEAT...?
W-WELL, IT'S TRUE THAT HE DOESN'T SEEM TO MAKE GIRLS MUCH OF A PRIORITY.
BUT YOU MIGHT SAY THAT THAT'S ONE OF NEGI-SENSEI'S GOOD QUALITIES.
YOU'R SO NAÏVE.
IT'S TALK LIKE THAT THAT LETS MEN GET AWAY WITH SO MUCH! YOU NEED TO BE MORE DEMANDING!
EXACTLY! WITH MEN LIKE HIM, YOU NEED TO FORCE HIM INTO A COMPROMISING POSITION AND MAKE UP ESTABLISHED FACTS! THAT'S JUST WHAT HE DESERVES!
YES! I WOULD GO SO FAR AS TO SAY HE MADE ME PREG--
EEEEK! I'M SORRY!
ANYWAY, I THINK NEGI-KUN NEEDS TO BE TAUGHT A LESSON.
RUMBLE RUMBLE RUMBLE
YEAH!
WE'LL HAVE TO ALL GANG UP...I MEAN CHASTISE HIM TOGETHER!
THERE'S NO TELLING HOW MANY WOMEN HE'LL DRIVE TO TEARS IF WE DON'T DO SOMETHING NOW!
YEAH! IT'S FOR HIS OWN GOOD! WE'RE ALL IN IT TOGETHER!
UHH....
WHAT ARE WE DECIDING HERE?
RIGHT.
WELL... IT'S TRUE...IT MIGHT BE BAD FOR NEGI-KUN TO LEAVE THINGS AS THEY ARE.
EVEN IF HE DOESN'T THINK SO.
SO ALLOW ME TO HELP ♫ HOW ABOUT THIS?
YOU ALL KNOW THAT CLASS REP'S FAMILY SPONSORS A BIG EVENT ON THE LAST DAY OF THE ATHLETIC MEET, RIGHT?

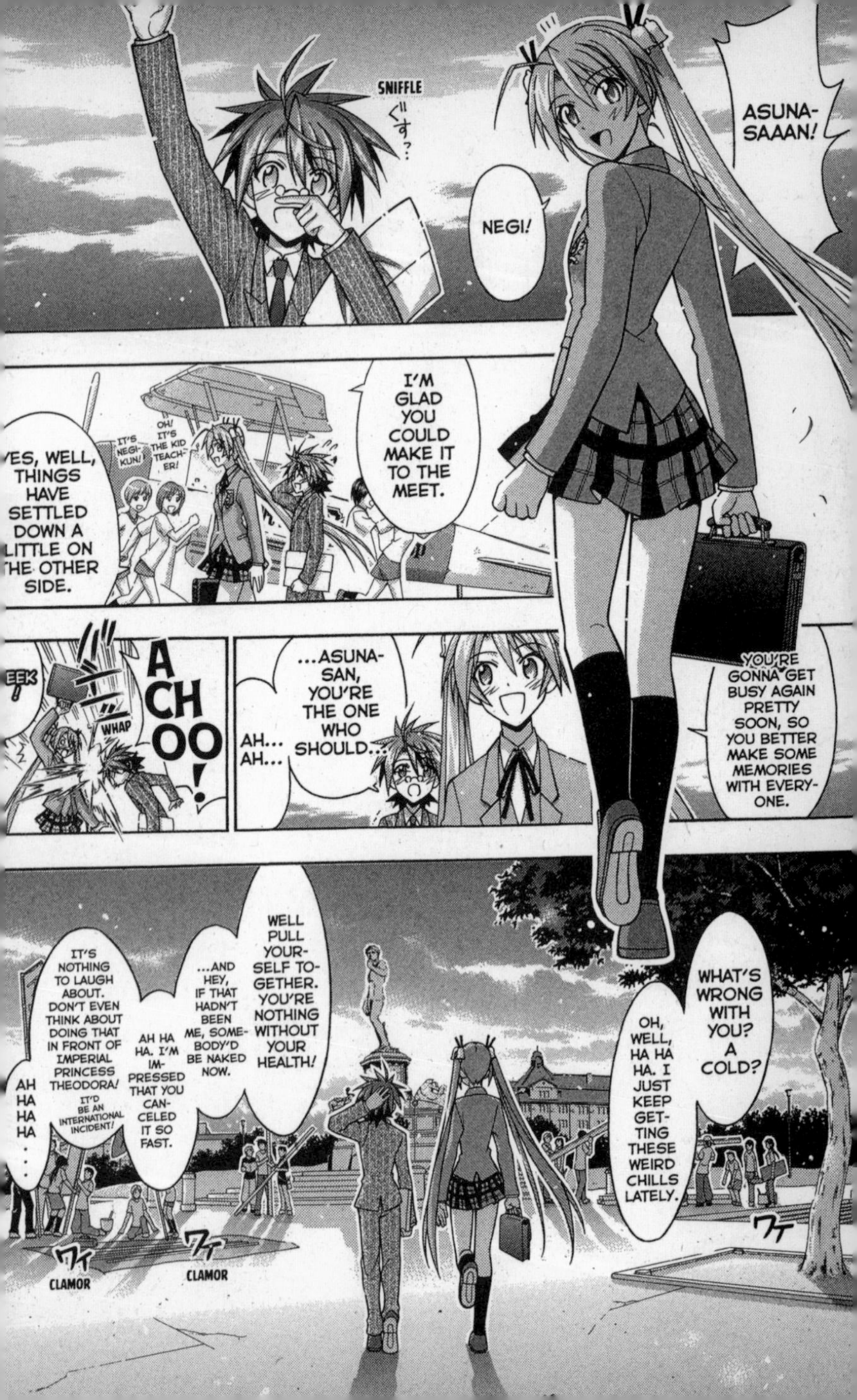
ASUNA-SAAAN!
NEGI!
SNIFFLE
ぐすっ
I'M GLAD YOU COULD MAKE IT TO THE MEET.
OH! IT'S THE KID TEACHER!
IT'S NEGI-KUN!
YES, WELL, THINGS HAVE SETTLED DOWN A LITTLE ON THE OTHER SIDE.
YOU'RE GONNA GET BUSY AGAIN PRETTY SOON, SO YOU BETTER MAKE SOME MEMORIES WITH EVERYONE.
...ASUNA-SAN, YOU'RE THE ONE WHO SHOULD...
AH... AH...
ACHOO!
WHAP
EEK!
WHAT'S WRONG WITH YOU? A COLD?
OH, WELL, HA HA HA. I JUST KEEP GETTING THESE WEIRD CHILLS LATELY.
ワイ
WELL PULL YOURSELF TOGETHER. YOU'RE NOTHING WITHOUT YOUR HEALTH!
...AND HEY, IF THAT HADN'T BEEN ME, SOMEBODY'D BE NAKED NOW.
AH HA HA. I'M IMPRESSED THAT YOU CANCELED IT SO FAST.
IT'S NOTHING TO LAUGH ABOUT. DON'T EVEN THINK ABOUT DOING THAT IN FRONT OF IMPERIAL PRINCESS THEODORA!
IT'D BE AN INTERNATIONAL INCIDENT!
AH HA HA HA...
ワイ
CLAMOR
ワイ
CLAMOR

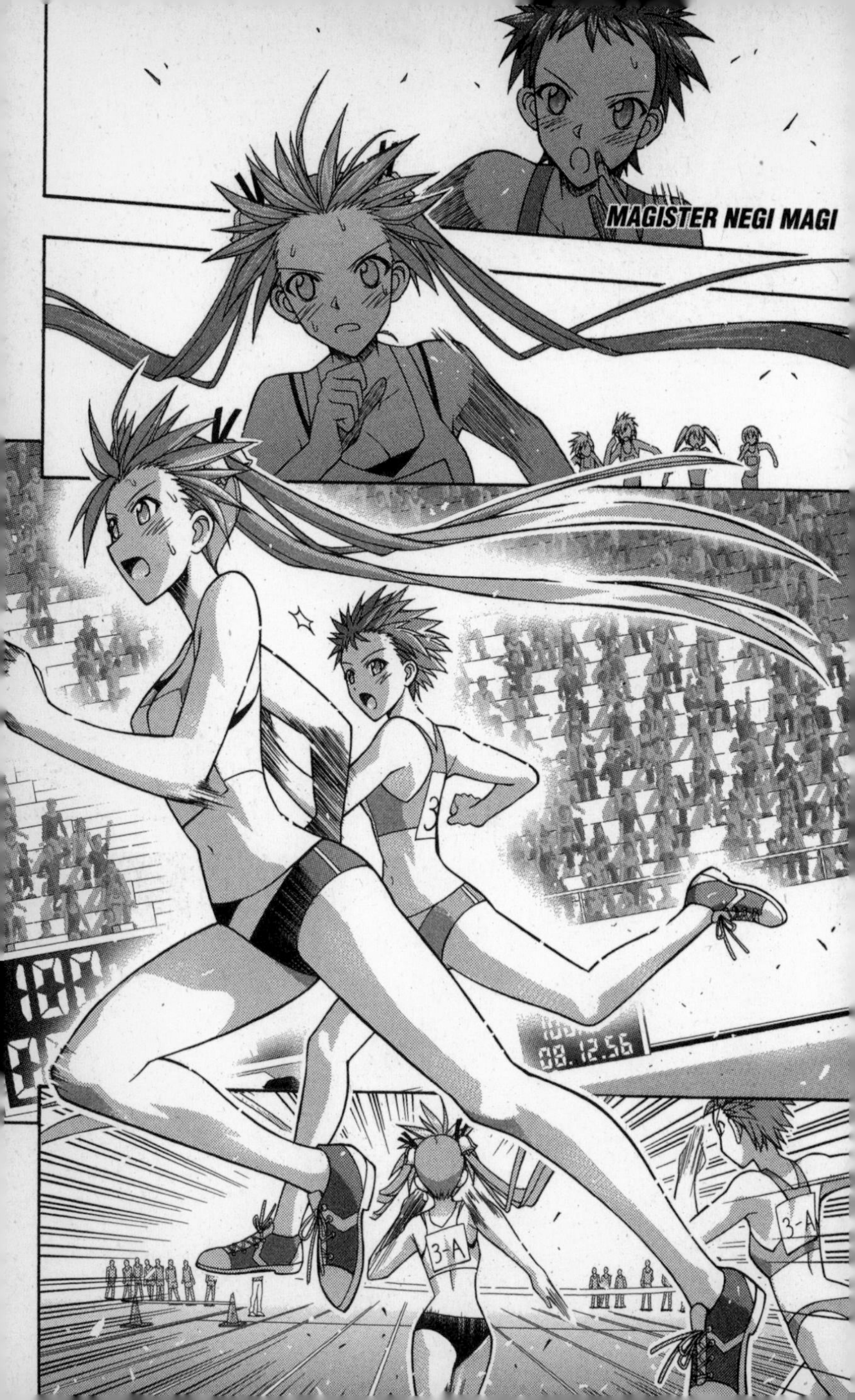
MAGISTER NEGI MAGI
08. 12. 56
3-A
3-A

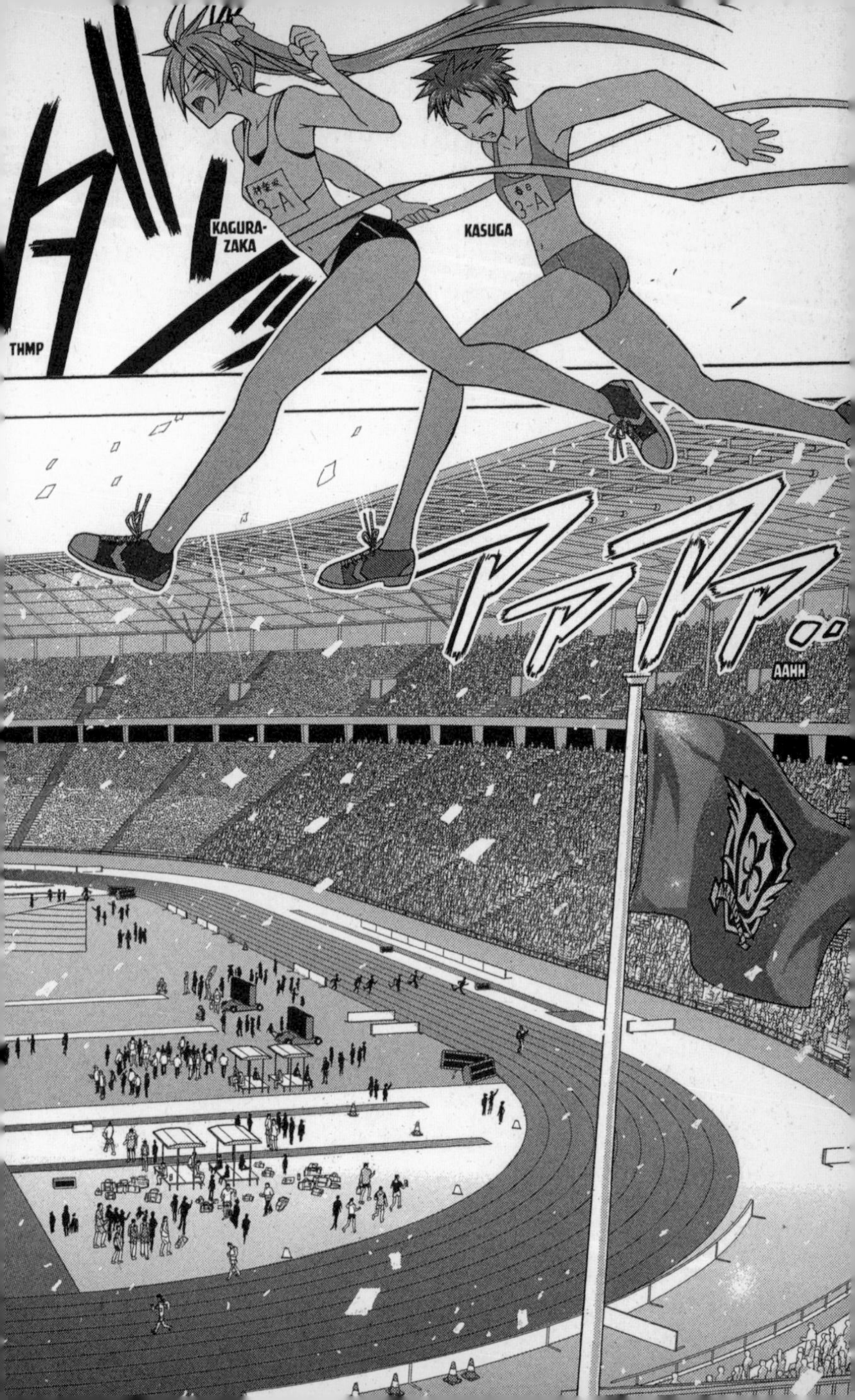

KAGURA-
ZAKA
KASUGA
THMP
AAHH

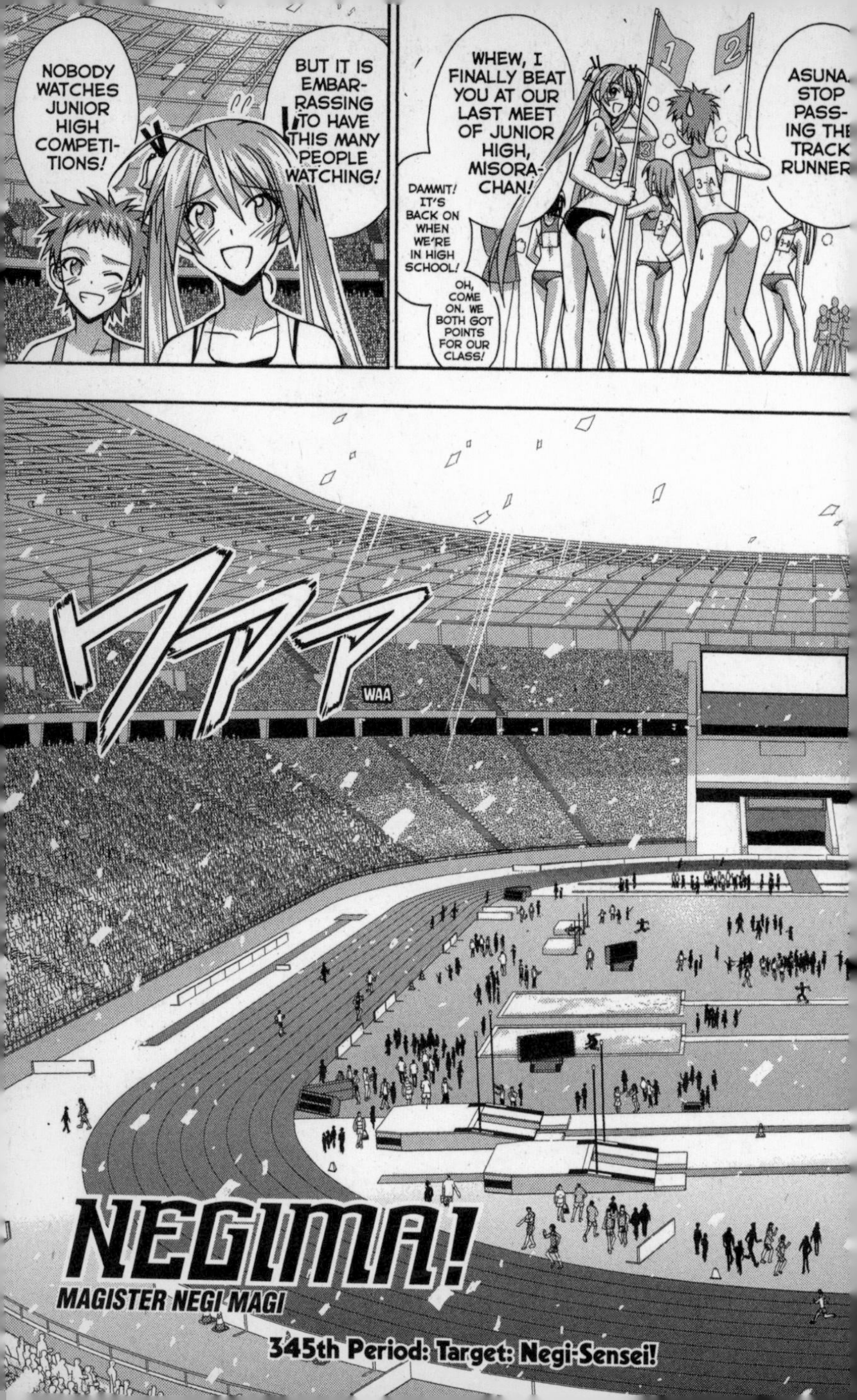
ASUNA. STOP PASS-ING THE TRACK RUNNER
WHEW, I FINALLY BEAT YOU AT OUR LAST MEET OF JUNIOR HIGH, MISORA-CHAN!
DAMMIT! IT'S BACK ON WHEN WE'RE IN HIGH SCHOOL!
OH, COME ON. WE BOTH GOT POINTS FOR OUR CLASS!
BUT IT IS EMBAR-RASSING TO HAVE THIS MANY PEOPLE WATCHING!
NOBODY WATCHES JUNIOR HIGH COMPETI-TIONS!
WAA
NEGIMA!
MAGISTER NEGI MAGI
345th Period: Target: Negi-Sensei!

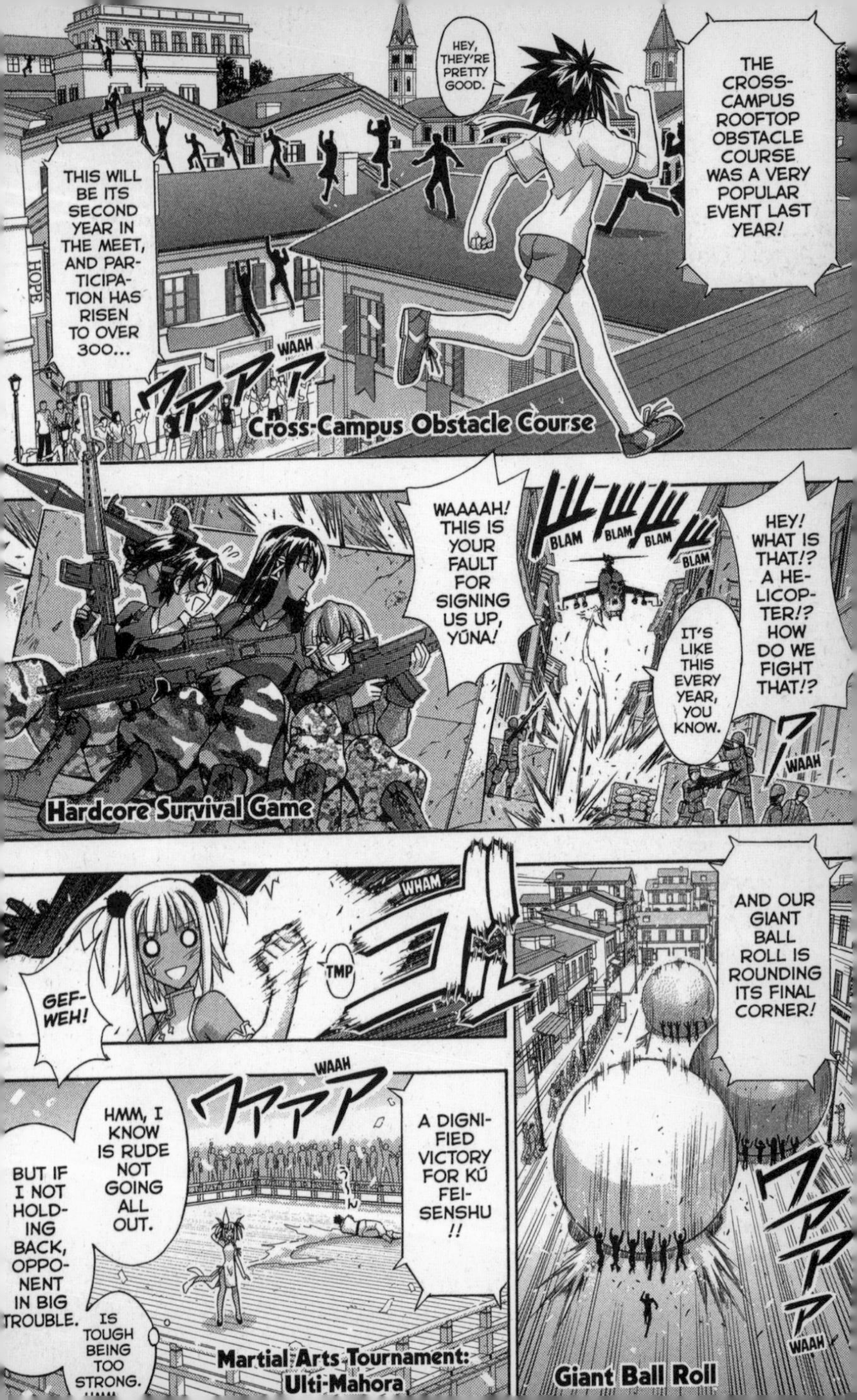
THE CROSS-CAMPUS ROOFTOP OBSTACLE COURSE WAS A VERY POPULAR EVENT LAST YEAR!
HEY, THEY'RE PRETTY GOOD.
THIS WILL BE ITS SECOND YEAR IN THE MEET, AND PARTICIPATION HAS RISEN TO OVER 300...
HOPE
WAAH
Cross-Campus Obstacle Course
HEY! WHAT IS THAT!? A HELICOPTER!? HOW DO WE FIGHT THAT!?
BLAM BLAM BLAM BLAM
IT'S LIKE THIS EVERY YEAR, YOU KNOW.
WAAH
WAAAAH! THIS IS YOUR FAULT FOR SIGNING US UP, YŪNA!
Hardcore Survival Game
AND OUR GIANT BALL ROLL IS ROUNDING ITS FINAL CORNER!
WAAH
Giant Ball Roll
WHAM
TMP
GEF-WEH!
A DIGNIFIED VICTORY FOR KŪ FEI-SENSHU!!
WAAH
HMM, I KNOW IS RUDE NOT GOING ALL OUT.
BUT IF I NOT HOLDING BACK, OPPONENT IN BIG TROUBLE.
IS TOUGH BEING TOO STRONG.
Martial Arts Tournament: Ulti-Mahora

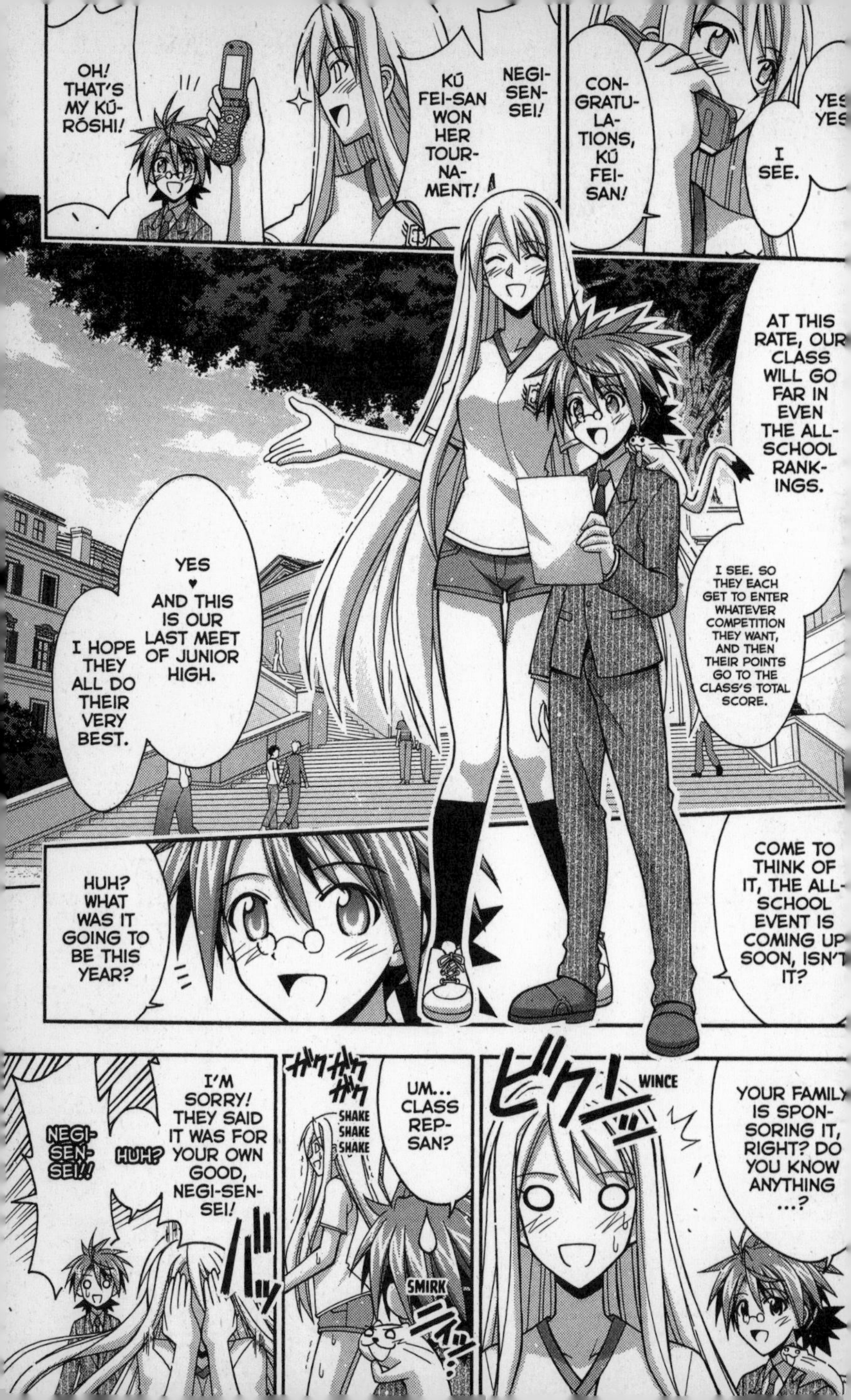
YES YES
I SEE.
CONGRATULATIONS, KŪ FEI-SAN!
NEGI-SENSEI!
KŪ FEI-SAN WON HER TOURNAMENT!
OH! THAT'S MY KŪRŌSHI!
AT THIS RATE, OUR CLASS WILL GO FAR IN EVEN THE ALL-SCHOOL RANKINGS.
I SEE. SO THEY EACH GET TO ENTER WHATEVER COMPETITION THEY WANT, AND THEN THEIR POINTS GO TO THE CLASS'S TOTAL SCORE.
YES ♥ AND THIS IS OUR LAST MEET OF JUNIOR HIGH.
I HOPE THEY ALL DO THEIR VERY BEST.
COME TO THINK OF IT, THE ALL-SCHOOL EVENT IS COMING UP SOON, ISN'T IT?
HUH? WHAT WAS IT GOING TO BE THIS YEAR?
YOUR FAMILY IS SPONSORING IT, RIGHT? DO YOU KNOW ANYTHING ...?
WINCE
UM... CLASS REP-SAN?
SHAKE SHAKE SHAKE
SMIRK
I'M SORRY! THEY SAID IT WAS FOR YOUR OWN GOOD, NEGI-SENSEI!
HUH?
NEGI-SENSEI!!

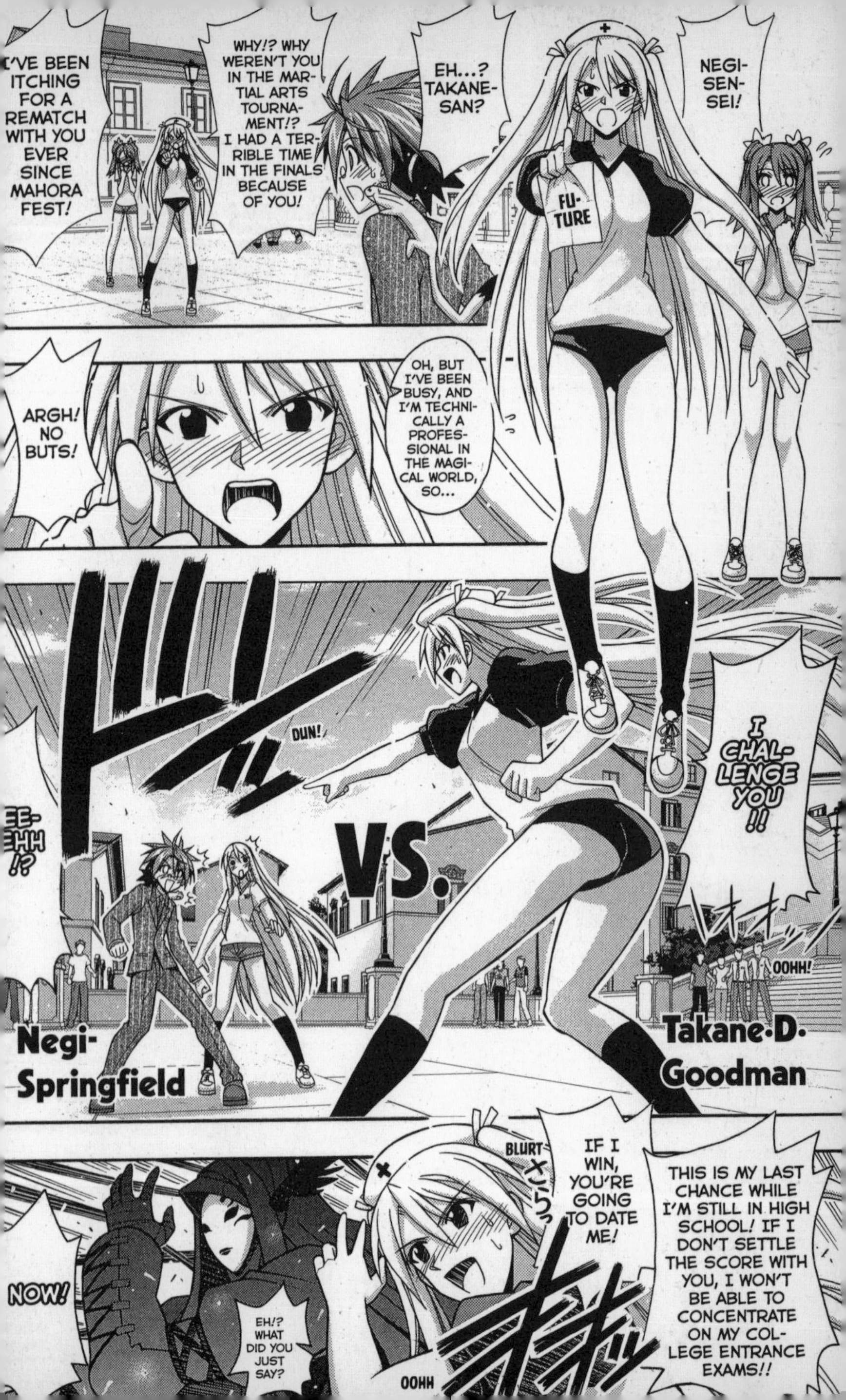
NEGI-SEN-SEI!
EH...? TAKANE-SAN?
WHY!? WHY WEREN'T YOU IN THE MARTIAL ARTS TOURNAMENT!? I HAD A TERRIBLE TIME IN THE FINALS BECAUSE OF YOU!
I'VE BEEN ITCHING FOR A REMATCH WITH YOU EVER SINCE MAHORA FEST!
FU-TURE
OH, BUT I'VE BEEN BUSY, AND I'M TECHNICALLY A PROFESSIONAL IN THE MAGICAL WORLD, SO...
ARGH! NO BUTS!
I CHALLENGE YOU!!
DUN!
VS.
EE-EHH!?
OOHH!
Takane·D·Goodman
Negi-Springfield
THIS IS MY LAST CHANCE WHILE I'M STILL IN HIGH SCHOOL! IF I DON'T SETTLE THE SCORE WITH YOU, I WON'T BE ABLE TO CONCENTRATE ON MY COLLEGE ENTRANCE EXAMS!!
IF I WIN, YOU'RE GOING TO DATE ME!
BLURT
OOHH
EH!? WHAT DID YOU JUST SAY?
NOW!

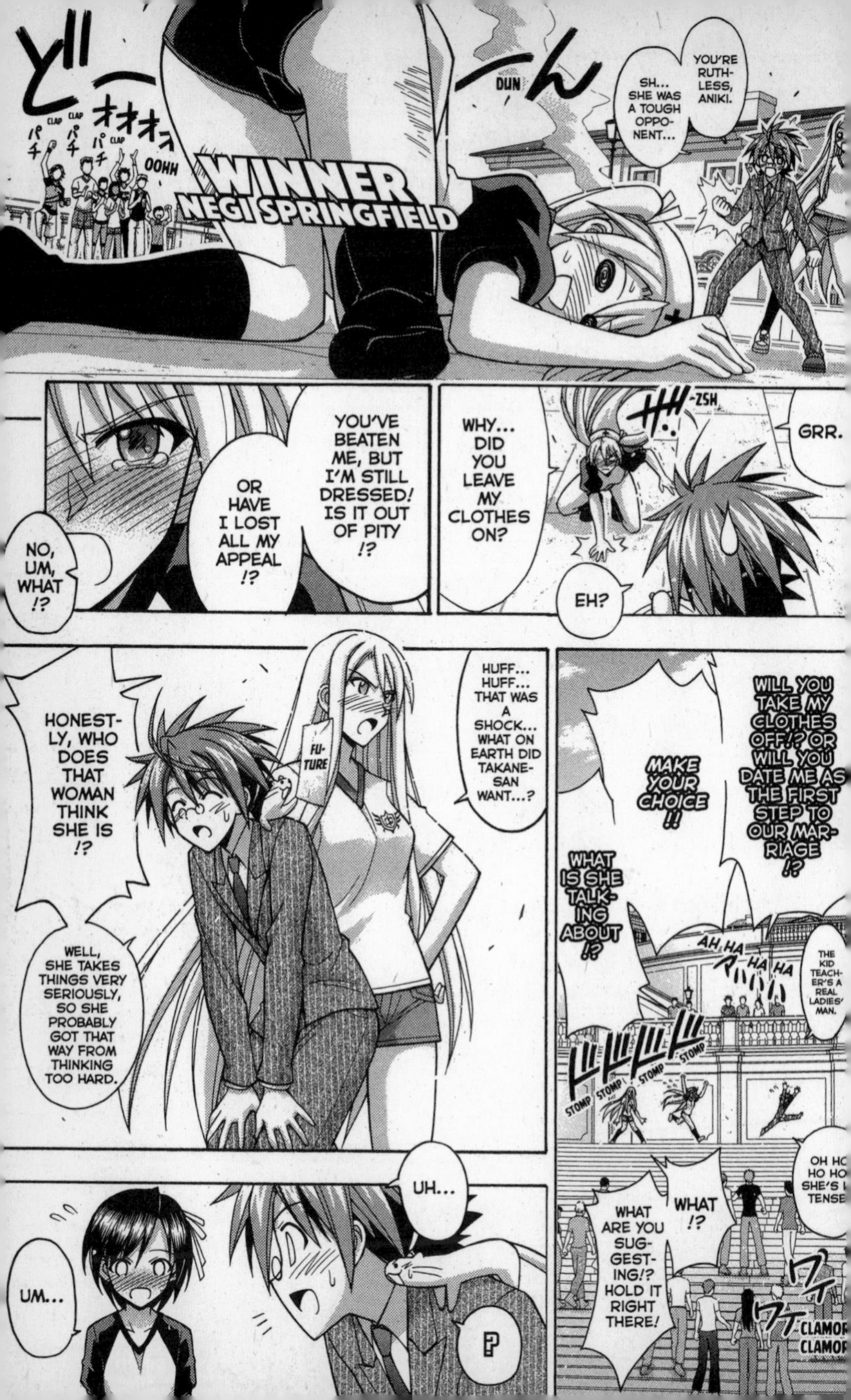

YOU'RE RUTHLESS, ANIKI.
SH... SHE WAS A TOUGH OPPONENT...
どーーん
DUN
オオオォ
OOHH
パチパチパチ
CLAP CLAP CLAP
WINNER NEGI SPRINGFIELD
GRR.
-ZSH
WHY... DID YOU LEAVE MY CLOTHES ON?
EH?
YOU'VE BEATEN ME, BUT I'M STILL DRESSED! IS IT OUT OF PITY!?
OR HAVE I LOST ALL MY APPEAL!?
NO, UM, WHAT!?
WILL YOU TAKE MY CLOTHES OFF!? OR WILL YOU DATE ME AS THE FIRST STEP TO OUR MARRIAGE!?
MAKE YOUR CHOICE!!
WHAT IS SHE TALKING ABOUT!?
AH HA HA HA
THE KID TEACHER'S A REAL LADIES' MAN.
STOMP STOMP STOMP STOMP
OH HO HO HO SHE'S TENSE
WHAT!?
WHAT ARE YOU SUGGESTING!? HOLD IT RIGHT THERE!
CLAMOR CLAMOR
HUFF... HUFF... THAT WAS A SHOCK... WHAT ON EARTH DID TAKANE-SAN WANT...?
FUTURE
HONESTLY, WHO DOES THAT WOMAN THINK SHE IS!?
WELL, SHE TAKES THINGS VERY SERIOUSLY, SO SHE PROBABLY GOT THAT WAY FROM THINKING TOO HARD.
UH...
?
UM...

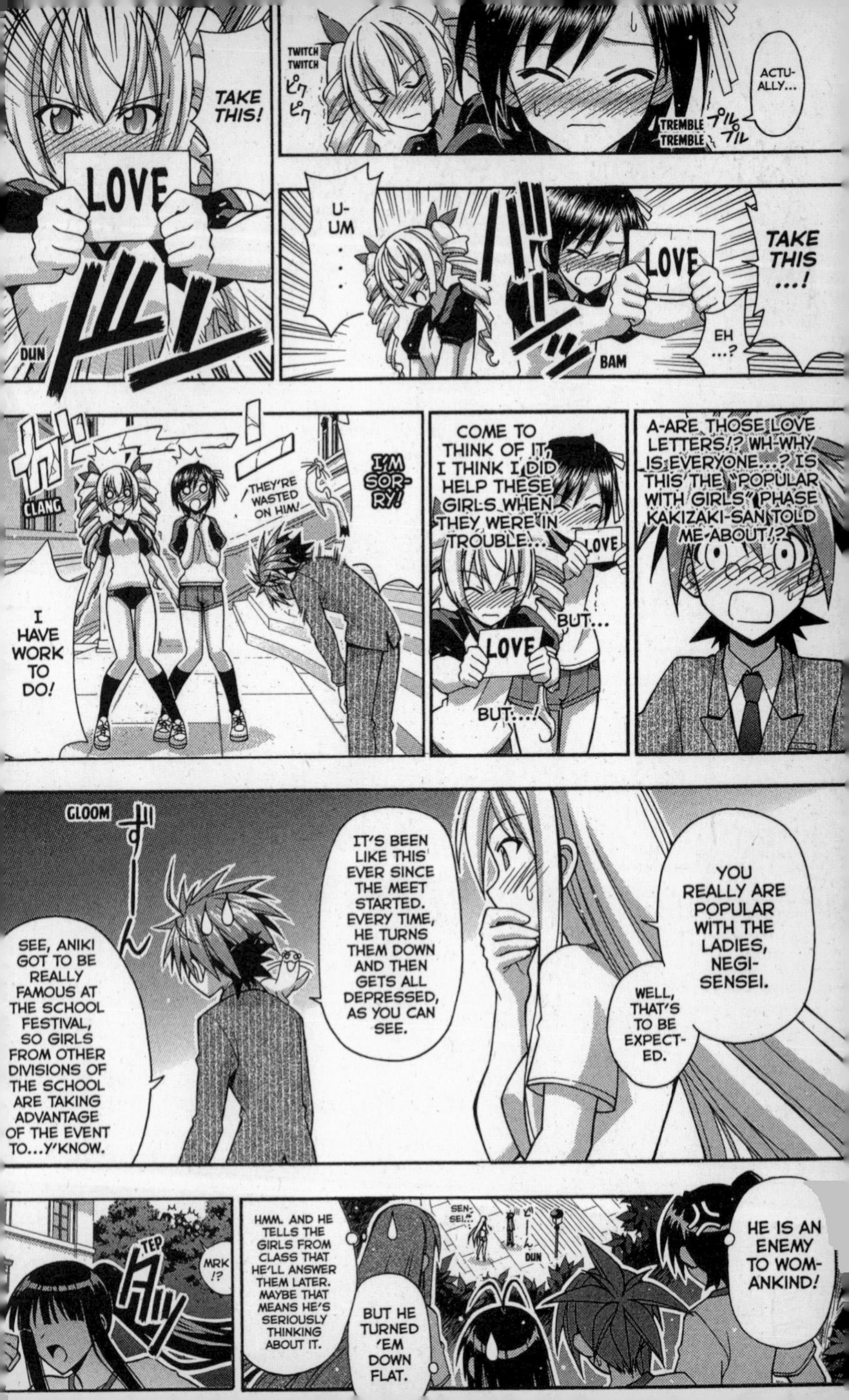
ACTU-ALLY...
TWITCH TWITCH
ピク ピク
TREMBLE TREMBLE
プルプル
TAKE THIS...!
LOVE
EH ...?
U-UM . . .
BAM
TAKE THIS!
LOVE
DUN
A-ARE THOSE LOVE LETTERS!? WH-WHY IS EVERYONE...? IS THIS THE "POPULAR WITH GIRLS" PHASE KAKIZAKI-SAN TOLD ME ABOUT!?
COME TO THINK OF IT, I THINK I DID HELP THESE GIRLS WHEN THEY WERE IN TROUBLE...
LOVE
BUT...
LOVE
BUT...!
I'M SOR-RY!
THEY'RE WASTED ON HIM!
CLANG
I HAVE WORK TO DO!
YOU REALLY ARE POPULAR WITH THE LADIES, NEGI-SENSEI.
WELL, THAT'S TO BE EXPECT-ED.
IT'S BEEN LIKE THIS EVER SINCE THE MEET STARTED. EVERY TIME, HE TURNS THEM DOWN AND THEN GETS ALL DEPRESSED, AS YOU CAN SEE.
GLOOM
SEE, ANIKI GOT TO BE REALLY FAMOUS AT THE SCHOOL FESTIVAL, SO GIRLS FROM OTHER DIVISIONS OF THE SCHOOL ARE TAKING ADVANTAGE OF THE EVENT TO...Y'KNOW.
HE IS AN ENEMY TO WOM-ANKIND!
SEN-SEI...
DUN
HMM. AND HE TELLS THE GIRLS FROM CLASS THAT HE'LL ANSWER THEM LATER. MAYBE THAT MEANS HE'S SERIOUSLY THINKING ABOUT IT.
BUT HE TURNED 'EM DOWN FLAT.
MRK !?
TEP

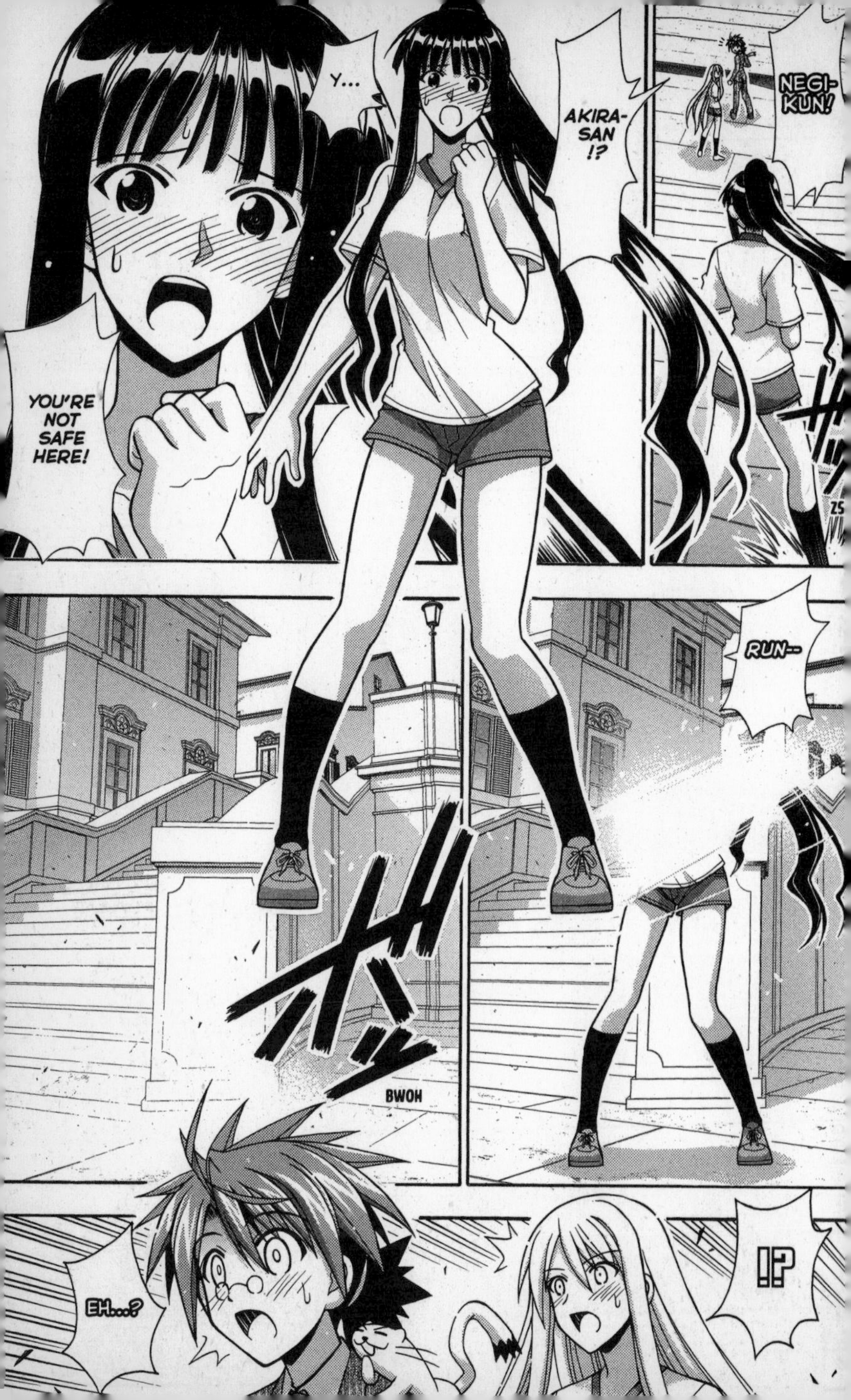

NEGI-KUN!
AKIRA-SAN !?
ZS
Y...
YOU'RE NOT SAFE HERE!
RUN--
BWOH
!?
EH...?

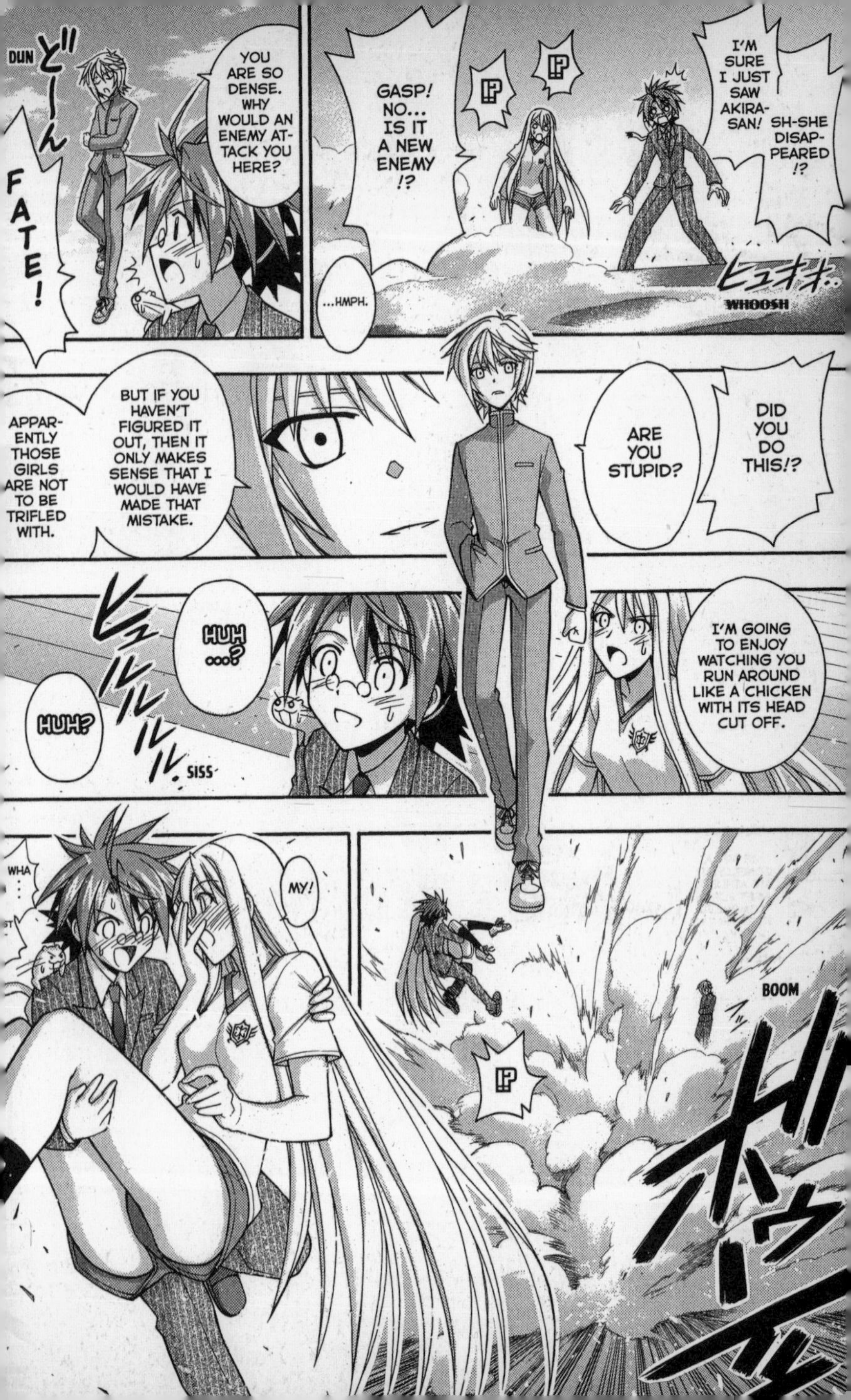
I'M SURE I JUST SAW AKIRA-SAN!
SH-SHE DISAPPEARED!?
!?
!?
GASP! NO... IS IT A NEW ENEMY!?
WHOOSH
...HMPH.
YOU ARE SO DENSE. WHY WOULD AN ENEMY ATTACK YOU HERE?
DUN
FATE!
DID YOU DO THIS!?
ARE YOU STUPID?
BUT IF YOU HAVEN'T FIGURED IT OUT, THEN IT ONLY MAKES SENSE THAT I WOULD HAVE MADE THAT MISTAKE.
APPARENTLY THOSE GIRLS ARE NOT TO BE TRIFLED WITH.
I'M GOING TO ENJOY WATCHING YOU RUN AROUND LIKE A CHICKEN WITH ITS HEAD CUT OFF.
HUH...?
HUH?
SISS
BOOM
!?
MY!
WHA...

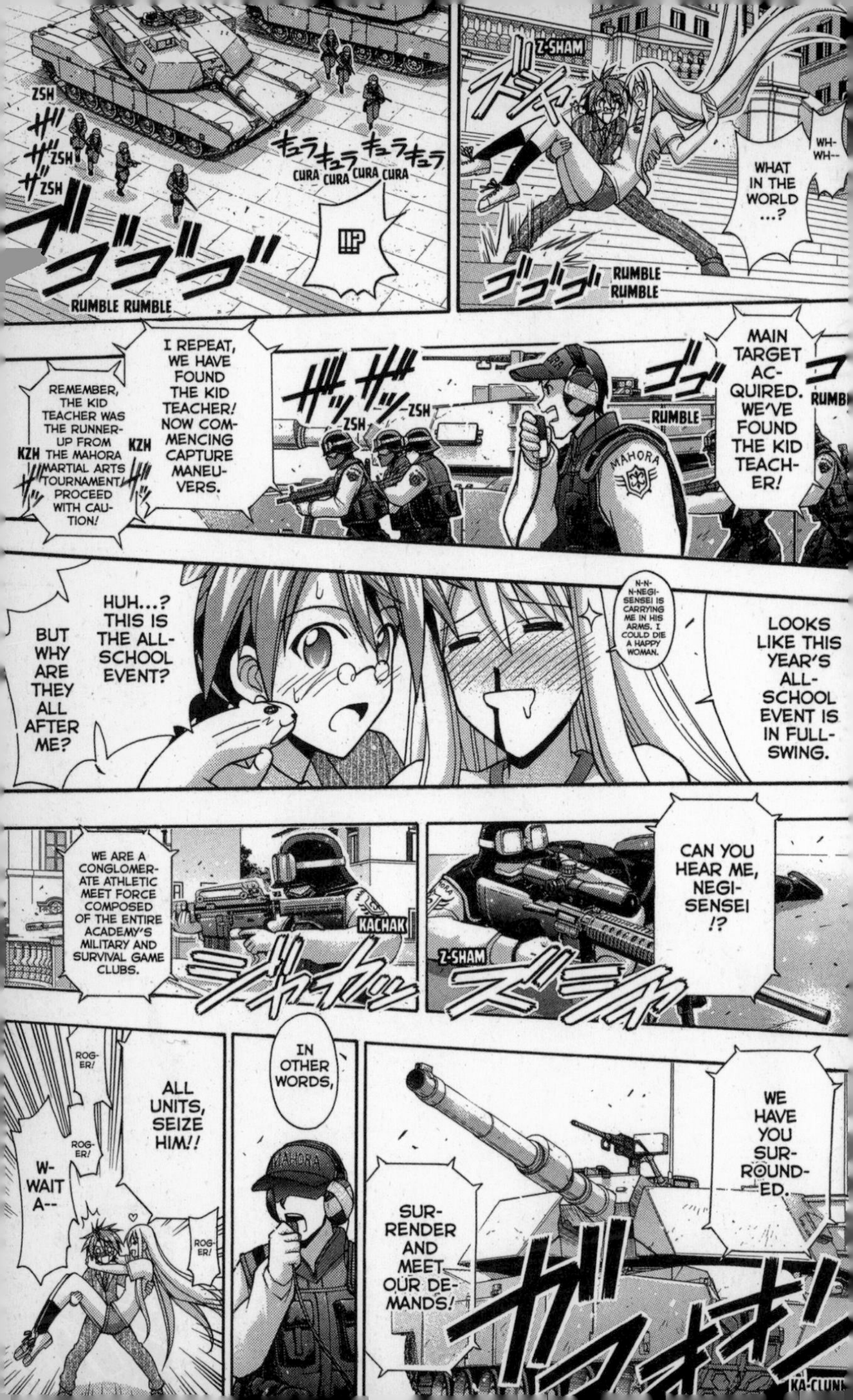

Z-SHAM
WH- WH--
WHAT IN THE WORLD ...?
RUMBLE RUMBLE
ZSH
ZSH
ZSH
CURA CURA CURA CURA
!!?
RUMBLE RUMBLE
MAIN TARGET ACQUIRED. WE'VE FOUND THE KID TEACHER!
RUMBLE
RUMBLE
ZSH
ZSH
I REPEAT, WE HAVE FOUND THE KID TEACHER! NOW COMMENCING CAPTURE MANEUVERS.
KZH
REMEMBER, THE KID TEACHER WAS THE RUNNER-UP FROM THE MAHORA MARTIAL ARTS TOURNAMENT! PROCEED WITH CAUTION!
KZH
LOOKS LIKE THIS YEAR'S ALL-SCHOOL EVENT IS IN FULL-SWING.
N-N-N-NEGI-SENSEI IS CARRYING ME IN HIS ARMS. I COULD DIE A HAPPY WOMAN.
HUH...? THIS IS THE ALL-SCHOOL EVENT?
BUT WHY ARE THEY ALL AFTER ME?
CAN YOU HEAR ME, NEGI-SENSEI!?
Z-SHAM
KACHAK
WE ARE A CONGLOMERATE ATHLETIC MEET FORCE COMPOSED OF THE ENTIRE ACADEMY'S MILITARY AND SURVIVAL GAME CLUBS.
WE HAVE YOU SURROUNDED.
KA-CLUNK
IN OTHER WORDS,
SURRENDER AND MEET OUR DEMANDS!
ALL UNITS, SEIZE HIM!!
ROGER!
ROGER!
ROGER!
W-WAIT A--

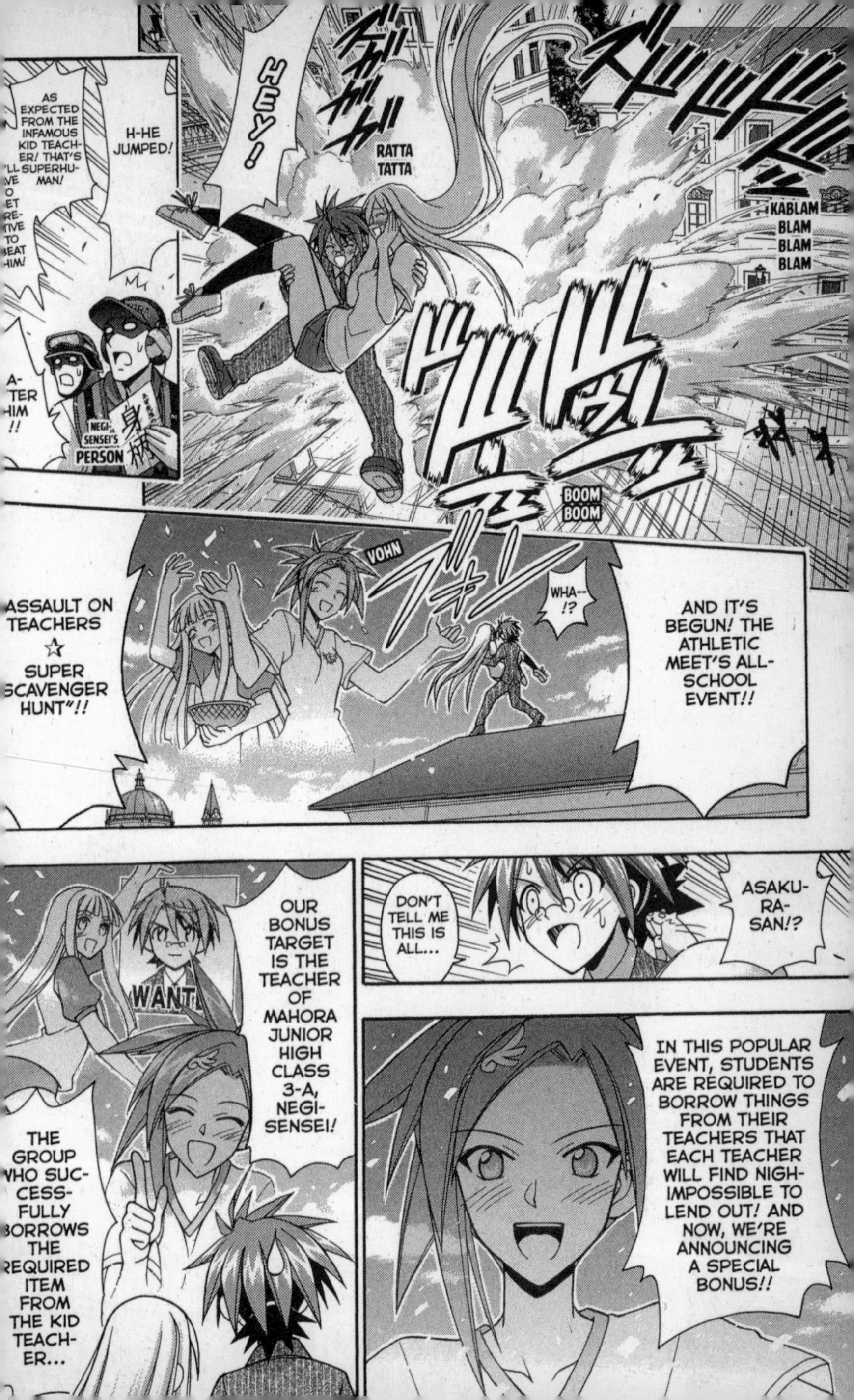
KABLAM BLAM BLAM BLAM
RATTA TATTA
HEY!
BOOM BOOM
H-HE JUMPED!
AS EXPECTED FROM THE INFAMOUS KID TEACHER! THAT'S SUPERHUMAN!
NEGI-SENSEI'S PERSON
VOHN
AND IT'S BEGUN! THE ATHLETIC MEET'S ALL-SCHOOL EVENT!!
WHA--!?
ASSAULT ON TEACHERS ☆ SUPER SCAVENGER HUNT"!!
ASAKURA-SAN!?
DON'T TELL ME THIS IS ALL...
IN THIS POPULAR EVENT, STUDENTS ARE REQUIRED TO BORROW THINGS FROM THEIR TEACHERS THAT EACH TEACHER WILL FIND NIGH-IMPOSSIBLE TO LEND OUT! AND NOW, WE'RE ANNOUNCING A SPECIAL BONUS!!
OUR BONUS TARGET IS THE TEACHER OF MAHORA JUNIOR HIGH CLASS 3-A, NEGI-SENSEI!
WANT
THE GROUP WHO SUCCESSFULLY BORROWS THE REQUIRED ITEM FROM THE KID TEACHER...

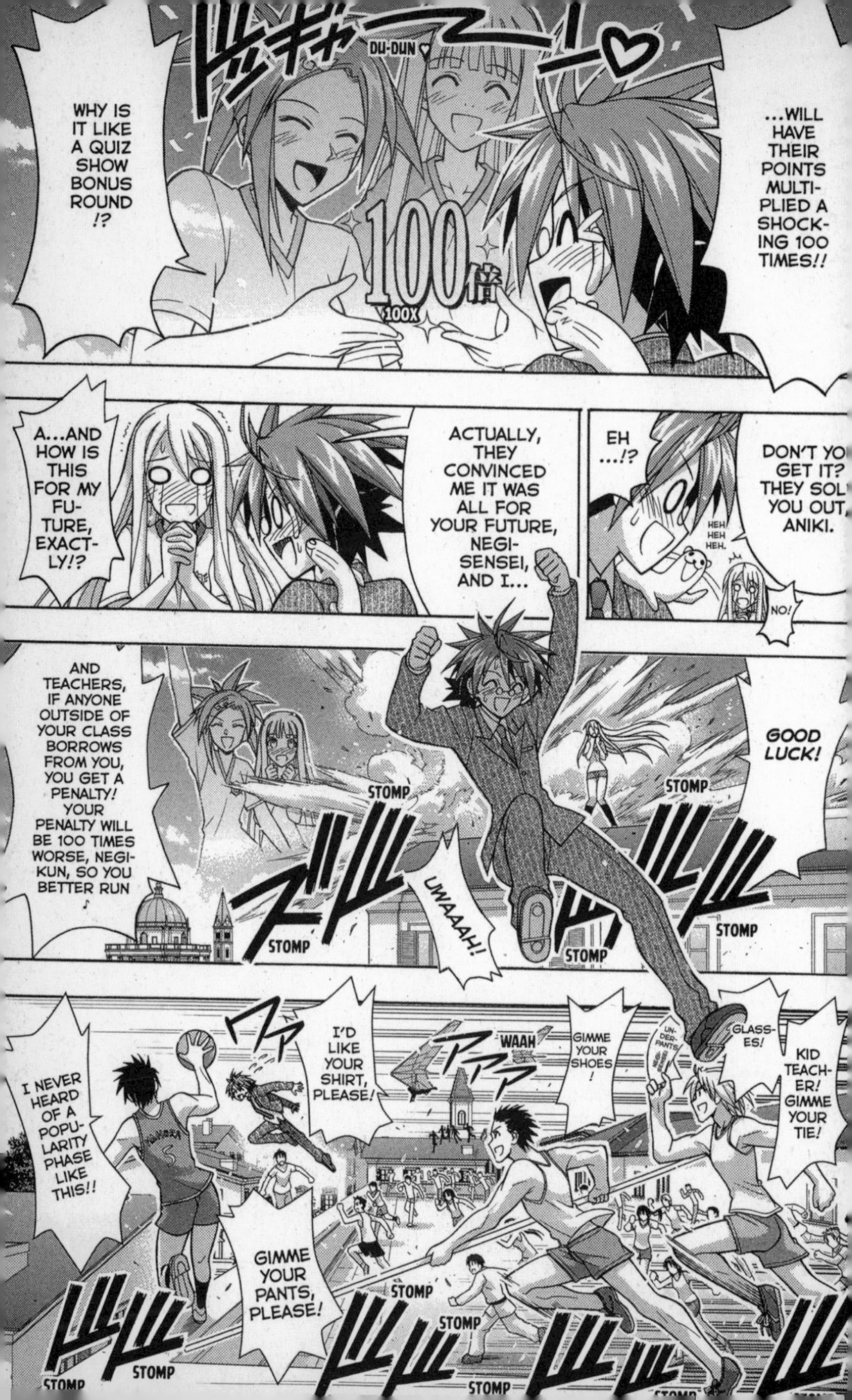
DU-DUN♥
...WILL HAVE THEIR POINTS MULTIPLIED A SHOCKING 100 TIMES!!
100倍
100X
WHY IS IT LIKE A QUIZ SHOW BONUS ROUND!?
DON'T YO GET IT? THEY SOL YOU OUT, ANIKI.
EH ...!?
HEH HEH HEH.
NO!
ACTUALLY, THEY CONVINCED ME IT WAS ALL FOR YOUR FUTURE, NEGI-SENSEI, AND I...
A...AND HOW IS THIS FOR MY FUTURE, EXACTLY!?
GOOD LUCK!
STOMP
STOMP
STOMP
UWAAAAH!
STOMP
STOMP
AND TEACHERS, IF ANYONE OUTSIDE OF YOUR CLASS BORROWS FROM YOU, YOU GET A PENALTY! YOUR PENALTY WILL BE 100 TIMES WORSE, NEGI-KUN, SO YOU BETTER RUN ♪
KID TEACHER! GIMME YOUR TIE!
GLASSES!
UNDER-PANTS!
GIMME YOUR SHOES!
WAAH
I'D LIKE YOUR SHIRT, PLEASE!
I NEVER HEARD OF A POPULARITY PHASE LIKE THIS!!
GIMME YOUR PANTS, PLEASE!
STOMP
STOMP
STOMP
STOMP
STOMP

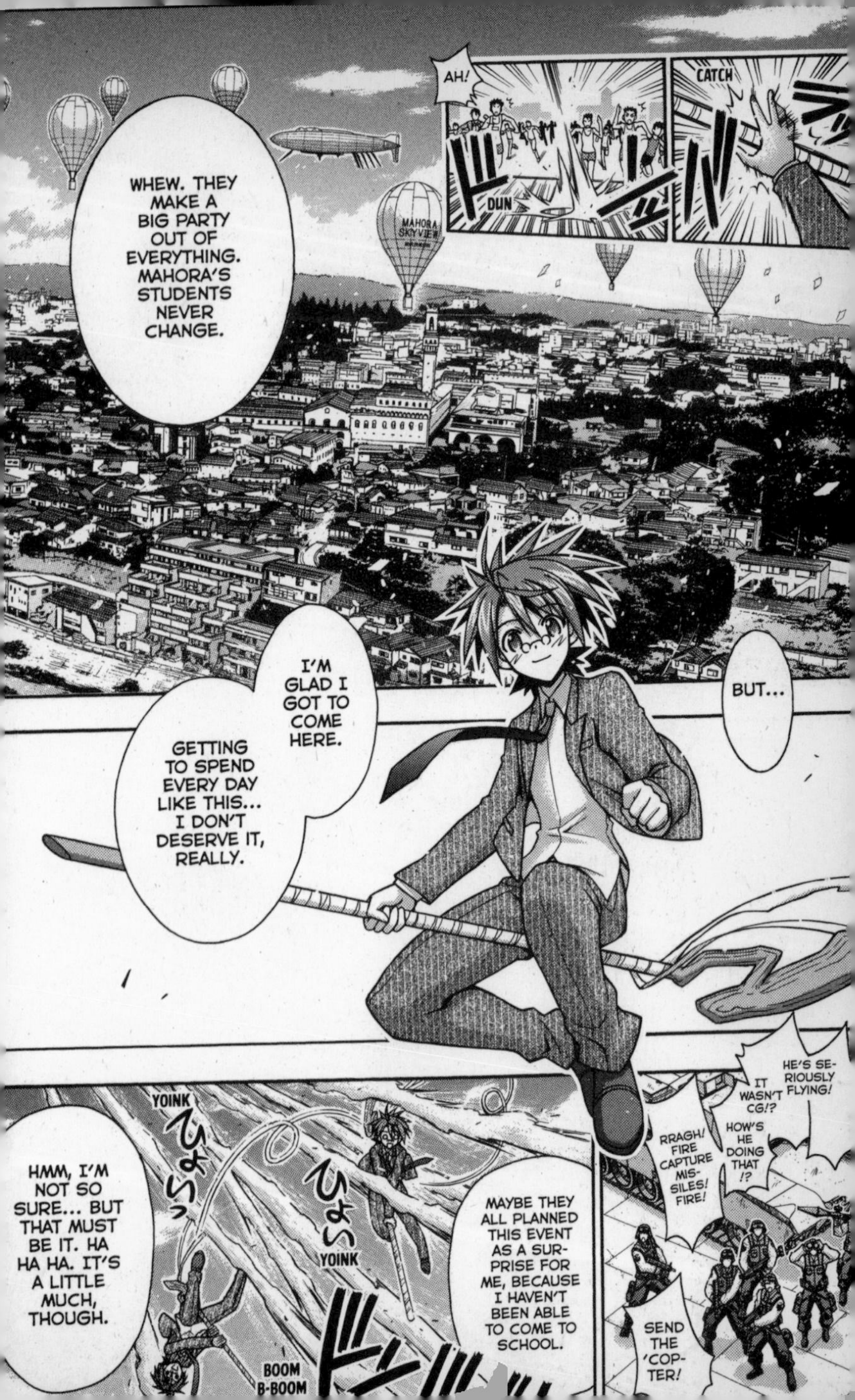
CATCH
AH!
DUN
WHEW. THEY MAKE A BIG PARTY OUT OF EVERYTHING. MAHORA'S STUDENTS NEVER CHANGE.
MAHORA SKYVIEW
BUT...
I'M GLAD I GOT TO COME HERE.
GETTING TO SPEND EVERY DAY LIKE THIS... I DON'T DESERVE IT, REALLY.
HE'S SERIOUSLY FLYING!
IT WASN'T CG!?
HOW'S HE DOING THAT!?
RRAGH! FIRE CAPTURE MISSILES! FIRE!
SEND THE 'COPTER!
MAYBE THEY ALL PLANNED THIS EVENT AS A SURPRISE FOR ME, BECAUSE I HAVEN'T BEEN ABLE TO COME TO SCHOOL.
YOINK
YOINK
HMM, I'M NOT SO SURE... BUT THAT MUST BE IT. HA HA HA. IT'S A LITTLE MUCH, THOUGH.
BOOM B-BOOM

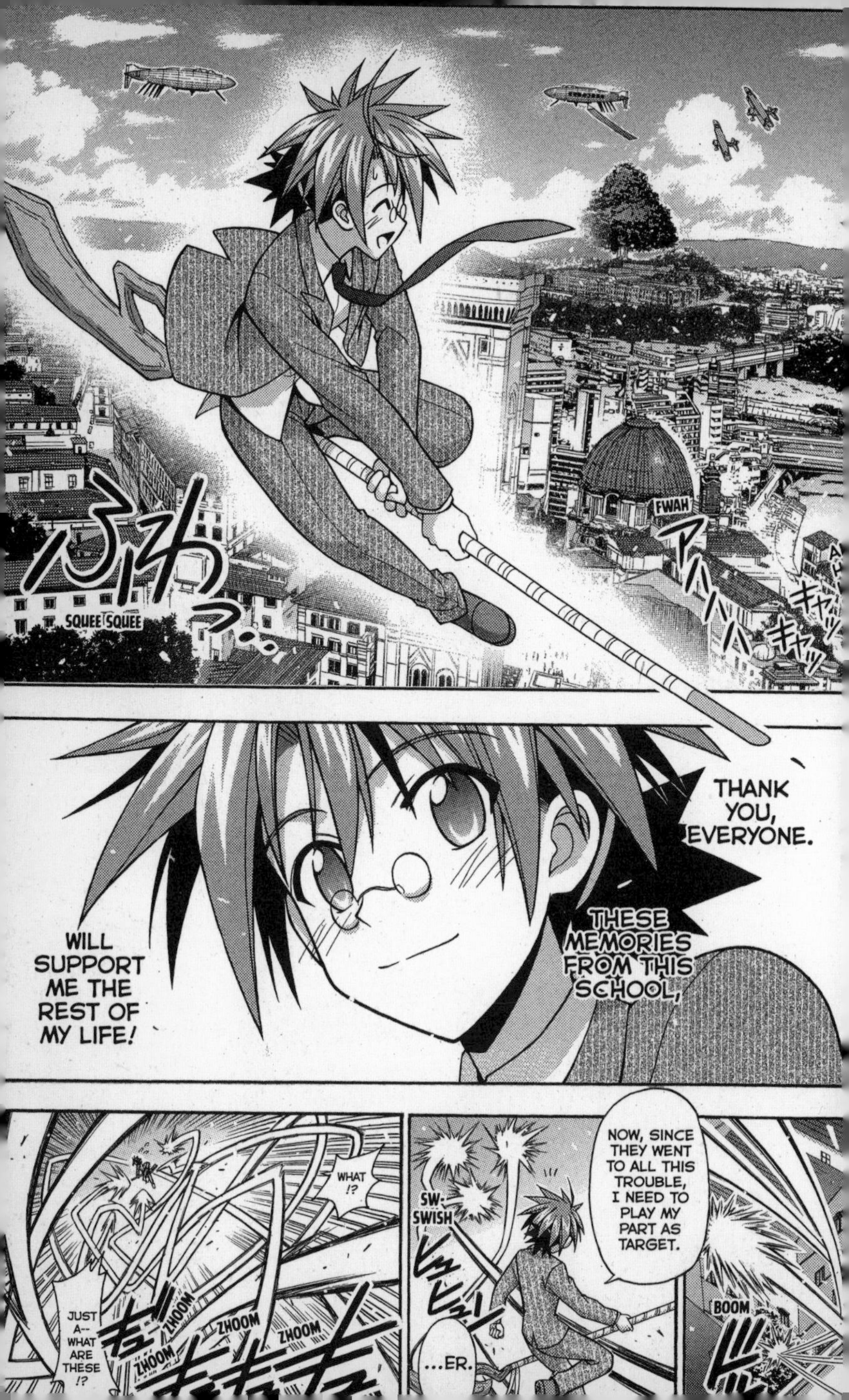
AH
キャッキャッ
FWAH
アハハハ
SQUEE SQUEE
ふわっ
THANK YOU, EVERYONE.
THESE MEMORIES FROM THIS SCHOOL,
WILL SUPPORT ME THE REST OF MY LIFE!
NOW, SINCE THEY WENT TO ALL THIS TROUBLE, I NEED TO PLAY MY PART AS TARGET.
BOOM
SW-SWISH
...ER.
WHAT !?
ZHOOM ZHOOM ZHOOM ZHOOM
JUST A-- WHAT ARE THESE !?

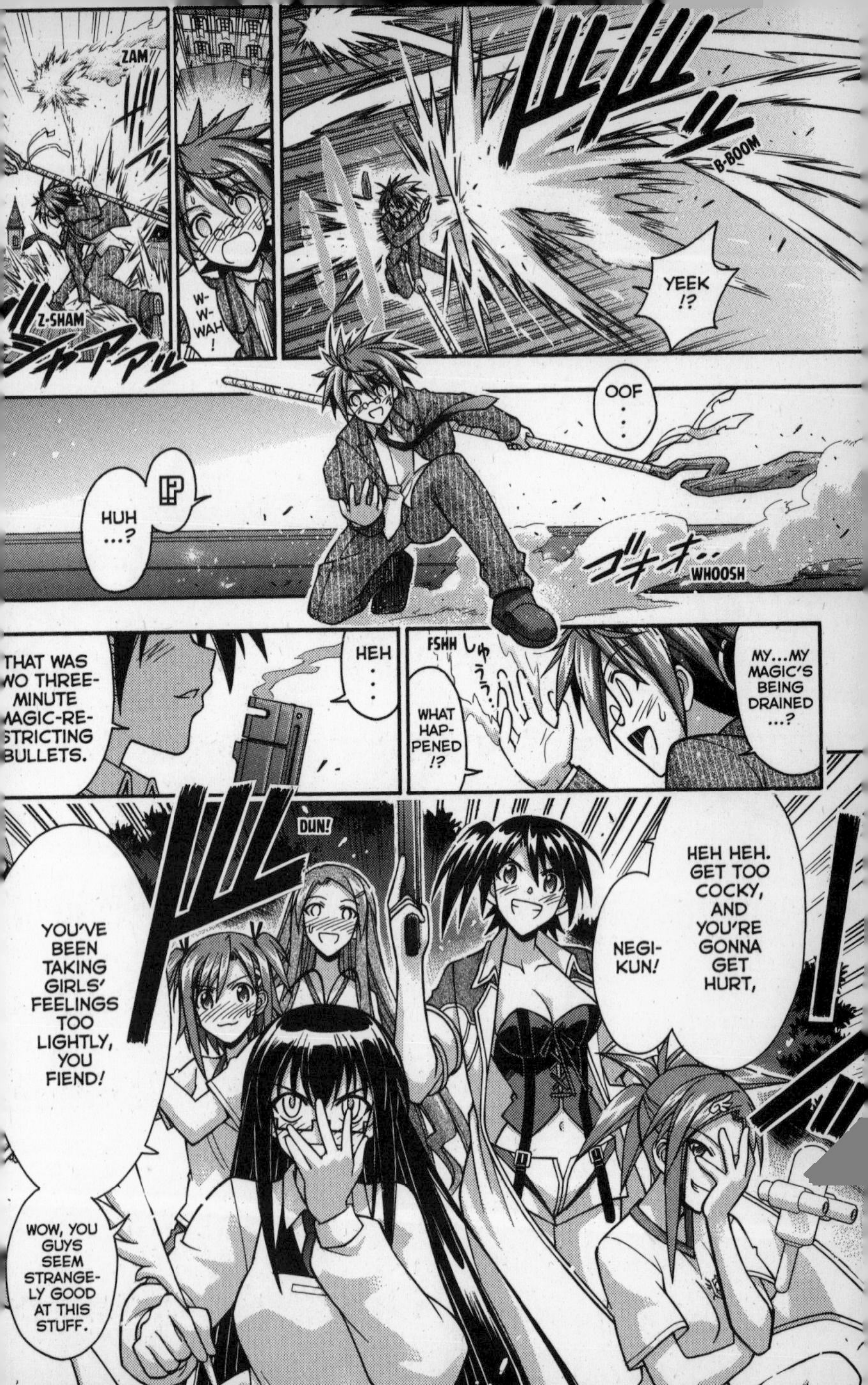
B-BOOM
YEEK!?
W-W-WAH!
ZAM
Z-SHAM
OOF...
WHOOSH
!?
HUH...?
MY...MY MAGIC'S BEING DRAINED...?
FSHH
WHAT HAPPENED!?
HEH...
THAT WAS WO THREE-MINUTE MAGIC-RESTRICTING BULLETS.
HEH HEH. GET TOO COCKY, AND YOU'RE GONNA GET HURT,
NEGI-KUN!
DUN!
YOU'VE BEEN TAKING GIRLS' FEELINGS TOO LIGHTLY, YOU FIEND!
WOW, YOU GUYS SEEM STRANGELY GOOD AT THIS STUFF.

o be continued in Volume 38

-STAFF-

Ken Akamatsu

Takashi Takemoto

Kenichi Nakamura

Keiichi Yamashita

Tohru Mitsuhashi

Yuichi Yoshida

Susumu Kuwabara

Thanks to

Ran Ayanaga

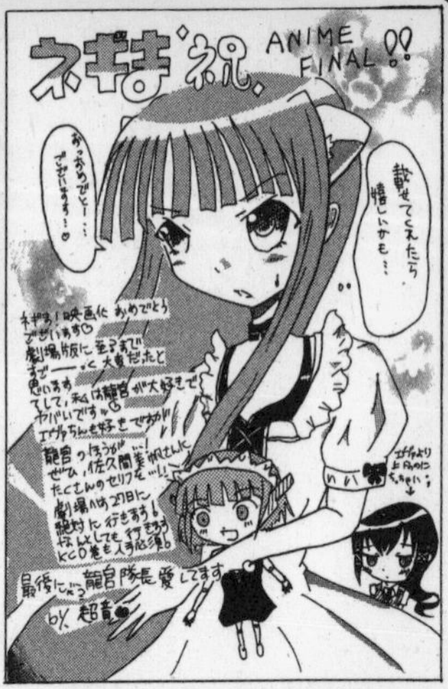
ANIME FINAL!!

THAT TATSUMIYA IN THE BACKGROUND IS ADORABLE. (LAUGH)

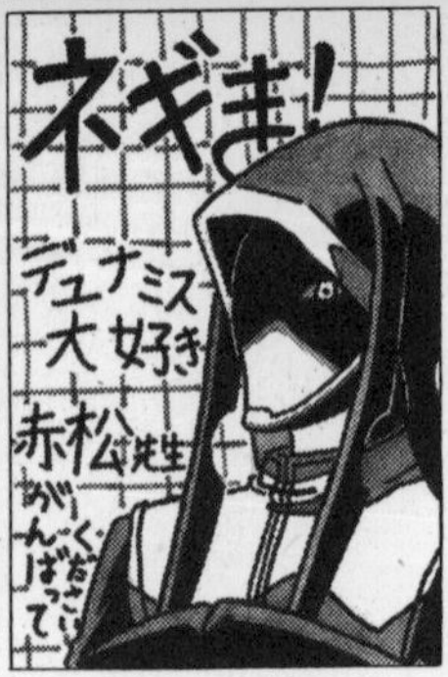
ネギま!
デュナミス大好き
赤松先生
がんばってください

LOOK! I FOUND A DYNAMIS FAN! (LAUGH)

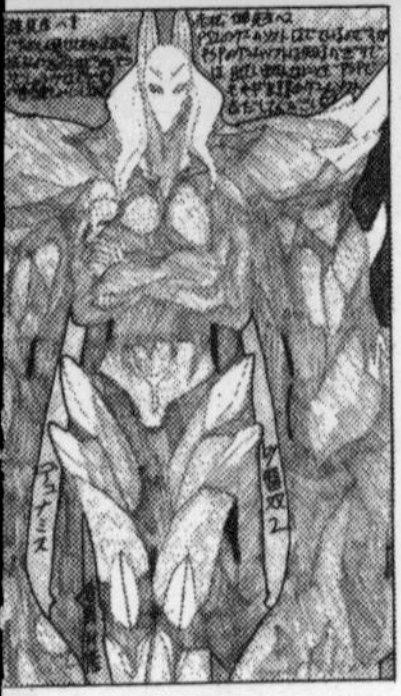

VERY POWERFUL.

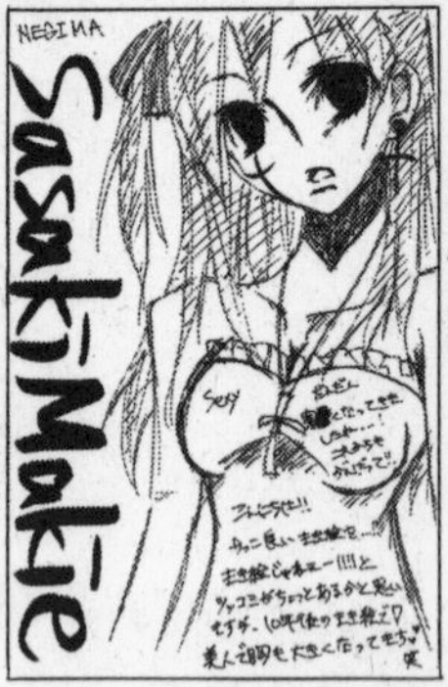
NEGIMA
Sasaki Makie

THIS IS A GOOD MAKIE.

NEGIMA! FAN ART CORNER

THIS TIME, WE GOT A LOT OF LETTERS AND DRAWINGS CONGRATULATING US ON THE NEW MOVIE! THANK YOU SO MUCH ♪ IS IT ME, OR DID THE NEGI DRAWINGS MULTIPLY EXPONENTIALLY!? WELL, HE IS THE MAIN CHARACTER, SO OF COURSE! (LAUGH) WELL, LET'S LOOK AT SOME FAN ART! PLEASE SEND ANY DRAWINGS OR LETTERS TO THE KODANSHA EDITORIAL DEPARTMENT (ADDRESS AT THE END OF THE BOOK). ♪

TEXT BY MAX.

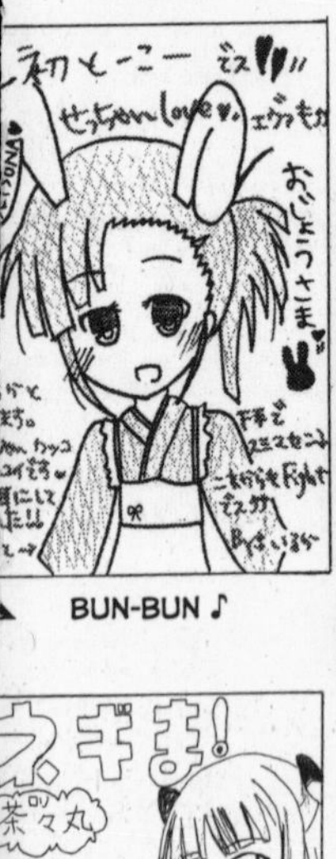
おじょうさま

BUN-BUN ♪

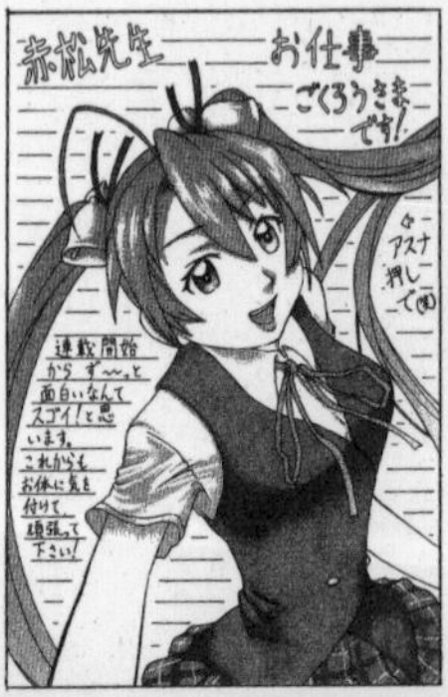
赤松先生
お仕事ごくろうさまです!

SUCH DETAILED TONE USAGE.

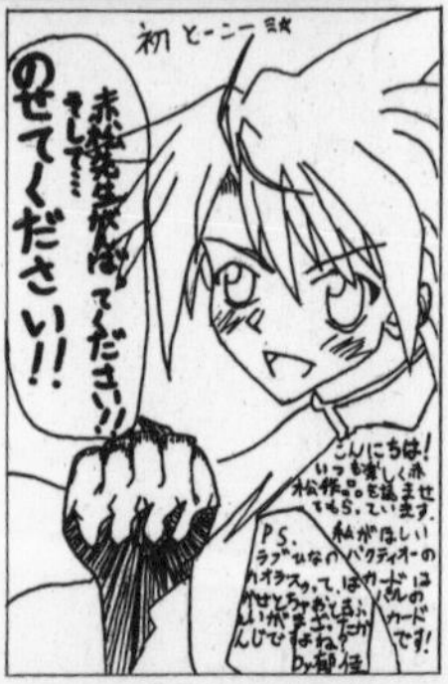
のせてください!!

A VERY POWERFUL NEGI!

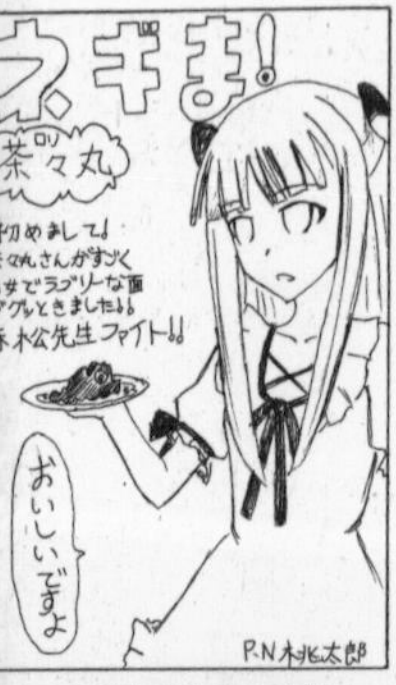
ネギま!
茶々丸
おいしいですよ

WHAT ON EARTH DID SHE COOK!? (LAUGH)

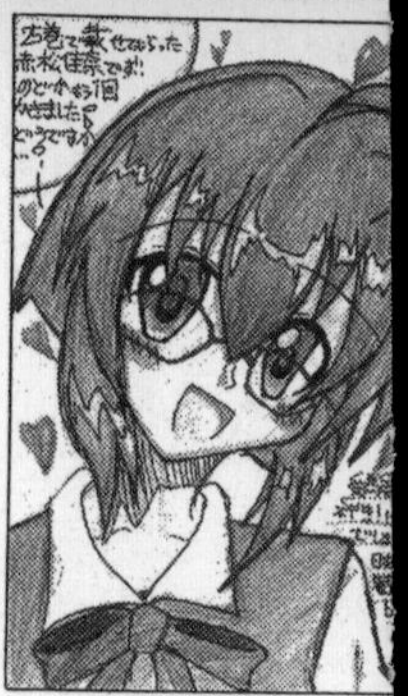

▲ GLASSES GIRL SMILE

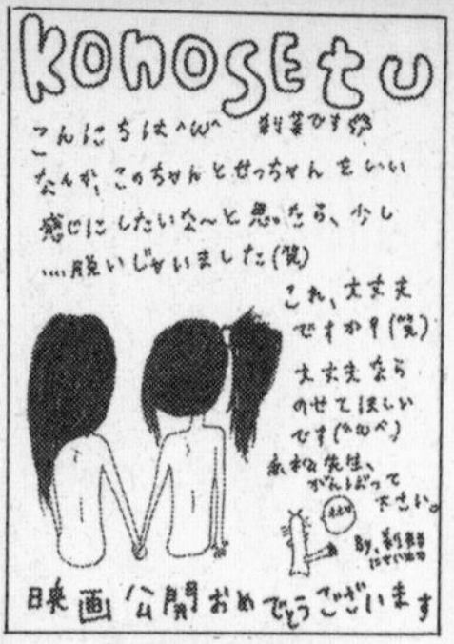
KONOSEtu
映画公開おめでとうございます

▲ D-BMP D-BMP ♪

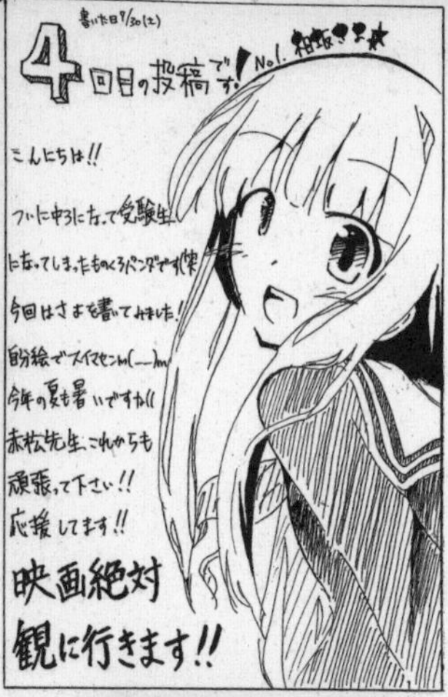
4回目の投稿です!
こんにちは!!
今年の夏も暑いですね
赤松先生、これからも頑張って下さい!!
応援してます!!
映画絶対観に行きます!!

◀ A LIVELY-LOOKING SAYO ♪

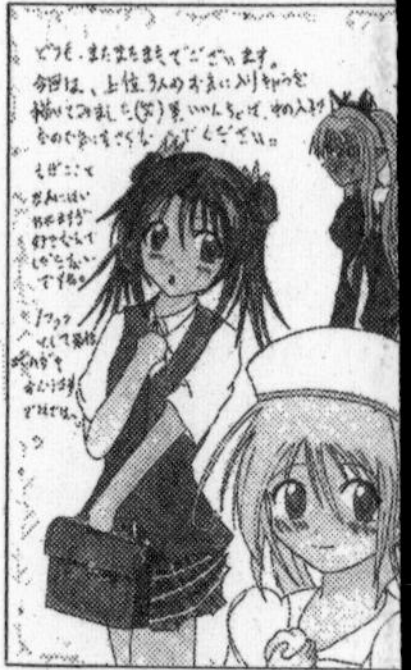

▲ THIS IS AN UNUSUAL GROUPING.

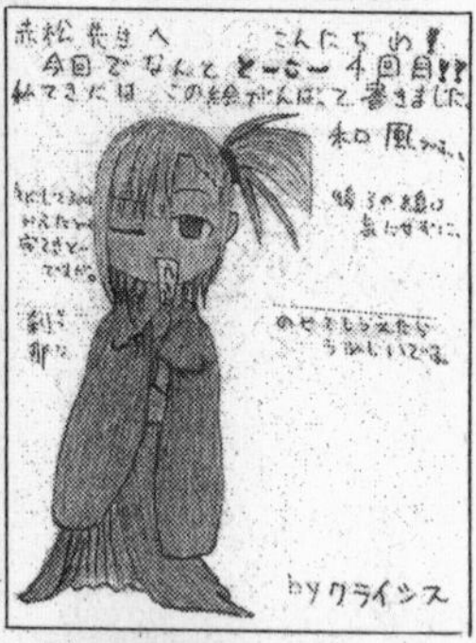

▼ SHE LOOKS LIKE A MOUNTAIN WIZARD.

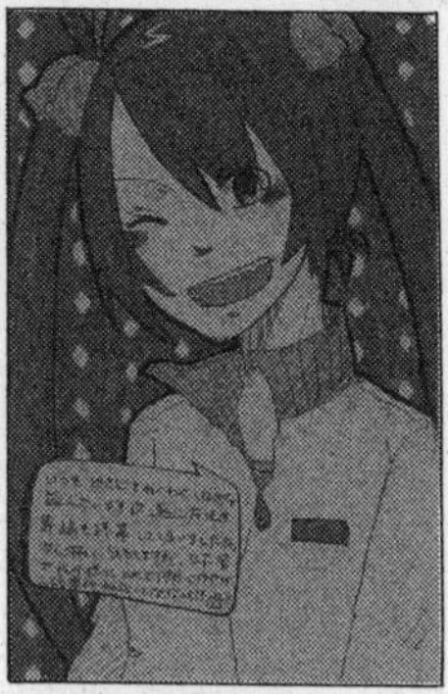

▶ SO FASHIONABLE ♪

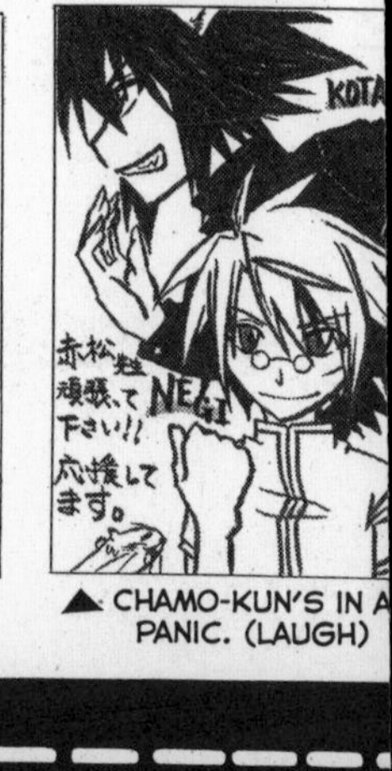
KOTA
NEGI
赤松先生頑張って下さい!!
応援してます。

▲ CHAMO-KUN'S IN A PANIC. (LAUGH)

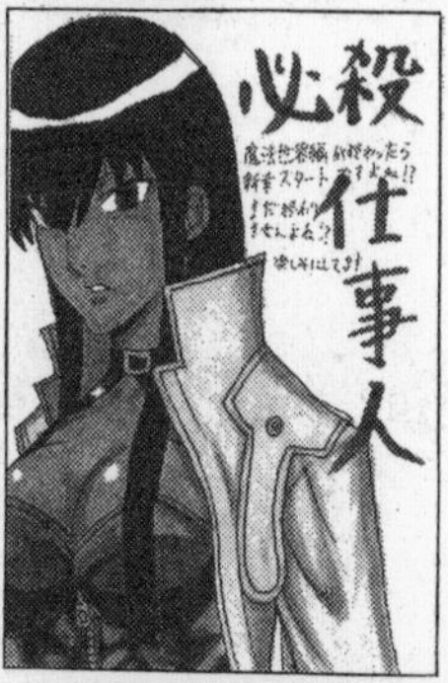
必殺仕事人

▲ DUH DU-DU-*DUH* ♪ (LAUGH)

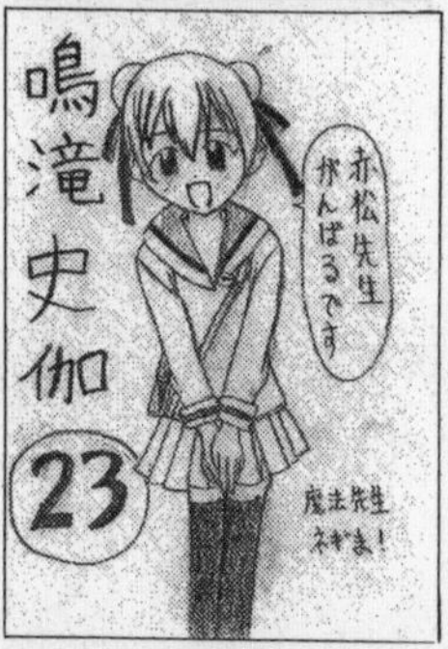
鳴滝史伽
23
赤松先生がんばるです
魔法先生ネギま!

▲ SHE'S SUCH A GOOD GIRL. (LAUGH)

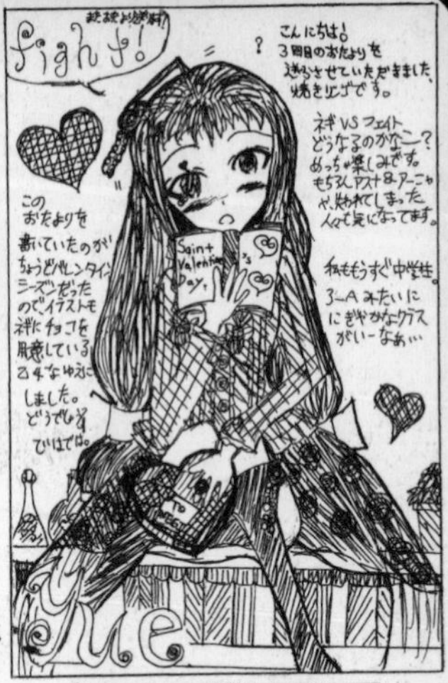

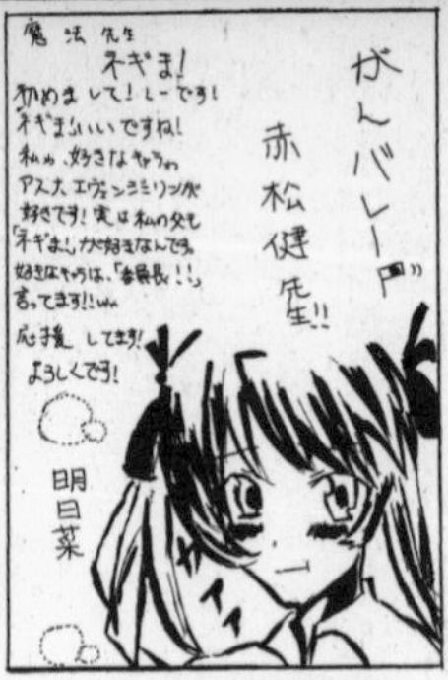

▲ SO YOUR FATHER LIKES NEGIMA!, TOO ♪

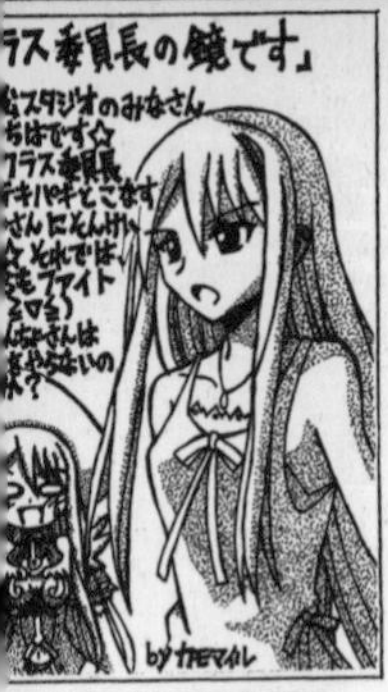

A VERY DRESSED-UP YUE.

LOOKING SHARP, CLASS REP. ▶

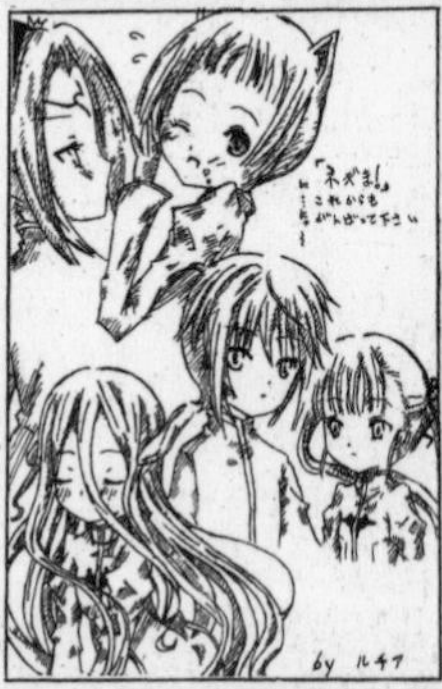

▲ SUCH AN ADORABLE TEAM.

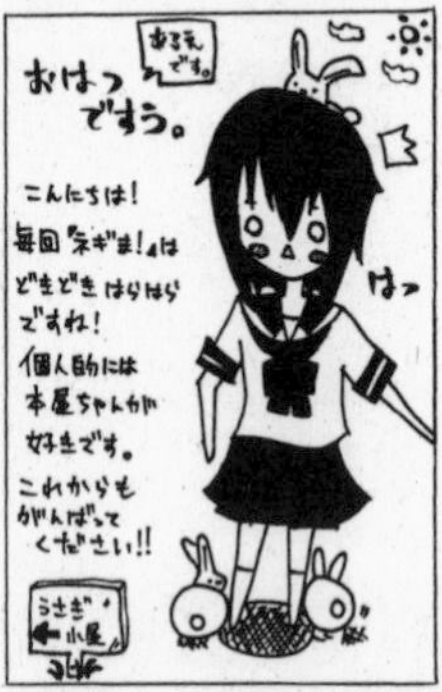

THOSE RABBITS ARE SO CUTE ♪ ▲

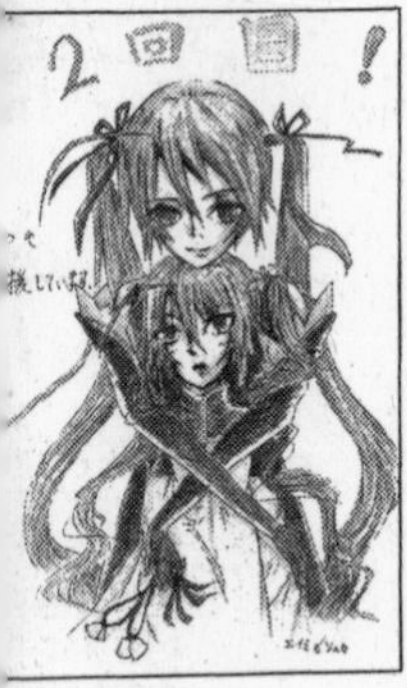

IT HAS A MYSTERIOUS FEELING TO IT.

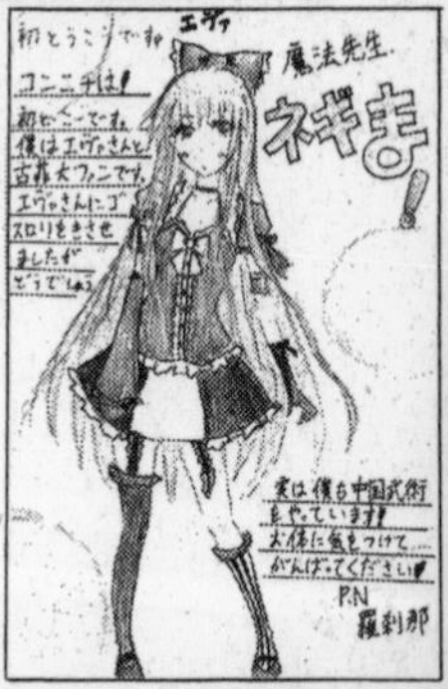

▲ SO SQUEE-ABLE ♪

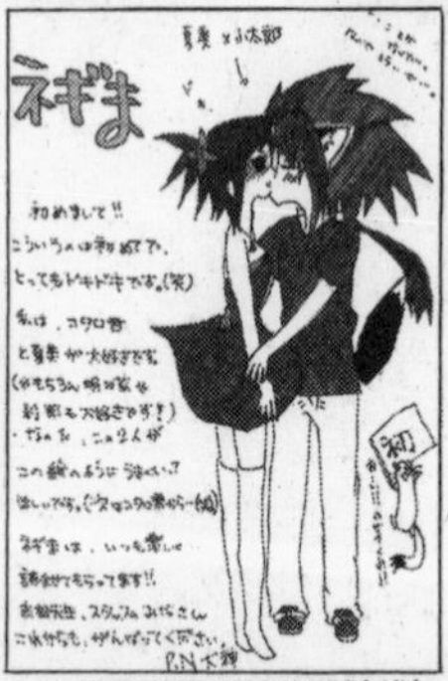

▲ I DON'T KNOW WHY MY HEART'S POUNDING SO MUCH.

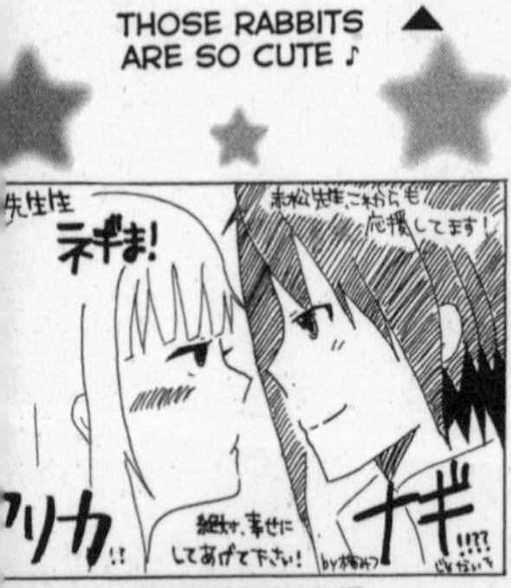

▲ IT LOOKS LIKE A LOVE STORY ♪

NEGI MA!

This volume's

MOST DRAWN CHARACTER!

Chisame Hasegawa

Ranking

第1位

A CHIBI CHIU IN A MAID OUTFIT! IT'S SO CUTE ♥ I CAN TELL YOU HAVE A REAL SENSE FOR THE HAIR HIGHLIGHTS!! (AKAMATSU)

ちびメイド♡
ちび千雨タン
ちう
かわいい!です!
赤松先生
がんばって下さい♥

MAGISTER NEGI MAGI

第2位

IT'S A GROWN-UP CHISAME, AND I THINK SHE MIGHT ACTUALLY LOOK LIKE THIS WHEN SHE'S OLDER. NICE JOB ON THE EYELASHES; VERY FEMININE!!

NO 25
千雨
ネギま!
映画化
おめでとう!!
赤松先生 こんにちは 今回は千雨を猫きました。
最初はロリの千雨を猫く予定だったんですけどね(汗)
これからもお仕事頑張ってください!! by中山チカ

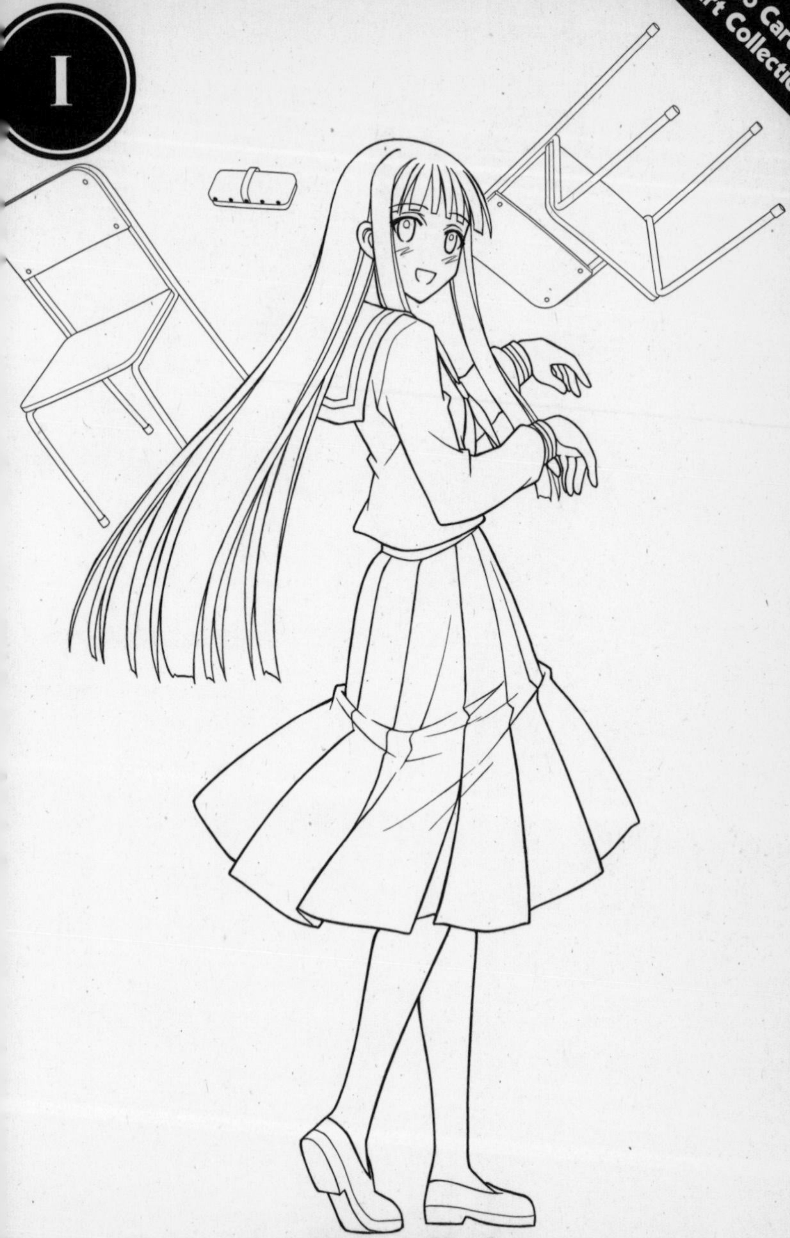
I

Unseen Shade

UMBRA INVISIBILIS

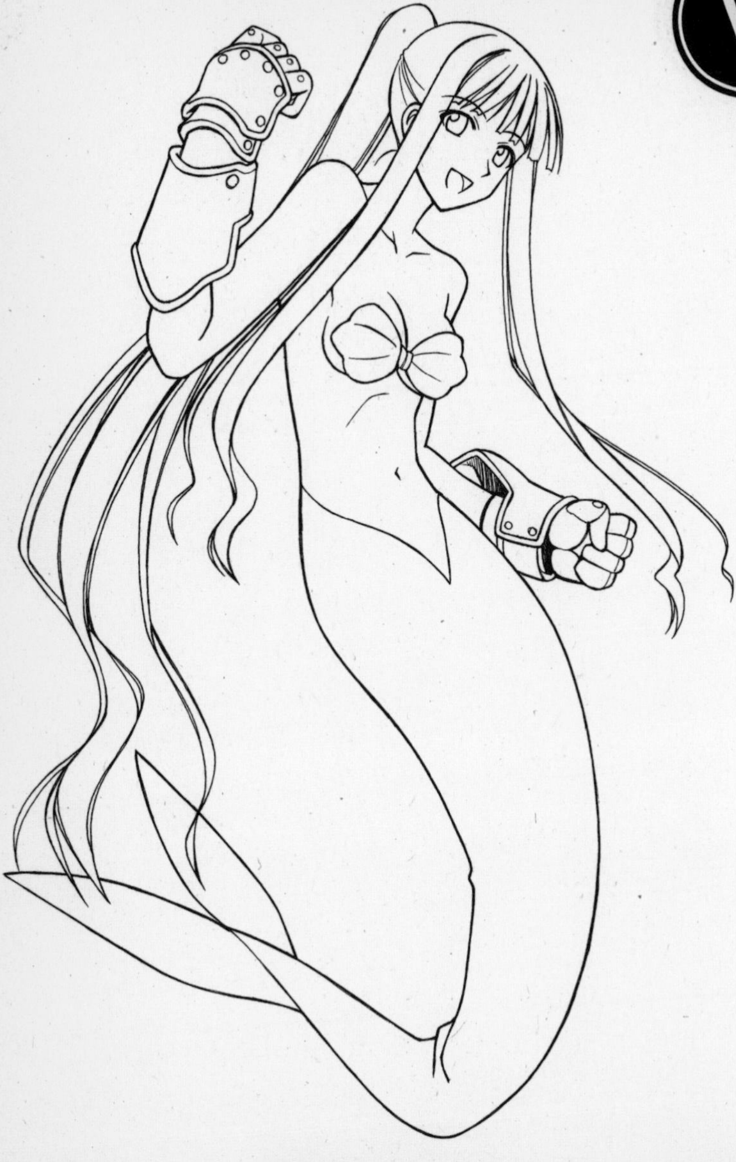

VI

Mighty Mermaid

SIREN VALIDA

VII

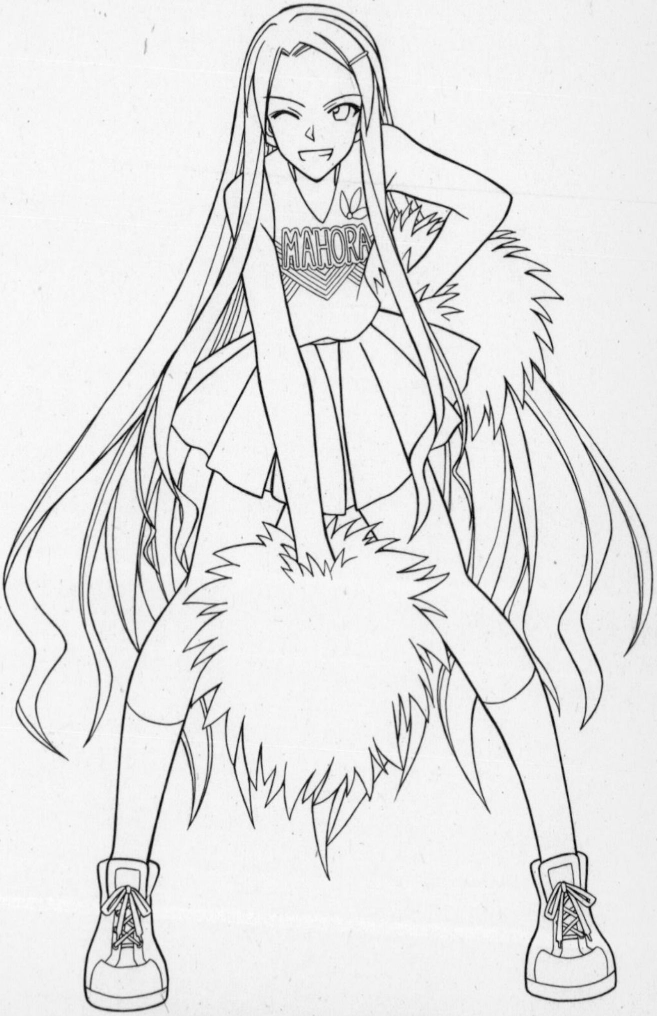
MAHORA

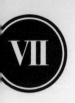

Rallying Cheerleader

HILARATRIX ACCENSA

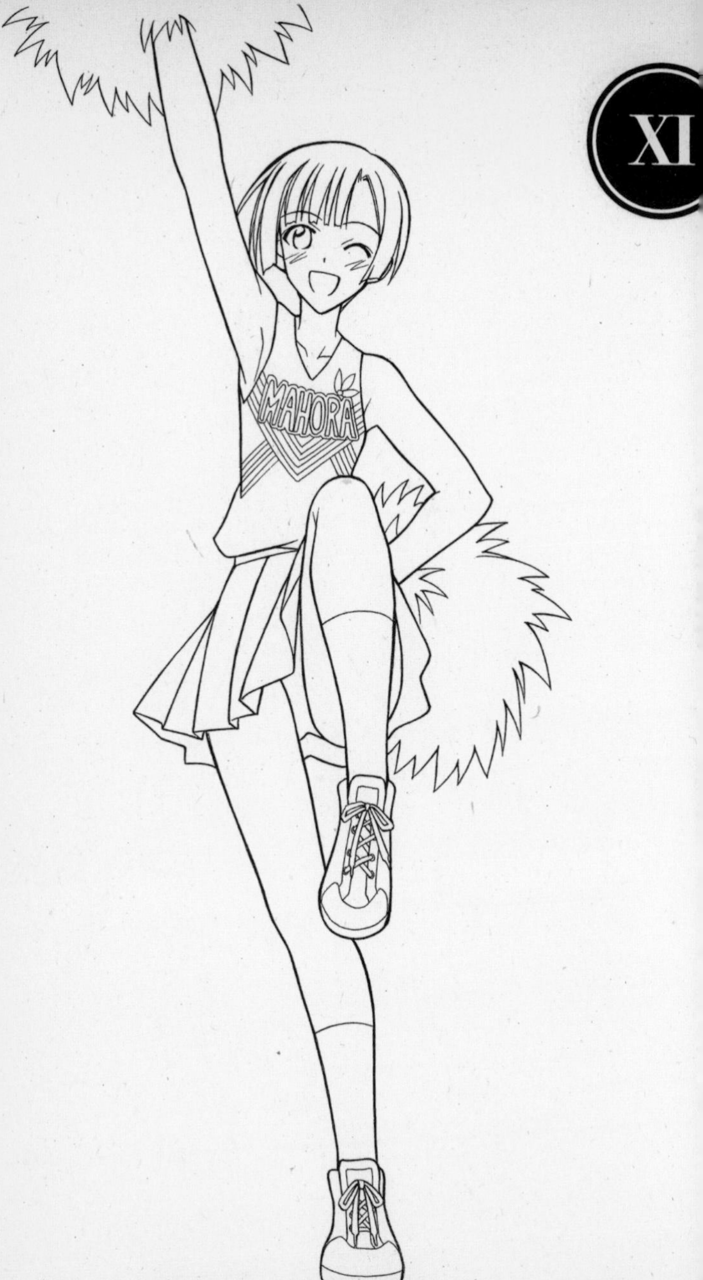
XI
MAHORA

Vitalizing Cheerleader

HILARATRIX DURANS

XVIII

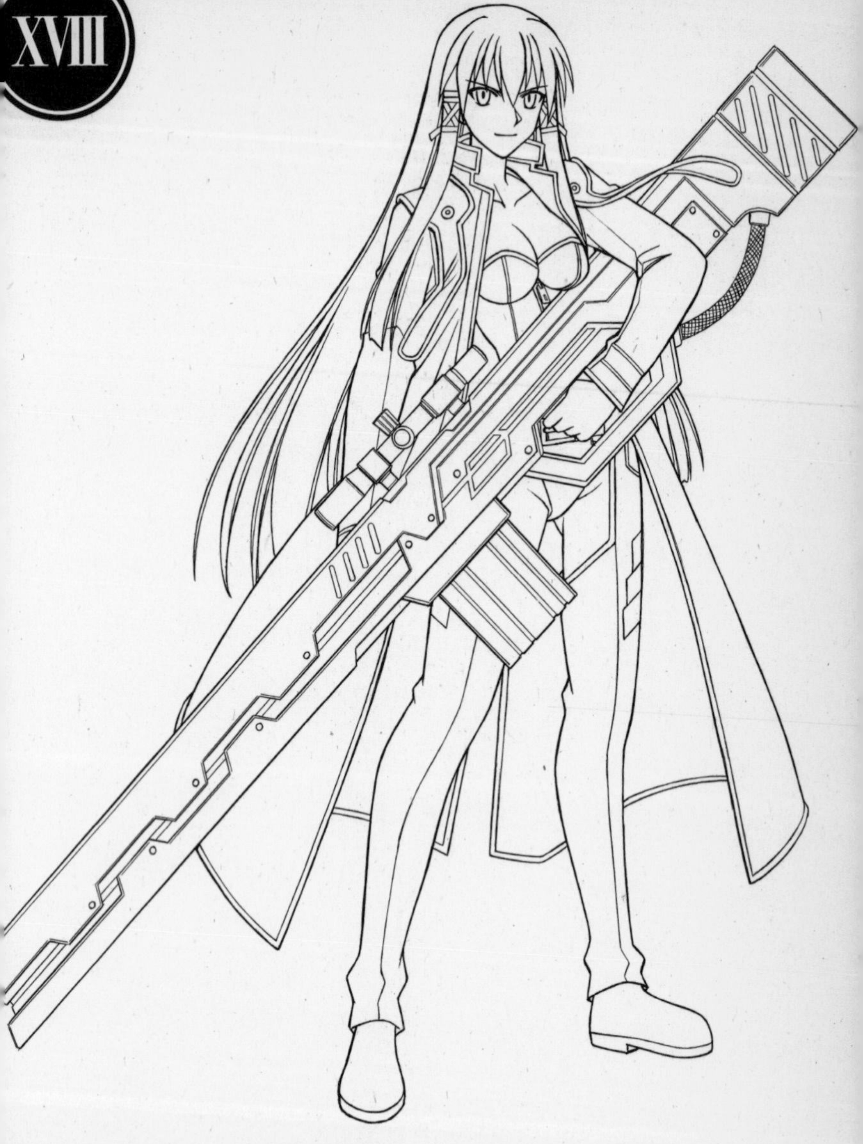

Half-Demon Sniper

VULNERANS SEMIDIABOLI

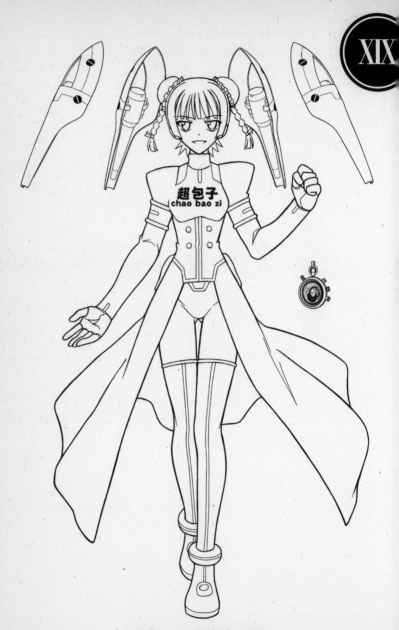

XIX

超包子
chao bao zi

All-Purpose Erudite

POLYMATHES UNIVERSALIS

XXI

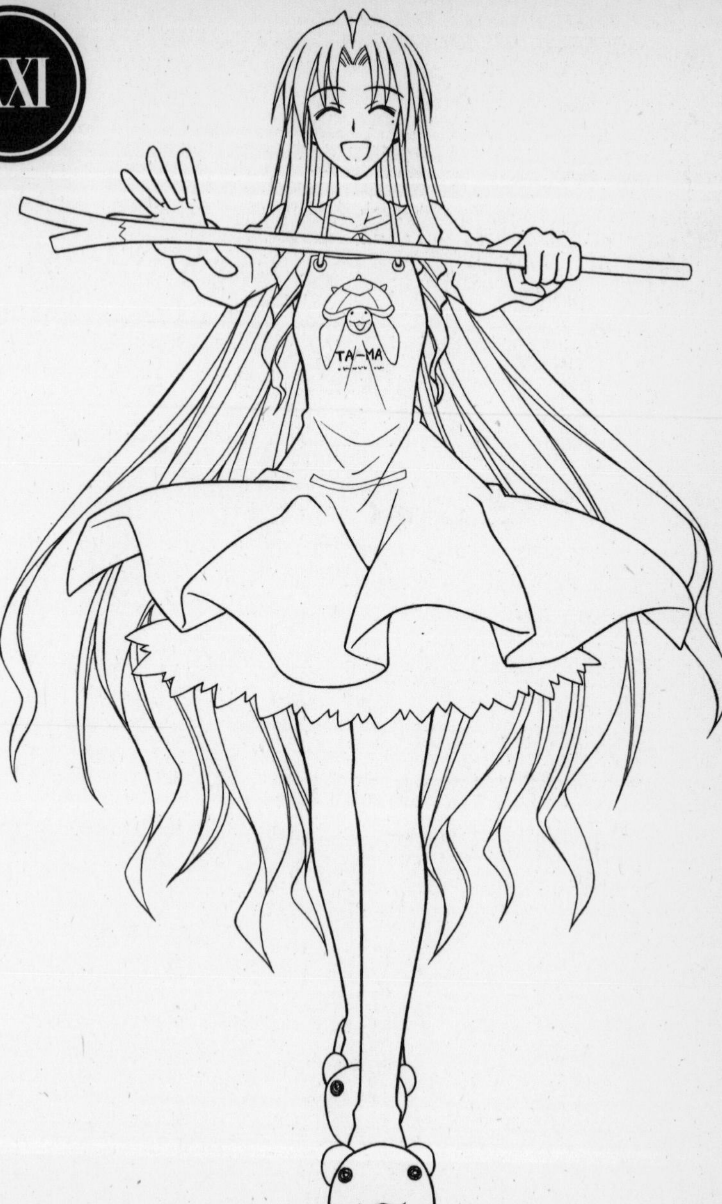
TA-MA

Astronomical Guardian

SERVATRIX STELLARUM

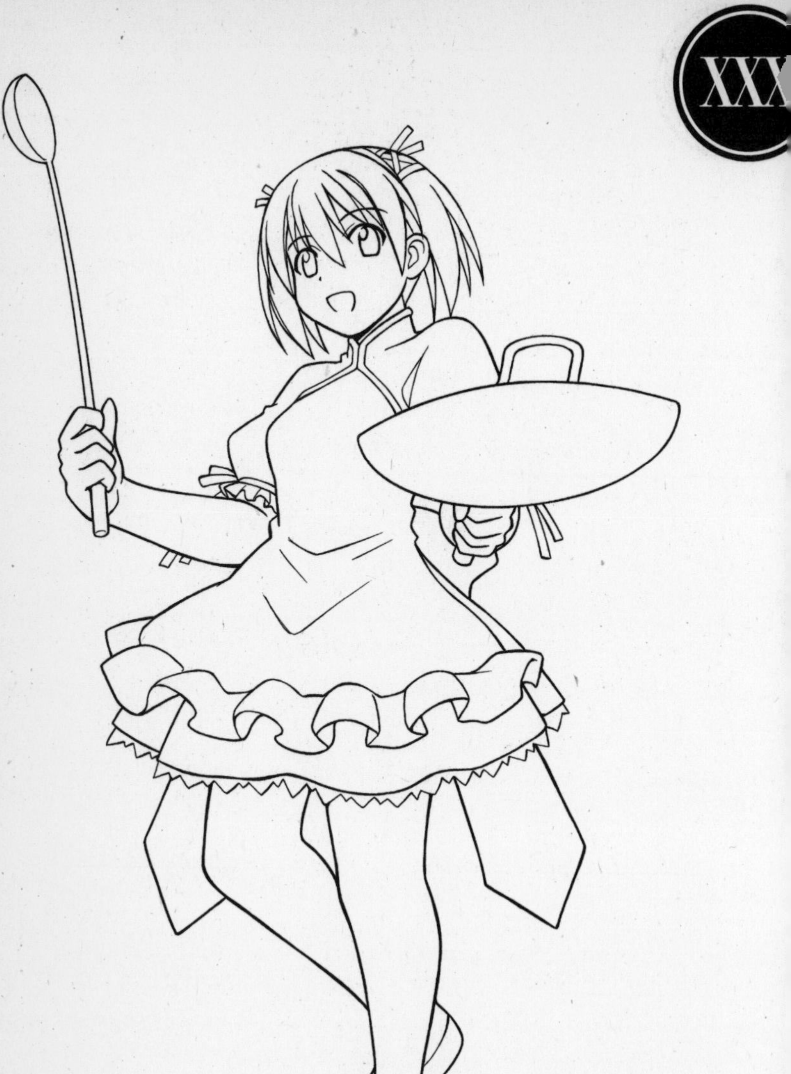
XXX

Legendary Chef

COQUA FABULOSA

XXXI

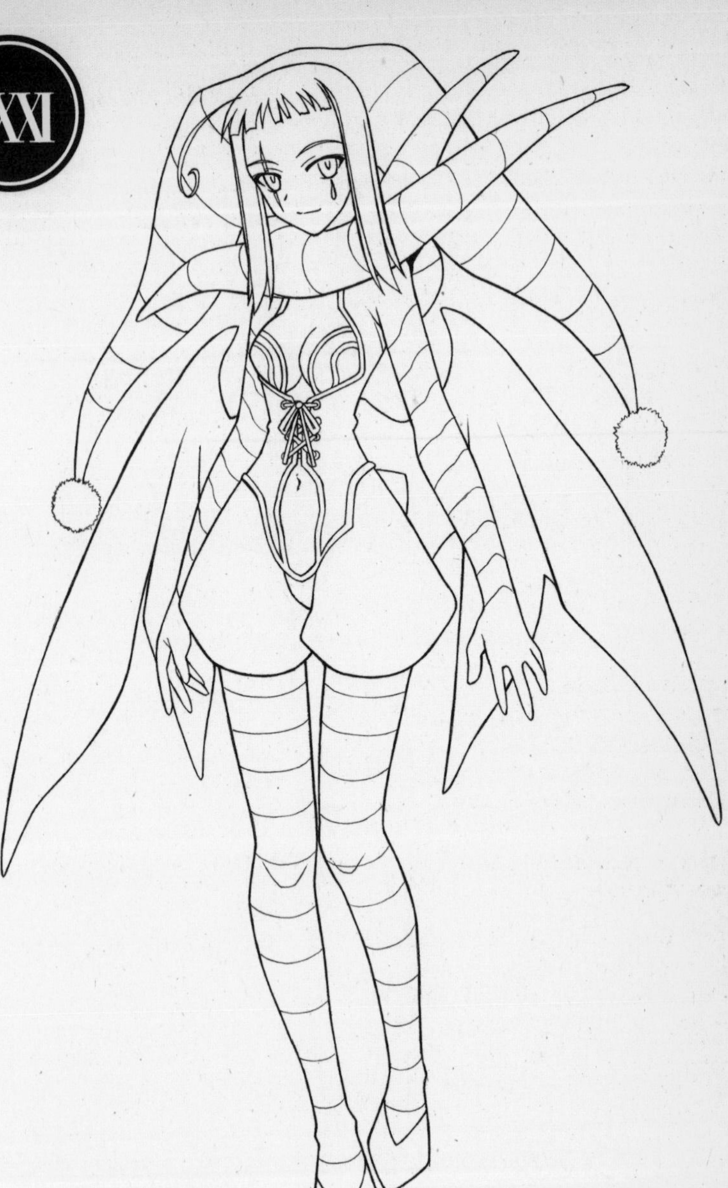

Princess of the Demon World

PRIMARIA IN DIABOLIMUNDO

Character
Profile

- Nagi Springfield

I don't need to tell you he's Negi's father. The name "Thousand Master" is something my studio staff just threw together; I kind of get the feeling that the English might be a little off. (laugh) (But no one from overseas has said anything to me.)

He's the typical main character type--strong, cheerful, and doesn't give up. All his friends trust him implicitly, and women love him. He's a bit of a punk, but that's because this is *Shonen Magazine*.

In the anime series, he was voiced by Takehito Koyasu-san. His dark yet mischievous nature made him a perfect choice!! (I may have requested him.) In *Negima!?*, Sawashiro-san played him and a few other characters.

In the live action drama, he's played by Hassei Takano-san. He's a good-looking actor who's Ultraman and Masked Rider! He's so cool!!

Akamatsu

魔法先生ネギま!
MAGISTER NEGI MAGI

赤松 健 SHONEN MAGAZINE COMICS
KEN AKAMATSU

37

The What and Why of Negima!?

Q. Negima!'s ending?

A. The next volume will be the last one.

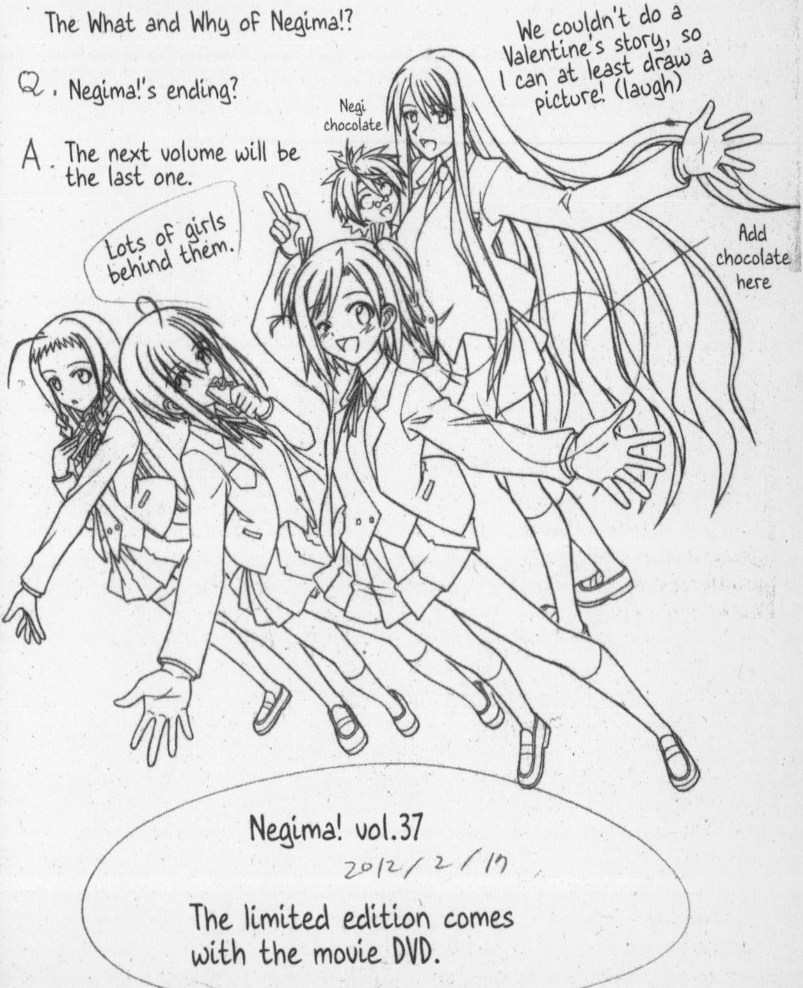
We couldn't do a Valentine's story, so I can at least draw a picture! (laugh)
Negi chocolate
Lots of girls behind them.
Add chocolate here
Negima! vol.37
2012/2/17
The limited edition comes with the movie DVD.

Translation Notes

Japanese is a tricky language for most Westerners, and translation is often more art than science. For your edification and reading pleasure, here are notes on some of the places where we could have gone in a different direction with our translation of the work, or where a Japanese cultural reference is used.

Megalo Manjū, page 45

A manjū is a type of bun with filling. When someone goes out of town, they will often buy the local manjū as a souvenir for friends and acquaintances, but it's also the kind of gift that doesn't require any thought.

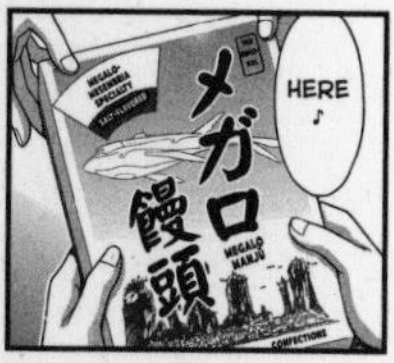
HERE ♪
メガロ饅頭
MEGALO MANJU
CONFECTIONS

Fate's karaoke, page 62

Madoka comments that Fate is singing a Japanese folk song. More accurately, she calls it an *enka*, which refers to a style of modern ballad, resembling Japanese traditional music. The song itself is remarkably similar to a popular *enka*, "Tsugaru Kaikyō : Winter Scene," sung by popular *enka* singer Sayuri Ishikawa. Whether the lyrics are different because it is in fact a different song, or whether Akamatsu-sensei changed the lyrics slightly to avoid copyright penalties, will remain a mystery.

Ayaka's confusion, page 77

You may be wondering why Ayaka didn't go berserk when she heard that Negi was on a date. The word that Fate used was *gōkon*, which is a slang term for what Americans would call a group date, but the meaning isn't obvious from the word itself. He also uses the term *gyaku-nan*, which is short for *gyaku-nanpa*, or "reverse *nanpa*." *Nanpa* is a slang term referring to a guy "picking up chicks," so *gyaku-nan* would be a girl picking up guys. Since none of these words give easy clues to their meaning, and Ayaka is very estranged from the world of people who use them on a regular basis, it makes sense that she would have no idea what they mean, or that she needs to give the cheerleaders a piece of her mind. The real mystery is: where did Fate learn those words?

Electric massager, page 106

This is a type of "game" played by Japanese bullies and/or older siblings on weaker/younger victims. It's exactly what Evangeline is doing, and gets its name from the fact that the victim vibrates uncontrollably, like an electric massager.

Junior, page 117

What Rakan really calls Negi here is *kōhai*, which is a Japanese word, referring to anyone who is a junior in relation to someone else. For example, a junior in high school in relation to a senior in high school. In this case, Negi started his training to save worlds after Goedel and Takahata, and so he is their junior.

Mundus Gelans, page 137

Here, Negi is incorporating one of Evangeline's spells into his attack. The difference is that Evangeline normally incants this spell in Greek (kosmike krystallopegia). The fact that Negi uses Latin may be an indication that he is not familiar with the spell, which is further demonstrated in the Japanese version, because the Japanese text uses only phonetic characters (as opposed to Chinese characters that represent ideas), as if Negi is sounding something out.

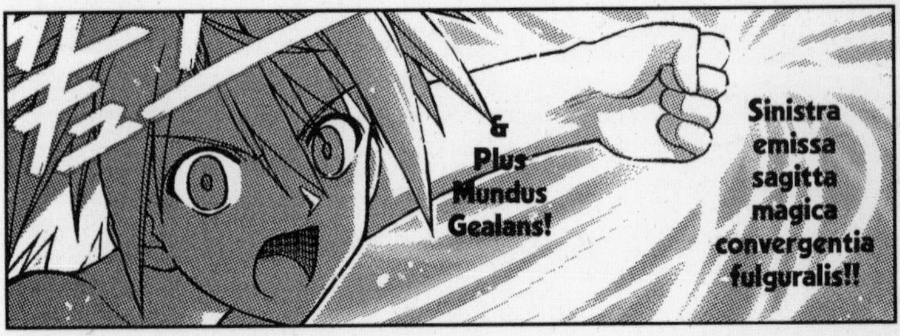
Sinistra emissa sagitta magica convergentia fulguralis!!
& Plus Mundus Gealans!

Negi's "cold," page 160

According to Japanese superstition, when a person sneezes, it's an indication that someone, somewhere, is talking about that person. Negi mentions these odd chills he's been getting, but those, and the sneezes, are most likely a psychic warning that people are plotting against him.

Preview for Volume 38

Enjoy these preview pages from Negima! volume 38 and check www.kodanshacomics.com to see when it'll be available!

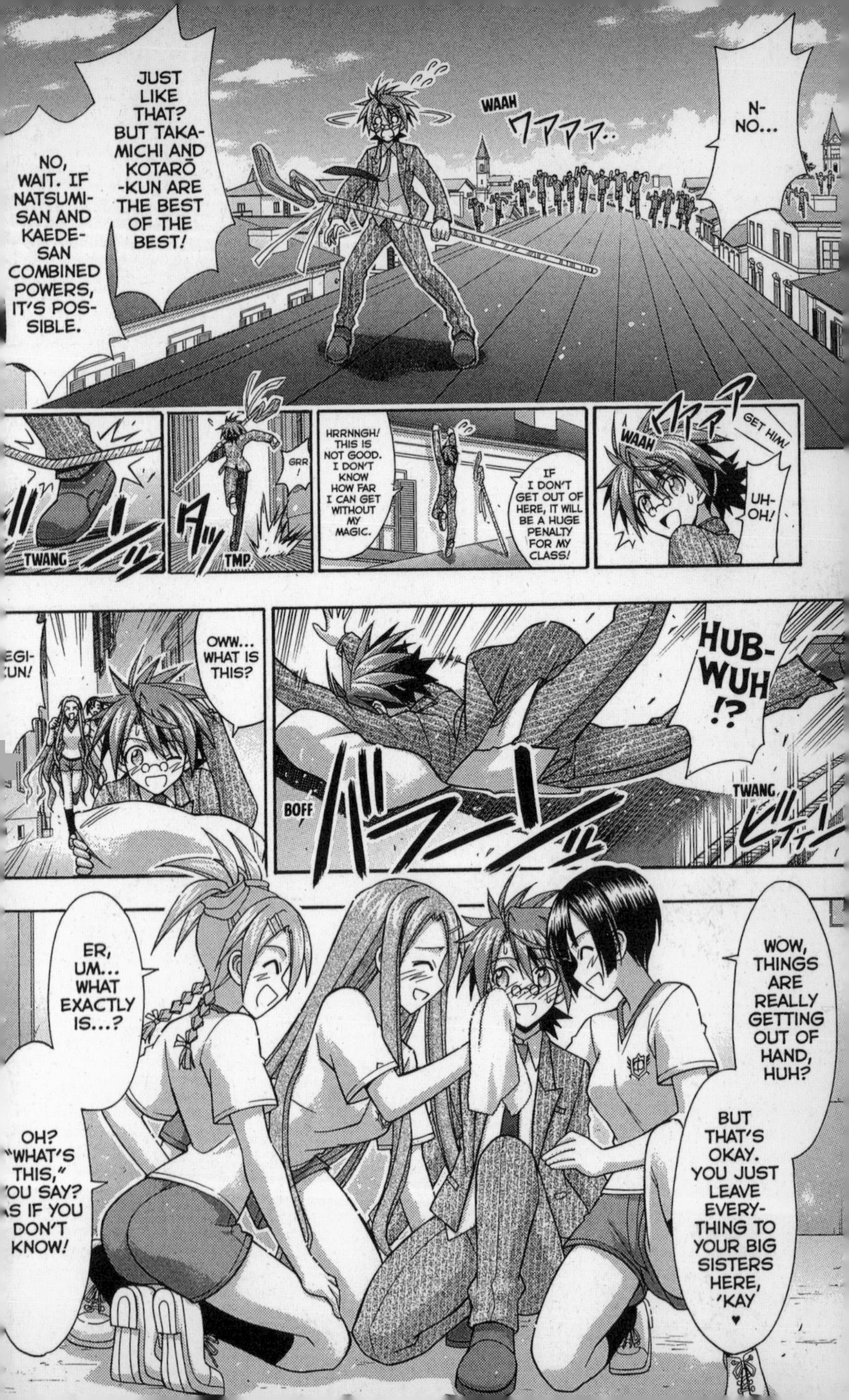
N-NO...
WAAH
JUST LIKE THAT? BUT TAKA-MICHI AND KOTARŌ-KUN ARE THE BEST OF THE BEST!
NO, WAIT. IF NATSUMI-SAN AND KAEDE-SAN COMBINED POWERS, IT'S POSSIBLE.
GET HIM!
WAAH
UH-OH!
HRRNNGH! THIS IS NOT GOOD. I DON'T KNOW HOW FAR I CAN GET WITHOUT MY MAGIC.
IF I DON'T GET OUT OF HERE, IT WILL BE A HUGE PENALTY FOR MY CLASS!
GRR!
TMP
TWANG
HUB-WUH!?
TWANG
BOFF
OWW... WHAT IS THIS?
EGI-KUN!
WOW, THINGS ARE REALLY GETTING OUT OF HAND, HUH?
BUT THAT'S OKAY. YOU JUST LEAVE EVERY-THING TO YOUR BIG SISTERS HERE, 'KAY ♥
ER, UM... WHAT EXACTLY IS...?
OH? "WHAT'S THIS," OU SAY? S IF YOU DON'T KNOW!

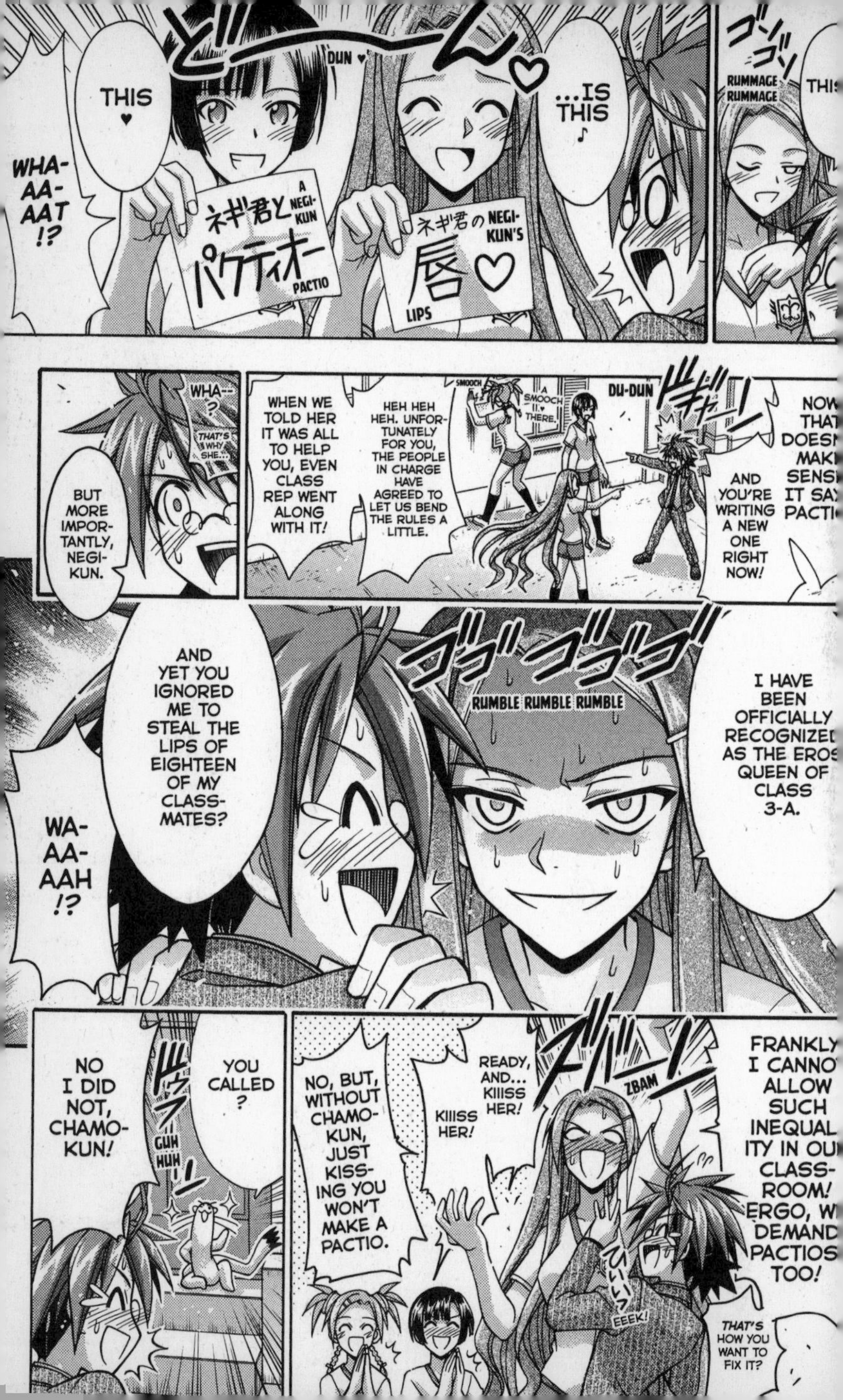

ゴソゴソ
RUMMAGE RUMMAGE
THIS
どどーーん♡
DUN ♥
...IS THIS ♪
ネギ君の唇♡
NEGI-KUN'S LIPS
THIS ♥
ネギ君とパクティオー
A NEGI-KUN PACTIO
WHA-AA-AAT!?
NOW THAT DOESN MAKE SENS IT SAY PACTIO
AND YOU'RE WRITING A NEW ONE RIGHT NOW!
DU-DUN
A SMOOCH ♥ THERE.
SMOOCH
HEH HEH HEH. UNFORTUNATELY FOR YOU, THE PEOPLE IN CHARGE HAVE AGREED TO LET US BEND THE RULES A LITTLE.
WHEN WE TOLD HER IT WAS ALL TO HELP YOU, EVEN CLASS REP WENT ALONG WITH IT!
WHA--?
THAT'S WHY SHE...
BUT MORE IMPORTANTLY, NEGI-KUN.
I HAVE BEEN OFFICIALLY RECOGNIZED AS THE EROS QUEEN OF CLASS 3-A.
ゴゴゴゴゴゴ
RUMBLE RUMBLE RUMBLE
AND YET YOU IGNORED ME TO STEAL THE LIPS OF EIGHTEEN OF MY CLASSMATES?
WA-AA-AAH!?
FRANKLY I CANNOT ALLOW SUCH INEQUALITY IN OUR CLASSROOM! ERGO, WE DEMAND PACTIOS TOO!
ZBAM
READY, AND... KIIISS HER!
KIIISS HER!
NO, BUT, WITHOUT CHAMO-KUN, JUST KISSING YOU WON'T MAKE A PACTIO.
EEEK!
THAT'S HOW YOU WANT TO FIX IT?
YOU CALLED?
GUH HUH
NO I DID NOT, CHAMO-KUN!

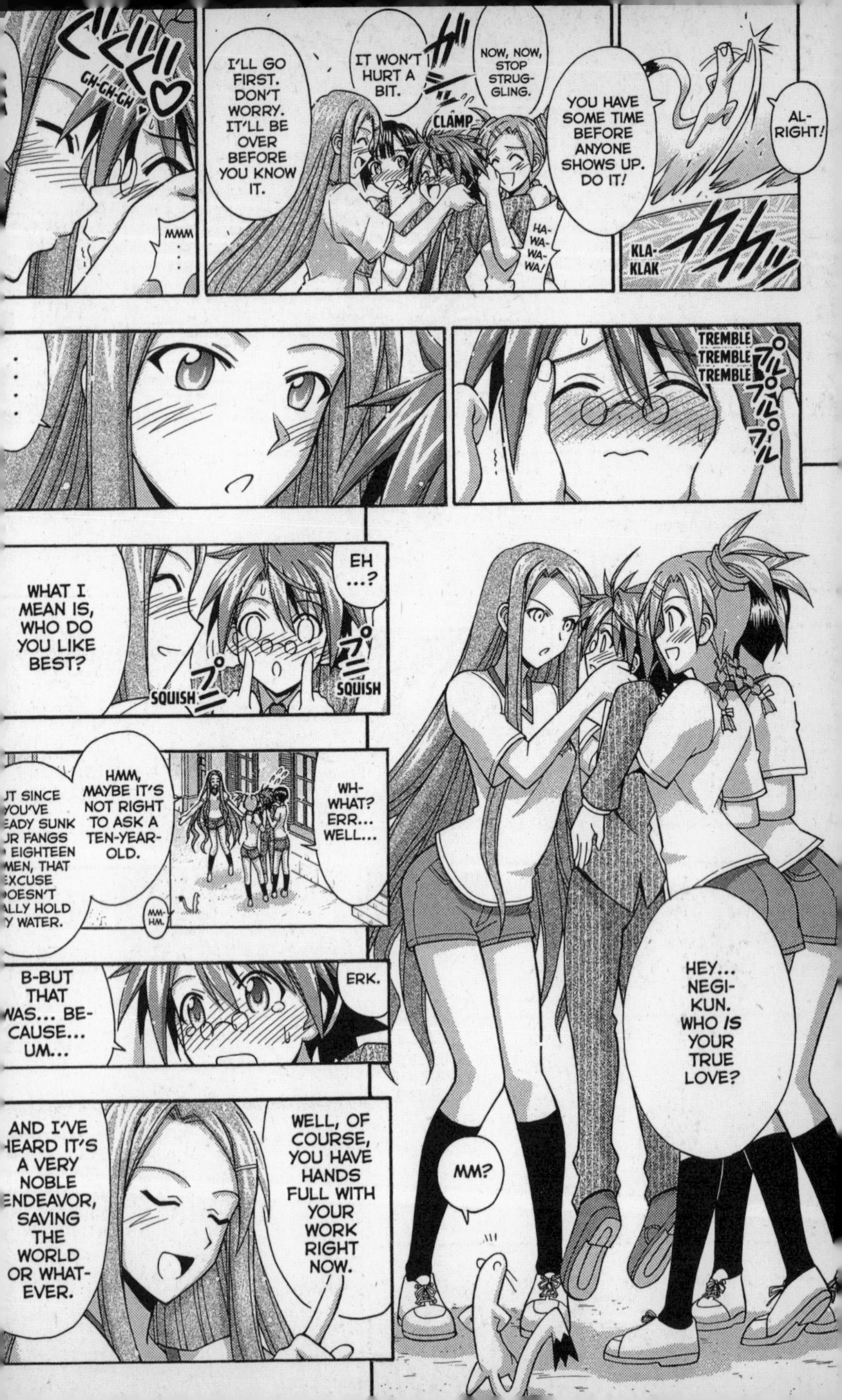

AL-RIGHT!
YOU HAVE SOME TIME BEFORE ANYONE SHOWS UP. DO IT!
KLA-KLAK
NOW, NOW, STOP STRUG-GLING.
IT WON'T HURT A BIT.
CLAMP
I'LL GO FIRST. DON'T WORRY. IT'LL BE OVER BEFORE YOU KNOW IT.
HA-WA-WA-WA!
GH-GH-GH
MMM...
TREMBLE TREMBLE TREMBLE
HEY... NEGI-KUN. WHO IS YOUR TRUE LOVE?
MM?
EH ...?
WHAT I MEAN IS, WHO DO YOU LIKE BEST?
SQUISH
SQUISH
WH-WHAT? ERR... WELL...
HMM, MAYBE IT'S NOT RIGHT TO ASK A TEN-YEAR-OLD.
JT SINCE YOU'VE EADY SUNK JR FANGS EIGHTEEN MEN, THAT EXCUSE OESN'T ALLY HOLD Y WATER.
MM-HM.
ERK.
B-BUT THAT WAS... BE-CAUSE... UM...
WELL, OF COURSE, YOU HAVE HANDS FULL WITH YOUR WORK RIGHT NOW.
AND I'VE HEARD IT'S A VERY NOBLE ENDEAVOR, SAVING THE WORLD OR WHAT-EVER.

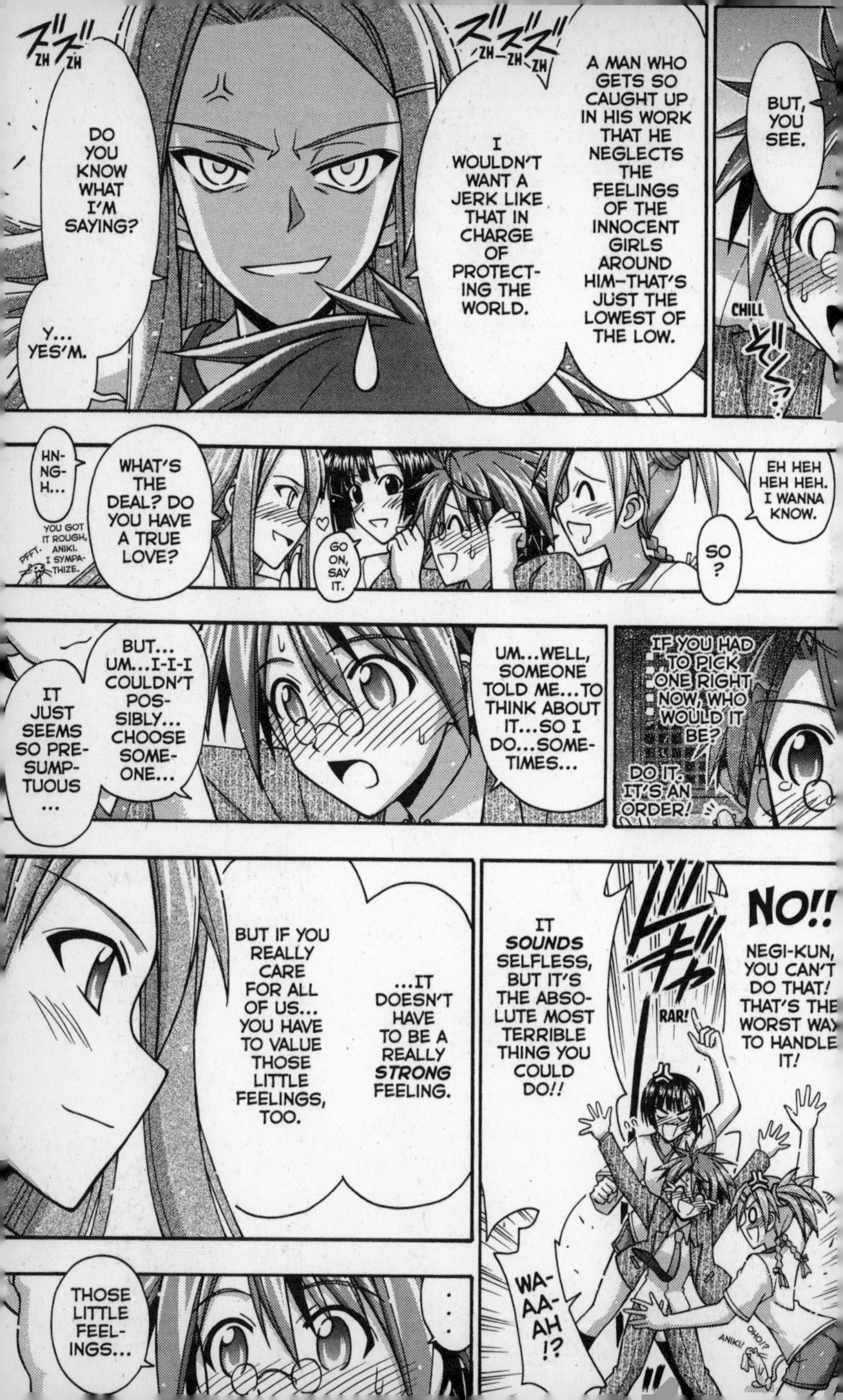
BUT, YOU SEE.
CHILL
ZH-ZH-ZH
A MAN WHO GETS SO CAUGHT UP IN HIS WORK THAT HE NEGLECTS THE FEELINGS OF THE INNOCENT GIRLS AROUND HIM—THAT'S JUST THE LOWEST OF THE LOW.
I WOULDN'T WANT A JERK LIKE THAT IN CHARGE OF PROTECTING THE WORLD.
ZH ZH
DO YOU KNOW WHAT I'M SAYING?
Y... YES'M.
EH HEH HEH HEH. I WANNA KNOW.
SO?
GO ON, SAY IT.
WHAT'S THE DEAL? DO YOU HAVE A TRUE LOVE?
HN-NG-H...
YOU GOT IT ROUGH, ANIKI. I SYMPATHIZE.
PFFT.
IF YOU HAD TO PICK ONE RIGHT NOW, WHO WOULD IT BE?
DO IT. IT'S AN ORDER!
UM...WELL, SOMEONE TOLD ME...TO THINK ABOUT IT...SO I DO...SOMETIMES...
BUT... UM...I-I-I COULDN'T POSSIBLY... CHOOSE SOMEONE...
IT JUST SEEMS SO PRESUMPTUOUS...
NO!!
NEGI-KUN, YOU CAN'T DO THAT! THAT'S THE WORST WAY TO HANDLE IT!
IT *SOUNDS* SELFLESS, BUT IT'S THE ABSOLUTE MOST TERRIBLE THING YOU COULD DO!!
RAR!
WAAAAH!?
OHO!?
ANIKI!
...IT DOESN'T HAVE TO BE A REALLY *STRONG* FEELING.
BUT IF YOU REALLY CARE FOR ALL OF US... YOU HAVE TO VALUE THOSE LITTLE FEELINGS, TOO.
...
THOSE LITTLE FEELINGS...

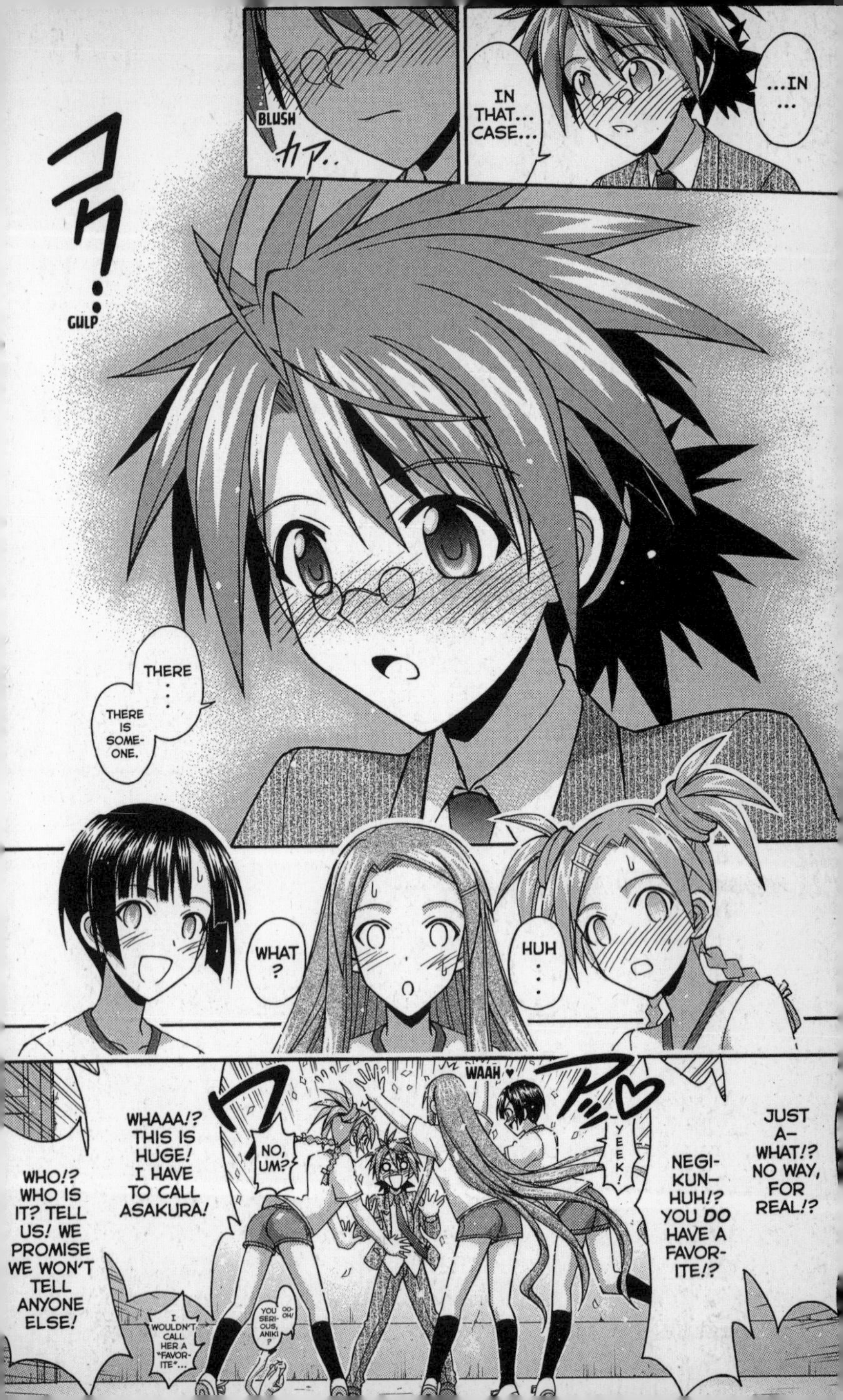

...IN ...
IN THAT... CASE...
BLUSH
カア..
コク..
GULP
THERE... THERE IS SOME-ONE.
HUH...
WHAT?
JUST A— WHAT!? NO WAY, FOR REAL!?
NEGI-KUN— HUH!? YOU DO HAVE A FAVOR-ITE!?
ワアッ♥
YEEK!
WAAH♥
NO, UM?
WHAAA!? THIS IS HUGE! I HAVE TO CALL ASAKURA!
OO-OH! YOU SERI-OUS, ANIKI?
I WOULDN'T CALL HER A "FAVOR-ITE"...
WHO!? WHO IS IT? TELL US! WE PROMISE WE WON'T TELL ANYONE ELSE!

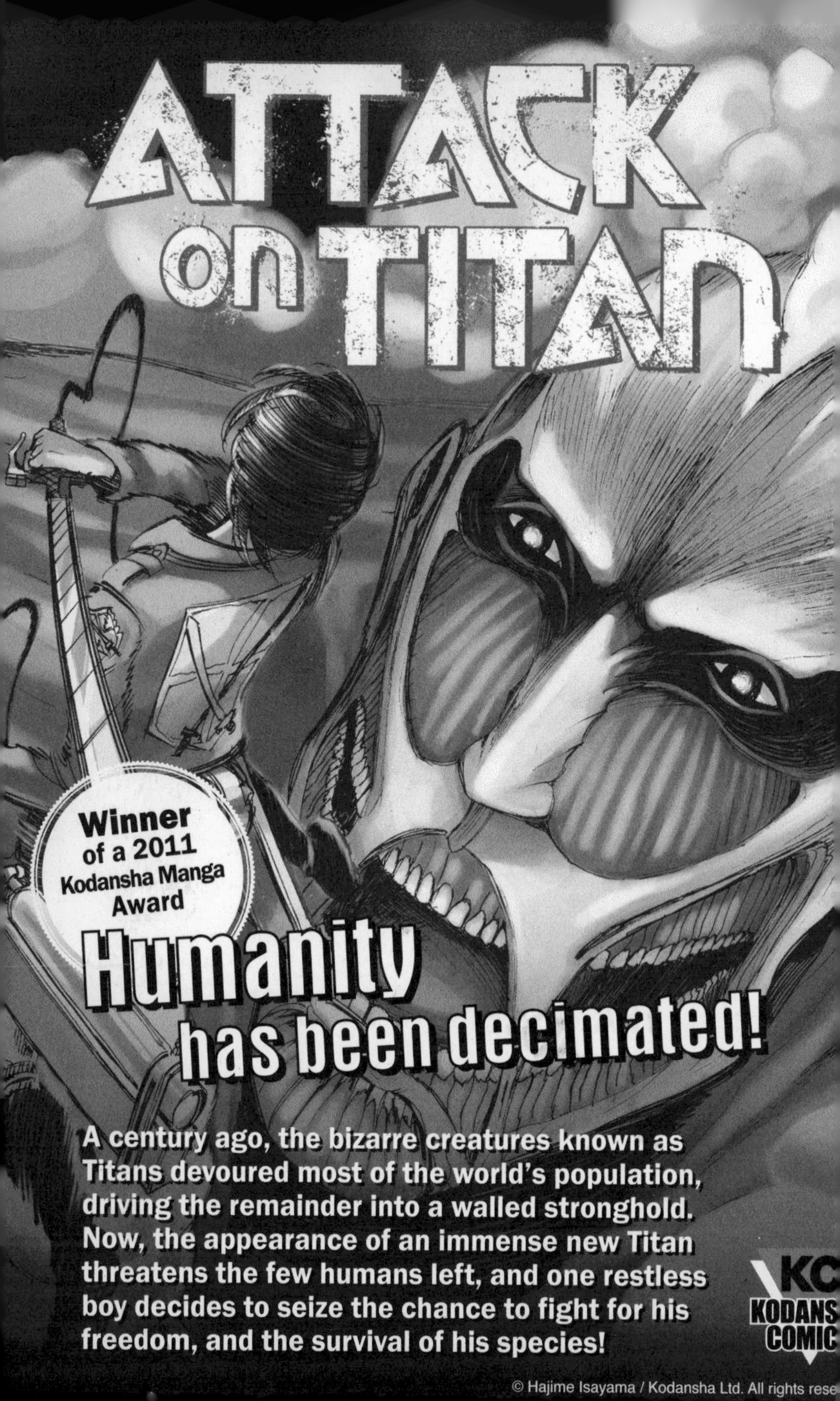
ATTACK on TITAN
Winner of a 2011 Kodansha Manga Award
Humanity has been decimated!
A century ago, the bizarre creatures known as Titans devoured most of the world's population, driving the remainder into a walled stronghold. Now, the appearance of an immense new Titan threatens the few humans left, and one restless boy decides to seize the chance to fight for his freedom, and the survival of his species!
KC KODANS COMIC
© Hajime Isayama / Kodansha Ltd. All rights rese

FROM HIRO MASHIMA, CREATOR OF RAVE MASTER

FAIRY TAIL

FAIRY TAIL 1
Hiro Mashima Creator of Rave Master

FAIRY TAIL 2
Hiro Mashima Creator of Rave Master

Lucy has always dreamed of joining the Fairy Tail, a club for the most powerful sorcerers in the land. But once she becomes a member, the fun really starts!

Special extras in each volume! Read them all!

RATING T AGES 13+

VISIT WWW.KODANSHACOMICS.COM TO:

- View release date calendars for upcoming volumes
- Find out the latest about new Kodansha Comics series

KC KODANSHA COMICS

Negima! volume 37 is a work of fiction. Names, characters, places, and incidents are the products of the author's imagination or are used fictitiously. Any resemblance to actual events, locales, or persons, living or dead, is entirely coincidental.

A Kodansha Comics Trade Paperback Original.

Published in the United States by Kodansha Comics, an imprint of Kodansha USA Publishing, LLC, New York.

Publication rights for this English edition arranged through Kodansha Ltd., Tokyo.

First published in Japan in 2012 by Kodansha Ltd., Tokyo, as *Maho sensei Negima!*, volume 37.

ISBN 978-1-61262-271-2

Printed in the United States of America.

www.kodanshacomics.com

9 8 7 6 5 4 3 2 1

Translator: Alethea Nibley & Athena Nibley
Lettering: Scott O. Brown

TOMARE!

[STOP!]

You're going the wrong way!

Manga is a completely different
type of reading experience.

To start at the *beginning*,
go to the *end*!

That's right! Authentic manga is read the traditional Japanese way—
from right to left. Exactly the *opposite* of how American books are read.
It's easy to follow: Just go to the other end of the book, and read each
page—and each panel—from the right side to the left side, starting at
the top right. Now you're experiencing manga as it was meant to be!